Tribes Of Nagaland And The Catholic Church

A Journey Together

Tribes Of Nagaland And The Catholic Church

A Journey Together

Fr Thomas John

Vitasta

Published by
Renu Kaul Verma
Vitasta Publishing Pvt Ltd
2/15, Ansari Road, Daryaganj
New Delhi-110 002
info@vitastapublishing.com

ISBN 978-93-90961-46-7

First Edition 2023

MRP ₹ 695

Edited by Dhanalakshmi Ayyer
Cover and Layout by Somesh Kumar Mishra
Printed by Chaman Enterprises, New Delhi

CONTENTS

FOREWORD

It is an accepted fact that Christianity had a huge impact in the Northeastern region of India. This impact produced a synergy that changed the entire landscape of the Northeast and the world view of the people of the region. Nagaland being one of the seven sister states of the region and a Christian majority state, Christianity has had much deeper and revolutionary impact on all aspects of the lives of the Naga people and it continues to do so even now. Some even describe this change in terms of "from headhunting to soul hunting."

The book *Tribes Of Nagaland And The Catholic Church: A Journey Together* has been an attempt at knowing how the Catholic Church took its roots in the state and the influence it has had on the people and the state in general. Though a few books on the Catholic Church in Nagaland have been written, this book is much more in depth in nature as it is supported by vast quantity of resources. Most part of the book is presented in a narrative form and hence various events are chronologically mentioned. It explores truth into history of the Church in the state. It shares with the readers the beginning and growth of the Catholic Church, which was very late to arrive in the scene and recalls the immense sacrifice the earlier Catholic missionaries and lay leaders made and struggles (like social isolation, indifference, threats and expulsion) they faced on account of being Catholics. They were the true torch-bearers of the Church especially in difficult times. A striking feature one notices in the book is that throughout the life of the Catholic Church the public in general including the administration worked as a team in order to defeat divisive elements and bring about cohesiveness and unity among the people of Nagaland and with rest of the country.

Even though the Catholic Church is quite young (around 70 years) in the state, it proved to be very significant in terms of its existence and impact. The book throws light on the great contributions the Church has made on the religious, educational, social, medical and economic life of the people of the state and thus becoming a key player and catalyst in the overall development of the state. The greatest achievement has been promotion of human development through its educational, social and healing ministry. As a great benefactor, therefore, no one can ignore the important role of the Catholic Church in the state. The book shares the hope that the Catholic Church will continue to serve the people of the state with commitment. By writing this book I am sure Fr. Thomas John has made a great contribution to the Naga society. No doubt it is an excellent work as it gives an overall picture of the Catholic Church in the state. I sincerely wish that all those who seek information about the Catholic Church in Nagaland and Naga society would find it immensely useful.

Most Rev. Dr. James Thoppil,
Bishop of Kohima, Nagaland.

MESSAGE

Church History holds an important place in exploring the truth of the Church and the people it represented in by gone times so that we can learn from them for the journey ahead. The penetrating insights it uncovers can become a driving force today and tomorrow for the People of God who look to adhere to the values of the Kingdom of God that inhere in their Church and faith. It can help clarify misconceptions or remove doubts and foster fresh dialogue with people of other faiths.

The book, *Tribes Of Nagaland And The Catholic Church: A Journey Together* by Fr. Thomas John is a valuable treatise on the history and contribution of the Catholic Church in Nagaland and the role it played in the development of the State. It offers a happy story of the implanting of the Church among the tribes of the Naga Hills and reminds us of how, from the time of the Apostles, the Church has been journeying all over the world in an apostolic mission that has now also witnessed the people of Nagaland embracing the Christian faith. May God bless Nagaland and its people.

With its simple narration, the book is easy to read and understand and I imagine its readers will be enriched by its scholarly nature and inspirational content, as well as being encouraged and strengthened to remain faithful, convinced and dedicated in their own Christian faith in the times to come.

Most Rev. John Keenan,
Bishop of Paisley, Scotland, UK.

INTRODUCTION

The British rule in North East India exposed the tribals of the region to Christianity. Thus they entered the world of knowledge and civilisation. The consequence of this remarkable shift was reflected in their everyday lives. The strenuous efforts of the Christian missionaries from America and Europe in the educational, religious, social, cultural and economic fields early in their contact with the tribals opened the minds of the latter to a fast changing world. The same work continued even when those missionaries were replaced by missionaries from mainland India.

The contribution of Christianity to the socio-economic development of the North East has been immense, although the main purpose of all the three major Christian denominations namely the Presbyterians, the Baptists and the Catholics, was evangelisation (Passah, 1996). The term 'evangelisation' in the ordinary sense is understood as 'preaching.' Hence in the beginning it was believed that the Church's involvement in socio-economic activities was a move away from its main mission. It all began in the 19th century with a shift from the traditional approach to a more holistic vision of evangelisation as the churches began to realise that their mission was not only spiritual but also the overall wellbeing of the whole person. Desrochers (1982) quotes the document 'Justice in the World', that "action on behalf of justice and participation in the transformation of the world is a constitutive dimension of the preaching of the Gospel" (pg. 21). Today, therefore, the Catholic Church's running of schools, colleges and hostels for boys, girls, working men and women, dispensaries, mobile clinics, rural health centres, hospitals, orphanages, crèches, homes for the aged and the destitute, social welfare and tribal welfare centres, leprosaria, agricultural, technical and vocational training centres, banks, cooperatives, rural developmental centres, etc. are all signs of its commitment to improving the living conditions of the people across the globe irrespective of religion, on the principle of holistic welfare to all that the Catholic Church embarked on the evangelisation of the state.

It is very interesting to note that the Nagas who were opposed to foreign rule or alien rule were not against foreign religion - Christianity. Notwithstanding the initial resistance in some places when Christianity was introduced in the late 19th century, there were mass movements in favour of this foreign religion. The Nagas were a warrior group challenging their enemy and fearing none even at the cost of personal sacrifice, yet they wanted a God who was close to them, willing to forgive their faults and showing them the path to truth. They fought the British till the Second World War, sending out a strong message that they were a different people who could not be subjugated under a tyrannical ruler and the policy of divide and rule. Their support was extended to the British only at the advancement of the Japanese towards their land.

The evangelisation work by the Catholic Church in Nagaland as in other places was directed towards the new role the Church assumed. The American Baptist Church's glorious history, work and evangelisation of the state over one hundred and forty years had great consequences for the people of the state and the entry of the Catholic Church only helped fulfill the aspirations of the people more realistically. It was the longing of many Naga people who expressed in clear terms their desire to have the Catholic Church planted in their soil to bring about all round development. Hence, all its efforts were aimed towards being a contributing Church in terms of effecting overall well-being of the people in their spiritual, educational, cultural, economic, and social life. It planned and coordinated all its activities towards that end. Notwithstanding the opposition and struggles it had to face, the Church invested all its available resources in terms of time, money and human capital to benefit all, especially the poor in rural areas. When examining and evaluating the efforts of the Church we come to know that the Church has positively responded to the aspirations of the people for which it has been founded. At the same time the Church is aware it has still many more miles in its journey to reach out to more people.

The people of Nagaland are indebted to the missionaries from abroad, rest of India and within the state for their selfless and humanitarian services that are reflected in the life of the people. It is undeniable that though a minority, the Catholic Church in Nagaland, through its spiritual, educational and social services, health care, promotion of culture, commitment to justice, peace and dialogue, and developmental activities has positively influenced this small hilly state within a span of sixty years. The Church takes these activities seriously in order to fulfill its commitment to the people. Among all the services rendered by the Catholic Church, it is the educational service that has changed the economic and social life of the people of the state. Notwithstanding the difficulties encountered, the Church continues to work for the welfare of all and its contribution cannot go unnoticed.

In order to place this study in its proper context, the first chapter deals with ***The Land and the Peoples.*** It is because of my personal interest to know in detail the history of the state that I have dedicated one full chapter in this book. In this, the topography of Nagaland, different races in India, origin and migration of the Nagas, the meaning of the term 'Naga,' settlement of the Nagas and their social, political, economic, and religious life are covered.

The second chapter, ***Christianity in Nagaland*** begins with Christianity in North East India, followed by the British policy in the North East and the beginning of the Catholic mission there. A short description of the beginning of Baptist mission in Nagaland is next in order, to place the beginning of Catholic mission in Nagaland. The arrival of the first Catholic missionaries and the starting of Catholic mission among the Angami tribe in Kohima are recounted. The move among the Lotha tribe in Lakhuti under Wokha district to embrace Catholicism is elucidated.

The growth of the Church is described in the third chapter under the title, ***Growth of the Catholic Church.*** In this chapter, the expansion of the Catholic Church to other parts of the state and its various activities are described.

The fourth chapter, ***Contribution of the Catholic Church in General*** is the central part of the book. Here, the contributions of the Church from the beginning till date with the support of primary and secondary sources have been narrated.

Chapter five titled, ***The Catholic Church and Nagaland Today*** gives a summary of the previous chapters with a few suggestions to look into the future. In the words of Bishop Robert Kerketta (1998), "we cannot foretell the future... we would want the Church to be vibrant in bringing peace, harmony and prosperity, both spiritual and temporal, to all people without any distinction of caste, creed and language, rendering glory to God and service to mankind (pg. 280).

This book is my revised doctoral thesis, 'Impact of the Catholic Church on Naga Society' done under Nagaland University in 2014. This work has been actualised due to the valuable assistance given by the following persons and I am indebted to them: Rev. Fr. Dr. Isaac Padinjarekuttu and Dr. Catherine Keogh for the correction of the manuscript; Dr David Wilson for his suggestions and the timeline; John Lowe for the typesetting and Rev. Fr. Tom Erambil for his help in the publication. I sincerely appreciate them for their time and help.

I dedicate this book to the pioneer Catholic missionaries of Nagaland.

Fr Thomas John

CHAPTER ONE

The Land And The People

1. Formation of the State

THE DECISION to form Nagaland, the then smallest state of Independent India, with a population of little above five lakhs, was taken by the Government of India in 1960. Prime Minister Jawaharlal Nehru announced on 1 August, 1960, in the Lok Sabha that his Government had decided to create a new state within the Indian Union, known as Nagaland because the Nagas had been longing and struggling for some sort of autonomy for years (Elwin, 1997). "India", Nehru said again, "achieved her independence thirteen years ago and the Nagas are as independent as other Indian citizens; we have not the slightest desire to interfere in the tribal customs and practices of the Nagas or their distinctive way of life" (Elwin, 1997, pg.1). To affirm his stand he further said, "Our policy has always been to give the fullest autonomy and opportunity of self-development to the Naga people, without interfering in any way in their internal affairs or way of life" (Ramunny, 1988, pg. 1). Hence Dr. S. Radhakrishnan, the President of India inaugurated Nagaland, the sixteenth state of the Indian Union at Kohima on 1st December, 1963.

1.1 Geographical Setting and Habitation

Nagaland, the third smallest state of the country in area, after Sikkim and Goa has an area of 16,579 square kilometer. The state has Assam all along its west from north to south, Manipur in the south, Burma on the east and Arunachal Pradesh on the northern side of the eastern border (Ghosh, 1982). It is situated approximately between 25° 11'55" and 27° 2'10" North Latitude and between 93° 0'20" and 95° 17'10" East Longitude (Sen, 1987).

The Naga Hills are not only beautiful and picturesque but also fertile and full of resources (Singh, 1987). The hills are inhabited by several tribes who are collectively called the Nagas (Shimmi, 1988). They inhabit the present state of Nagaland, parts of Manipur, Assam, the north-eastern parts of Arunachal Pradesh, and the Somra tract in neighbouring Myanmar (Lotsüro, 2000). The state with its rich diverse cultures and festivities of its various tribes and sub-tribes is distinct from other states.

The topography of Nagaland is just like any other mountainous state with high hills, sharp edges, steep ridges, with deep and narrow gorges. As Joshi (2001) describes, "It is endowed with rich natural flora and fauna, lush green hills and valleys, rivers, … with many rich resources like forests, minerals, fertile soil, abundant rainfall, moderate cool climate, etc." (pg. 4). Except a few hundred square kilometers of the plains in Dimapur, Naginimara, and Tijit area, the foothills of Chumukedima, Borjan Colliery to Dikhu valley and several other valleys of the river-beds like Ghaspani (Medziphema), Baghty, Bhandari, etc., (Sen, 1987), the entire state is hilly and mountainous. The terrain of Nagaland can be sub-divided into three zones: (i) high hill-ranges in the east, (ii) medium high hill-ranges in immediate zone, and (iii) outer foothill areas in the west.

The Naga Hills in general are surrounded by Patkai Bum in the North-East, Barail Range in the South-West, Saramati Range on the East (Sen, 1987). The Barail range enters the state from North Cachar and after passing through Kohima runs in the direction of Wokha. Japava (Japfu) which lies to the south of Kohima is the highest peak of Barail Range at a height of 3,804 metres above the sea level. The Patkai range constitutes the international boundary between India and Burma (Hussain, 1988). There are seven mountain-peaks in Nagaland. Mount Saramati, with a height of 12,598 feet in Kiphire district, the highest peak in the state is situated on the Burma-Nagaland border. Mount Japfü in Kohima district is at a height of 9,890 feet. Mount Ezupu stands at 9,320 feet while Mount Kapu is 9,315 feet. Mount Paona at 9,150 feet, Mount Zephu at 8,408 feet and Mount Kapamesu at 7,964 feet is the seventh peak. The altitudes vary between 914 metres and 3,048 metres above sea level (Saleh, 1989).

The geography of the area is also responsible for the isolation of the Naga people from the rest of the country. In the beginning the Nagas did not choose the hot, damp and malaria infested low-lying areas and valleys for human habitations. They preferred hill tops as places for village settlements because of strategic reasons, (Hussain, 1988), as a defence against enemies. This type of natural setting has a great bearing on the population distribution in Nagaland particularly in the extreme eastern part adjoining Myanmar, which is less developed and inaccessible because of the formidable physical terrain.

Nagaland is blessed with a number of serpentine flowing rivers and streams. Dhansiri, Doyang, Dikhu, Milak, Zungki and Tizu are the main rivers of Nagaland (Hussain, 1988), among a number of other minor rivers, all of which play a significant role in the economy of the state. They flow either into the Brahmaputra in the west in Assam or into the Chindwin in the east in Myanmar (*Nagaland*, 2001). Of these, Dhansiri, Doyang and Dikhu flow towards west and fall into the Brahmaputra, while the Tizu river flows towards the east and south-east and joins the Irrawady in Myanmar (Venuh, 2005). The Dhansiri (Temeki) river forms a natural boundary between Nagaland and North Cachar Hills of Assam and joins another river Doyang from Nagaland near Golaghat in Assam and then flows into the Brahmaputra (Nagaland, 2001). The Doyang is the largest and the longest river of the state, originating from the Barail Range near Mao (Imnayongsang, 1990) and is the most important river in the state in terms of utility.

Literature on the geology of Nagaland is scanty. The rocks of this region, geologically speaking, are comparatively young—about 140 million years old (Ghosh, 1982). According to the geoscientists of various departments, the north-eastern region of the country was under the ocean which existed between India and Burma, and the land which now joins India and Burma did not exist at that time but originated much later. Marine deposition took place on that sea floor layer after layer and now we have the sandstone, slate and limestone formation (Imnayongdang, 1990). The Geological Survey of India in the North-Eastern Region has recently discovered some mammal fossils which belong to about twenty million years ago (Sen, 1987). Coal, oil and gas, chromite, nickel, iron ore, lime-stone, base-metal, are the mineral wealth of Nagaland. Coal has been located in several regions of Mokokchung district, and oil and gas in the foothills of Wokha district.

Nagaland has a typical monsoon climate ranging from tropical to temperate. Over the foothills it is warm and humid, and over the high hills it is cool and temperate or moderate climate. In December, January and February, the coldest months in the year, the night temperature comes down between 4° c to 0° c. Over 75% of the total rainfall in the state occurs during the rainy season of mid-June to mid-October. The average annual rainfall varies from 150 cms to 280 cms and the temperature varies from 0°c in winter to about 35°c in summer (Imnayongdang, 1990). According to Changkija (2006), the climatic condition ranges from wet-tropical in the plains, sub-tropical in the middle and temperate in the high hills of monsoon with excessive rainfall.

1.2 Flora and Fauna

Nagaland bears testimony to the presence of large varieties of flora and fauna as the greater part of her hills are still covered with evergreen monsoon forests. There are varieties of plants in the mountain ranges as in some of the South American countries where the green vegetation is thickly grown. However, the unmindful and unlawful felling down of trees and clearing of forests for habitation and burning jungles for cultivation in recent times have caused the extinction of many protected and valuable species. Some of the species which grow continuously without any dormant period are the alders (*Alnus Nepalensis*) and some Cedrellas that outgrow even the fastest growing Eucalyptus (Nagaland, 2001). Other important plant species found in the hills are oak, chestnut, birch, magnolia, laurel, bonsum, gamari, hollock, koroi, khokan, peepul, creepers, cactus, cotton, etc. Rice, maize, wheat, millet, gram, mustard, potato, tapioca, pineapple, apple, sugar-cane, apricot, plantain, chillies, etc. are grown here in large quantity (Sen, 1987). Tea grows all along the low northern slopes at the foot of the Barail (Yonuo 1984). Different varieties of orchids and a good variety of plants bearing beautiful flowers like Shiroi Lily (*Lilum Shirohi*) is a common sight in the state especially in Dzuku valley. While the bamboo Dzüli *(Pstenoatachium)* is found only in Nagaland, the tallest Rhododendron in the world (108'8") is found on Mt. Japfü (Nagaland, 2001). The land is blessed with abundance of edible and medicinal plants and fruits.

Fauna of any region is of great importance so far as the ecological life is concerned. Even today many parts of Nagaland are covered by thick forests and jungles. However, in the recent past de-forestation has overtaken afforestation. On account of indiscriminate hunting in the forests including in the wildlife sanctuaries namely, Intanki National Wildlife Sanctuary, there has been a rapid depletion of wildlife in the state. The free use of guns in the state is another reason for the extinction of different species.

The fauna consists of Mithun *(Bos frontalis)* which is a semi-domesticated animal (Sen, 1987). Animals like wild elephants, buffalo, tiger, bison, barking deer, swamp deer, four horned antelope, pangolin, flying fox, leopard, monkey, jackal, wild pig, wild bear, wild cat, golden cat, porcupine, etc., are found in the forests of Nagaland. Reptiles like Indian python, Chinese green tree viper, eastern green mamba, etc. are common in Nagaland. Hornbill and tragopan are some rare birds found in the state. A notable feature of the Shiloi Lake at the foot of the Saramati Mountain is that it attracts migrating birds from Siberia on their way to lakes in Manipur and Myanmar (Nagaland, 2001).

1.3 Migrations to India and Racial Affinities

History bears testimony to great achievements of civilisations that flourished from time immemorial. Attempts to trace the origin and history of every race and tribe arouse curiosity in the minds of the people. This is often studied with the help of unwritten records like stories, folklore, hymns, signs and symbols, rare written materials, artifacts etc. Migrations and settlements are unique characteristics of all the lands and hence there is no land in the world without this phenomenon. For example, no one can claim India to be a land only of the Hindus as claimed by some Hindu fanatics. Muslims and Christians have been accused of having their roots in some foreign lands and so they are considered as agents of disunity and disharmony in the country. One cannot forget the fact that India has had a long history of migrations starting from the Aryans who crossed over from Central Asia and settled in India. It is evident from the words of Stanley Wolpert (1989):

> Around 2000 B.C. the original Indo-European-speaking, semi nomadic barbarians, who most probably lived in the

> region between the Caspian and the Black seas, were driven from their homeland by some natural disaster, possibly drought, prolonged frost, or plague. Whatever the cause of their dispersion…..the ancestors of the Italic, Greek, Germanic, English, Celtic, Iranian, Sanskritic, and modern Hindi-speaking people were forced to flee from southern Russia to survive. These tribes moved in every direction, splitting up into smaller, more cohesive units, driving their herds of cattle, sheep, goats, and domesticated horses with them and opening a new chapter in the history of Europe, as well as of India, …by about 1500 B.C. However, they (the Indo-Iranians) appear to have split once more and pastoral tribes known to history as the Indo-Aryans or simply Aryans, advanced still further east, across the perilous Hindu Kush Mountains, into India (pg. 24).

Jha (1977) is of the opinion that Sanskrit, Latin, Greek, Germanic (German, English, Swedish, etc), Slav (Russian, Polish, etc.) and Romance (Italian, Spanish, French, Rumanian, etc.) are languages that belong to the Aryan family. The scholars have named this language group as Indo-European or Indo-German language group (Chaudhuri, 1993). On the basis of similarity between these languages, it has been postulated that the original Aryans had a common homeland located most likely in the great steppe land stretching from Poland to Central Asia. From this region, Aryans may have migrated to different parts of Europe and Asia (Jha, 1977). The overwhelming majority of historians are of the opinion that the Aryans as a people had migrated to India. After they entered Punjab, the 'land of the five rivers' or 'of the seven rivers', they moved in a south-easterly direction (Smith, 1990).

India is a land of mixed races and communities. She represents unity in diversity from the North to the South and from the East to the West. It is quite amazing for a foreigner to wonder at this incredible unity characteristic of India through the past twenty centuries or more. There are a number of theories expounded by scholars on the existing races in India. Chief among the scholars is Sir Herbert Risley who classified the races in India into seven groups, while Dr. J. H. Hutton grouped them into eight. The latest view, however, generally accepted by all today, has been put forward by Dr. B. S. Guha, the former director of the Anthropological Survey of India in his book Racial Elements in the Population. He is of the opinion that, the six main races that came to India are: 1. Negrito; 2. Proto-Australoid; 3. Mongoloid; 4. Mediterranean; 5. Western Brachycephale and 6. Nordic. He has classified the Mongoloids into three sub-groups, namely, (i) Palaeo-Mongoloids of long-headed; (ii) Palaeo-Mongoloids of broad-headed; and (iii) Tibeto-Mongoloids. The Nagas in India have their affinity with the Mongoloids. Mahajan (1993) writes, "They were the most ancient stratum of the population and formed a dominant element in the tribes living in Assam and the Indo-Burmese frontiers" (pg. 45).

1.3.1 India and the Nagas

The Nagas did not have written records and chronicles till the arrival of the British. Many of the British administrators to the North-East, particularly to this hilly region, were writers. The scanty information we have of the Naga society in the pre-British period does not throw much credible light on the past history of the Nagas. Hence, information about origin, migration and settlement of the Nagas remains obscure. One of the myths circulated regarding the absence of written records among the Nagas is that at the beginning of creation God imparted knowledge of reading and writing both to the hill-man and the plains-man. The plains-man was given paper to write upon, while the hill-man was given skin. The hill-man devoured the skin when he found it edible. As a result, the Nagas have no record of their past (Joshi, 2001).

The Nagas live in the North East of India. They are a group of tribes racially and culturally distinct from other tribal groups living in North-Eastern India (D Souza, 2001). They are an Indo-Mongoloid people, divided into many major tribes, speaking different languages and dialects that are more than double the number of tribes (Alemchiba, 1970).

1.3.2 The Name *'Naga'*

The term 'Naga' appears to have been given not by the Nagas themselves but by outsiders. Imchen (1993) is of the view that the term was not used by them until the advent of the British, for each tribe or village in some cases was a sovereign independent entity known as the Aos, Semas, Angamis, Konyaks, etc. They were not called Ao Naga, or Angami Naga but each tribe was known by its given name. For example, the Aos were known as Aor, while the Angamis as Tenyimi, the Semas as Sumi and the Lothas as Kyon. All the other tribes, whether in Burma, Arunachal Pradesh, Manipur, Assam, or Nagaland, have their own distinct names (Sema, 1986). On the other hand, Horam (1974) describes the Angami tribe as Tenyimia, the Sema tribe as Semi, the Rengma tribe as

Mezama, the Lhotha tribe as Chizima, the Chang tribe as Mochumi, the Sangtam tribe as Lophomi, the Yachimi tribe as Yamsongar, the Konyak tribe as Taprongumi, the Ao tribe as Metikumi, the Mao tribe as Sopomi, and so on. The word, *mi, ma, mia*—all mean 'people' in the various Naga dialects. Alemchiba (1970) quotes V. Elwin, "Even as late as 1954, I found the people of Tuensang rarely speaking of themselves as Nagas but as Konyaks, Changs, Phoms and so on,... Gradually, however, as the Nagas became more united they began to use the name for themselves " (pg. 24). In Burma the Khiamungan, the Tikhir, the Chirr, and Mokori form a sizable population. These four tribes and some Pochuri villages were collectively called Kalyo Kengyu by the British. Khiamungans are a major tribe in Nagaland but the majority of them live on the Burma side. Lotha (2007) writes, "At present, Tikir, Chirr and Makori are considered 'sub-tribes' of Yimchunger tribe. The majority of the Makori live on the Burmese side but in Nagaland they are considered a 'sub-tribe' of Yimchunger" (pg. 2). Some of the tribes are clubbed together and known by a new name. For example, the tribe Zeliang-Rong is a combination of Zemi, Liangmai and Rongmai tribes living in a compact area. Similarly, Chakhesang is a compilation of three tribes, namely Chakru, Kheza and Sangtam (Sema, 1986). According to Horam (1974) even the present tribal names, like Angami, Ao, Lhotha, Sema and Tangkhul seem to have been coined by outsiders, most probably by the British administrators. In many cases these tribes existed in complete isolation. Their contact with one another was restricted to head-hunting and frequent warfare (Sema, 1986). Imchen (1993) concluded that the term 'Naga' came into common usage during British rule and became more evident during the rise of the Naga Club (NC) in 1918, and subsequently, at the formation of the Naga National Council (NNC) as a united Naga political institution in February 1946.

Many authors have defined the term 'Naga' but all in diverse ways. Namo (1987) writes, "The word *'Naga'* is derived from a Burmese word *'Na-ka'* meaning 'earring' (Na-Ear and Ka-Ring). The Burmese still call us *'Naka'*. Even before our ancestors migrated from Burma to present day Nagaland, we were a distinct tribe, called *Nakas or Nagas* in the present form" (pg. 17). Piercing of the ear-lobes is a widespread practice among the Naga tribes. A. Z. Phizo, the legendary Naga leader also maintained that the Burmese word, *'Naka'*, is the origin of the word 'Naga'. Perhaps the Burmese word *'Naka'* became *'Naga'* due to either phonetic perversion or when it was used in Roman script.

According to Maitra (1991), the word 'Naga' has been derived from the Sanskrit word *'Nanga'* which means 'naked.' Of course in the earlier days Nagas in the remote areas of the state were comfortable with scanty clothes. Many, however, agree with the view that the origin of the word Naga is associated with the Assamese people as they are the immediate neighbours of the Nagas. In Assamese, the word *Noga* means 'naked'. They use this word even today for the Nagas. Throughout Assamese literature one finds the use of this word (Sema, 1986). Similarly, quoting from J. H. Hutton's book 'Angami Nagas,' Chutia (2002, May 9) writes, "The word 'Naga' has been given all sorts of derivations, the most probable explanation of it is that it is merely a European lengthening of the Assamese 'Naga' (pronounced *noga*) meaning naked" (pg. 4).

The general belief is that the name was given by the Aryans to mean naked hill people. It is a fact that the word 'Naga' remained a terror to the Aryan-origin Assamese for ages. Quoting from E. A. Gait, Imchen (1993) suggests, "The word known to the Assamese seems to be derived from *Nok,* meaning folk, in some local dialects. Thus *onok,* 'we'; *nenok,* 'you' (plural) *parnok,* 'they' meaning, we people, you people, those people, etc as is found in the Ao dialect" (pg. 16). The Bengali word, *Nangta,* with the meaning 'crude and barbarous' is also associated with the word 'Naga' (Imchen, 1993). According to Philip (1983), "*Nok* in the Ao language is *dao*—a sharp, long knife used for head hunting...and also an implement of daily work. *'Ka'* means 'to have'. Hence the word 'Naga' may have derived from the words of *'nok-ka'* meaning 'a man with a *dao"* (pg. 5). Thong (1997) describes, "The head-hunters inhabiting the hilly regions between the Brahmaputra river in India and the Chindwin river in Myanmar (Burma); who practice rituals with the head of their victims are called 'Nagas', which was originally derived from the word *'Naüga'* as expressed by the Cachari King Dima of Dimapur" (pg. 3). On the other hand, for the Manipuris from the valley, the word *'Nag'* means 'Jewel' and hence the Nagas are called the Jewels of the Hills (Horam, 1974). It is evident, therefore, from the views of different writers that the origin and meaning of the word 'Naga' is more speculative than authentic.

1.3.3 Migration and Recorded History of the Nagas

One of the features of every tribe is to trace its origin lest it remains in obscurity. The Nagas, too, try to identify their roots through their own myths and stories, written and unwritten sources. From the available remnants of ornaments, tools and cutlery one can only presume the possibilities of their whereabouts in the past. It appears that the Nagas living in the North East have come from outside the region. Daili-Mao (1992) writes:

> Most of the scholars believe that originally the Naga people came from Central Asia. These people of Central Asia were known as the non-Chinese Chinang Tribes and were barbarous. They first came to north-west border of China many centuries before the Christian era. Later on these tribes spread over to China, Indonesia, Philippines, Bhutan, Burma, other South-East Asian countries and to the present Naga Hills/land (pg. 12).

This is evident from the fact that the Nagas bear similarity with some tribal groups such as Dyaks and Koyans of Indo-China as their social customs and culture resemble the latter (Singh, 1981). Kaka D. Iralu believes that the Nagas came from southern China by relying on the available oral traditions and legends which are corroborated by written documents of their neighbours, who had learned the art of writing long before them. Iralu (2010, June 2) writes:

> The Nagas, Kachins and Karens are considered to be blood brothers who came in the same migratory wave from southern China during the building of the Great Wall of China (403-221 B.C.). Their forefathers probably ran away from the forced labour that was used for building the wall. The Chinese have a word for the Nagas which means 'the runaway people.' Before these events, their forefathers along with the Kachins and Karens migrated from Mongolia along

> with the other Mongolian Asian races in 2617 B.C. and entered the Yunan Province of China in 1385 B.C. This was after their migration across Turkistan and Tibet (pg. 6).

Various ornaments and weapons used by the Nagas have similarity with that of the people from outside the North East. For example, Raatan (2006) is of the view that their love of marine shells points to a past settlement near the sea, their spears with ornamental barb curling outward from a shaft suggests some relationship with the residents of the Philippine Islands and Indonesian people. Alemchiba (1970) is of the opinion that some places in the said areas bearing similar names like 'Naga' and *'Nabas'* of Philippines, *'Naka'* of Malaya, *'Naiga'* of Burma, *'Nagreg'* of Java Island, etc., suggest cultural and physical similarities among these people.

There are conflicting stories regarding the origin, migration and settlement of the Nagas. Hence, it is difficult to say with precision when the Nagas entered the North-East. Dr. S. K. Chatterjee, a writer and scholar is of the opinion that the Mongoloids made their entry by 10th century B.C., when the Vedas were compiled. Their earlier history, however, remains obscure. Anand (1980) observed that the Nagas belonged to the Indo-Mongoloid group and spoke the Tibeto-Burman dialects of the Sino-Tibetan family. Their earliest presence appeared to have been noted in Yajurveda about a thousand years before Christ, which mentions the tribal group *'Kirata'* that occupied the North-East, particularly NEFA (now Aunachal Pradesh), Nagaland, Manipur and Burma. Sunguist (2001) writes, "Elwin traces the origin of the Nagas back to the northwest part of China. They migrated during the conflict between the Chinese and Tartars in the 13th and 14th centuries" (pg. 581), from the Sinkiang Province in China and crossed the Brahmaputra river west-wards.

The routes these immigrant tribes took were different. Sanyu (1996) writes, "Some took the Himalayan section which extends down through the Patkai, Arakan Yoma, and Banda Arch towards Sumatra and Java, and some took the Pacific section which extends from Formosa through the Philippines, Borneo and on to Japan" (pg. 11). According to Singh (1987), different Naga tribes came to Nagaland after crossing the Irawaddy and the Chindwin rivers of Burma. Some of the allied tribes of the Nagas like Karen, Shan, Chin, Singpho and others who had come from western China settled in Burma.

Yonuo (1984) is of the opinion that the Nagas came to Nagaland and Manipur sometime between the last century B.C. and the beginning of the Christian era from the modern Yunnan through Burma. It is from there they moved to Tibet to Assam and then entered the Naga Hills. The Royal Chronicles of Manipur recorded by King Meidingu Nongda Lairen Phakhamba of Manipur mention about Naga Haochang village of Kabui (Impui) Nagas around 33-150 A.D. Another mention of the same village was later made by the Manipuri king Ningthourel Lamba during his reign around 662-762 A.D (Nuh, 2002). So, the Nagas must have occupied the land at about the beginning of the Christian era. Their migration might have been caused by the need for more agricultural land. The other factor which added to this migration within Asia was the expansion of the Chinese Han people pushing southwards as population grew in the cradle of the Yellow River valley (Sanyu, 1996). So, from these above descriptions and presumptions one can conclude that the Nagas were a Mongolian stock that migrated from China before the Christian era through the Patkai range and settled in different areas of the present Naga Hills.

Sanyu (1996) quotes Huang Tsang, the Chinese pilgrim who visited Assam during Bhaskaravarman's rule in 645 A.D), "The east of this country is bounded by a line of hills, so there is no great city to the kingdom. The frontiers are contiguous to the barbarians of south-west China. These tribes are in fact akin to those of the Mon people in their customs" (pg. 7). In the Buranjis or chronicles of Assam, the Nagas are not referred to by their tribal or modern names. They are usually described by the broad name 'Naga' (Barpujari, 2003). However, nothing much is known about the history of the Nagas prior to the advent of the Ahoms to Assam in 1228. With the gradual establishment of the Ahom kingdom, the Ahoms came into contact with the Ao, the Lotha and the Rengma Nagas who were closer to Assam (Barpujari, 2003). Ahom Buranjis also record that by the time the Ahoms came to Assam in the thirteenth century, Nagas were already settled in Naga Hills.

1.4 Settlement

The history of how the Naga tribes came to occupy their present places is yet to be established, (Alemchiba, 1970), as there are incompatible legends, theories and claims of migration by various writers and tribes. However, the studies based on all of them reveal that the area had been peopled by successive waves of migration from different directions. Yonuo (1984) writes:

> Yet, it looks possible that the first wave of migrants were the Maos (Shipoumai), Angamis, Semas, Rengmas,

> Rongmai and Lothas who moved from the south through the mountain-fringes touching the valley of Manipur to the north. Then, they settled down at Makhriphfü, a village in Mao area near the hills of Japfu. After living there for some years, Shipoumai, now better called Maos, settled permanently down in this area where Maharmai or Marams closely allied to Meiteis also came in latterly, whereas the rest went through different directions to different places where the Angamis, Semas, Rengmas, Chakhesangs, Zeliangrongs and Lothas are today. The second wave of immigrants comprised the Aos, Changs, Kheinmunghans, Sangtams, Yimchungers and Tangkhuls. They are believed to have migrated from Thangdut, near the Chindwin River in Burma by different routes and at different times. The Konyak Nagas came to their present area of occupation in the hills from the north-east of Burma. The Aos' migration route is believed to be from Burma through the Tangkhul, Chakhesang and Tuensang areas to the present Ao villages. This is how all of the Naga tribes came to settle in their respective areas in the hills and mountains (pg. 39).

It is clear that the migration of Nagas did not take place all at once. It must have gone on for some years or centuries before they came to settle down in their present places in India and Burma. Perhaps the break-up into different tribes must have also taken place not only in the present habitat but also on the way to their settlements. Sema (1986) writes, "The above view is substantiated by the present location of tribes like the Konyaks, Phoms, Changs, Sangtams, Kheimungans, Yimchungers, and especially that of Konyaks and Kheimungans. These tribes are still living in parts of Burma adjacent to Nagaland" (pg. 5). Various oral traditions, folklore, legendary sources and writings by well known authors also support this view.

Khezhakenoma appears to be an important migration route of many of the tribes living in Nagaland. Various traditions speak of the Nagas who have lived there for years before their departure to other places for settlement. Sema (1986) writes, "According to a legend, the Aos went first and were followed by the Lothas and the Semas. After them, came the Rengmas, the Angamis and the Chakhesangs " (pg. 5). In the words of Hutton (1969), "The Angamis, the Aos, the Lothas and the Semas, they say, are descended from four brothers" (pg. 18).

1.5 Language

The language of the Indo-Mongoloid people, except those of the Khasis and the Jaintias, belongs to Sino-Tibetan or Tibeto-Chinese speech-family. These languages have been classified into two groups, namely, Tibeto-Burman and Siamese-Chinese and all the Naga dialects are included in the former group. These dialects not only vary from tribe to tribe and area to area, but also from village to village in some regions. The inter-village feuds and existence of many tribes also undoubtedly contributed to the rise of different dialects.

Nagas don't have a common language or a script, even where each tribe has its own language or dialect. They have adopted the Roman script. Sema (1986) writes, "Each tribe has a separate dialect and often some tribes have two to three dialects. For example, the Aos have four dialects - Mongsen, Chungli, Changki and Merinokpu"(pg.12). Among these, Chungli is accepted as the mother-tongue of the Aos. According to one legend, the Nagas had their own script written in an animal skin, but they cooked it by mistake and ate it up. Another legend says it was a dog that ate the skin in the absence of its master (Imchen, 1993). English is the official language of the state. Nagamese, a broken form of Assamese, is the lingua-franca among the Nagas.

1.6 Social, Economic and Political life

The Naga society is an aggregate of communities composed of multiple tribes. They are all known by a common name 'Naga', which inherently displays their name, language, customs, culture, practices etc. But the real identity of a Naga is revealed in the tribe he belongs to. Sunguist (2001) writes, "The Nagas are a non-caste, classless, autonomous and free hill-dwelling people" (pg. 581). Ghosh (1982), quoting from W. C. Smith's book, 'Ao Naga tribes of Assam,' highlights some of the characteristics of the Tibeto-Burman tribes of Assam that are also found among the tribes of South-East Asian countries:

> They are: head-hunting, common sleeping houses (*Morung*) for the unmarried men which are taboo to women, dwelling houses built on posts and piles, disposal of the dead on raised platforms, a sort of trial marriage, great freedom of intercourse between the sexes before marriage, betel-chewing, aversion of milk as an article of diet, tattooing by pricking, absence of any powerful political organisation, the double-cylinder vertical forge, the simple loom for weaving cloth, a large quadrangular or hexagonal shield, residence in hilly regions with a crude form of agriculture (pg. 42).

Rice is the staple diet of the people. They eat any kind of

meat and boiled leafy vegetables. They also eat millet and barley. Ramunny (1988) writes, "They never used to drink milk. Their favourite beverage is rice beer. This had very little alcoholic content but provided sufficient kick and contained essential nutrients for energy and strength" (pg. 7). Coffee, cardamom and tea as plantation crops and sugarcane and potato as cash crops are grown in some parts of the state in a small scale. The people rear buffaloes, mithuns, cows, pigs, dogs and chickens for food as well as for commercial purposes.

The economy of the state is agricultural as the majority of the population is directly dependent on agriculture. The main crops are rice, millet, maize and pulses. Even though the state produces a considerable amount of rice, it still depends on import. The two methods of cultivation practiced by the Nagas are *jhum*, sometimes known as the 'slash-and-burn' or 'shifting' cultivation which is practised by the majority population and terraced cultivation (Lotsüro, 2000). Jhum cultivation is a method in which a piece of land is cleared of all trees and grasses, burnt and then a variety of crops like rice, maize, millet, chilies, potatoes, ginger etc and different kinds of vegetables are grown. The land is then allowed to lie fallow for some years till the soil regains its fertility. The people then look for another fresh plot of land for cultivation. The terraced cultivation is mostly followed by the Angami tribe. This method of cultivation is also found in Malaya, Indonesia, Philippines, Formosa, Japan, etc. Terraces are cut on the slopes of the hills and the fields are irrigated with running water from the mountain side or from streams.

The Nagas are a self-sufficient people who produce everything for their survival be it food items, tools, ornaments, clothing etc. Marine shells, particularly white shells closely strung with types of beads form part of the ornaments meant for men and women. Shimmi (1988) writes, "Ivory armlets were worn by the well-to-do but in most tribes men wore white wooden armlets in the upper arms and heavy brass rings in the lower arms. The girls generally wore coiled brass armlets in the upper arms and brass rings in each lower arm" (pg. 17). Both men and women wore ear rings of different types and kinds. The patterns of the textiles were distinct and different for each tribe. For each occasion they have different costumes. One could make out the position one holds in the village by the costumes worn by them. Nagas are very protocol-minded about dress. In the olden days the finest cloth could be worn only by the head-hunter or the donor of feasts of merit (Ramunny, 1988).

A special characteristic of a Naga village is the Morung or the bachelors' dormitory, which is situated at the centre of the village. It was actually a training place for the youth of the village. Women were not allowed inside. At a young age of six or seven, a boy enters the morung and remains there till he marries and sets up his own independent house (Raatan, 2006). The young people attain maturity here and are taught folk tales and songs. In the words of Elwin (1997), "The 'Morungs' are guard-houses, recreation clubs, centres of education, art and discipline and have an important ceremonial purpose" (pg. 8). Important decisions relating to war and peace were taken in the Morung. However, the Morung is not a common feature in all the Naga tribes. Angami villages do not have a Morung but the Ao, Lotha, Konyak and the Phom villages do have them.

Recently, the Government of Nagaland declared the state

as the 'Land of Festivals'. The Naga people celebrate a number of festivals. Most of them revolve round agriculture. During festivals they observe different *genna* (day of prohibition). Dance and music draw the attention of the people during festivals. The important festivals are Sekrenyi (Angami tribe), Sühkrühnye (Chakhesang tribe), Aoleang Monyu (Konyak tribe), Monyu (Phom tribe), Moatsü and Tsüngremmong (Ao tribe), Miu and Tsokum (Khiamniungan tribe), Naknyu Lem (Chang tribe), Tuluni (Sema tribe), Metumniu (Yimchungrü tribe), Amongmong (Sangtam tribe), Tokhü Emong (Lotha tribe), Ngadah (Rengma tribe), Hega and Chega Gadi (Zeliang tribe), Yemshe (Pochuri tribe), and others (Sen, 1987).

A village is an independent autonomous unit. Philip (1983) writes, "Among all Nagas the real political unit of the tribe is the village" (pg. 29). A common bond namely, 'an individual is for the village and the village is for the individual' binds all people together. Hence they are socially, politically and religiously united. Raatan (2006) writes, "More than four-fifths of the population lives in small, isolated villages. The villages are usually divided into *khels* or quarters, each with its own headman and administration" (pg. 228). The number of khels depends on the size of the village. Philip (1983) quotes the words of Elwin, "The basic interest of every Naga is in his family, the clan, the khel and the village" (p. 29). All Naga villages can be termed petty republics in themselves. Tribal administration is democratic. The constitution of a village is based on the principles of justice and equality. The village council consisting of *Gaon Buras* and elders generally decide all disputes in the village. The decisions have to be unanimous (Singh, 1987). Once a decision is taken it is binding on all.

Each village was more or less self-sufficient. Villages had their own cultivable land, sufficient to support its population. The houses were built on hill tops for security reasons as various tribes were engaged in inter-village feuds. As Raatan (2006) mentions, "Selection of the sites for the village was largely influenced by considerations of defensive strategy,… well-fortified with stone walls, sharp pointed bamboo spikes, heavy wooden gates and deep ditches around" (pg. 229). One of the features of most villages was the xylophone or the log drum meant to give an alarm or celebrate a victory.

The organisation of the village community differs from tribe to tribe. There is a system of hereditary chieftainship among the Semas and Changs. On the other hand, the Konyaks have very powerful Chiefs or Angs who are regarded as sacred and whose word is law (Elwin, 1997). Raatan (2006) writes:

> Among the Angamis, although the chief is chosen for his wealth, physical prowess and skill in diplomacy, the decisions are taken collectively by all the villagers. The Semas have a system of hereditary village chief. The chief is called *'Kukami,'* who rules over a village but has no control over other villages. He is overlord of the village and all others are 'mighimis' or dependants. The chief looks after *the mighmi,* gives him land, helps him financially, protects him and even arranges a bride for him if the mighimi is not in a position to pay the marriage price. On the other hand, the mighimi looks upon the chief as his father, works for him, fights for him and obeys him in all matters of village administration. It was customary for the eldest son of a Sema chief to establish a village of his own out of his father's estate. In case, the village did not admit to further division, the son could go

to another area, clear or conquer that place and establish his authority. Thus the Sema society encouraged expansionist colonisation (pg. 230).

1.7 Religion

The traditional Naga religion is animistic. Nuh (2003) writes, "Nagas did not belong to any major religion of the world but like any other tribal of the world they believed in and feared spirits" (pg. 16). However, various types of beliefs and rituals of the Nagas suggest that their religion was a mixture of animism and polytheism. They had a vaguely imagined supreme creator, ghosts and spirits of trees, rivers, hills, unseen forces etc (Elwin, 1997). Their belief was expressed through the worship of nature and through their faith in the power of magic and of omens. In order to propitiate and exorcise them (malignant demons), the Nagas usually offer efficacious things like egg, fowl, giblets, spirituous liquor, pig, cattle, mithun, cloth, pieces of iron, etc (Yonuo, 1984).

Superstitious beliefs, following good or bad omens at the time of important undertakings like starting a war, beginning a journey, first sowing or harvesting or in the event of an illness, etc. control the life of a Naga. Besides, during festivals and other auspicious days a few grains of food and rice beer are offered to the departed souls with the belief that they would visit the people and bring good fortune if they are pleased with the offerings. Yonuo (1984) writes, "Individuals pray to God to avert bad luck, cure sickness, promise victory in life and assure a propitious passage from this world to the next" (pg. 23). However, idol worship was unknown to them.

According to Philip (1983), "The Naga religion is not a

moral code. It is a system of ceremonies" (pg 39). There are priests and medicine men that play an important role in the life of the people. The Nagas believe in life after death. The good soul goes to a Village of the Dead towards the sunrise, the bad to a less pleasant place towards the sunset (Elwin, 1997). Added to that, observances of a large number of gennas, (some call the day of prohibition as genna) for the propitiation of the spirits also form part of the Naga belief system. They are observed for the benefit of everybody—the individual, household, clan, village, and members of a certain age-group or sex-group (Philip, 1983). It is believed that breaking of the norms may bring curses and hence their strict observance is essential for the health, wealth and progress of both the individual and society. These gennas varied from tribe to tribe and from region to region (Sema, 1986).

1.8 Headhunting

It is assumed that the practice of head-hunting was prevalent in many countries like Europe, British Islands, Ireland, Nigeria, Balkan Peninsula, Malaysia, Indonesia, Indo-China, Philippines, North America, Burma etc in earlier days. It was not a mere exercise to display one's courage and valour but was also associated with religious ritual practices. Nagas too from time immemorial have practiced head-hunting for various reasons. According to a legend, the Nagas learnt the practice of head hunting from the fight between an ant and a lizard over a berry. In the course of the fight the ant cut off the lizard's head and thus men learnt to take heads (Elwin, 1997). The reasons cited for head-hunting are complicated and interesting. Head-hunting culture was a part of the lives of the Nagas when all the villages were independent and sovereign. The village had to be located on top of a hill for good defence (Thong, 1997). In the words of Lotsüro (2000), "Inter-village wars culminating in the taking of the enemy's head were part of everyday life until the *Pax Britannica* established its sway over the Naga Hills" (pg. 19). Headhunting was expected to bring individual glory to a man and prosperity to his village in the form of good harvest, birth of many children and rich hunting (Lotsüro, 2000). It was said that heads were needed for several religious ceremonies and rituals. Whenever a chief's house or Morung or such abodes were to be built, a head was needed to appease ancestral ghosts (Thong, 1997). This practice was also aimed at the acquisition of more land and water for cultivation, hunting, fishing and food gathering. Bishop Stephen Ferrando (1947) attaches a religious flavor to this practice when he writes:

> We hear stories of brutal massacres when the Nagas were not yet under the British and the present Indian administration. But the outlook of the people was never as entirely brutal as some journalists would make it appear. The heads were not cut for pleasure, but for religious reasons, to bring fertility to crops, to obtain spiritual benefits (pg. 94).

Elwin (1997) writes:

> The practice is probably based on a belief in a soul-matter or vital essence of great power which resides in the human head. By taking the head from another village, therefore, it was believed that a new injection of vital and creative energy would come to the aggressor's village when he brought the head home. This was valuable for human and animal fertility. It stimulated the crops to grow better, especially when the

> head was that of a woman with long hair. Moreover, the Nagas have always been a warlike race and the warrior, especially the young warrior, who had taken a head held a great advantage over his fellows in attracting the most beautiful girl of his village for marriage. Indeed, it is said that a youth who had not taken a head found considerable difficulty in obtaining a wife at all (pg. 11).

In the words of Horam (1977), "It was that a young man, eager to prove his mettle, would long to take a head, bring it home in triumph to be feted as a warrior, gain the wearing of the coveted warrior's ornaments and having at last proved his worth and manhood, acquire a bride" (pg. 88). The head-hunting practice had an adverse effect on the people as it actually isolated villages from one another. This restricted free movement of people from village to village and increased suspicion among different tribes. Gradually with the prohibition enforced by the British and the influence of Christianity most tribes have discontinued this abominable practice.

CHAPTER TWO

Christianity In Nagaland

CHRISTIANITY HAS a long history of nearly 2000 years in India, however, in the North East it became known only from the 18th century especially after the conquest of the region by the British. For many people in mainland India information about the North East and Christianity is minimal. It comes as a great shock to the people of the North East when they learn that many are still ignorant of this region as being part of India. A misconception about this region passed on to successive generations is that it is Christianised and is infested with insurgency. However, the truth of the matter is that the whole region is not Christianised and the areas that have embraced Christianity are not as wide as is claimed. If the whole population of Mizoram and Nagaland, the two Christian states in the Indian Union and the Christian population of other North Eastern States is compared with the total population of other Indian states, their number is like a few drops in

CHRISTIANITY IN NAGALAND

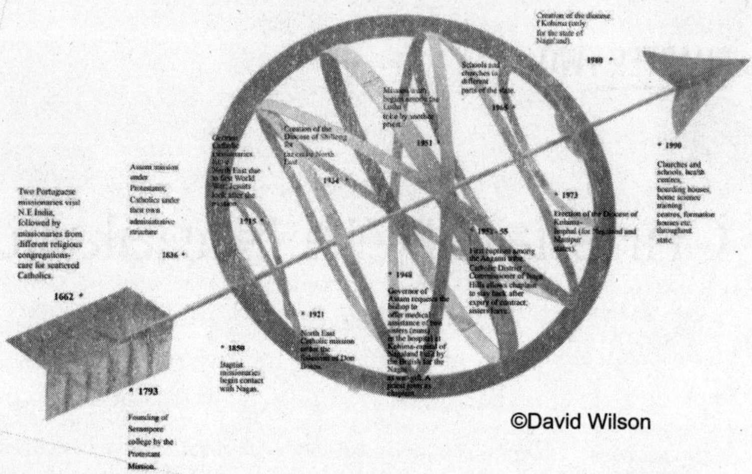

the mighty ocean of great India. In other words, compared to the non-Christian population in other states the Christian population is negligible. It is a fact that this region is a different world in itself because of its distinct races and culture.

The North East is home to various tribes like the Ahoms, Bodos, Chutiyas, Garos, Jaintias, Kacharis, Khasis, Kochs, Kukis, Mizos, Nagas, etc. and a host of minor and sub - tribes. Much before the Christian influence was felt in the region, many parts of Manipur and Assam had already been Sanskritised. Understanding this region with its own belief systems and practices, therefore, is an enormous task and it needs a thorough and an in-depth study. Insurgency in the region is not because of its contact with Christianity but due to geographical, economic, cultural and political factors. However, the untiring efforts and contributions made by hundreds of Christian missionaries of various denominations for the development of the region needs to be recorded in the annals of the history of the North East. The Christian missions deserve much recognition for the development of this region and exposing it to the world.

Overall knowledge and influence of Christianity gradually spread in the North East from the 19th century onwards. In the words of Philip (1983), "The nineteenth century witnessed an amazing growth of Christianity in Asia. North East India with its diversities, inaccessibility and problems of communication was no exception" (pg. 46). The North East, isolated from the world as well as mainland India, was united with the latter in the first quarter of the century. Undoubtedly a significant step towards Christianization of the region was the Treaty of Yandabo, concluded between the British East India Company and the Kingdom of Burma on 24th February 1826. Downs (1983) writes, "For the first time in its history the region was now linked politically with a major Indian power and hence brought within the mainstream of Indian history" (pg. 1). However, even much before this Treaty was concluded there had been cultural contacts with the rest of India. Within a short span of time the entire North East, previously fragmented politically, was brought under the control of the British and this provided a favorable climate for the spread of Christianity.

2.1 Earliest Christian Contact with North East India

While the North East came into contact with Christianity only about three hundred years ago, some parts of India mainly South India have a history of association of about two thousand years. Even though the Catholic Church took the first initiative to keep in contact with the North East, it was often irregular with a number of intervals in between. In the

North East, as Syiemlieh (2004) writes, "The Catholics were the first of the foreign Christian missions to come to North East India but amongst the last to stay on and grow" (pg. 113). Supporting this view Sangma (1987) mentions that the earliest visit by the Christian missionaries to North East India was in 1626, by two Jesuit missionaries, Fr. Stephen Cacella and Fr. John Cabral. O. Paviotti (1987) writes on the detailed account of their journey and purpose:

> On August 2, (1626) three Jesuits, two Portuguese and one Italian, Fr. Cacella, Fr. Cabral and Fr. Fontemona set out from Hooghly (Bengal) on their way to Tibet. On September 26, only Frs. Cacella and Cabral reached Hajo (near Guwahati), then the seat of the Mughal Governor. At Pandu they met the Raja of Busna. By him they were introduced to the Raja of Cooch Behar at Hajo itself, who advised them to meet his son at Cooch Behar for help in their journey. They reached Cooch Behar on October 21. Then resuming their journey, they made for Rangamati. There Fr. Cabral was taken seriously ill. On his recovery on February 21, 1627, they left for Paro (Bhutan). There they met the Raja who welcomed them. They obtained permission to build a chapel and preach the gospel. But as their apostolate bore no fruit, they took to the road again. Eventually they reached Lhasa and returned to Bandel via Kathmandu and Patna (pg. 2).

2.2 The Mughal Invasion and Beginning of Christianity

In the second half of the 17th century the Mughal army invaded Assam to conquer the Ahoms. In the army there was a sizeable group of Indo-Portuguese Christians, who lived at Rangamati (the present day Goalpara in Assam) for many decades as border guards of the Mughals (Kottuppallil, 1991). So here the origin of the Catholic community dates back to the end of the 17th century, and most of the Christians were soldiers. This view is supported by the Chronicle of the Augustinian Friars of Bandel, near Hooghly in Bengal in 1682, which makes reference to a flourishing community of 7,000 Christians at a place called Rangamati in Goalpara district of Lower Assam. Again in 1696 an Augustinian, Frey Sicardo makes further reference to the Christian community of Rangamati, "In the Camp of Bencomatis on the confines of Assam, in the country subject to the king of the Mughals, there are two Churches, one dedicated to Our Lady of the Rosary, the other to Our Lady of Guadelupe" (Sangma, 1987, pg. 15).

There is a report of a visit by Bishop F. T. Laynez of S. Tome-Mylapore to Rangamati community in January 1715 who spent 25 days in the area. Fr. C. A. Barbier who accompanied Bishop Laynez reported that the latter had confirmed 1,000 persons during his visit (Sangma, 1987). Thus Rangamati, is said to have been the first place in the North East inhabited by the Christian community. Unfortunately the descendants of this community can no longer be traced. In successive years the Augustinian friars made periodic visits to minister these Catholics who were in the service of Mughal, Cachar and Tripura rulers. Muttumana (1984) mentions, "During the Burmese war in Cachar in 1824 a garrison of Christian soldiers belonging to the former Mughal army had been maintained by the Cachar king against the Burmese " (pg. 5). Again after the annexation of Assam by the British in 1838, some of those Christian soldiers and families did not leave Assam.

They were occasionally looked after by priests from Calcutta (Muttumana, 1984). The records of Barbier who accompanied Bishop Laynez also mentioned that during the visit of latter he spent time with the community at Ossumpur where Catholics were present and administered the sacrament of confirmation to them in a Church dedicated to St. Nicholas of Tolento (Muttumana, 1984). There are also Catholics in the present day Tripura. In the words of Syiemlieh (2004), "Tripura which was closer to Bengal had Augustinian and Holy Cross priests visiting Catholics in the village of Mariamnagar just out of Agartala. The earliest visit to the Christians in this native state was that of Fr. Ignatius Gomes in 1683" (pg. 114).

Another area that had a significant presence of Christians was Bondashill of Cachar district in Assam, situated on the left bank of the Barak River (Barak Valley). "Throughout the vast Surma valley this was the only settlement of Catholics for decades and formed what we may call an oasis in the midst of a pagan population" (Muttumana, 1984, pg. 5). However, the origin of this Catholic settlement is shrouded in obscurity. According to the tradition of the Catholics of Bondashill, their ancestors were Christian soldiers who, around the year 1790, emigrated from Meerut (Uttar Pradesh), under the leadership of a petty prince. Sangma (1987) writes:

> Their number was about 500 and about 600 Muslim soldiers. While the struggles were going on between the Mughals and the British, these Catholics immigrated into the Surma valley and settled down at Bondashill. The still common family names of Pinero, Fernandez, etc. indicate their Portuguese origin. It may be also that these Catholic soldiers of Bondashill were under the service of the Mughal

> Emperor and were sent by him from Meerut to Bengal and Sylhet to fight against the British, but when in 1765, Bengal and Sylhet were finally transferred to the British, they found refuge in the kingdom of the Raja of Cachar, who, allotted to them this area which may be the beginning of the Catholic Christian village of Bondashill. This Catholic community still exists today (pg. 16).

There was no mention of the presence of any other Christian denomination in the North East till 1790 other than the Roman Catholics. We can thus conclude that the first contact with the North East India was made by the Catholic missionaries and the first Christian communities in North East India were also the Catholics.

It is a known fact that Christianity spread to the region comfortably when the territories were incorporated under the British Empire after the Anglo-Burmese war. Thereafter, we find a steady progress in missionary activities by different denominations in the region. However, in their enthusiasm to do missionary work, priests of various orders like the Society of Jesus (Jesuits), the Augustinians and the Holy Cross travelling to and through Assam, Cachar and Tripura apparently were not interested in proselytizing; but their focus was China and Tibet (Syiemlieh, 2004). While travelling to these places through Assam they administered sacraments to the scattered Christian communities of the region. In the words of Syiemlieh (2004), "They were more interested in Bengal and North India where they set up missions. Consequently, the real beginning of the establishment of the Christian Church in the region has to be attributed to the Protestant foreign missions" (pg. 2004).

2.3 Protestant Missions in the North East

The arrival of William Carey, a Protestant missionary on 11 November 1793 at Calcutta was an important milestone for the Church in this part of the country. Since then this region has witnessed a dramatic growth and spread of Christianity through various missionary activities. With a view to train the Indians for missionary work he founded the Serampore College in 1818 (Sangma, 1987) and this English Baptist mission was a pioneer in the opening of the region to Baptist Christianity.

2.3.1 The Charter Act of 1813 and the Beginning of American Baptist Mission

The Charter Act of 1813 passed by the British Government, that permitted the Missionaries to carry out ministries in India, was a blessing for the Serampore mission which made use of the opportunity to reach out to the North Eastern region (Sangma, 1987). From 1813, the Serampore mission started taking interest in evangelising the Khasis at the request of W. N. Garrett, a judge at Sylhet. William Carey sent Krishna Chandra Pal, the first Serampore convert who was baptised in 1800 as the first missionary to the Khasi Hills. In the course of time, Cherrapunjee was selected as the site for the mission station as the local leader/chief (Syiem) was very close to the British. Their next area of interest was Guwahati where they opened the mission centre and a school in 1829 at the request of David Scott, the Commissioner of Assam. James Rae, the first missionary to this mission had made some significant breakthrough. The main reason for the success of the Church at the initial stage was the active participation of and collaboration extended by the civil servants to the missionaries. Many of the civil servants believed in the overall development of the people and the region and so they were actually missionaries in their work and beliefs. They, therefore, greatly assisted the work of the Church through their personal effort. Supporting this view Kuriakose (2003) mentions, "Charles Trevelyan, civil servant and liberal reformer, and Francis Jenkins, the evangelical Governor-General's Agent and Commissioner in Assam, played an active role in the establishment and, in the latter case, the continuing development of the Baptist mission in Assam" (pg. 132). Meanwhile for the smooth functioning and better coordination among the workers, the Serampore mission was amalgamated with the Baptist Missionary Society. The Serampore Mission station at Guwahati was then eventually handed over to the American Baptist Mission in 1838 which helped them concentrate fully on the North East.

In 1836 the American Baptist Mission began their work in Assam. According to Downs (1983), "Ironically, the first American Baptist Mission stations in North East India were not established for the purpose of evangelising the people of that area but as strategic outposts for reaching the Shan tribes of northern Burma and southern China" (pg. 97). (The Ahoms too are a Shan people who migrated into Upper Assam in the early thirteenth century). With this end in mind for several years after its establishment the mission first centered at Sadiya and later at Jaipur was known officially as the Shan Mission (Downs, 1983). The efforts of the American Baptists to enter northern Burma, however, proved futile as the Burmese kings had fortified their territories against intrusion. Meanwhile the publication of a book titled, "Journal of Two Voyages along the Coast of China in 1831 and 1832," written by Charles

Gutzlaff in 1834 aroused curiosity among the Americans to establish mission stations in China. The Chinese authorities on the other hand guarded the eastern Chinese coasts closely and would not allow missionaries to enter China. So the mission authorities in America thought of a possibility to enter from the south, through Thailand. Finding that they were unable to enter China or Burma through known passes they turned their attention towards the North East and ventured into Arunachal Pradesh through Sadiya to work among the Adis. Perhaps they thought it was possible to enter China later on through Arunachal Pradesh, bordering China. Since then the Baptist mission concentrated its work in Assam. Captain Francis Jenkins, the Commissioner of Assam was instrumental in setting up mission centres in Assam particularly among the two tribes of the Shan family—the Khamtis and the Singphos. By 1843 the American Baptist Mission had started mission stations in Upper, Central and Lower Assam, namely Sibsagar, Nowgong and Guwahati. This is how they began to exercise their sway over Arunachal Pradesh, Naga Hills, Manipur Hills, Garo Hills, Mikir Hills and most of Brahmaputra valley.

2.3.2 The Welsh Calvinist Methodists

One of the earliest groups of missionaries to work in the North East was the Welsh Calvinist Methodist Foreign Mission (Welsh Presbyterian) that began working in the Khasi-Jaintia hills in 1841 with the arrival of Thomas Jones. Within the span of a few years it became well established in the whole of the Khasi Hills, the Jaintia Hills, Cachar, and Sylhet in the Barak valley and in Lushai Hills (Mizoram) after its annexation into British India in the early part of 1890. The first Welsh missionary to arrive in Aizawl, the present day capital of Mizoram, was D. E. Jones, in September 1879. Meanwhile the mission work in Manipur began in the year 1894 by an Englishman by the name of William Pettigrew. He took up his residence in Ukhrul and started his work. The American Baptist missionaries in Assam worked out a device to make a local church. Kuriakose (2003) writes, "The 'Guwahati Policy' (1895 A.D.) as it is known is based on a three-self formula. It aims at 'the development of native churches with a view to their ultimate settlement upon a self-supporting, self-governing, self-extending system" (p. 266).

2.4 British Policy and Annexation of the North East

The British colonial rule did not favour the Catholic Church in India over the Protestants. Ever since the Reformation movement began in Germany the Catholic faith suffered setbacks in most of the European countries. From being a staunch supporter of papal causes and the one who vehemently condemned Martin Luther and his teachings, Henry VIII (1509-1547), the Tudor King of England, turned out to be an arch enemy of the papacy when Pope Clement VII declined to accept Henry's request for a dispensation annulling his marriage with Catherine of Aragon. In this marriage he had no male issue to succeed him. He avenged the papacy's disapproval by becoming the head of the Church in England. As Bhattacharjee (1993) writes, "Henry caused the Parliament to pass the Act of Supremacy which declared the king to be the 'Supreme Head of the Church of England" (pg. 96). His successor, Edward VI (1547-1553) through a series of reforms made England a Protestant country. Various attempts made by James II (1685-1688) to restore Catholicism in England finally led to the Glorious Revolution (1688). This also resulted in the expulsion of the king and the accession of Mary and William (Mary was James II's daughter, but married to a Protestant, William of Orange) as the joint sovereigns of England. Through the 'Declaration of Rights' enacted in 1689, the new government upheld the official status of the Protestant religion in England. On record there are a number of official statements made by highly placed British officials, pointing to one of their paramount interests in India as promotion of Christianity. One of such examples is found in the writings of Downs (1983) when he writes:

> In 1806, when the East India Company officially opposed missionaries, Lord William Bentinck wrote, 'Our first wish must be to see the followers of Mahomet and Brahma embrace Christianity'. Ten years later the British representative in Travancore-Cochin, Col. Munro, declared in a letter to the C.M.S., 'I regard the diffusion of genuine Christianity in India as a measure equally important to the interests of humanity and to the stability of our power.' In 1854 Lord Palmerstone, the British Prime Minister, used the following words, 'It is not only our duty, but it is our interest to promote the diffusion of Christianity as far as possible throughout the length and breadth of India (pg. 50).

The above mentioned written record amply points to the support given by the British administration in promoting Christian missions, particularly the Baptist missions in India. This was further enhanced by various policies of the British Government such as appointment of chaplains to the service of the East India Company, extension of the company's rule in India, assignment of school education to missionaries in some areas, support to the British and American Protestants in mission work, etc. The end of the Napoleonic wars further enabled them to concentrate more on Christian missions. A common maxim, 'Missionary followed the British flag,' indicates that it was the policy of the British Government to propagate the religion, consolidate the empire and strengthen the trade.

Before the British arrived in North East India in the early nineteenth century, the whole region was in a state of disunity and isolation. In the hill areas the basic unit of administration was the village. "Tribal and village feuds, head-hunting and village raids were frequent. In the plains, on the other hand, there were several rival kingdoms" (Puthenpurakal, 1984, pg. 146). Since the region was fragmented on many accounts, both the Burmese and the British wanted to exploit the existing situation. In the course of time the British managed to expel the Burmese from Assam and both sides ended the hostility by the Treaty of Yandaboo signed on 24 February 1826. Soon Assam became a part of the British province of Bengal.

In a few years' time the British managed to bring most part of the North East under their control. For example, between 1829 and 1833 they extended their political control into the Khasi Hills. By 1858 they extended their sway over the most valuable revenue producing territories of the North East, including the Brahmaputra and Surma valleys (Downs, 1983). Cachar was annexed in 1832 after the murder of its Raja. The Rajas of Manipur and Tripura had submitted to the British without much resistance. The Jaintia Hills and a portion of the Khasi Hills were annexed before 1858. In the Naga Hills, the

Angami area was occupied in 1866; the Lotha area in 1875 and the Ao area in 1889. It was during the Kuki rebellion of 1917-19 that the tract between Kohima and Manipur was brought under the British rule (Puthenpurakal, 1984). By 1914, Assam and nearly all the hill areas of today were brought under the British administration (Downs, 1983).

In order to enhance the British position, promote their religion and control free movements, the Government promulgated an important regulation known as the Inner Line Regulation of 1873. By this regulation entry into the hill areas was restricted. The central thrust of this regulation is found in the writings of Downs (1983):

> The Government could now prescribe, and from time to time alter by notification a line to be called the Inner Line and to prohibit any subject living outside the area from living or moving therein. Beyond this line the tribes are left to manage their own affairs with only such interference on the part of the frontier officers in their political capacity as may be considered advisable with the view to establishing personal influence for good among the chiefs and the tribes (pg. 41).

This regulation was extended to many places except Mikir, Khasi, Jaintia and Garo Hills. Downs (1983) again writes:

> It was under these regulations that the entrance of missionaries into the hills areas was controlled. As a general rule the government seems to have adopted a policy of allowing only one mission to work in each hill district. This policy worked in favour of the older Protestant missions, the American Baptist and the Welsh Presbyterian, and against

others like the Roman Catholics. Throughout the British period Catholic missionaries were only permitted to work in the hill areas that now constitute Meghalaya (pg. 41).

2.5 Catholic Church in North East India

As a whole the British in India did not extend any tangible support to the Catholic Church. So much so, even the English employees of the government were not given leave on Catholic holy days till 1890 (Bhattacharjee, 1993). However, lack of support and restrictions imposed on the Catholic Church did not deter her from discharging religious and social responsibilities towards the people and gradually she emerged a major player in the North East. Downs (1983) says, "By far the most important denomination to begin missionary work in the North East during the second half of the nineteenth century was the Roman Catholic Church" (pg. 115). At that time the entire North East was under the jurisdiction of the Vicar Apostolic of Calcutta since its establishment in 1834. The Vicariate never had sufficient personnel to spare for the pastoral ministry of its small flock scattered in and around Assam. In 1845 Mgr. Patrick Joseph Carew, the Vicar Apostolic of Calcutta (Bengal, 1841-1856) had the Vicariate divided into the Vicariates of West Bengal and East Bengal, Assam then became part of the East Bengal Vicariate which facilitated easy administration and outreach. In 1844 two missionaries, Everista Huc and Joseph Gabet, French Lazarists passed through Lower Assam on their way to Tibet (Downs, 1983). Meanwhile, the Vicariate of Tibet-Hindustan was divided and Tibet was separated from Agra and made into the Vicariate Apostolic of Lhasa in 1846 and it was entrusted to the Missionaries Etrangeres de Paris -

the Foreign Missions of Paris (MEP). Paviotti (1987) writes, "As access to Tibet was not possible through China, which was hostile, the MEP Society asked the Calcutta Vicar Apostolic (Bengal) to transfer Assam to the Lhasa Vicariate as a base for the evangelisation of Tibet" (pg. 3). On 16 February, 1850, Assam became part of the Lhasa vicariate.

2.5.1 Assam and the Foreign Missionaries

From 1850 to 1854, Assam was the centre of missionary activity for the Foreign Missions of Paris. The MEP, however, tried in vain to enter Tibet as the Chinese military kept strict vigilance to prevent any foreign influence. On 27 June 1850, Francis Jenkins, the Commissioner of Assam, welcomed Fr. Julien Rabin, Fr. Nicholas Michael Krick and Fr. Louis-Marie-Noel Bernard, the first three French men, destined for the missions of Tibet (Kottuppallil, 1990). From Guwahati they looked after the spiritual needs of the scattered Catholics of Assam. In 1851 Fr. Krick made his first attempt to enter Tibet, passing through the present Arunachal Pradesh inhabited by Mishmis (Downs, 1983). The Abors or Adis blocked his way while the Mishmis let him through. On 16 January, 1852, Fr. Krick entered Walong, the first Tibetan village on the frontiers (Menamparampil, 1981). He, however, could not proceed ahead as he was ordered back by the Tibetan Governor at the border. The successive attempts by the missionaries to reach Tibet via Mongoldai, Udalguri and Bhutan also failed. In 1853 when Fr. Rabin had fallen ill and left India, Fr. Bourry came to join the mission. In February 1854, another attempt was made by Fr. Krick and Fr. Bourry. They were accompanied by two Mishmis, Kroussa and Powasing. "They reached Somme, a Tibetan village, exactly on 25 July 1854, the feast of St. James the Apostle. As it was a Saturday, Fr. Krick dedicated the Mission to Our Lady and wrote to his superior in Paris about it all" (Menamparampil, 1981, p. 28). There, at Somme, they were murdered by a Mishmi chief Kaisha/Kaisa. It was said that the fathers had offended the chief. This was not, apparently, their fault. Becker (1989) writes:

> They had invited Kaisa to take them over the Tho Chu Pass and had promised him money and guns as reward. But another Chief double-crossed Kaisa and got the reward instead, at the same time ensuring that the fathers did not pay the expected friendly visit to Kaisa's house. The angry Chief followed the fathers into Tibet and killed them as they came up the Tellu path by the mouth of the Tho Chu. He carried off their property and took their Singpho servant as a slave (p. 206).

They were the first two martyrs who shed blood for Christianity in North East India. Of course on hearing about their death the British undertook an expedition and captured the chief and put him to death. After the tragic death of these two missionaries, the Paris Mission withdrew from Assam and it was reverted back to the ecclesiastical jurisdiction of Dacca, with the intention of entering Tibet through Darjeeling or Simla. When requested, the Holy Cross missionaries of Dacca had neither personnel nor resources to look after the scattered Catholics of North East. All other efforts to get personnel to keep in touch with the Catholics did not succeed. Assam was once again placed under the care of the Vicariate of Bengal.

In 1860, however, a Holy Cross missionary Fr. Mercier,

CSC from Dacca, visited Catholics at Guwahati and Dibrugarh (Kottupallil, 1991). Since there was a shortage of personnel, the spiritual care of the people of Assam could not be carried out until 1870. The Apostolic Visitor to the Bengal missions, Mgr. Charbonneaux and his assessors took note of the utter neglect of the Assam mission and recommended to Rome to entrust it to the pastoral care of the Foreign Missionaries of Milan (PIME - Pontificium Institutum pro Missionibus Esteris) (Kottuppallil, 1993). So in 1870 Assam and Bhutan were included within the Prefecture Apostolic of Krishnagar and it was entrusted to the care of the PIME, who were already working in Central Bengal. The Prefect Apostolic, Mgr. Antonio Marietti sent Father Jacopo Broy of PIME mission, to pioneer the Assam missions. He reached Guwahati on 20 June, 1872. He was the first resident missionary in this area and worked for 18 years between 1872 and 1890 (*Diocese of Kohima-Imphal,* 1973), alone in Assam with no companion priest to work with him. In 1883, he built a Church and dedicated it to St. Joseph. Meanwhile in the latter half of the 19th century, the migration of coolie workers from Bihar and Madhya Pradesh into the tea gardens of Assam had already started (Kottuppallil, 1988). Before Broy could do anything tangible for them, about 200 of them had left for their native villages in Madhya Pradesh and Bihar. His mission was limited to the care of the Catholic families of the Brahmaputra valley. However, the creation of two Dioceses of Dacca and Krishnagar which encompassed the whole territory of North East India in 1886 made it possible for the Church to take better care of the people (Bednarz, 1993).

2.5.2 Creation of a New Prefecture Apostolic of Assam

In the meantime, the success of the American Baptists and the Welsh Presbyterians among the hill people of Assam reached the ears of the Roman Catholic bishops. At the Synod of the Catholic Bishops of North India held in 1887, the PIME congregation expressed its inability to spare either personnel or money for the evangelisation of Assam. It was also decided to request Rome to separate the Assam mission and create a new Prefecture Apostolic of Assam. Accordingly the Prefecture Apostolic of Assam, Bhutan and Manipur, comprising the Brahmaputra Valley, the Surma Valley (Cachar and Sylhet Districts), and the Hill Districts, with the exception of Mizoram, which still belonged to the Dhaka Vicariate was formed on 13 December, 1889 by Pope Leo XIII and handed over to the Society of the Divine Saviour, popularly known as the Salvatorians. The Society of the Divine Saviour, earlier known as the Catholic Teaching Society, was founded by Rev. John Baptist Jordan in Rome. In 1904 the Society took its present name. The new Prefecture Apostolic of Assam was to be carved out of the two Dioceses of Dacca and Krishnagar. With the arrival of the Salvatorians and the creation of the Prefecture Apostolic of Assam, Bhutan and Manipur, serious Catholic missionary work began (Downs, 1983). The Propaganda Fide had suggested that the centre of the Prefecture Apostolic of Assam should be in Shillong. It was also felt by the administrator of the Diocese of Dacca, as well as Bishop Pozzi of Krishnagar, that the hill tribals were more ready to accept Christianity than the Assamese (Becker, 1980). Accordingly the centre was shifted to Shillong and the first missionaries moved from Guwahati to Shillong on 27 February, 1890 under the leadership of Fr. Otto Hopfenmueller. In the words of Curran

(1993), "The arrival of the Salvatorian missionaries in March 1890 marked the beginning of the Catholic mission in whole of North East India" (pg. 345).

One of the problems, among many, faced by the missionaries was lack of personnel. The Protestant missions, on the other hand, had enough personnel at their disposal and so people began to flock to them. By now the Protestant churches were established in the Khasi and Jaintia Hills. They had many schools, hospitals, and self-supporting infrastructure with indigenous pastors, leaders and teachers. In comparison the Catholic Church was just a beginner there. As a result she had to face the fury of the Protestants who unleashed hate campaigns against her in Shillong. Kottuppallil (1993) writes, "The government supported the Protestants by forbidding the establishment of Catholic schools in areas where the Protestants objected to them and this often disheartened the Catholic missionary" (pg. 45). Fr. Otto Hopfenmueller wrote on 4th August 1890 on the hate campaigns of the Protestants about the Catholics: "They attacked the Catholics as usual in their newspaper...they accuse us of adoring Mary, St. Peter, the saints and of worshipping holy pictures. They deny the perpetual virginity of Mary" (Becker, 1980, pg. 254). In December 1890, the first group of three Sisters of the Congregation of the Sisters of Divine Saviour (SDS) arrived in Assam (they were the first group of Sisters who reached Assam). Their presence further accelerated the activities of the Church. Despite many allegations, the Catholic missionaries continued their good work and as a result of their hard work the first group of Khasis was received into the Catholic Church on 8 December 1891 in Shillong. On 9 January, 1906, Fr. Christopher Becker from

Frankfurt was appointed the first Prefect Apostolic of Assam by the Propaganda Fide.

2.5.3 World War I and Catholic Missionaries in the North East

The first German Salvatorian missionaries set foot in Assam in February 1890 and their committed service lasted for twenty five years until the outbreak of the World War I in 1914. About the war Maliekal (2005) writes, "Towards the beginning of 1914 Europe sunk into a deep crisis ...two thirds of the Catholics of the time were directly involved in the war, 124 million on the side of the Allies and 64 million on the side of the Central Powers" (pg. 111). In the beginning of 1914 itself the British Government in India had imposed vigilance and restrictions on German and Austrian citizens in India (Maliekal, 2005), including both Catholic and Protestant missionaries. The missionaries were accused of being the enemies of Britain and spies of Germany. In June 1915, the missionaries were given orders by the British Government to quit India. It was stated that the Catholic priests and the ordained Protestant ministers were to be repatriated. The war, therefore, put an end to mission of the Salvatorians as they were Germans. They had to leave for Ahmednagar prison camp and then to Germany. Finally the German and Austrian missionaries, both Catholics and Protestants were expatriated on 27 March 1916. Soon the SDS Sisters too were served Government order to leave the country and on 18 November they too left for their homeland.

The growth of the Roman Catholic Church in North East India, therefore, is essentially a post-war phenomenon, although Catholic missionaries were familiar with this region ever since 1627. At the departure of the German missionaries the young Catholic Church in the North East was at the point of becoming an orphan once again. At the request of Becker, Archbishop Meuleman, S. J., of Calcutta sent his own Secretary, Fr. Lefebvre, S. J., on 24 June, 1915, to take charge of the Assam mission. Soon four more Jesuit priests A. Boone, J. Vial, N. Krier and A. Grignard joined the caretaker missionary group of Assam. They were too small a group to man such a big mission territory and so they were unable to maintain all mission stations managed by the Salvatorians. Of the nine resident stations managed by the Salvatorians, the Jesuits could reside at only four stations. Despite the hard work and self-sacrifice of the experienced Belgian Jesuit missionaries, particularly their outstanding leader Paul Lefebvre, the Catholic communities of Khasi and Jaintia Hills suffered losses as they could not reach out to many places (Kottuppallil, 1991). The Jesuits expressed their unwillingness to continue after 1921 as they were short of personnel in Calcutta. As a result the North East was once again left with no priests to serve the Catholic community.

The First World War adversely affected the Catholic mission work in the region. The Jesuits' inability to continue, eventually, paved the way for the change of guard to the Salesians of Don Bosco/Societas S. Francisci Salesii (SDB) (Aluckal, 2006). It was after repeated requests by the Propaganda Fide that the Salesians of Don Bosco agreed to come to India and take charge of the Assam mission in 1921. Eleven Salesians including six priests and five brothers led by Fr. Louis Mathias reached Shillong on 13 January 1922. Before the end of the same year Fr. Louis Mathias was appointed the new Prefect Apostolic of Assam, on 15 December 1922. Bishop Ferrando in the chronicle mentioned that the Salesians took charge of the vast region which had little more than 5000 Catholics, and the Christian life at this juncture was at an ebb due to the disastrous period of the war with its consequent drain on the missionary strength (Ferrando, 1935, Chronicle).

On 8 December 1923 the first group of Salesian Sisters (FMA-Figlie di Maria Ausiliatrice) arrived in Shillong at the insistence of Mgr. Mathias. It was from Guwahati that they began their missionary activities which included visiting families in nearby villages and the sick at the government hospital, and opening an oratory and a workroom for the girls (Maliekal, 2005). Towards the end of 1926 more missionaries joined the mission. The government found the Sisters good at nursing the sick and running the administration and so handed over the Guwahati Civil Hospital to them in 1932. Based on the ten years' (1922-1932) report of missionary activities in the Prefecture Apostolic of Assam, Bhutan and Burma sent to Rome, the Holy See decided to make the Prefecture of Assam into a Diocese. On 9 July 1934 Monsignor Louis Mathias was appointed Bishop of Shillong for the whole North Eastern Region (Paviotti, 1987). The Episcopal consecration of Monsignor Mathias along with that of Fr. Stephen Ferrando, the Bishop elect of Krishnagar, took place in Shillong on 10 November, 1934 (Aluckal, 2006). Upon his transfer to Madras, Monsignor Bars was elected Vicar Capitular of the Diocese of Shillong on 9 June 1935. In November 1935, Bishop Stephen Ferrando of Krishnagar was transferred and appointed Bishop of Shillong and he took possession of the Diocese on 24 January 1936. With his appointment a new chapter began for the Church in the North East, particularly Nagaland.

2.6 Baptist Church's Contact with the People of Nagaland

Before we speak of the Catholic Church in Nagaland it is essential to know the Baptist church's contact with the people of the states wherein the latter was the first to begin interaction with them. The arrival of William Carey, a prominent Protestant missionary, in 1793 and the founding of the Serampore College in 1818 were the most important steps towards the establishment of the Protestant Mission in the North East. The Treaty of Yandaboo signed in February 1826 after the first Anglo-Burmese war could be considered the next important step to the introduction of Christianity in the North East.

The English then annexed hills after hills and added them to their vast empire. Towards the end of the nineteenth century they had almost the entire North Eastern territories under their control. The considerable involvement of British officials in missionary work helped the mission to grow step by step. Some of the British officials had great interest in religious matters and so they were the proponents of Protestant Christianity in the region. One among them was Major Jenkins, Commissioner General of Assam who invited the Baptist missionaries of Bengal to come to the North East. They in turn thought that it was more convenient for the American Baptist missionaries in Burma to work there and the latter readily accepted the invitation.

The first American Baptist missionaries to enter Assam were Reverend Nathan Brown and his wife and Reverend Oliver T. Cutter and his wife (Philip, 1983) from Calcutta and they reached Sadiya on 23 March 1836. In July 1837 they were joined by Mr. and Mrs. Miles Bronson and Mrs. Jacob Thomas. Due to the hostility of the Kamptis in Sadiya they abandoned their work there and went to Jaipur on the edge of the Naga Hills and settled

there in May 1839. The Baptist mission had a very strong presence in Sibsagar and Nowgong.

Through the policy of annexation, the British formed the Naga Hills District in 1866 and founded its headquarters in Kohima in 1878. In 1890 Mokokchung became the sub-division headquarters of the Naga Hills District. Even much before the establishment of the Hill District the missionaries came to know of the Nagas of the Hills. The American Baptists stationed at Guwahati since 1836 and in Sibsagar since early 1840's had contacted the Ao Nagas of Nagaland from 1850.

The Nagas used to come down to Sibsagar on market days and out of curiosity they used to visit the mission centre at Sibsagar where the missionaries had a small printing press. So the missionaries kept up their contact with them and as a result the first Naga convert, Hube, a Konyak Naga, was baptised on 12 September, 1847. He, however, died shortly after his baptism on 10 October, 1847 (Philip, 1983). Three years later the first Ao Naga convert, Longjanglepzük from Merangkong village was baptised on 7 September 1851 at Sibsagar by Rev. S. W. Witting.

2.6.1 Baptist Mission to the Ao Nagas

Naga Hills is a land of different tribes who speak innumerable dialects besides preserving different social customs and practices. People like Verrier Elwin, a well-known writer on Nagas had, therefore, doubted the success of missionary work in the midst of diversity in the Hills. In support of this view he quotes a remark made by John Butler in 1847, "Vain endeavour to awake in them (the Nagas) a sense of the saving virtues of Christianity" (Downs, 1983, p. 81). Against all pessimism and speculation the Baptist Church in Nagaland began to take roots. The credit for sowing the seeds of Christianity in Nagaland goes to three important missionaries of Sibsagar mission namely, Edward Winter Clark (Dr. Clark), his wife, Mary Mead and Godhula Rufus Brown, an Assamese convert evangelist. Dr. Clark reached Sibsagar on 30 March 1869 and was the missionary in charge of the mission and the printing press. It is believed that he abandoned the Assamese mission, in favour of the Nagas of Nagaland due to poor response from the Assamese. It had been noticed that there were just about a hundred converts after thirty seven years of work in Assam. To express his total disillusionment at the poor response in the mission he once wrote to the missionary union, "Can it be believed, that Paul or other New Testament evangelists would have spent so long a time on such a field and not tried hard to find a heathen people more favourable to Christianity than the Assamese" (Puthenpurakal, 1984, pg. 58).

In the beginning of 1871, with the objective to begin the mission work among the Nagas, Dr. Clark had asked Godhula, his Assamese assistant to learn a dialect of the Nagas who occasionally visited Sibsagar and the mission compound (Puthenpurakal, 1984). On being asked to go to the Ao country, Godhula expressed his willingness and so he was the first to undertake Christian work among the Nagas. An added reason for Dr. Clark to venture into this strange land was Godhula's acquaintance with one Subongmeren, Ao, who lived with him for some time. He was baptised after being inspired by the exemplary Christian life of Godhula and his family by Dr.

Clark in early 1871 at Sibsagar.

Godhula's first visit to the village of Deka Haimong (Molungkimong) was in the winter of 1871 with Subongmeren and some Ao traders. On his entry into the Ao area the people took him for a government spy and assumed that he had come to occupy their land. Meanwhile, the people heard that the British had forcefully occupied Angami, Zeliang, Lotha and Rengma areas of Naga Hills and were moving forward to occupy the Ao areas. But this distrust was put to rest by his amiable behavior and the broken Ao dialect he had earlier learned. In Clark's writings, Molungkimong is known by its Assamese name 'Deka Haimong' or simply, Haimong. In November 1872, Godhula and his wife led a group of Nagas to Sibsagar, of whom nine were baptised by Dr. Clark on 10 November 1872 in the Dikho River.

Despite Government restriction and denial of permission by the Home Mission Board in the USA to visit the Naga Hills, Dr. Clark decided to go ahead at the risk of his very life. He was escorted by a group of sixty warriors sent by the Molungkimong village council and reached the village on 18 December, 1872. There, to his heart's content he saw a chapel built by the new converts. Philip (1983) describes the baptism of fifteen men by Dr. Clark on 23 December 1872 in the following words, "This was the first baptismal service ever held in Nagaland" (pg. 53). With this opening a solid foundation of the American Baptist Mission work was laid in Nagaland.

From May 1876, Dr. Clark took up his residence in Molungkimong. Meanwhile as the mission work was progressing he decided to establish a new village solely for his new converts due to pagan opposition.[1]

They moved to an uninhabited mountain top, about three miles west of Molungkimong on 24 October 1876. The village was named as Molungyimsen (New Molung). Neiphiu Rio, the Chief Minister of the state once called Molungyimsen 'Bethlehem of Nagaland' and said that it could become a pilgrimage site because of its history ("Molungyimsen, Bethlehem of Nagaland," 2011, March 20, pg. 1).[2]

After a few years of work and contact Godhula built a church at Merangkong village in 1881. In 1894 Dr. Clark moved the mission centre to Impur which is presently known as Ao Baptist Arogo Mungdang ("Baptists of Nagaland," 2008, August 24). It was from here that the Baptist movement spread among the Ao Nagas and to the neighbouring tribes.

2.6.2 Baptist Mission to the Angami Nagas

After the establishment of the Baptist church in several Ao villages, attention was paid to the Angami areas to establish the same there. The British Government managed to occupy Kohima, the centre of the Angamis despite strong resistance from them. Even after the occupation of Kohima in 1878 the

---

1 The pagans were against any new religion being brought into the village. When Christianity was introduced there started persecution against the converts. Similar treatment was meted out to the Catholics in a few villages by the non-Catholics/ Baptists. When this happened, the Catholics moved to a new place or village, abandoning their ancestral property and wealth.

2 Rio delved on the mission works carried out by Dr. Clark and his wife Mary Mead and said that both were not only missionaries but also educators. He further remarked that this changed the Naga history by leading the Nagas from 'darkness to light.' He also declared this as a Naga Educational Heritage . The Ao Students Conference earlier in 2003 named this as 'Cradle of Education.'

Angamis inflicted a number of raids on the British. Dr. Clark himself requested the committee in the US to send a missionary to the Angami area to initiate Christianity among them. Following his request, Charles DeWitt King (C. D. King) was sent and he and his wife Anna Sweet reached Samaguting, now Chumukedima on 27 June 1879. They settled themselves at Samaguting because the people there were the "only Angamis who were then quiet, peaceful, friendly and accessible" (Philip, 1983, p. 80). His experience and association made C.D. King to pass a remark later on the Angamis as the "most independent, enterprising, warlike and treacherous of all the numerous hill tribes of southern Assam" (Philip, 1983, pg. 79).

However, in November C. D. King and his wife had to flee to Sibsagar when the Angami uprising at Kohima started in the middle of October 1879, "to extirpate every European and every trace of European supremacy in the Angami Hill" (Puthenpurakal, 1984, pg. 94). His next attempt to work among the Lothas in Wokha at the advice of Dr. Clark was objected to by Major Michell, the then Political Officer of the Naga Hills District at Kohima who said that the former would be the only white person among the Lothas. Major Michell then advised him to take up his residence in Kohima when things improved. Back in Kohima in April 1880 he found it hard to learn the Angami dialect. He, however, understood the importance of schools in relation to preaching. He had written even before he reached Kohima, "Something must be done for the Nagas, and I suspect it will cost money and that educational work will constitute an important branch of the work of the missionary who tries to save souls among them" (Puthenpurakal, 1984, pg. 96). With the assurance of all possible help from the Government and the Inspector of Schools, he started a school with eleven Naga boys and two Assamese Christians namely Henry Goldsmith and Sarbey from the Church of Nowgong to teach in the school. The work was carried on with much success until 1886, when the number of students gradually declined. One of the reasons for the decline could be that the teaching was done in Assamese which was not understood by the students as there were no books in the Naga language (Sangma, 1992). In the meantime he had organised a church at Kohima on 29 March 1883. And this first church among the Angamis had Mr. and Mrs. King, Mr. and Mrs. Henry Goldsmith, Messers Sarbey and Robi as members but not a single Naga as member. King's labours however, bore fruit when S. Sieliezhu of Kohima, the first Angami was baptised in 1885. Dr. Rivenburg, King's successor, continued the mission after the latter's departure. It had been observed that the growth among the Angamis was at a low pace compared to the Aos and later on among other tribes. Even after forty years of work there were only two Angami churches—one at Kohima and the other at Nerhema. And the reason for this could be that the Angamis were more independent and individualistic in character (Philip, 1983), they were also more resistant to change.

2.6.3 Baptist Mission to the Lotha Nagas

The initiative to open a mission centre at Wokha came from Dr. Clark himself because he wrote in 1876 that he had a plan to settle down among the Lotha Nagas (Puthenpurakal, 1984). Interestingly in 1885 C. D. King had also expressed his desire to work there. Perhaps the missionaries found Wokha a prosmising place for evangelisation. Mr. and Mrs. W. E. Witter, transferred from Sibsagar, reached Wokha on 9 April 1885. At Wokha, they initiated literary activities and opened a school on 25 August 1886 with three Naga boys. Ill health forced the Witters to leave Wokha for America in March 1888. After their departure, Wokha did not have regular missionaries till 1947, so the missionaries from Impur and Kohima attended to the needs of the Lotha church. According to some reports, though doubtful, the first baptised person among the Lothas was Mmohomo in 1891.

2.6.4 Baptist Mission to the Sema Nagas and other Tribes

It is amazing to note how the Semas became Christians as Christianity was a mass movement among them. Philip (1983) observes that, "without the work of a missionary or the preaching of a native evangelist, people became Christians and organised themselves into churches" (pg. 102). The first contact with the Semas was through Sema boys who frequented the Impur mission school started by Perrine and the Kohima mission school ran by Rivenburg (Puthenpurakal, 1984). It was the Dicksons, who were appointed in Kohima in place of the Rivenburgs who took interest to convert the Semas with the help of one Avilhu Sema and one Lucitzu Angami who used to visit the Sema villages. Dickson kept up the contact with different villages. From the visits of Dickson from 1907 he came to realise that many villages were ready to accept Christianity. A positive change noticed among the Semas was that the non-Christians had stopped persecuting the Christians because, "the crops of the Christians were the best" (Puthenpurakal, 1984, pg. 103). Ivilho of the Ghokimi village was the first Sema convert around the year 1906.

Among the other tribes only the Chakhesangs had an earlier contact with Christianity in the beginning of the twentieth century and the rest much later. It is believed that Sieliezhu, the first Angami convert, preached Christianity among them from 1893 to 1894. Through his efforts a church was founded at Chazouba village, with three members (Philip, 1983). Christianity was preached to the Kukis, one of the smallest tribes of Nagaland starting from 1897.

On the occasion of the 50th anniversary of the Kuki Baptist Association of Nagaland and Mikir Hills it was stated that the first Kuki conversion to Christianity took place in 1897 and the first Kuki church was inaugurated at Sirhima on 7 February 1912.

The beginning of Christianity among the Rengmas began in 1918 with the conversion of Lokin of Tseminyu. Among the Zeliangrongs the missionary work was slow as there was the influence of Rani Gaidinlu who opposed conversion. It is said that she was worshipped as a goddess for her extraordinary powers and her stiff opposition to the British occupation. Despite her opposition the first conversion to Christianity took place on 31 December 1905, when three students who were studying at the Kohima Mission Training School were baptised.

In the unadministered district of Tuensang, the British administration had prohibited all kinds of missionary activities. Even though the British claimed sovereignty over the area, they had left the administration with the people. This was done to avoid any kind of disturbance that might lead them to annex and administer the area. Even in the 1940s the Government of Assam denied permission to the Ao Baptist Association to undertake any missionary activities in the Sangtam area.

Contact with the Konyak Nagas started in the 1840s. Hubi, the first Naga convert baptised in 1847 may have belonged to the Konyak tribe, the largest of the tribe in Nagaland. The murder of Longjanglepzuk, the first Ao Christian probably from Merangkong village, at the hands of the Konyak warriors of Tamlu village speaks about the early contact the missionaries had with this tribe. According to Syiemlieh (1990), "Christianity came only late to the Sangtams, Konyaks, Changs, Phoms, Yimchungers and Kheamungans. These tribes got their Bible only after independence" (pg. 34).

Today, majority of the Naga people in the state are Christians except for a few who still follow their traditional religion. The Aos were the first to embrace Christianity and by the beginning of the twentieth century a good number of them became Christians. Downs (1983) writes, "The second largest 'Christian' tribe, the Semas, started becoming Christians in significant numbers in the late 1920s and were followed by the Lothas in the 1930s. These three tribes represent the main concentration of Christians" (pg. 133). In the early part of 1950s when the Baptist missionaries had to leave the Naga Hills, the leadership of the Baptist church passed into local hands (Puthenpurakal, 1993). As a result the churches grew in large numbers and work was extended to nearby tribes as well.

2.7 Catholic Church in Nagaland

It was only after India got Independence from Britain in 1947 that the Catholic Church could make her entry into Nagaland. It is learnt that the first Nagas who embraced Christianity belonged to the Baptist denomination owing to the British policy that did not allow other Christian sects into Nagaland. Syiemlieh (1990) writes:

> The different Christian missions had almost distinctly marked out areas of their operation. The Baptists were in Upper Assam, the Naga Hills and the Garo Hills. The Presbyterians were in the North Lushai Hills, the Khasi and Jaintia Hills and had some activity in Cachar. The Lutherans and the Anglicans worked among the plains people in Assam, particularly the tea garden labourers. These missions had generally agreed not to encroach upon each other's fields (pg. 35).

The Bishop and priests stationed at Shillong and in parts of Assam had longed to venture into the picturesque Hills for years. They hoped that this would happen sooner or later as the Baptist missionaries had already started working there for decades and India might reconsider their request for an entry. Besides, the entry into Naga Hills and Manipur Hills would not be as difficult as the erstwhile N.E.F.A (North East Frontier Territory), the present Arunachal Pradesh was considered forbidden territory for Christian missionaries. It was the government's policy to protect the tribes from outside influence, except government educational and welfare agencies, and to allow them to develop inwardly according to their customs and "culture", whatever they may mean (Marengo, Assam Church History, unpublished).

When the Catholic missionaries came, they were considered as 'intruders.' Aluckal (1982) writes:

> Missionaries belonging to non-Catholic denominations

> came to this part of our country long before the Catholics, and often, they enjoyed the patronage of the colonial power, so much so, in some cases, territories were divided and given to them for evangelisation and Catholics were nowhere in the picture. When the Catholics arrived on the scene they were addressed as 'intruders.' Whatever may be, the Catholic Church struck root in the soil and grew rapidly (pg. 26).

One of the reasons for assigning an area to a particular denomination is believed to have been to avoid rivalries among different denominations. In Nagaland the Government had even insisted on the Baptist missionaries to seek their permission prior to the exploration of new areas because of the hostile nature of the Nagas especially towards foreigners. For example, the Government had warned the missionaries not to venture into the unadministered areas where people themselves had their say in administration and not the Government.

The Baptist leadership was not pleased to have the Catholic missionaries in Nagaland; as it was evident from the remarks made by Dr. Clark in 1873 when he compared the non-responsive Assamese Hindus to the "… stiff, bigoted Roman Catholics of America" (Puthenpurakal, 1984, pg. 88). He also did not want any part of Assam or the Naga Hills being occupied by other Christian denominations (Puthenpurakal, 1984). He was shocked to hear the plan of Major Michell to ask the Bishop of Calcutta to "send one or two missionaries to open a school in Kohima" (Puthenpurakal, 1984, pg. 89). Dr. Clark and other missionaries also decided to prevent the Church of Scotland from opening a mission station among the Lotha Nagas. Perhaps that may be the reason why he was in haste to send W. E. Witter and family to establish a mission at Wokha. Meanwhile the Catholic Church in Assam and Meghalaya was growing alongside the Baptist and the Presbyterian churches. It was through the Diocese of Shillong (now Archdiocese), the mother Diocese of the North Eastern Dioceses, that the Catholic Church made her contact with Nagaland. She made her first contact with the Angami tribe and then the Lotha tribe. Abolition of Chin Hills Regulation actually came handy and facilitated the opportunity to move into the hills for the opening of the Catholic Church among the Naga tribes. The words of Puthenpurakal (2000) point to this reality:

> It is true that the so-called Chin Hills Regulations was abolished in 1946, thus removing from the police sweeping powers to expel from the North East anyone they thought harmful and who was not a native of the place. Thus, the law that kept the Church out of the region was finally abolished. So, with the dawn of independence the Church was free, in principle, to enter anywhere in the North East to preach the Good News (pg. 281).

2.7.1 Terms 'Catholic' and 'the Roman Catholic Church'

A lot of arguments and counter arguments for and against the Catholic Church have been leveled by some people. Strange and derogatory remarks by some sections of the people of other denominations such as 'Catholics are not Christians', 'worshippers of Mary', 'Satan worshippers', 'idol worshippers', 'anti-Christ' etc. were a blot on the very nature and spirit of Christianity that have confused ordinary people. The meaning of the word 'Catholic' will perhaps clear some of the doubts people have about the Catholic Church. Jesus did not give any name to his followers or the church but it evolved in history. Just as the name 'Christian' originated in Antioch, so also the name 'Catholic' was used for the first time by St. Ignatius of Antioch, in 109 A.D. In his letter to the Smyrnians, he said, "Where Jesus Christ is, there is the Catholic Church." ("Searching for the Truth", 1985, pg. 5). He also said, "Where the bishop is to be seen, there let all his people be; just as wherever Jesus Christ is present, we have the Catholic Church" (Mcbrien, 1994, pg. 3). St. Cyril of Jerusalem (315-386 A.D) said, "If you are sojourning in cities, enquire not... merely where the Church is, but where is the Catholic Church. For this is the particular name of the Holy Church, the Mother of us all" ("Searching for the Truth", 1985, pg. 5). St. Augustine (354-430 A.D) one of the great defenders of the early Church also used the term, 'Catholic Church.' The Encyclopedia Britannica says the term 'Catholic' was used since the 2nd century A.D. to distinguish the Christian Church at large from local communities or from heretical and schismatic sects. The gradual use of the word 'Catholic' was due to the negative attitude of the Jewish Christians towards the non-Jewish Christians who were considered as inferior. Some of the early Jewish Christians insisted that non-Jewish Christians should follow the rules, traditions and customs of the Jews. To counteract these unhealthy feelings, the early Fathers of the Church, especially Bishop Ignatius of Antioch, stressed the universal aspect of Christ's Church and called it the Church Catholic (i.e. universal or equally meant for all people) (Chacko, 1990). Another explanation is that Jesus Christ founded a church of which he made Peter the head (Mt. 16: 13-19) and which he intended to last for all time (Mt.

28:20), thus presupposing successors to Peter. This apostolic Church became known as the Catholic (universal) Church and Peter's successors are known as Popes (Sheedy, 1978).

As the headquarters of the Church from St. Peter onwards was in Rome, the Church began to be called Roman Catholic especially by other denominations (Chacko, 1990).[3] The word Catholic is derived from the Greek adjective, *katholikos,* meaning "universal" and from the adverbial phrase, *kath' holou,* meaning "on the whole" (Mcbrien, 1994, pg. 3). Hence, it means "according to or in relationship to the fullness of (means)" which Jesus gave to the Church he founded. Plathottam (2001) writes:

3 Fr. T. J. Chacko further explains the schism in the church and how the name 'Roman Catholic Church' came to be attributed to her in 'Searching for the Truth,' (unpublished) on p. 6 in the following words: The 11th century A.D. marked the split of the Church into two groups due to geographical, cultural, linguistic and political factors. In 330 A.D. Emperor Constantine transferred his capital from Rome to Constantinople and stayed there. Since the Emperor resided in Constantinople, the Patriarch (bishop) of Constantinople began to grow convinced of his importance. He wanted to rival the Pope in authority, since he was the bishop of the new capital of the Empire. He resented Papal intervention in matters of faith. In addition, there were differences of culture, character and language between the East and the West; the East spoke Greek and the West, Latin. The actual split between the East and the West was brought about by ambitious churchmen who strongly resented Papal authority. A layman, called Photius, got himself elected as the Patriarch of Constantinople while St. Ignatius, the legitimate Patriarch, was still reigning. When the Pope refused to accept his election, Photius broke away from communion with Rome and made all kinds of charges against the Latin Church. This schism was temporarily healed in 877 A.D., after the death of Ignatius. When Michael Caerularius became the Patriarch, he accused the Latin Church of heresy for adding the word 'Filioque' (and from the son) to the Nicean Creed. He condemned the Latin use of unleavened bread for mass, and even the Latin practice of priests not keeping a beard (at that time). On 16 the July, 1054, he finally led the Greek Church into schism. His church was called the Greek Orthodox Church. The Church of the West, which remained faithful to the Bishop of Rome, the Pope, was called the Roman Catholic Church, since its head was in Rome. Thus, the Church got the name 'The Roman Catholic Church'.

> We may also add that the word "Catholic" does not have anything to do really with geography or statistics. The first group of Christians about whom we read in the Acts of the Apostles (1: 14-15) too were "Catholic", because they possessed as in a seed the fullness of the means given by Jesus to His Church. It is because of this fullness of means that the Church is "universal", and not necessarily because it is "all over the world"! It becomes present all over the world, because it is "universal" (*uni-versare* = moving to the same goal marked out by Jesus) (pg. 33).

2.7.2 The First Contact and Visits

The first contact the Nagas of Nagaland had with the Catholic missionaries was in the middle of the nineteenth century and then later after a gap of fifty years. On 4 September 1847, Fr. Freycenon of Dhaka paid a visit to the foot of the Naga Hills after paying a visit to the Christians of Bondashill (present Bangladesh). He reported that he found Naga tribes (Zeliangrongs?), well disposed to Catholic religion (Menamparampil, 2006). The first Catholic missionary to enter Nagaland was Fr. Marcellinus Molz, a German Salvatorian from Bondashill (Puthenpurakal, 1993), who reached Tamlu in the Phom Naga area under Longleng District in 1908. He stayed with the Aos for some time to get acquainted with this tribe and to explore the possibility of introducing the Catholic missionary work among them. "He was the guest of the British officer of Mokokchung and was at Tamlu, a military outpost, twenty-five miles from Nazira" (Syiemlieh, 1990, p. 38). Becker (1980) quotes the words of Fr. Molz which he wrote to the Prefect Apostolic of Assam from Tamlu on 15 May 1908 regarding the possibility of evangelisation among these tribals:

> It was very tiring to travel in these areas up and down hills and valleys. Tamlu is a military outpost, twenty five miles from Nazira. Around the fort there is a Naga village with about 1000 inhabitants. I am completely fascinated by these Nagas. Not far from here there is an area still independent of the British where all the people go about almost naked. They wear a small leather apron in front about the waist. For the rest they have no clothing at all. I could write many pages about the great hopes and possibilities of evangelisation among the Nagas, but what is the use? You know better than I do how things stand and what can we achieve without adequate means! The American Baptists are making great progress in their missionary work here. I think the Naga Hills are sparsely populated. Yet there are villages ten to fifteen miles distant from each other and each one has at least 500 inhabitants! (p. 132).

Fr. Molz was followed by another Catholic missionary Fr. Ansgar Koenigsbauer, also a Salvatorian, (Puthenpurakal, 1993), on his way to Manipur via Dimapur in 1912. It has also been reported that a fourth missionary to have had contact with Naga Hills was Leo Piasezcki in 1920, who made a number of visits to Manipur (George, 1990). What aroused curiosity and adventure among those missionaries might have been some invaluable resources perhaps known only to them in the far away hills. Undoubtedly, their visits proved an impetus for the Church in the days to come. Bishop Ferrando had been longing for an opening to give the Hill tribes the message of the Catholic Church. The information and knowledge he gathered for years to make his dream come true might have also come from the visits of the said priests and the casual contacts he had had with the Naga students studying in the colleges of Shillong. All these sources undoubtedly led him to believe that the Manipur Hills, the Garo Hills and the Naga Hills would probably be the most fruitful fields in India for the growth of Christianity. Bishop Ferrando (1949) writes:

> These words are true after ten years, but we could not yet start our work in the Manipur and Naga Hills. How great is our responsibility before God. These tribes are ready for the good seed…in spite of many difficulties, the prospects of our entering in the Naga Hills are much brighter than two years ago. From many villages we receive invitation. These messages say: 'We like the Catholic Fathers because they love the children, enter our houses, stay with us and do not destroy our tribal life.' We are in touch with the highest authorities and we hope that this day will come soon, as it came for another Hill-Tribe, the Lushai, where after long years of expectation a beautiful spring has begun. But we can scarcely run our actual missions because we have no money and other means…Yet God wills it! A good friend of ours who by order of the Central Government is always travelling amongst the hill-tribes of Assam to study their conditions told me: 'Monsignor! Now or it will be too late.' Dear Benefactor, help us to open the Naga Mission, to win to Our Lord one of the most picturesque primitive Tribes of the earth (p. 2).

On the one hand the Church was eager to enter this land; on the other hand, there were restrictions both external and internal that she was faced with. The external was the British restriction imposed on the Catholic missionaries and the internal included lack of personnel and material resources.

2.7.3 World War II and the Civil Hospital

World War II had been the turning point for the Nagas in general and the Catholic Church in particular. A sovereign state, independent of India had been the demand of the Nagas for decades but even after India attained independence from Britain in 1947, the Naga territory remained a part of Assam and hence they continued their demand. The voice of this demand echoed by different factions for many decades did not die down but is heard louder and louder today. On the other hand, efforts were made and policies were renewed for an amicable solution.[4]

Prior to the World War, Great Britain was a great enemy of the Nagas which was reflected in the bitterly fought battles in the past. However, during the War, Britain won over the Nagas and was able to count on the trust of the latter to fight the Japanese, their enemy in April 1944. The Nagas cooperated efficiently and loyally with the British and the American forces to repulse the enemy who had to retreat (Ferrando, 1949),

4 In 1957 an agreement was signed between the Naga leaders and the Indian government, following which the Naga Hills district and the Tuensang division were brought together under a single unit, directly administered by the Indian Government. However, unrest continued and another record was reached at the Naga Peoples Convention meeting of July 1960. According to this accord, it was decided that Nagaland should become a constituent state of the Indian Union (Vattoth, 2010, p. 33).

forever from this land after the 64 days of battle.[5]

The War Cemetery at Kohima is a memorial of this war where hundreds of American, British, Indian and Japanese soldiers died in that battle lay interred. The dead included Reverend Callahan, an Irish Catholic and Chaplain of the forces. A thought provoking caption in the cemetery reads, 'When you go home tell them of us and say for your tomorrow we gave our today.' It inspires one to rededicate his life and love for his motherland.

Actually the Civil Hospital at Kohima was a gift from the British to the Nagas for their loyalty and dedication during the War.[6] The people helped in various ways: some were porters, others worked as guides, some were interpreters, others acted as spies and helped in disclosing enemy hideouts, while some who were in the forces joined the British fighting the enemy

---

5 After the Second World War, everything was new at Kohima because everything was destroyed during the last Japanese offensive when they threatened to invade India. It was here that the decisive battle of the campaign was fought in 1944. The English garrison at Kohima surprised by the sudden advance of the enemy was surrounded on a hillock and was reduced to extremities, but after three months of fierce fighting the invaders began to give way and commenced that retreat which was never to stop again. But Kohima cost the British army a heavy price as is evident from the countless crosses in the soldiers' cemetery and the monoliths, crosses and slabs, scattered all over commemorating this or that corps (Nagas of Assam by Rev. A. Pianazzi in History of the Diocese of Shillong 1951-1953 Chronicle).

6 The government had constructed a hospital in gratitude to the Nagas who stopped the entry of the Japanese into the Indian territory and the Superintendent of health asked the Bishop of Shillong for sister nurses, to be in-charge of the new hospital. This was offered to them and the Institute accepted the invitation (Extract from the History of the Institute). (The British had built a 10 bedded dispensary in 1905-06, they later upgraded it to a hospital).

(Suosahie, 1994).[7] A hospital was a much needed requirement for this hilly state as there weren't any good health care units in the state at that time. The British built the hospital but it was left without manpower to administer it. Syiemlieh (1990) writes, "The British soon left the hills without filling in the requirement and the district administration of the Naga Hills had then to look for suitable staff" (pg. 41). The Government of Assam appreciated the noble service by the two trained Salesian nuns at Guwahati Civil Hospital and they were looking for Roman Catholic nuns to be appointed in Dibrugarh hospital as well. Perhaps the nuns' contribution in the field of health prompted the Governor of Assam to request the assistance of trained nuns at Naga Hospital, Kohima too.[8] At the time

---

7 In the article titled 'God's Guiding Ways' in the Silver Jubilee souvenir of Christ King School Kohima, 1969-1994, p. 44, Philip Suosahie, Vincent Visielie and Nicholas Neinguzolie mentioned that the British managed to defeat the Japanese. The Nagas helped the British not because they were their friends and the Japanese their enemies but since they were under the British Government they were forced to help them. They also believed that many Nagas helped the Japanese as well. But in a war there has to be a winner and here the British won. In recognition of the service of the Nagas during the war, the British built a good hospital for the people of Kohima, and named it the 'Naga Hospital.'

8 "I am glad to find that the sick attendants assist in the nursing of serious cases... are receiving some instructions in their duties as such. In a hospital of this size, good nursing is absolutely essential; and I hope it will be possible at the distant date to introduce the same system as has favourably been established in the Guwahati hospital where two trained Roman Catholic sisters give their services daily for a nominal sum. Major Allen is advised to address Monsignaur Mathias, the Roman Catholic Bishop of Shillong with whom I have already discussed the matter (Louis Mathias became bishop only in 1934; and in 1932 he was the Prefect Apostolic of Assam, the head of the Catholic Church in the North East)....it will be possible to provide 3 trained nursing sisters of his order for the Dibrugarh Hospital. It will take some time for those nursing sisters to be found as they will probably have to be brought from Italy or from Madras Presidency..." (Extract from the Inspection remarks made by the Inspector General of Civil Hospitals Assam, in the Visitors' book of the Dibrugarh State Hospital in February, 1932).

Akbar Hydari was the Governor of Assam and the two Princely states of Manipur and Tripura (George, 2007). Hoping that the Church might respond positively to the request, Hydari appealed to Bishop Stephen Ferrando of Shillong for help.[9] The Diocese of Shillong then comprised a very vast territory which included the whole of the North East (Puthenpurakal & Mampra, 2006). Never to miss this opportunity, which was considered the gateway for the Church to the future, the Bishop agreed to the request. Upon his request the congregation of the Sisters of Christ Jesus from Spain came forward to help. Below is the letter written by N. K. Rustomji, Advisor to the Governor of Assam, on 14 July 1948 requesting the Bishop of Shillong to depute a sister to the Civil Hospital/Naga Hospital at Kohima.

On receiving the letter Bishop through his secretary Fr. M. Bianchi wrote on 17 July 1948 assuring him of the medical service of two Sisters at Civil Hospital.

2.7.4 Arrival of the Spanish Sisters and their Chaplain

The Congregation of the Sisters of Christ Jesus obliged the request of the Bishop and on 25 November, 1948 five Sisters arrived in Shillong.[10]

---

9 Bishop Stephen Ferrando (1895-1978) was born on 28 September 1895 in Italy. He was ordained a priest on 18 March 1923. He reached Shillong on 23 December 1923 together with eight other Salesians. His first appointment was at the novitiate in Shillong. In the absence of Mgr. Mathias, he had to take his place as Pro-Prefect Apostolic on several occasions. On 10 November 1934 he became Bishop of Krishnagar and Louis Mathias, Bishop of Shillong. Upon the transfer of Bishop Mathias to Madras in 1935 Ferrando became the Bishop of Shillong (1935-1969).

10 The Missionaries of Christ Jesus started their service in Kohima in 1948. In 1948, the Catholic Church was not established there and neither were the Catholics granted permission to enter (Extract form the History of the Institute, titled 'Kohima-Nagaland).

Letter 2.1 Letter to the Secretary to the Bishop

OFFICE OF THE ADVISER TO THE GOVERNOR
OF ASSAM FOR EXCLUDEDX AREAS & STATES.

Shillong, Assam.

No: 6214/48-AL. The 14th July,1948.

From: N.K.Rustomji, Esq., ICS.,
Adviser to the Governor of Assam,

To: The Secretary to the Bishop of Shillong,
Bishop's House,
SHILLONG.

Sir,

With reference to your letter dated the 12th May,1948, I am to enquire whether you would be so good as to depute a Sister to Kohima as early as possible to help in the new Hospital which is shortly to be opened. I should be grateful for an early reply confirming that a Sister will proceed accordingly and letting me know the date on which she may be expected to reach Kohima.

Yours faithfully,

(N.K.Rustomji)
ADVISER TO THE GOVERNOR
OF ASSAM.

Three of them were sent to Tura Leprosy colony and two others, Sisters Margarita Cifre and Guadalupe to Kohima. While they were in Shillong, they had expressed their request to the Bishop to send a chaplain along with them for their spiritual care. Hence the Bishop had to compel the administration to grant permission for a priest to stay at Kohima although the latter had allowed only two Sisters to stay. They left for

From: Rev. Fr. M. Bianchi, S.D.B.,
Secretary to the Lord Bishop of Shillong,
Bishop's House,
Shillong.

To : N.K. Rustomji, Esq., ICS.
Adviser to the Governor of Assam,

Shillong 17th July 1948

Dear Sir,

With reference to your letter No-6214/48-Ad dated the 14th July, I beg to inform you that two Sisters will be deputed to Kohima, to work in the hospital.

As regards the date on which the Sisters may be expected to reach Kohima, I am not in a position to say it now, because the two Sisters have not yet arrived from Europe. As I told you during our conversation at your offices, the Sisters were expected to arrive last May. Having not yet obtained the visa on their passports, they are still in Madrid. But we hope that the Visas will not any longer be delayed and the Sisters will fly at once to India.

Yours faithfully,

Secry. to the Lord Bishop of Shillong.

P.S.- I should be much obliged if a pass could be granted for myself(Rev.Fr.M.Bianchi,S.D.B.) and Rev. Fr. F. Mellino, S.D.B., to visit Kohima , so as to report to the Lord Bishop.

maarig 0/4

Kohima on 29 December, 1948 and reached Kohima on 31 December along with their chaplain Monsignor Emmanuel Bars (Mgr. Bars).[11] Mgr. Bars was the first resident Catholic priest in Nagaland. They were accompanied by one S. John Longyao, a Tangkhul Naga boy who was studying in Shillong and who would be helping them and studying in Kohima ("Kohima-Nagaland", 1984).[12] The following is an account of their journey from Shillong to Kohima found in the diary of Sr. Magarita Cifre (2 January 1949), translated from Spanish:

> 29th December (1948) early morning, Guadalupe, Mgr. Bars and I left Shillong in a military van. We stopped by Bishop's house to collect our luggage and say goodbye to Bishop and Fr. Bianchi. Mgr. Emmanuel Bars who was permitted to accompany the sisters as Chaplain was an

---

11 The Society of Christ Jesus, is a Spanish religious Institute founded by Archbishop Marcellinus Oloachea and Mother Camino Sanz Orio. Like many other congregations in India and abroad they could adapt their religious dress or habit according to the requirements of the local situations.

12 "Thus the first Catholics to enter Naga Hills were two of our sisters, a priest and a Catholic boy who was taken as a helper and who belonged to one of the Naga tribes. Later a third Sister, also a nurse joined them" (Extract from the History of the Institute).

On being asked about the background of this boy in order to identify him, Sr. Guadalupe said that she only knew his name as John. Later on he was identified as S. John Longyao. He worked with Rev. Fr. Mgr. Bars SDB and Rev. Fr. Marocchino for a short time in Kohima. After leaving the hospital he went back to his native place Ukhrul and became the first volunteer catechist of the Ukhrul Catholic Church in 1952.

On 14 February 1953, Fr. Ravalico blessed his wedding. It was the first Catholic wedding there (Sebastian, 1999, p. 67).

He became the touring catechist of Tangkhul area in 1957. He was the first touring catechist who sowed the seeds of faith in Hunphun village (under Ukhrul district). When a small community was formed in Maram Khullen in 1957 he was sent there to instruct people. It is also said that he was a close companion of Fr. Peter Bianchi and so both toured the Mao area. Although an active leader in the Church he was unable to carry on with his work as he became a victim of tuberculosis and died on 1 February 1964 (personal communication, November 23, 2011, Sr. Joy msmhc, daughter of John Longyao).

experienced missionary by then. He had come to India in 1922 with the first group of Salesian Fathers and Brothers. He was a teacher, touring missionary, writer and Apostolic Administrator of Krishnagar in West Bengal and Vicar General of Shillong Diocese for forty years before the Lord called him Home on April 4, 1974 at the benevolent age of 85. On 31 after a 13 hour journey the train halted at Dimapur….we were shocked to see the terrible poverty of the people. Mgr. Bars met an English Catholic gentleman and then we mounted the bus….As we were arriving we could see men and women working along the road, they were very poor but looked strong and well built, we kept looking and suddenly, we saw they were "our Nagas"…. We entered the only hotel in Kohima and stayed there for a few days…..2nd January was the first day of our work in the hospital. The first thing we did was to prepare the beds of the patients….we gave good baths to some of the patients….tended to the wounds….5th January we changed our residence to the hospital campus….Mgr. Bars encouraged us and told us not to worry, that even if we do not know the language to preach to the Nagas, it is enough for them to see us and know that we are their sisters who work in the hospital…..we were just happy and gave thanks to God for bringing us to this mission (pg.3).[13]

---

13 Sr. Guadalupe started her work when she was 24 years. In the hospital, the Sisters were also asked to teach the wives of the Assam Rifles officers and soldiers.The public in general were happy with the three. After two years of service she was transferred to the Leprosy Colony, Tura in Meghalaya State. Sr. Pilar took her place in the hospital. Sr. Guadalupe came back to Nagaland to visit the hospital on 9 August 2004 and received the memento of the Golden Jubilee of the Hospital. She visited Kohima again on 2 December, 2008.

Prior to the arrival of the Sisters the Government had signed a six year contract with the Church. The condition laid down by the government was that the Sisters and their chaplain were forbidden from exercising any pastoral ministry other than medical care (Kottuppallil, 1990). Since their arrival, the Naga Hill was unofficially opened to the Catholic Church.

The following letter written by Bishop Ferrando (1951) tells us about the hospital and the service of the Sisters:

> During the last war the Japs opened a new road through the jungle carrying their cannon and ammunition on elephants. After fierce battles the Japs were stopped at Kohima. Masters in jungle warfare, the Nagas made no small contribution toward the victory. As a reward for their (Nagas') services, the government gave them the most up-to-date hospital in Assam. I am happy to tell you that this hospital is run by a new order of Spanish nuns. Right Reverend Monsignor Bars is their chaplain and our pioneer missionary among the Nagas (pg. 6).[14]

14 From the Mission of Assam' found in the Chronicle-History of the Diocese of Shillong 1951-1953 under the title, 'Bishop Ferrando writes from Assam' it is stated that Monsignor E. Bars hailed from Spain. He belonged to the first batch of missionaries that came to the North-East in 1922. O. Paviotti in his book, 'The Work of His Hands' p. 22, describes Monsignor Bars as a man who has a penchant for language and scientific knowledge of fauna, flora, geology and medicine. He was successively a teacher, a touring missionary, a parish priest, Administrator Apostolic of the Diocese of Krishnagar for six years and for some 40 years Vicar General of the Diocese of Shillong. On page 49, he is affectionately called Fr. Motor-car for his fast walking up and down the War Hills. In 1973 he published his monumental English-Khasi Dictionary. In addition to this, he left a valuable Garo-English dictionary in manuscript form. He along with Fr. H. Elias translated the New Testament into Khasi. When the Lord called him on April 4, 1974, at the age of 85 he was engaged in revising the New Khasi translation of the Bible. He was a missionary in India for 52 years.

After the entry of the Catholic Church into the Naga Hills Bishop Ferrando (1951) wrote in the chronicle of the Diocese about the possibility of evangelization, in these words:

> The American Baptists have worked here among the Nagas for 100 years. It has always been closed territory to Catholics. However, now we have Catholic nuns running the hospital at Kohima, and Msgr. E. Bars, the resident Chaplain, is making many useful contacts. As yet Catholic Missionaries cannot preach in the Naga Hills. But the Nagas themselves repeatedly petition the Government to allow us to open schools and churches.

Sr. Guadalupe said, that since there was a contract signed between the Government and the Bishop, they could not openly propagate the Catholic faith as it would lead to violation of the agreement. Under such circumstances, however, she felt that doing good to someone was equal to preaching. She said, Mgr. Bars used to tell us, "let us go to the town and Kohima village to preach in silence" (Personal communication, December 2, 2008). Mass was celebrated in a small chapel in the hospital and at times in the open-air attended by some people of the village out of curiosity. By witnessing their life and work people started enquiring about the Catholic faith and in the course of time a few people came into contact with Mgr. Bars and expressed their desire to receive Catholic faith. Sr. Guadalupe said, one day a Baptist told Mgr. Bars that while reading the Bible he had an inspiration that 'true religion is the religion of the Sisters.' She could not remember his name but said he came draped in a red shawl. After she had left the hospital she was told he became a Catholic (Personal communication, December 2, 2008).

Sr. Guadalupe was happy to learn that patients loved and appreciated their works even though the only language they knew then was the language of love and service. Since they had been forbidden from doing pastoral ministry like preaching and teaching catechism and knowing there were no Catholics in Nagaland Mgr. Bars took a photo of him, John and two Sisters and said jokingly, 'This is the first Catholic Church in Naga Hills' (Personal communication, December 2, 2008). While in the hospital, Mgr. Bars became acquainted with some local people who had often invited him to their homes. He would distribute books on Catholic religion and many expressed their liking for the new faith (Suosahie, 1994).

Mgr. E. Bars, S.D.B.

Sr. Guad[illegible]e SCJ.

Sr. Margarita Cifre, SCJ.

John Longyao

The Sisters' service in the hospital was also a healing remedy to cool down hatred and prejudice people had had of the Catholic Church over the years. It was not possible to wipe out the stigma attached to the Catholic Church within a span of two to three years. However, over this period, the suspicious nature of the people had been narrowed down, curiosity about the Church aroused and a bridge of friendship built. Quoting the words of Thepfünilhu, Vattoth (2010) writes, "They really changed the attitude of the Baptists, though they did not go about preaching. They took good care of the patients... changed the attitude about the Catholics" (pg. 52). A few young people, like, Suosahie Philip, Sasielie Belho, Khriesalie Antony etc. used to visit Mgr. Bars in the hospital, and their interaction with him made them come closer to the new faith and later on Fr. Marocchino baptised them. On her second coming to Nagaland, 9 August 2004, after the long gap of fifty four years, Sr. Guadalupe once again recalled her experiences in Nagaland and shared the joy of how the Church took roots in Kohima village. Vattoth (2010) recalls the words of Sr. Guadalupe, "We were strictly forbidden by the authority and other Christian denominations of the area to teach the Bible or speak about the Catholic Church, yet day by day they found us Christians with a difference worth following,... and the seed of Catholic faith was sown" (pg. 55). Mgr. Bars and the Sisters thus sowed the seeds of the Catholic faith in this forbidden land during their short stay and work in the hospital.

Mgr. Bars and the Sisters strictly adhered to the orders of the administration not to involve in the religious affairs of the people of the state. It is evident from the chronicle of Catholic Mission Golaghat (1941-1958) which stated that they used to attend Christmas and Easter services in the Church at Golaghat during 1950 and 1951. Again in the same chronicle dated 10 March 1949, Fr. Neyens mentions, "It is a pity that no direct work can be done for the conversion of the Nagas, at present, but we hope the difficulties will disappear and so we shall have a good field wherein there is much hope."

2.7.5 Arrival of Fr. Marocchino

In 1952 Mgr. Bars was succeeded by Fr. Marocchino as the chaplain of the Sisters (Kerketta, 1998). Vattoth (2010) describes Fr. Marocchino in the following words, "One person who is responsible for the beginning of the Catholic Church in Kohima, Nagaland, is none other than Fr. Umberto (Albert) Marocchino, (1909-1991) who alone as a one man force struggled to get a foothold in the American Baptist Mission stronghold" (pg. 38).[15] According to the chronicle of Catholic Mission, Golaghat (1941-1958) dated 4 February 1952 he took charge of the new assignment in January 1952.[16] During

---

15 Fr. Marocchino was born on February 3, 1909 in Italy. He came to Assam in 1924 at a tender age of 15 to become a missionary. He was ordained a priest on 29 April 1933 at the age of 24. He started his priestly ministry in Krishnagar Diocese where Mgr. Emmanuel Bars was the Apostolic Administrator (1928-1934) before he came to Shillong as Vicar General and later on as the first resident priest in Kohima, Nagaland. He was just 42 years old when he came to Nagaland. He was well built and robust, over 6 feet tall.

16 The Chronicle of 1941-1958, Catholic Mission Golaghat says on 10 December 1951 Fr. Marocchino came from Shillong and from there he went to Kohima to take the place of Mons. Bars. It further says, on 23 December 1951 Mons. Bars and Sisters came down to Golaghat for Christmas. 4 February 1952 version of the chronicle says 'Fr. Marocchino who has taken the place of Mons. Bars in Kohima arrives from Kohima through Mokokchung and Mariani.

World War II (1939-1945) he, along with several other Italian missionaries were taken from Sonada, Darjeeling, and kept in the concentration camp at Deoli (1942), and later on shifted to the concentration camp at Dehra Dun and remained there till October 1946. After two years of ministry in the Diocese of Agra he was appointed in Tezpur, Assam as a touring missionary in the Tea Gardens. It was followed by his ministry in Golaghat, Assam. When he was the assistant priest in Shillong he was transferred to Kohima to replace Mgr. Bars who was transferred from Kohima to Shillong.

When Fr. Marocchino began his ministry in Kohima in 1952, he was faced with a lot of rumours and allegations leveled by the non-Catholics against the Catholics. Yet he braved all with his perseverance and trust in God. He was destined to make history as far as the Catholic Church in Nagaland was concerned. With his arrival in Kohima, a new era dawned for the Church.

Fr. Marocchino too had been given strict orders not to go out to do any mission work outside the hospital or in the villages by the then Deputy Commissioner, Pawsey. As he landed in a new land with a totally different situation, his consolation was meeting with a few friends of Mgr. Bars. It was from his residence in the hospital that he started distributing literature on 'Catholicism' to his new friends and asked them to translate them into Angami dialect. Slowly a small group was formed around him and they began to participate in Sunday services in the hospital chapel ("Christ King Parish, Kohima", 1999). Thus, as a missionary to the Angamis, he began his 'silent' mission work.

Bishop Ferrando was optimistic about the opening of the Naga Hills to the Catholic Mission. He wrote in the chronicle of the Diocese (1951-53): "Nagas seeing the self-sacrificing and humanitarian work of the Sisters and the Salesian father began to take interest in Catholic religion and are attracted to embrace the Catholic faith. Many Nagas came to me asking about the true religion of Jesus Christ and wanted us to enter the Naga Hills." It had been confirmed by the Bishop that for two years the Naga people had been sending letters to the Governor seeking his permission for the Catholic missionaries to enter and begin the mission work in Nagaland. But the Governor said that the permission to work in the Naga Hills would not be granted as the Nagas' determination to remain independent troubled the administration. The Naga people, however, opined that the permission to enter the Naga Hills was nearer. What saddened the Bishop was that the Catholic religion was known only through the false teachings of the American Baptists who were in the Naga Hills. He mentions also in the same chronicle, "Many Naga students studying at Shillong are preparing themselves to become missionaries to their own villages. They are translating the catechism and small prayer books."

2.7.6 New District Commissioner

The new District Commissioner (DC) to the Naga Hills, S. J. D. Carvalho a devout Goan, whose presence in Kohima was indeed a solace to Fr. Marocchino and his close associates who were intending to become Catholics. He served as DC from

1953-1957.[17] He helped Fr. Marocchino to stay on in Kohima, even after the Sisters had left at the expiry of their contract in 1955 (Kottuppallil, 1990). Suosahie (2002) has this to say: "On Sundays he used to come for mass which was celebrated outside Father's residence and impressed many by kneeling on the bare ground with his well pressed suit. It was an inspiration for many and perhaps for the first time people had come to know that even Catholics have such respectable officer" (p. 1). Fr. Marocchino and the Sisters breathed a sigh of relief when the new Commissioner allowed them to visit Kohima Village. Just like the joy of a bird freed from its cage, they started visiting Kohima village on Sundays and at other free times.[18] Meeting and interacting with the people brought them closer and gradually people began to shed their feelings of antagonism and prejudice against the Catholics. The DC Carvalho was sympathetic not only towards Fr. Marocchino and Sisters but also the Bishop. While recalling his experiences in the Naga Hills with the new Catholic DC, Bishop Marango, the former

---

17 S. J. D. Carvalho was born in 1919. He became an I.A.S. officer in 1948. He was the Deputy Commissioner of the Naga Hills District from 1953 to 1957. On 18 March 1956 when he was returning from Chiesama, where the Assam Rifles and Police had destroyed a Naga hideout killing 8 Nagas and injuring several others, there was an unsuccessful attempt on his life by hostile tribesmen near Narhema village in Naga Hills District (Source:Internet). According to Fr. Marocchino, Carvalho was transferred to the Naga Hills by the personal order of Jawaharlal Nehru (Source:Don Bosco Mandaluyong)

18 But by now familiar figures in Kohima, the three Sisters, another having joined the first two, were slowly permitted to extend the area of their medical work to the Kohima village, above the town. In time, a small group of people became interested in the Catholic teachings and attended the Sunday services at the hospital chapel. Among the first of the Angami Catholics were Paulus Keviprale, Louis Neizo and Philip Suosahie (source: Memoirs from Sisters of Christ Jesus, Shilling, p.6).

Bishop of the Diocese of Dibrugarh wrote in the Silver Jubilee magazine of the Sacerdotal Silver Jubilee of Bishop Abraham in 1989, "I visited Kohima the first time when Carvalho, the then DC granted me permit to visit the Catholic Community of Lakhuti. He wanted me to meet him at Wokha where he happened to be visiting with the Kohima S.P" (pg. 34).

It is appropriate to mention here some of Fr. Marocchino's close friends who from the start of his stay in the hospital, continued to be a band of faithful supporters and showed their unquestioned loyalty to him and the Church even after his departure in 1963. They include Kevipralie Paulus Belho, Neizo Louis, Sasielie Samuel Belho, Suosahie Philip, Kezesuohie Sylvester, Vayolie Valentine, Deinuo Diana, Viesielie Vincent, Vilasalie James, Visakhuo Simeon, Khriesalie Anthony, Mezhuvilie Dominic, Dietho-o Dominic, Lhouze-ü Lucy, etc. Among them his closest friend was Kevipralie Paulus, who took the initiative and leadership in Kohima community. It was he and Neizo Louis who closely collaborated with Fr. Marocchino for the promotion of the Catholic faith in and outside the Angami area.

2.7.7 First Baptism, Christmas and Easter Celebrations

The gradual opening to the new faith resulted in the baptism of a child. It has been stated that, "14th December 1952 remains a red letter day in the history of Catholic Church in Nagaland" ("Christ King Parish, Kohima", 1999, p. 15). On that day, Kevipele, son of Kevipralie Paulus was baptised and took the name 'John Bosco' in the Sisters' chapel in the Naga hospital. What prompted the parents who were non-Christians at the time of the baptism of their child to get it baptised in the Catholic Church is not known. Most probably the child was not keeping good health after the birth and Sisters in the hospital must have advised the parents to let the baby be baptised. The child's parents, Kevipralie Paulus and his wife Deinuo, and the Spanish sisters were the only witnesses to this sacrament of Baptism which was given in the Sisters' chapel in Naga hospital (Vattoth, 2010). The effect of the first baptism was already reflected in the attitude of the people who agreed to the suggestion to have Christmas and Easter celebrations in Kohima village the following year. Accordingly, unlike other years, Christmas and Easter celebrations of 1953 were celebrated in the village. In the words of Fr. Marocchino:

> This year Christmas was not kept at the hospital but in the heart of the Naga village of Kohima. A school building was placed at our disposal and was adapted as a Church for the occasion. Everybody gave a helping hand in the preparations and decorations in the true Christmas spirit. At midnight Mass the Church was filled to capacity, even though the only Christians were me, the sisters and a few soldiers. There was no lack of Christmas carols as the Naga children had learnt several of them in their already musical language. The mass was preceded by a magic-lantern show, followed by distribution of prizes to the children. Trumpets and whistles were prominent so that after some time the village was 'awakened' to the fact of Nativity. One of the main attractions was a large sized crib and many catechetical charts stuck up all over the wall. We had appointed Cicerone to explain the one and the others. On the 25th there was a powerful "bara khana" for our friends and sympathisers at the exclusion of "Zu" (Naga beer)... At the end of the day

> everybody remarked that the "Catholic Christmas" with its service, prizes, sports, games and even the large star lifted high on a bamboo pole at night, were the "non plus ultra" (Family News, February, 1954, pg. 3).

The presence of a large number of people at these two gatherings was quite encouraging. Dr. Das, the Naga Civil Hospital surgeon who was from Bengal had all praise and appreciation for the Sisters who worked there. He got permission from the police to let Sr. Annie and Sr. Pilar distribute clothes to the poor children in Kohima Village and to visit and care for pregnant women.

2.7.8 Alumni Requests

St. Anthony's College and St. Edmund's College, Shillong, have been the first choice for many students of the North East, including Nagaland and Manipur, as these colleges offer quality education since their inception. By 1953 many of the Naga students returned to the home states after their studies, convinced of the values of quality education and the faith that the Catholic Church represents. The deep rooted sincerity of those students is found in the words of Syiemlieh (1990), "They did much to dispel the illusions of what the Catholic Church stood for and were convinced that the Roman Catholics, as they were called till recently, were not as bad as what the people were made to believe" (pg. 44). Fr. Marocchino was optimistic that the work among the Nagas especially with the help of these students would not go rewardless. He looked forward, with hope, to the abrogation of the law which forbids Catholic propaganda among the Naga tribes. Ferrando (1953) quotes the words of Fr. Marocchino:

> Since the past 6 years there is a real movement towards the Catholic faith going on in the Naga tribes and the Tangkhuls of Manipur. We might say that the movement was "self-started", that is we almost did not mean it. It was due to some few Naga students who chanced to be reading at the Shillong Catholic schools and there discovered the 'Romans' and of course they found out by first-hand experience that they were not those that crucified Our Lord!,...The factor that we have such Catholic Schools at Shillong where Non-Christians and Non-Catholic students are attracted must therefore be given its due credit (pg. 2).

The following letter had been written by the former Catholic pupils of Shillong requesting the administration and the Bishop to send Catholic priests to Nagaland.

In the year 1954 on the occasion of the blessing of the new Church of St. Paul at Marbisu, Fr. Marocchino took eight representatives, all pagans, from three different villages to Shillong from Kohima. It was for the obvious consideration that, a first-hand contact and acquaintance with such a Catholic centre as Shillong and its nearby districts might make a favourable impression on them and prove to be a true "Object-lesson" (Family News, 1954). "The results were superior even to our expectation: all that they saw and heard seems to have made a great impact on their mind as I could gather from their remarks and appreciation" (Family News, 1954, pg. 6). Fr. Marocchino continues:

> One of them, a pagan holding the office of member of a tribal Panchayat was heard laughing and uttering happy

Letter to the Bishop of Shillong

Letter No. AR/PRC/51/136,
Dated Akuluto the 15th August, 1951.

To,

The Secretary,
to the Government of Assam for Tribal Areas, Shillong.

Sir,

We the Baptised Roman Catholics beg to lay down the following few facts for your kind consideration and generous order.

That Sir, nearly three years have elapsed since we asked for permission to be granted to Catholic Priests to go over the Naga Hills as well, for preaching their faith. We beg to point out to your honour that it was not through the agency of R.C. Fathers but we ourselves became converted into R.C. religion; and now we want to acquire our knowledge both spiritually and educationally.

That Sir, it is officially learnt that the Government would permit the R.C. Priests to go over to the Naga Hills after one year only: ie after deciding the political situation of Naga Hills. It is very difficult to understand why Government should intervene in religious matter. However, we assure your honour that R.C. Priests are not coming to Naga HILLS to interfere in Naga Politics, but we want them just for religious service-ministration: in accordance with the freedom of religion granted to us under the constitution of India. Consequently, we request your honour to give permission to any R.C. Father to come to Akuluto Range of Mokokchung Sub-division, Naga Hills; for our religious service-ministration.

We shall be highly obliged if you would kindly treat it as <u>EXTREMELY URGENT</u>.

Yours faithfully,

1. [signature]
2. [signature]
3. [signature]

On behalf of whole Akuluto Range.

Letter No. AR/PRC/51/136, dated Akuluto the 15th August, 1951.

Copy forwarded to:-

1. H.E. Bishop's Secretary, Shillong for favour of H.E. Bishop's information and necessary action. He is further requested to send one Priest to Akuluto as soon as permission is g[iven].

2. H.E. the Governor of Assam, Shillong for information and necessary action. We should be most grateful for any assistance that your honour could give in this connectio[n].

3. The Deputy Commissioner, Naga Hills, Kohima for information.

4. The Sub-divisional Officer, Mokokchung for information. (Civil).

[signature] 15-8-[5]1

Akuluto M.E. School
Compound
P.O. Mokokchung
Naga Hills.

Sir,

We the people of Ak[illegible] Range beg most humbly and respectfull[illegible], to state that we have been expecting and looking forward [illegible] the best result out of everything from you. But it is our great surprised that no attention has been paid to our an[illegible] with you by our two representatives whom we have send to you from last month.

As we have been informing you that most of the people have determined to convert if you kindly allow a priest to visit our Akuluto Range and to construct us the new faith and the way of worship. we are not yet given the last decision, but have great hope that you are trying to enter in the Naga hills also.

we beg to add, that the Govt. also given us permission to accept the new faith and informed us that the Roman Catholic may enter in the Naga Hills for the religious metter. So it is your will, whether it possible to come or not. As you know well, we the Semas are the centre in the Naga Hills and we are sure, that your faith may spread to all tribe in our places, if you possible to come. We the people are ready now to accept your faith and it is our earnest hope and we trust that you will give this metter your immediate attention.

Your faithfully,
X. Shikhu
Secretary of Akul[illegible]

exclamations even in his dreams! Asked for an explanation by his fellow Nagas he had to confess that he had dreamt of a most beautiful Church just like the one in Marbisu, standing on a slope right above his village! Let's hope he had the right kind of prophetic dream. What struck them most and "won the day" is the contact they had directly with the different phases of Catholic life as lived by Hill-men like themselves. After the visit to the beautiful Shillong cemetery, one of them remarked: "this religion is beautiful to live and to die in!" It reflects on the care and the cult of the dead which the Nagas seem to share in common with the Khasis. They have also witnessed the happiness and serenity which transpires from all people and Catholic ways and have been comparing it with other "ways" of a non-Catholic denomination. "The Catholic worship has most of the things that we Nagas would like to have" they say. These are the few highlights of the visit of our 'Naga Squad' to Shillong and Marbisu (Family News, "Kohima" March 1954, pg. 6).

A faith evoking experience for the Catholics has been the annual Corpus Christi procession in Shillong. Fr. Marocchino continued to take several Nagas on this pilgrimage every year as it helped to instill a deeper faith.

It was during the midnight of 24 December 1954 that nine young people led by Kevipralie Belho, who was very closely associated with Fr. Marocchino and often received instructions from him on Catholic faith, received baptism. So, officially the Catholic Church came into being in the Angami area on that day. These nine people, prior to their baptism, had obtained permission from their parents to become Catholics despite the latter expressing their fear that they were following a wrong religion. Those who received baptism on that day were: 1. Kevipralie Paulus, 2. Neizo Louis, 3. Deinuo Diana (Kevipralie's wife), 4. Sasilie Samuel, 5. Kezesuohie Sylvester, 6. Vayolie Valentine, 7. Suosahie Philip, 8. Miapho Marcus, and 9. Neipieü Noemi (Vattoth, 2010).[19] Fr. Marocchino did not administer baptism to several other boys even though they too had received instruction and got permission from their parents as they were too young. As the new members joined the Church, there erupted a special joy among the members to celebrate Christmas more meaningfully. Ferrando in Family News "Kohima" February (1955) quoting the words of Fr. Marocchino, described the exciting Christmas celebration of 1954 in the following words:

> Also this year we had the grace and happiness of celebrating Christmas up at the Naga village of Kohima: in the heart of the Angami Tribe. As the school building was at our disposal the Sisters could transform it into a well decorated chapel. Previous to midnight Mass we had a sing-song session to which a group of pagan boys and girls asked spontaneously

---

19 Vattoth in his book, A Star Over Tenyimia, p. 72 says that Kevipralie Paulus was a leading light for the infant Church in kohima. During his study in Shillong in 1946, as a student of Agriculture Training Centre, Upper Shillong he came to know more about the Catholic Church especially by reading books like 'The Truth About the Catholic Church, What is the Bible' etc. After meeting Mgr. Bars sometime in 1949 in Kohima, he collected more books about the Church and he distributed them among his friends and they took a keen interest. While he was studying at Baptist School, Kohima, one day his teacher happened to utter the words, 'Protestants and Catholics' in the class. In response to his questions, the teacher replied that the former were 'refined Christians' and latter were 'not refined.' This answer, however, did not satisfy him. Finally his search for the truth led him to enter the Catholic Church.

to participate as a home to us, their guests at Christmas. They sang their tribal songs in their unusual system of chords of drones: they were about such subjects as: going to the fields, planting rice, drawing water etc. The projector show attracted quite a large crowd and so we had the best of opportunities towards the presentation of Catholic faith. At midnight mass most of the people remained in the Church and mingled with our Catholics and catechumens. They (people-both Christians and non-Christians) were following all the proceedings with interest and respect. We know that they are greatly attracted by the vestments, ornaments and ceremonies used in the Catholic worship. At Mass the Naga children sang two carols in their own language and with great 'gusto' even though the original music seemed to have been lost in the intrusive tones and accents of the Naga text. After Mass followed the distribution of prizes to the children who had been faithful to Sunday Mass throughout the year: some 50 of them. That day 'Bara Khana' (Naga fashion) with plenty of pig meat and lavish savoring of chilies... the only pity of it all during that 'Zu' (Naga beer) was not allowed as digestive!!! For us the best aspect of this 'Naga Christmas' was the baptisms of adults and children: the real first-fruits of this lead Tribe among the Nagas (pg. 5).

On being asked the reasons for his conversion to Catholicism, Philip Suosahie, said that Samuel Belho, brother of late Kevipralie Paulose, who was his classmate used to attend Holy Mass regularly at the hospital and he invited him to join him. This participation gradually led him to the Catholic Church (personal communication, June 14, 2011). He also said that the people who became Catholics were mostly from non-Christian religions as well as a few from the Baptist Christianity.

2.7.9 Sisters' Departure

On 22 January 1955 the Sisters left the Naga Hospital on the expiry of a six year contract (Puthenpurakal, 2000). It was a time of political turmoil in Nagaland and the Central Government was apprehensive of the Christian missionaries whom they suspected to be the force behind the political upheaval. Since the fledgling Catholic Church was caught in between, the Bishop of Assam felt he could not take responsibility for the foreign sisters ("Kohima-Nagaland", 1984). It had also been mentioned in the institute's biography that the Government asked them to leave on completion of their six years' contract with the hospital. When it was time to renew the contract the Government refused to do so and the Sisters had to leave in distress (Missionaries of Christ Jesus, 1988).[20] During the

20 In spite of the great difficulties of the language, the professional experience of the Sisters and optimism which they had, made their work highly valued. Nevertheless, the Government asked the Sisters to leave on completion of their six years contract with the hospital probably due to the influence of the Baptists, who had the upper hand in the place and tried to prevent work wherever possible. The patients and personnel of the military blocks, where one of the Sisters was working, were ready to ask for permission, to the authority, to enable this Sister to remain. On the part of the Institute there was no inconvenience, as long as another Sister could stay with her, but probably there were some other difficulties, so the Sisters didn't continue. The priest, nevertheless could remain in Kohima and the Church went ahead...... Our stay there was short,-six years-but the going of the Sisters was instrumental for opening the way for the Church in Nagaland (Extract form the History of the Institute, titled 'Kohima-Nagaland,' unpublished). This was also confirmed by Sr. Maria Camino Sanz-Orrio, who was one of the pioneers of the Missionaries of Christ Jesus and worked in Tura, who in a written reply to Fr. Joseph Puthenpurackal's enquiries on the activities of their Sisters in the North-East on 23rd June 1988, says 'when it was time to renew it the Government did not want to renew it again and the Sisters had to leave. They left crying. The people were wonderful and we have great love for them.'

meetings of the heads of the Hill Districts of Manipur and Nagaland of the Diocese of Dibrugarh held from 17 to 18 February 1965, Fr. Bernick said that the Sisters were told by the Union Government of India that their services were not required any more and as a result they had to leave (Rosario, 1965). He also mentioned that after the 1956 attack (between the Naga Home Guards and the Indian Army at Kohima Village), Fr. Marocchino lost favour with the underground. Sr. Pilar Gonsalez who worked in the Naga Hospital went to her eternal reward in the diamond jubilee year (2008) of the arrival

Mary Help of Christians Cathedral in Kohima

While Bishop Marengo was in Kohima one Mr. Zopianga, who was Secretary to the Nagaland Government, came to see him with a request. "Bishop", he said, "your Sisters were doing splendid work in the Kohima hospital and to this day I don't know why they have been asked to go and by whom. I would be grateful if you could arrange for those same Sisters to come back. We would like to do justice to them." I wrote to Sr. Joaquina, the then provincial of the Spanish Sisters of Christ Jesus, but her reply was that she could not see her way to comply as all her Sisters were already engaged elsewhere. (Bishop Marengo in the souvenir of the Sacerdotal Silver Jubilee of Bishop Abraham Alangimattathil, 1989, pg. 36).

in Nagaland and was accorded a fitting tribute by Fr. Graviour Augustine. He writes:

> A stranger she came and a friend she left. The dialect she could not speak, but with a smile she could communicate, Spaniard by birth and an Indian she was in death. Unknown her service to many but known to God what she did for Nagaland that too in those years when the country India was just born.....Belonging to the group of pioneering Catholic missionaries who served in the Naga Hospital, her life was not all that could give happiness. It was like that of a flying bird with disabled wings. She was a missionary but only within four walls of the hospital. She was a preacher but without speaking. She was a communicator but only with smiles. And she was a doer, but only with her healing touch...(Extract from the History of the Institute, Sisters of Christ Jesus, pg. 6).

2.7.10 Continuation of the Works by Fr. Marocchino

By the time the Sisters left the hospital there had already been a number of Catholics in Kohima, mostly soldiers serving in the army and also civil servants in the administration who came from different parts of India. Some of them used to attend Mass whenever it was celebrated either in the hospital chapel or in Kohima Village. It was essential, therefore, to have a priest to take care of the pastoral needs of these people. It is believed that Fr. Marocchino was granted permission by the DC to stay on either at the former's discretion or the latter's request after the Sisters had left the hospital. The DC's role in establishing the Catholic Church is highly appreciable as he helped the Church in many ways and impressed many people who previously did not like the new religion in their area (Suosahie, 1994).

Fr. Marocchino was also granted permission by the DC for free movement and this permit helped him to reach out to many adjacent Angami villages. After the Sisters' departure, he moved into a small shed in the war cemetery, close to Samuel Mezhur's quarters. Vattoth (2010) writes: "On some Sundays the service was shifted from the hospital to the War Cemetery, where there is an altar, which could be very conveniently used and the custodian of the War Cemetery, Samuel Mezhur, had no objection to Fr. Marocchino conducting his service there" (pg. 69). Seeing the need for a school in Kohima both of them started the 'Kohima English School', presently known as Mezhur Higher Secondary School.[21]

Fr. Marocchino continued to face opposition from the public despite the permission to remain. One day the Superintendent of Police invited Fr. Marocchino to his office and asked many questions and sought much information about the Catholic Church. One of the questions he asked was, "Tell us if you feel safe for your life here in Kohima or if you encounter any sort of opposition from the Naga Hostiles." He replied: "The only opposition I meet is the Baptist warriors"

---

21 Vattoth in his book A Star Over Tenyimia, p. 69 says that in those days, seeing the need for a school in Kohima, both of them together started the 'Kohima English School' presently known as 'Mezhur Higher Secondary School' in the hope that one day Sisters would take over the school and run it. In fact when the Little Flower Sisters first came, they started teaching there, but gave up the idea of taking charge of the school, as the place was not sufficient and suitable to them.
Fr. Marocchino was taken down to the school and around the class rooms when he visited Kohima in 1981. The students were told by Atu-o, Samuel's son that Fr. Marocchino was the founder of the school (Interview given by Fr. Marocchino on 22nd November 1981).

("Civil Hospital Kohima II", 1950, pg. 1). The police officer was pleased with his answer.

Before he moved out of Nagaland he had stayed at six different places - hospital, War Cemetery, a house below Baptist Mission compound, Levi's house in D' Block, Neizo Louis' house at the Veterinary hospital and Kohima Village. Since it was inconvenient for the people of Kohima village to go to the War Cemetery for the services he conducted them from Neizo Louis's house at T. Khel. In his search for a suitable place to gather people for worship with the increase in the number of Catholics especially after the baptism of 51 people in 1955, the T. Khel elders allowed him to have the ground floor of the Lower Primary School for the purpose. Soon he took up his residence below the Baptist Mission Compound, in Kitsubozou. Meanwhile the search for a leader for full time work with Fr. Marocchino ended with the appointment of Suosahie Philip, a lower division clerk, at Government High School who was free to work from 2 o'clock in the afternoon (Vattoth, 2010). Although Kevipralie Paulus and Neizo Louis were the first and second choices to lead the community, their professional commitments demanded more time from them and as such they would not be available for reasonable pastoral work.

The sacramental and non-sacramental rites and rituals of the Catholic Church attracted a great many Baptists and non-Christians of Kohima. For example, the funeral rites of the Catholics accompanied by holy mass, prayers, use of candles, flowers, and incense always won the appreciation and admiration of the people as they felt that their dead have been duly paid honour and respect for the next life. This gesture increased the appreciation of the non-Christians for the Catholic Church. In the year 1958, two important people of Kohima Village asked for baptism at the point of death and so they were baptised ("Civil Hospital Kohima II", 1950).

2.7.11 The Attack of 1956

Nagas consider the years between 1950 and 1970 as the most disturbing period in their lives as it was mired by insurgency in the state. The Indian government deployed a large number of military personnel to suppress the independent movement and there was strong resentment from the people. Uncertainties and an unknown future awaited the people especially the Angamis. Imchen (2008) describes the situation at the time in the following words, "These decades saw the emergence of the Naga freedom fighters against the defiance of the inalienable rights of the Nagas to sovereignty. The consequence was, the deployment of the Indian armed forces in the Hills and hostilities between the Nagas and the Indian army" (pg. 164). Despite a bleak future ahead, Fr. Marocchino decided to stay on in the village. Before he moved into Vilanuo's rented house, he had shifted most of his belongings to Philip Suosahie's house. On 8 June 1956, he went to Imphal by bus escorted by a convoy to get some hosts and wine for the daily celebration of the Mass. He reached his destination safely but the following day the bus was attacked by militants. Back home on Monday the 11 June, the Naga Home Guards attacked the Indian Army stationed at Kohima Village. As a consequence, those who supported the Naga cause left for the jungles while others took refuge in the town and sought help from the Indian army

(Suosahie, 2002).[22] In the course of the fighting the homes of those who joined the underground army, as well as others, were looted and burned down. In this attack, Fr. Marocchino's belongings which were in the house of Suosahie Philip were also looted and burnt ("Kohima", 1957).[23] After fleeing from the village to the nearby forest, it is said that the Catholics were the first ones to return to the village. Ferrando in Family News "Kohima" October (1956) describes the dreadful attack of 1956 in the following words:

> In the month of June bands of Naga rebels attacked Kohima by surprise. As a consequence Fr. Marocchino's house was thoroughly looted and burnt down. Being temporarily absent just at that time, Fr. Marocchino had what he calls 'his second escape.' What grieves him most is the loss of manuscripts in the Angami language. All the Catholics together with other villagers had fled and remained in hiding for several days. Most of them are back now, but a few have to lament the loss of their houses and

---

22 Christ King Church, Kohima, Golden Jubilee Magazine, p. 2. The Nagas' repeated attempts to settle the Naga issue with the Indian Government for total independence failed even before and after Independence of India. In 1945 the Nagas changed the name of the Naga Hills District Tribal Council into the Naga National Council (NNC) which would soon become the umbrella organization for the fight for Naga independence. In 1956 A. Z. Phizo formed the 'Naga Central Government' to replace the earlier 'Sovereign Republic of Nagaland.' In 1959, this was changed to the 'Federal Government of Nagaland or FGN. The 'Naga Home Guards,' the armed wing, was also formed (courtesy: A Star Over Tenyimia).

23 In his interview in November 1981 during his visit to Nagaland Fr. Marocchino said that it was when he went to Imphal to get some hosts that his house was looted and burnt down. Even his cassocks had been taken away and found in the jungle torn. Then, the rumor that spread about him was that he had taken off the cassock, put on the uniform and was leading the undergrounds and was killed in the fighting. His typewriter and the small Geloso tape recorder etc. disappeared ('Fr. Marocchino Visits kohima Again, pg. 3).

their belongings. A little Angami lad, who is still a pagan, succeeded in bringing back to Fr. Marocchino the green-red chausable and other pagans recovered the large painted picture of Our Lady Help of Christians. The site of our chapel is at present occupied by the military who are also using the C.I. sheets meant for the roof. Fr. Marocchino hopes to bring the chapel to a finish by Christmas, if things return to normal. Meanwhile, on Sundays mass is said in the beautiful setting of the War-Cemetery, at the foot of the great Memorial Cross. A group of Catholic servicemen has increased the Catholic congregation there (pg.5).

Fr. Marocchino eagerly waited for the situation to cool down and after a few months took a flight to Guwahati and reached Golaghat. He joined a convoy that was coming towards Kohima and when he reached he was shocked to see the vast devastation of the village. As he had no place to stay, Carvalho, the DC accommodated him happily as his guest in his bungalow for a few days before he moved to the house of Levi Zeliang who was a head assistant in DC's office, in D'Block, where he stayed for four years till 1960.

This unfortunate event did not dampen the spirit of Fr. Marocchino or his faithful flock. As in previous years they had a beautiful and meaningful celebration of Christmas in Kohima village. Fr. Marocchino writes:

Our Christmas was kept with greater success this year at Kohima. Our chapel (43x32 ft.) still unfinished was decorated and fitted for the celebration. Midnight Mass could not be had due to curfew orders, but the turnout was great at the Mass on the 25th morning. A group of servicemen also attended. At the ceremony of the kissing of the Baby Jesus just after Mass, it was touching to see the number of non-Christians who came devoutly to pay homage to the born Saviour. One little child wanted more than that: he wanted to take away the Child Jesus with him at all costs! At the fraternal meal there were 200 mouths feasting with the usual very good Naga appetite! The Publicity Department kindly provided us with the extra-loud musical background which lasted up to the evening. From our chapel, which is on a commanding height of the village, we certainly got the whole of Kohima laughing with the irresistible Neapolitan Recording of "La Risata!" The girls of our incipient choir gave also a recital of Catholic songs at the microphone. Our songs must have brought up to the chapel quite a number of people from the town below: even the Brigadier and other high officers graced the games and sports with their presence and kind interest. We brought this successful Naga Christmas to a close by carol-singing and prayers before the camp-fire and at the foot of a very high bamboo bearing the illuminated Christmas Star and a great Cross-flag. One of the great attractions for everybody was the exhibition throughout the day of a large Christmas Crib with not less than 40 statuettes: a dozen of them represented usual Naga characters (Family News, 1957, pg. 8).

Nothing of the chapel was left in the war. At this time the number of Catholics and the catechumens began to increase and this period could be considered a period of conversion. Those who came forward first to receive Catholic faith were from the T. Khel Kohima and, therefore, it was decided to build the Church there. It was Keviselie Sekhose, then a non-Christian, who offered a plot of land in Sozieba, the second highest viewpoint in Kohima Village, when everyone else turned down the request. Through the collective efforts of the Catholics and with help from one Major D'Souza and one Colonel Adam the Church was constructed and it was blessed on 20 April 1957 by Bishop Marengo. To his great surprise and joy he found that the number of neophytes had increased fourfold. The same evening, after blessing the chapel, the bishop received sixteen people into the fold. He celebrated Mass on the morning of Sunday 21st April when he also administered Confirmation to over a hundred of the flock. It was especially for the blessing of this first Catholic Church in the Naga Hills that the Bishop was allowed to visit Kohima again after two years (Family News, "Kohima", November 1957). On the façade he had written 'One Lord, One Faith and One Baptism' ("Fr. Marocchino Visists Kohima Again", 1984, p. 3). Thus with the blessing of this Church the Catholic Church made her visible presence for the first time in Kohima.

2.7.12 Bosco Primary School

Fr. Marocchino

While staying at Levi's house in D' Block, Fr. Marocchino founded the Don Bosco Elementary School in 1959. This new venture was appreciated by all, irrespective of religious affiliations. The school imparted basic education to about 60 students. The teachers included Ms. Dierheninuo Helena, Ms. Lhouze-ü

Lucy, Ms. Sabina Belho, Fr. Marocchino and few others. One of the teachers Ms. Dierheninuo Helena who taught for two years from 1959-1960 said that Ms. Lhouze-ü Lucy and Ms. Sabina Belho were sent to Calcutta for Montessori training ("Civil Hospital Kohima II", 1950, p. 1). The school was later shifted to the present Veterinary compound at Pezielietsie. All the teachers of this school were also good missionaries as they used to tour villages with Fr. Marocchino for evangelisation works.

There were also many young Catholic boys and girls in Kohima who closely collaborated with Fr. Marocchino in teaching catechism and doing other missionary works. When he was staying at D' Block, many boys from Kohima and Khonoma stayed with him; while pursuing their high school studies they also helped him with domestic chores. Among them Vilasalie James, Thepfünilhu Francis Kuotsu and Rüünguto Augustine received baptism from him. Vilasalie James who stayed with him for three years was also a touring companion of Fr. Marocchino (personal communication, April 24, 2012).

Fr. Marocchino had sent some young Naga boys to Assam to get educated in a multicultural setting. They learned Assamese fluently and their ability was appreciated by the authorities in Nagaland. They observed that language could bridge the people of Nagaland and Assam and that they could live in peace with each other. Once the District Commissioner in one of his meetings with his subjects said: "The only person who can change the Nagas is the Catholic Priest" ("Civil Hospital Kohima II", 1950, p. 1). The Catholic community was now spread over to a number of villages in and around Kohima and it received a big morale boost with the baptism of Jasokie, popularly known as J. B. Jasokie. On 20 September

1963, Jasokie John Bosco Zinyü, who eventually became the Chief Minister of Nagaland, joined the Church together with his wife and three children (Vattoth, 2010).

In 1963, the Government of India declared the area a sensitive and exclusive zone as a result of warfare. As a foreigner, Fr. Marocchino had to leave Nagaland. So after 12 years of hard work he left on 3 October 1963 for Golaghat. While he was in Damra, Assam, the Indian Government decided to expel foreign missionaries from Assam. He had to leave Assam in 1969 and after a year of rest in Italy he moved to the Philippines to continue missionary work. In his place Fr. Felix and Fr. Bernick who were Indian citizens came in to continue the work.

2.8 Catholic Church in the Lotha Area

After years of waiting, the Hills, particularly Nagaland and Manipur gradually began opening to the Catholic Church. This was made easier with the creation of a separate Diocese of Dibrugarh which comprised of the entire Nagaland and Manipur and parts of Assam. On 12 July 1951 the Diocese of Dibrugarh was formed by a special decree of Pope Pius XII with Fr. Marengo as its first bishop; but his installation as Bishop took place only in May 1952. From the writings of Bishop Marengo it has been learnt that Nagaland and Manipur were opening to the Catholic Church on the very day of his installation itself because there were two Naga delegations that came to meet him - one composed of Lotha Nagas from Lakhuti (Nagaland) and the other Tangkhul Nagas from Hundung (Manipur) with a request to begin the work of the Church in the said areas. Marengo writes:

> One composed of Lotha Nagas from Lakhuti, the other of Tangkhul Nagas from Hundung. Nagaland and Manipur were at last opening to the Catholic Church. Although most of our work and of our modest achievements were in the plains among our Adivasi Christians who were the first and the bulk of our flock, I must plead guilty to a particular interest and solicitude for the field in the hills that was just opening to us. I felt we had to make the most of the opportunity which presented itself after years on the tiptoe of expectation for something to happen in this direction. Now something was happening and we could not fail God's hour (Silver Jubilee: Diocese of Dibrugarh 1951-1976, pg. 36).

At the time of the creation of the new Diocese, even though it was geographically a vast region, Catholics were concentrated only in the plains consisting of the Adivasi flocks, while the hills were devoid of Catholics, but open to the work of evangelisation.

The plains of Assam provided the basis for the hill evangelisation. In the words of Bishop Marengo (1976), "the vast Diocese of Dibrugarh has today been trimmed down to its Adivasi flock. But our plains Christians must be happy to have served as spring board for our venture among the hill-tribes of Nagaland and Manipur" (pg. 38). He poured out his heart for the hill people when he (1976) writes:

> I have said, as in truth bound, that as Bishop of Dibrugarh my greatest concern were the hill tribes of Nagaland and Manipur who were beckoning to us for the first time, and for lack of personnel I had to assume direct care of our Lotha neophytes until God sent His man and their man in the person of Fr.

Larrea whom they called 'our Lotha Father' (pg. 37).

When the Church began to establish contact with the Angami tribe, the Lotha tribe on the other side longed for the Catholic mission. Providence has its way and so, the Lotha tribe further towards the north and closer to Assam on the other side of the state invited the Catholic priests from Golaghat to open a mission among them (Syiemlieh, 1990). "The Angamis had the Church start in their hills not from a call by that tribe. Some Lothas, on the other hand, invited the Catholic priests from Golaghat to open a mission among them" (Syiemlieh, 1990, pg. 48).

The Lothas used to come down to Furkating and Golaghat, two towns in Assam bordering Nagaland to sell their produce of fruits, vegetables and manufactured goods. The first known contacts of the priests at Golaghat with the Lothas go back to 1946, when Fr. Nyans, the priest in charge of the mission at that time engaged a large number of Lothas to clear the jungle in the mission compound (Pallikunnel, n.d). He had hoped that one day the Catholic Church would be implanted in the hills particularly among the Lotha tribe.

In the course of a conversation, Fr. Nyans, told them: 'One day your children will come to study here.' Prophecy or not, these words were narrated to Fr. J. Larrea in 1963 by one of the workers, a Baptist who came to Golaghat with some Catholic friends, when he saw the Lotha boys happily playing after class. 'I am really surprised', he said, 'to see how the words of Fr. Nyans pronounced 17 years ago have become true' (Larrea, 1963, pg. 2).

2.8.1 The Golaghat Mission: The Gateway

The Golaghat Mission, the gateway to the Lotha mission, was inaugurated and blessed on the 24 of August 1941 by Bishop Stephen Ferrando of Shillong. Recalling the beginning of the Lotha mission from Golaghat, Fr. Felix Bollini SDB, who spent 23 years in the Golaghat mission writes: "On December 28th, 1950 I had a surprise visit by five Lotha Nagas. They invited me to go to Lakhuti" (Bollini, 1991, pg. 7).[24] None present on the occasion could have imagined that their visit would lead to a breakthrough for the Catholic Church among the Lotha tribe. Puthenpurakal (2000) says: "In the providence of God they became the nucleus of the first Catholic community of Nagaland. When Fr. Marengo met them in Golaghat he could never have imagined that within a few months they would be part of his flock" (pg. 269). The names of the five are Shanpano Humtsoe, Yantsao Lucas Yanthan, Yanpansao Humtsoe, Niemsao Humtsoe and Renzamo Humtsoe. Among them three had been expelled from the Baptist church. Kottupallil (1990) wrote that after two days of lengthy discussions, they left Golaghat with rosaries, medals and crucifixes and holy water, for their village of Lakhuti where the Baptists had expelled them from their church sometime back.

24 The visit to Golaghat by five Lothas from Lakhuti has been mentioned in an article written by Fr. Felix Bollini in the Golden Jubilee of the Catholic Church Golaghat, 1941-1991, and the same has also been mentioned in the Chronicle 1941-1958, of the Catholic Mission Golaghat. Fr. Bollini could reach Lakhuti only on the feast of St. Joseph in 1951. He describes the visit as an occasion of tremendous joy, however, he was unable to tour regularly due to physical impossibility as well as many restrictions imposed by the government.

2.8.2 Background of the Expulsion

Lakhuti is a village situated about 45 kilometers away from Wokha district headquarter. When the American Baptist missionaries came into contact with this village in the year 1920, the people were non-Christians (pagans). Prior to the arrival of the Catholic missionaries, the people were fed with wrong information about the Catholic Church. M. Humtsoe, one of the pioneer Catholics of the village said the Baptists had spread the rumor that "the Roman Catholics crucified Christ. So they are not Christians" (Personal communication, January 10, 2007). By the time the people came to know of the Catholic Church many people in the village had already embraced Christianity.

Nkomo mentioned in his letter, 'Establishment of Catholic Church in Nagaland' that in 1949 the Lotha Baptist Church Council passed an order to the Lakhuti Baptist Church that its pastor Tsumongo Yanthan's salary should be increased by Rs. 2.50 per month. It is said that this order was made known to other Lotha Baptist churches throughout the Lotha region.[25] Following the order, the Lakhuti Lotha Baptist Church discussed the matter two to three times. But in all the meetings they could not arrive at a decision as some were in favour while others against it. The reason for opposing the increment is even now known only to them (Yanthan, Personal communication,

25 According to J. Humtsoe, the increment in the salary was recognition to Pastor Tsumongo for his role in getting Lakhuti Baptist Church first position in singing among Lotha Churches consecutively for three years. The decision to increase the salary of the pastor was taken by the Lakhuti Baptist church and not by the Lotha Baptist Church council (personal communication 5, May 2012).

May 1, 2012).[26] Anyway it is evident that there had been some confusion and misunderstanding that cropped up in the church before and after Christmas 1949 and as a result some deacons had resigned and subsequently the church functioned without a pastor and deacons for six months. Ntheo Louis said that during the interim period he took over the overall responsibility of the church and presided over all the functions including funeral and marriage ceremonies. On 19 March 1950 Ntheo was appointed pastor of Lakhuti Baptist Church by Rev. Ahamo (Ntheo, personal communication, January 10, 2007). On 29 August 1950, another meeting of the Lakhuti Baptist Church Council was called to discuss the matter again in which Chenisao Humtsoe, the deacon, Shanpano Humtsoe, the treasurer and Yantsao Yanthan, the chowkidar suggested to have the salary of the pastor increased as other churches had already done it as per the directives of the Lotha Baptist Church Council and also on the ground that their pastor was doing well in his duty. At this suggestion deacon Nyansao, the key holder, angrily threw away the key of the church at the door of the church and walked away (Ntheo, personal communication, January 10, 2007). Shampano the church treasurer, however, expressed his displeasure over the incident and said that such people should be corrected then and there and that his behavior was unacceptable to the council. He then expressed his inability to continue as treasurer of the church and asked the council to take away the chest from his house. Meanwhile, the group that

---

26 According to D. Yanthan, the above view was shared by many others too. Most probably it was due to jealousy or some 'isms' as it happens among many Naga tribes particularly among various clans.

was against the increment of the salary selected Nyansao as the treasurer of the church. Upon his appointment, Shanpano took the chest from his house and kept it at the house of the former (Humtsoe, 1976).[27] When this petty quarrel reached a volatile situation the church at Lakhuti requested the Lotha Baptist Church Council to settle it amicably. Yantsao and Shanpano reported to the council the facts of the trouble in Lakhuti and warned them if they sided with the other group they would fight to the end. But the council without studying the pros and cons of the situation favoured the opposition and accused the three of betraying the faithful in the name of the church. They were also branded as anti-church and excommunicated from the church. The Council published the excommunication of these three people in the Lotha news in October 1950 and circulated this information all over the Naga Hills (Humtsoe, 1976).[28] Discouraged and unhappy with the unpleasant turn of events the three members pleaded with the Council and community not to do so and also not to strike off their names from the church but their pleas fell on deaf ears.

---

27 It was decided to hand over this petty case to the 'Mission Field' to find a solution. The council was somehow biased and decided that functions of the office bearers should be discontinued. At this Shanpano protested and said that if something happened to such a big village like Lakhuti who would come forward to solve it. He suggested that only those found guilty should be asked to discontinue. The community replied, 'if we die now who cares about it.' So they decided to approach the chairman of the church council; but the latter without any consultation favoured the majority. So finally the rebels decided to give information to the Lotha Church Council so that they might solve the problem amicably. They also argued that those who serve the church wholeheartedly are neglected (Silver Jubilee, Lakhuti Catholic Church).

28 At that time Rev. Phantheo Okotso was the Chairman of the Council and Nphyu Kikon, the Secretary. Rev. Ahamo Patton was the Chairman of the Lotha Baptist Church (Siver Jubilee, Lakhuti Catholic church).

Disheartened by the state of affairs the expelled members asked pardon from the church as they didn't want to go back to a pagan religion. However, they were denied membership again. The Gaon Buras said: "Go to the pagan priests as you have been handed over to them. Pay your tithes to them and they will solve your problems. You are free to follow any religion." They were also told "even during jubilee you will be excluded" (Ntheo & Marcus, Personal communication, January 10, 2007).

2.8.3 Contact with the Catholic Church

Despite the setback, the three took a firm resolution that on no account were they ready to go back to their ancient religion. Until then no Lotha in Lakhuti had heard of the Catholic Church. During the most trying moments of their life they remembered having heard of a 'Christian Church' at Golaghat from their friend, Rhansümo Humtsoe. He had told them that he had heard of a Church called 'Catholic' in Dibrugarh when he had worked first as a servant with an Anglican Bishop and then as a servant of Fr. L. Piasecski, a Catholic missionary from Poland, when the latter was building a new Church there, which is now called the Catholic Cathedral of Dibrugarh. He also told them that this Catholic Church had a mission centre at Golaghat (Larrea, 1988).[29]

29 Rhansümo was a non-christian when he told his friends about the Catholic Church. Children of the three expelled members say he was a cook of a foreign tea garden manager and later on became a helper or a servant of a priest at Dibrugarh. After his baptism in the Catholic Church he took the name as Lawrence (J Humtsoe, personal communication, 5 May 2012).

Soon there began a new turn of events in the life of these three expelled members. A great desire to launch into the deep to a new Christian Church began to take roots in them. With firm determination, they discussed and resolved on 2 April 1951 that they would 'not to go back'. In a resolution written by them, they said that they had repeatedly requested their church to take them back but to no avail. It was decided therefore, that they would join a new denomination that they had recently heard about (Appendix: Document A).

On 4 April 1951 the three – Yantsao, Shanpano and Chenisao signed with thumb impression, their decision to join the Catholic Church (Appendix: Document B). They said that it was in deep sorrow that they took this firm decision to join the Catholic Church which no Naga had accepted or believed in. 'Then what shall we do?' One of them asked the other two and they answered, 'We will bring (accept) the religion which no Naga has accepted, that is the Catholic religion to Nagaland. Are you ready to stand by at any cost'? The other two replied 'yes.' He again asked, 'After accepting it, will we practice it or not'? They said, 'yes'. 'Whatever it may be, even if no one follows us we will remain.' Then they wrote their names and vouched with their thumb impression on the document.[30]

30 First time when they met Fr. Bollini in Golaghat on 28 December 1950 there were five persons. But when they signed the document on 4 April 1951 there were only three. When asked about the absence of the other two it was reported that most probably when they went to meet the first time they had taken their own companions who might have been their sympathetic friends. But when they realised the hardships or alienation from the Church the other two might have backed out for reasons known only to them (personal communication, Ntheo and Daniel, May 1, 2012).

2.8.4 Meeting with the Lotha Baptist Church Council

Since they were law abiding citizens they decided to inform the Lotha Baptist Church headquarters of their firm decision to embrace a new faith and to enquire if anything was wrong in doing so. On 7 April Yantsao and Shanpano left for Vankosung Mission, near Wokha, which is the mission centre of the Lotha Baptist Church Association and asked Rev. Houston, the Lotha Baptist missionary whether they committed a sin by joining the Catholic Church. Rev. Houston told them, "This is something you must decide for yourselves; I will tell you nothing. I cannot forbid you to join the Catholic Church, since this is the original church" (Larrea, 1988, pg. 3).[31] Then, they approached Nchemo Kinghen, the Lotha Bench Court Chairman and sought his opinion about their intention to become Catholics and he said, "According to the Indian constitution one is free to practice his or her religion" (Ntheo, Personal communication May 1, 2012). They were very much pleased when they got the same reply from the third person M. Mhondamo Kithan, Lotha Tribal President.

They went back to Lakhuti on the next day having obtained a 'No Objection Certificate' from the Baptist church authority. They then signed another document based on the consent of the latter to have another faith in the village. The document

31 According to Ntheo, Rev. Houston told them, "My father is a Catholic and I am also a Catholic. But because my wife is a Baptist I became a Baptist" (personal communication, January 10, 2007).
Vankosung is the mission centre of the Lotha Baptist Church Association, very close to Wokha town.

says, they reported the matter to the Lotha Bench Court about the acceptance of the Catholic faith and their reply was 'As you wish.' They also reported to the Tribal President whose reply was also 'It is up to you.' Finally the missionary of the Baptist Church also said, 'I won't tell you to accept or not to accept.' From the replies of the three it is understood that none had any objection to their decision (unpublished script). Having obtained the permission and officially completing the formalities they decided to meet the priests at Golaghat.

2.8.5 Meeting at the Catholic Mission, Golaghat

Yantsao, Shanpano and Chenisao left for Golaghat on 10 April on foot and reached Kurajan (Gorajan), border between Nagaland and Assam, close to Champang, where a considerable number of Adivasi Catholic population looked after by the priests from Golaghat lived. They met with the Catholics of the place to get morally and spiritually strengthened before they embraced the new faith. On 11 April Fr. Bollini in Golaghat received them kindly and they narrated the hardships they faced in the past few months. Most probably during their two day stay (12 and 13 April 1951), they were instructed in Catholic faith and received baptism. In their own words, 'We accepted Catholic religion in the year 1951. Father prayed over us and presented us with holy water and crucifix' (unpublished manuscript).[32] It is said that they were gifted with religious articles like rosary, holy water and crucifix. Thus officially,

32 There are some discrepancies about the dates told by the elders. Most probably the three new members wrote about their meeting, experiences, baptism etc., after they reached back from Golaghat. Perhaps they could not recollect exact days and time.

Chenisao Humtsoe, Shanpano Humtsoe and Yantsao Yanthan were Nagaland's first Catholics. Fr. Marengo who had gone to Golaghat to preach a retreat to the nuns was present there at the baptism of these three men (Syiemlieh, 1990). After their return from Golaghat on 14 April as Catholics their main concern was to find a place to put up a church for them and their families. They were prepared to face the worst and mounting opposition from their own people for bringing in a new faith. It is said that the people of Humtsoe Khel opposed them tooth and nail from the inception. Any way in the midst of all the expected troubles, they selected a place for the construction of a church and blessed the site with holy water on 15 April. On 1 May they held their first religious service in the new church. (Larrea, 1988). After the erection of the 'House of God' the news spread all over the Lotha areas that 'Lakhuti village has brought in the Roman Catholic Church.'

After a while there was an epidemic in the village and it mainly affected the Catholic families. Rumors began doing the round in the village that since they brought in the Catholic faith, God was punishing them. Soon they were excluded from going together with the Baptists to the field for jhum cultivation. The Baptists refused to attend the funeral service of the Catholics and were even unwilling to visit the sick. They were deprived of Government grants and in the school the students were told not to become Catholics lest they lose government jobs (Joseph, Personal communication, May 5, 2012).

2.8.6 General Meeting

A new chapter was opened in the lives of the people of Lakhuti with the dawn of a new faith. Perhaps in the beginning when those three embraced Catholicism nobody might have thought of its serious consequences for the future. However, soon the new faith became a subject of concern, discussion and deliberations for various organisations including the Baptist Church. Hence, a lot of groundwork might have been done before a letter was drafted by K. Yanthan (Khodao Yanthan), addressed to Fr. Bollini in Golaghat asking him to wait to venture into the Lotha mission as it is a concern for the Baptists and the Naga administration in general. Sensing the seriousness of the chain of events the Baptist Church thought it was not too late to appeal to the expelled members to return back to their fold lest the latter pull many more members to theirs. So, in earnest pursuance to rectify the error and to remedy the situation and concern over the new Church, the Lotha Baptist Church Council convoked a general meeting of Wokha public and students at Wokha Church, on 16 May 1951 in which 36 delegates from 15 villages took part. The subject matter of the meeting, which was presided over by Rev. Ahamo, Chairman and Khodao Yanthan, Secretary, was 'Remedy for the Roman Catholic Members of Lakhuti Village.' In the meeting, the following resolutions were passed: (i) to send a selected body with a letter to Lakhuti on behalf of this General Meeting (ii) the selected body would consist of two members from each of the villages present; including the members of the Church Council, Rev. Houston, Rev. Ahamo and some other older members from the churches and (iii) the selected body was authorised to settle the matter (Larrea, 1960). It was also agreed that the selected body would meet on the 26 May 1951 at Lakhuti. In the said meeting the Catholic members stood firm in their resolve not to go back to the Baptist fold again.

They told them that despite repeated requests and apologies from their side to take them back, the latter refused. Hence even if they cut their heads off, they won't go back. From the Baptist church's side they were promised various positions in the church. As they were not yielding to the pressure, Khodao, in conclusion uttered the concluding words: 'The Catholic Church will never die away' (Ntheo, personal communication, January 10, 2007).[33] The meeting was a futile exercise as is evident from the words of Syimlieh (1990), "Nothing came of the delegation that went to Lakhuti on 26 May to try to convince the 'dissidents' not to become Catholics" (pg. 51).

2.8.7 Information to the Public

In order to settle the dust arising from the expulsion of the members and to bring about a settlement to the misunderstanding and rumors, the Lotha Baptist Church decided to send information to all the churches under its jurisdiction as a warning and precaution. So the following had been published in the October 1950 edition of the publication from Vankosung, the Lotha Baptist headquarters:

---

33 There is a twist in the episode that followed. After the meeting, the Lotha delegation asked one of the learned Catholics, Nkonsheo Humtsoe to renounce the Catholic faith for a good position like the post of a missionary in the Baptist Church. He agreed and sent a letter to Fr. Bollini through his son not to come back to Lakhuti village as there were no more Catholics left in the village. Having come to know of this letter Yantsao and Shanpano went to apprise the priest of the situation but the latter refused to listen to them because he had already received the letter. Discouraged, they retured to Kurajan and shared their grievances with them. Feeling one with them, the Catholics of Kurajan had a meeting and resolved to request the priest once again not to close down the Lotha mission through a letter. On receiving the letter he understood that those Catholics were serious minded and he received them back (personal communication, Ntheo, 10 January 2007).

> Notification: It is in view of the misunderstanding arisen in the Baptist Church at Lakhuti. The Baptist Church Council from Vankosung had gone to Lakhuti on 29th August and stayed there until 31st August with a view to settle the matter amicably. In the name of the church, if any person writes against the Church and spreads it without its permission they shall be excluded from the church's membership. Accordingly three members were found guilty who went against the resolution. So the Church council resolved that henceforth if anybody is going against the church without the consent of the pastors, council, church, they will be excommunicated. Dear brethren, we regret the loss of the members. Some people made mistakes yet they point fingers at others. Those persons who commit mistakes and not admitting are Christians in the flesh and not in the spirit. Good Christians don't do that (Kithan, 1950, pg. 1 (Appendix: Document C).[34]

2.8.8 The New Diocese

The Catholic Diocese of Shillong comprised of the entire North East India until 1951. With the ever increasing number of Catholics in the region it was extremely difficult to reach out and cater to their spiritual and material needs. So, the need for the bifurcation of existing Diocese to create a new one was felt. On 23 July 1951, the Vatican accepted Bishop Ferrando's suggestion to divide the Diocese: "A new Diocese was created, with its headquarters at Dibrugarh and comprised

34 Loose translation of the text.

the Dibrugarh and Sibsagar districts of Assam, the Lohit and Tirap districts of the then N.E.F.A., Naga Hills and Manipur" (Syielieh, 1990, pg. 52). Fr. Orestes Marengo, a zealous priest working among the Adivasis and who had a fair knowledge about the Lotha mission was appointed the first bishop of the new Diocese. In the course of his ministry as bishop he would learn the Lotha dialect, translate prayers into their dialect, take special care of the catechists and appoint Fr. Larrea, a full time priest exclusively for the Lothas. Thus, the Catholic Church in the Lotha area entered into a new era of missionary work.

2.8.9 Beginning of the Mission

Despite the absence of resident priests and trained catechists the Church in Lakhuti began to grow in number and vitality owing to the guidance of the pioneers and the constant encouragement the Lothas received from the priests whenever they visited them at Golaghat. The pagans in the village found the Catholics vibrant and united and hence they extended help during the construction of the temporary church building. Initially there were only six Catholic families but during the construction of the church twenty four pagan families extended their help (Larrea, 1988). Fr. Bollini from Golaghat, the first Catholic priest to visit Lakhuti, under whose care the new promising community of Lakhuti came under, could visit only two years after the formation of the community, from 16 to 19 March 1953. The elders of Lakhuti told that during his stay, Fr. Bollini instructed the new community in faith and visited a few pagan families in preparation for the first visit of the new bishop of Dibrugarh. Meanwhile the new bishop started preparing for his upcoming visit to Lakhuti by learning the Lotha dialect. One of the great missionaries of the region, particularly of Manipur Hills, Fr. Ravalico whose great desire to visit the Lotha area, was met with success when he visited Lakhuti on 24 November 1953, which coincided with the first visit of the Bishop Marengo. He began his work by instructing the people in faith and preparing them to receive the bishop. Bishop Marengo (1989) writes about his visit to Lakhuti in the following words:

> I visited Kohima the first time when Mr. Carvalho, the then D.C. granted me permit to visit the Catholic community of Lakhuti. He wanted me to meet him in Wokha where he happened to be visiting with the Kohima SP. My plan was to leave for Wokha after one night in Kohima where I offered mass for the sisters, then nursing in the Military Hospital, but the truck on which Fr. Marocchino had booked a seat for me would not start unless I was prepared to help the owner to get new tyres. After hours of waiting, an old Khasi friend from Malki, Shillong, who was a mechanic in one of the military posts, got me a seat in a military truck that took me to the Sema area, to Pokoboto, where I had to spend the night. Next morning I said Holy Mass for a motley congregation of Catholics, Baptists and Pagan soldiers before proceeding to Wokha where I had to spend one more night before starting my long strenuous trek to Lakhuti (pg. 34).

Syiemlieh (1990) describes further in detail the journey of Bishop Marengo to Lakhuti for the baptism in the following words: "On 27 November, after a night's rest at Wokha, he walked (32 miles) all the way to Lakhuti. He remembers the ascent to this large village…'I crawled with my hands and feet the steep hill and I really don't know how I managed to reach the summit.' Fr. Ravalico had gone down to Sunglap, a small village some six kilometers below Lakhuti, where the Bishop was welcomed by a small but fervent community. After a short rest in the small Church the last stretch of the uphill path was completed before nightfall" (pg.53).

On 28 November, the Bishop and Fr. Ravalico baptised 240 men, women and children of Lakhuti including those who came from Sunglup, and Akuk villages. On the following day, they administered Holy Communion and Confirmation to the newly baptised Christians. During his stay and ceremonies no objection was raised from any quarter. It was reported that even the pagan priests were happy and they praised Catholic Christianity and in subsequent years many became Catholics. In the words of one of the pagan priests, "Sir, I am happy that you have come to Lakhuti…I respect Christianity and am glad that my people follow you. I am the priest of all this area. I only offer sacrifices to the God of Heaven as you do" (Puthenpurakal, 2000, pg. 275). Three years later he became a Catholic. In the same year 1953, the bishop sent some young men to Dibrugarh for training and a prayer book was printed with the help of Peter Yanthan (Pallikunnel, n.d).

It was indeed difficult for the priests from Golaghat to go and look after the community often as they were foreign nationals and many restrictions were placed on them by the government. Even though Fr. Ravalico had Indian citizenship, he was already assigned to the Manipur Hills. So, the need for the service of a catechist was felt and Nkomo Humtsoe was made the first catechist of the new community. He was somewhat a learned person and knew Assamese well (Marcus, Personal communication, May 2, 2012).[35] For the next two years the Bishop personally looked after the Lotha mission. Being a promising area the need for a full time priest was felt and so Bishop Marengo requested Fr. J. Larrea in Salesian College, Sonada (near Darjeeling) to serve the growing Lotha community. Fr. Larrea came to help Bishop Marengo (Puthenpurakal, 2000), and joined the Diocese of Dibrugarh and moved to Golaghat, the base of Lotha mission in September 1955.[36] He paid his first visit to Lotha area, together with Bishop Marengo, from 26 March to 2 April 1954 visiting Lakhuti, Sunglup, Yimpang and Longayim villages (Larrea, 1988). With his appointment as priest in charge of the Lotha mission, the Catholic Church in Nagaland entered a new era.

2.9 Church in Dimapur

Much before the Church officially came into being among the two major tribes of Nagaland, Angami and Lotha in the early part of 1950s, the Church made her presence already in Dimapur (earlier known as Manipur Road) in the three smaller communities of Advasis, Garos and Rongmeis. Priests from Golaghat and later on from Kohima used to visit these

---

35 There is no clear information regarding who the first catechist was. Some say in the initial stage Yantsao Yanthan looked after the community as catechist, while others say it was Renzamo Humtsoe. Any way in the Golden Jubilee souvenir of the Catholic Church Lakhuti, the name of Nkomo is mentioned as the first catechist.

36 Fr. John Larrea is fondly called by the Lotha Catholics as 'Our Lotha Father, as he was the one who in the initial stages looked after and nurtured the community. Most of the present Lotha Catholic villages were contacted and communities were founded due to his efforts. Even now many of the Lothas who have known him and benefited from him spiritually and materially do visit him at Pastoral Centre, Shillong where he has been residing on retirement as well as doing a number of literary and pastoral works.

communities and cared for their spiritual needs. The presence of the Catholic Church and community was evident from the writings of Fr. Neyens of Golaghat who wrote to Bishop of Shillong as follows:

> Not long ago I wrote to you, Monsignor, saying that R. C. Chaplain Moss urges us to take over the Church in Dimapur and Imphal and if possible to send for that purpose a father of Irish nationality. The matter is urgent, the buildings are pukkah, and it would be our nicest chance to contact the Nagas and to start NOW a mission amongst them. I am convinced also, that any father residing now in Dimapur or nearby, would find there stocks of building material, enough to build 2 large missions. Please, have a talk with Fr. Provincial. With kindest regards, Fr. Neyens (Chronicle, 1941-1947, Archdiocese of Shilong).

Before people accepted Catholicism in Lakhuti and Kohima, some people, in all probability, at Burma Camp had already been baptised by priests from Golaghat. The chronicle of the Catholic Mission, Golaghat, records that there was a church at Dimapur. On 15 September 1946, Fr. Florenzo Mellino from Golaghat went to Dimapur and enquired from the officer in charge about the Church there. The latter in turn told him to let the Bishop send an application to the D. C. of Kohima to obtain the permit for buying the land on which the church stands (Chronicle 1941-1958, Catholic Mission, Golaghat).[37] It is a clear indication that there was already a

37 Fr. F.Mellino was an Italian who served at Catholic Mission Golaghat from 1941to 1952. The available records are not sufficient to prove the site of the Church; however, people believe it was in the present Burma camp.

church and there were Catholics living in Dimapur. However, no one can say with precision the exact year the Catholics had been in Dimapur and the exact location of the Church; it is assumed that it was at Burma Camp. Again the same chronicle reported that on 18 December 1946 Fr. Mellino went to Dimapur and there he was told that there were no more objections to having the church built there. It was decided, therefore, to have a good church constructed at the site and different building materials for the Church construction were bought and kept there. However, contrary to the suggestion given or permission granted earlier, Fr. Mellino was told on 5 January 1947 in Dimapur that the D. C. of Kohima was strongly against the Catholic Church in having the plot of land for the church and the permission to build the same in Dimapur. This decision perhaps, was necessitated by the policy of the administration to have only one denomination in the Naga Hills. Fr. Mellino mentioned that there was no more hope of building the church there. At the same time an application had been sent in order to have the church removed and build the mission in Golaghat. Fr. Mellino went to Dimapur on 10 March 1947 to take back the materials still left in the Church. On 12 May 1947, Brother Joseph was sent to Dimapur to dismantle the church, but was stopped from doing so as the D. C. of Kohima had sold it to the Dimapur village people (Chronicle 1941-1958, Catholic mission, Golaghat). Thus, the administration stopped the mission from building a church but couldn't stop them from gathering for prayer and worship. The priests from Golaghat continued visiting these people on a regular basis to celebrate Holy Mass and contacted a group of Garos who wanted to become Catholics. On 13 May 1947

Fr. Bollini went to Dimapur where he visited three villages of Garos who expressed desire to become Catholics. And on 10 June 1948 Fr. Mellino paid a visit to the few Christians of Dimapur and to a Garo village where some people wanted to become Catholics.

It is believed, therefore, from the above narrative that there were Catholics already in Dimapur much before the official baptism took place among the Lothas and the Angamis. The above chronicle dated 31 October 1950 showed that Fr. Bollini celebrated the Holy Mass and baptised the first four Nagas: one Angami boy of 16 years, three Kabuis (Rongmeis) - a boy of 12 years, a girl of 6 years and another girl of 2 years.[38] Unfortunately the pioneers of the Catholic Church in Dimapur had been dead for many years.

Nevertheless the earliest visible presence of the Catholic Church in Dimapur was at Burma Camp, where there were few Catholics living. Burma Camp is the Bethlehem of present day Holy Cross parish. Lawrence Gudinho, a devout Catholic from Burma who was an English teacher in Dimapur led the community of Burma Camp to the Catholic faith. Being a learned person and staying at Burma Camp he instructed some boys into Catholic faith. Subsequently two of them namely, Lawrence Rongmei and Paulus Rongmei were baptised in

38 This is perhaps the most accurate information regarding the first baptism of the Nagas in the Catholic Church in Nagaland because this is a chronicle proof. Nobody knew the availability of this record; hence everybody thought the first baptism in Nagaland in the Catholic Church was in the year 1951 in Lakhuti and 1952 in Kohima. As in any other case the non-availability of records would lead to confusion and inaccuracy of facts and might lead to presumption. It is not possible to trace who that Angami boy was as all of my researches could not lead to any clue (Catholic Mission Golaghat, Chronicle 1941-1958).

Golaghat in 1953 (Mandal, 1993).[39] He built a chapel for the community. The priests from Golaghat and Kohima, used to celebrate Mass in this chapel. Later on, the land where the church stood was taken over by the Government.

Singrijan, a few miles away from Dimapur is perhaps the oldest Catholic community of Nagaland. A few Adivasis, originally from Jharkhand, but settled down under Golaghat district and Upper Assam as tea garden labourers, came to the present place under the leadership of the first catechist Joseph Chelekchela in 1948. At that time the Forest Department was in need of labourers to work in the department. One Nandi, a Bengali Forest ranger, told Joseph that there was plenty of forest land available in Singrijan area and that he would demarcate land to every family if they came to work in the forest department. Accordingly, 30 families came to settle down and the land was allocated to them as per the promise (personal communication, E. Kindo, B. Kindo and P. Dung Dung, May 10, 2012). They built a chapel and named it as 'St. Mary's Catholic Church,' and it was blessed by Rev. Fr. Frassi from Golaghat parish.

Another earlier Catholic community of Nagaland is the community at Samaguri, Dimapur. They belong to the 'Garo' tribe who are a scheduled tribe. The majority of the Garos are inhabitants of the State of Meghalaya. But, a good number of

---

39 Both of them died long ago and some of their family members have already shifted from Dimapur. Lawrence built a chapel for the community but later the land was taken over by the Government. According to the Silver Jubilee souvenir of the Holy Cross Church the present APO office and storeroom is the location where the chapel was originally built.

them are also settled in the State of Assam. The chronicle of the Catholic Mission, Golaghat records the presence of the Garos in Dimapur area as early as 1946-47 who wished to become Catholics and priests cater to their spiritual need by visiting and evangelising them often. Six Garo families with some twenty members settled down in Erali Beel in 1949 under the leadership of Racansing Sangma (Mandal, 1993).[40] Their present settlement at Samaguri has a short but interesting background. Magaia Marak was the founder of Reking Sakware area (with about 10 to 15 villages) under present East Garo Hills. There was a land case and an arrest warrant was issued against him. To escape the arrest and the subsequent consequences he fled to Nagaland in 1949 to stay with one of his younger brothers by name Simka Marak who was a farmer with his family at Erali Beel.

Within just two years' of their stay at Erali Beel, the Garo settlers got into trouble with the local people of the place who were Baptists. They were accused of misbehavior and blamed of stealing. They also reported to the Gaon Bura to send them away from the place. Shocked by such attitude of the people Racansing reported to Fr. Marocchino who used to visit them and celebrate Mass in their small chapel, to search some land for them. Fr. Marocchino, in turn asked land surveyor, R. K. Bora whether some undisputable land was available for

40 According to the Chronicle of Golaghat Catholic Mission 1941-1958, on 13 May 1947, Fr. Bollini visited three Garo villages in Dimapur area as some people wished to become Catholics. Then on 10 June 1948, Fr. Mellino paid a visit to the Christians of Dimapur and to a Garo village for same purpose. In the following months and years priests continued their visits and offered mass and conducted service for them. When a priest started staying at Kohima, he started visiting and catechising them.

these people. As per Bora's advice, Dunkan, the then Deputy Commissioner allotted 60 'bighas' of land (10 bighas of land for one family as per Assam rule). Six families who were Catholics and close relatives came to settle down under the leadership of Magaia Marak and Racansing at the new place. They named this place as 'Samaguri' and moved into it in 1952 (Personal communication, P. Sangma and E. Sangma, May 11, 2012).

Though they were Catholics, they didn't know about the presence of any Catholic community in Dimapur area. One day in 1950, Rokensing Sangma came to sell fish in the town and he happened to reach the house of Lawrence Gudinho. Seeing a Holy Bible and a rosary on his table, he understood Gudinho was a Catholic. The latter directed him to Golaghat parish and Fr. Bollini agreed to come after three days. Fr. Bollini informed the priests at Kohima about this community (Mandal, 1993).

Thus the Catholic Church in Nagaland took root despite various challenges from different corners. It is from this small beginning among the Angamis and the Lothas that the Church could reach out to other tribes of Nagaland.

CHAPTER THREE

Growth Of The Catholic Church

FROM A humble beginning at Kohima and Lakhuti in Wokha district in the early part of 1950 the Catholic Church began to establish itself in other parts of the state at the invitation of the people. This journey, however, was not without hurdles as it often met with both acceptance and rejection. Lack of personnel and finance, inaccessibility to the villages, poor transportation and communication, insufficient knowledge of the customs and culture of the people, absence of proper lingua-franca, hostility and persecution from the Baptist Church, indifferent attitude of the people, vast area etc. were some of the hurdles the church had to face. At the same time God's providence, love for people and mission, people's desire for quality education, leadership of the bishops, the indomitable spirit of the missionaries and the Catholic community and collaboration from bureaucrats, village elders and the public in general helped the Church to grow. In forty years' time, against all odds the Church got rooted in the soil.

3.1 Growth of the Church in Lotha Areas

From Lakhuti, the Catholic Church began to reach out to its neighbouring villages in the Lotha area. Even from the very beginning, many people in the villages voluntarily expressed their desire to embrace the new faith. The beginning of the Catholic Church at Sunglup village, about nine kilometers away from Lakhuti towards Sanis coincided with the establishment of the Catholic Church at Lakhuti. Sunglup was the first Lotha village Bishop Marengo had entered. Recalling his visit, Fr. Larrea (2003) writes: "In November 1953, on his way from Wokha to Lakhuti, which he did on foot all the way, yours was the first Lotha village he entered. Thus in the Bishop's journey, we could compare Sunglup to Bethany, the village where Jesus stopped on his way to Jerusalem (Mt 26:6) a village He loved" (pg. 4). Shanpano Humtsoe and Yantsao Yanthan, the two pioneer Catholics of Lakhuti made effort to catechise the people of Sunglup about the Catholic faith in the midst of misunderstandings. In response to their preaching, Ashio Abraham Yanthan and Kilosao David Ezung and their families became catechumens in the year 1952. So the community of Sunglup was started with just two families and they were baptised on 28 November 1953 together with others at Lakhuti. As the pagans in the village decided not to extend any help when the small community wanted to build a church the Catholics of Lakhuti came forward. The relationship got further strained on the day of the dedication of the church as elders of Sunglup claimed that as per pagan traditions such celebrations were not allowed as that year was the year of building the 'morung.' The Catholics, however, began to use the Church building from that day without the blessing. Later some elders of the village informed the Government that they would not allow the Catholic Church to remain in the village and if anyone was found practising they would be expelled. So the Catholics in order to strengthen their position approached Nchemo Kinghen, Wokha Bench Court Chairman who told them if they expelled anyone from the village for accepting Catholic faith then the village was responsible to build the latter's houses and shift their belongings wherever they went (Yanthan, 2003). With this ruling things settled down and henceforth no further harassment was reported from the village.

3.1.1 Appointment of Fr. Larrea to the Lotha Mission

The opposition from the Baptists, the ban on the entry of foreign missionaries and the absence of a priest or a catechist did not deter the community from growing in numbers. Instead, more people started embracing the new faith because of the firm stand of the tiny group of Catholics and the encouragement they received from the priests at Golaghat. Bishop Marengo decided to care for the Lotha Nagas personally as he had no other personnel to spare. In order to reach out to these people he started studying the Lotha dialect and translating prayers into the same. Mattappally (2007) writes, "To this end, he studied the Lotha dialect and got the first catechism, prayer books and hymn books ready" (pg. 252). Then he realised that there was indeed a great need to appoint a full time priest for the promising Lotha mission. In December 1953 Fr. Larrea, fondly called 'Our Lotha Father,' by the Lotha Catholics joined the diocese of Dibrugarh, and was put in charge of the Lotha area. But only in September 1955 could he move to Golaghat to take care of the Lotha mission as a full time job (Pallikunnel, n.d). He paid his first visit to Lotha area with Bishop Marengo, from 26 March to 2 April, 1954, visiting Lakhuti, Sunglup, Yimpang and Longayim. Again in 1955 he visited the Lotha area twice including during Christmas. In 2005 he writes, "But then for two long years, 1956 and 1957, I could not obtain permit to visit the Lotha area until March, 1958. So, the only way to instruct you in the Catholic faith was the leaflet NTSA which I wrote in Golaghat, with the help of Ngheo Humtsoe, my previous helper there" (pg.5).

A successful missionary effort was the opening of the Naga School for the Lotha children at Golaghat on 15 February 1958 with 17 boys. By end of 1953 onwards, Fr. Larrea started sending Lotha children (boys and girls) to different schools at Dibruagarh, Tezpur, Naharkhatia and Shillong. In 1958, however, he brought these children back to the school at Golaghat. This school was shifted to Wokha in August 1965. Many Lotha girls too had been sent to Golaghat from time to time for training in Home Science along with catechesis while staying with the sisters.

On 4 May 1955 a small community at Mekokla village was formed with the baptism of two persons by Fr. Larrea at the initiative of the Catholics of Lakhuti village. They were told by the village that only the Baptist religion would be allowed there and if anyone was found breaking this law would be expelled. When the situation calmed down, they built a small church with the help of the young people of the village. "On 25 September 1956 the whole Mekokla village was attacked by the Indian army and people fled to nearby jungles for safety. In the inferno, houses, animals and property were burnt to ashes except the Catholic Church" (St. Paul Church Mekokla, 2005, pg. 28).

Following the baptism of three members of Lakhuti, the Lotha Church Council had a meeting in Lakhuti on 27 May 1951, attended by people from Lakhuti and Akuk to discuss ways to discourage people from becoming Catholics. The general impression expressed by members at the meeting was that no one could be prevented from embracing the Catholic faith. It was said that even the American Baptist church leaders who came once to suppress the Catholic faith could not, which meant the Catholic Church came to exist in Nagaland. After the said meeting some people from Akuk started enquiring about the new religion. Shanpano Humtsoe and Yantsao Ynthan the two pioneers, started visiting Akuk regularly to catechise them in the Catholic faith. Also from 1951 to 1954 some people from Akuk used to visit priests and Catholic families of Lakhuti. Consequently three families were received into the Catholic Church in 1955 by Fr. Larrea. On being asked why he embraced Catholic faith, Azamô Humtsoe, in his late eighties, said that he had heard from his friends about a church called the Catholic Church that was not against people drinking rice beer, while the Baptist Church had placed strict restrictions on people regarding drinking (Personal communication, January 11, 2007).

From 1954 to 1955, Fr. Larrea got permit to enter only six times, and in the next two years he was denied a permit. He had often heard from Peter Yanthan, his first catechist in Lakhuti about Lungsa village where some people had expressed their desire to become Catholics. But it took him another six long years to reach Lungsa village as he had been denied a permit by the government. Fr. Larrea's journey to Lungsa has been narrated in the following way: "But God has his time fixed and, finally, on January 22, 1960, Friday, he set out from Sunglup early morning on his way to Lungsa. Elithung Ezung, then political officer at Wokha, a sincere friend, and past pupil of our St. Anthony's college, Shillong, had told Father he would send his jeep to pick up Father half way. Hence, Fr. Larrea started all along the new road, accompanied by Wosemo Kithan and Rilumo Paton from Akuk. The jeep never arrived and Father Larrea walked all the way to Wokha and then to Lungsa on the same day" (Lungsa yano katholik ekhumko chi motsü chi, pg. 12).[41]

Fr Larrea

But refusing to give up, he walked for 12 hours to the destination only to be told he was not welcome. He and his team, however, were lodged at the house of one Nyamo, who was a police officer and a citizen of Dimapur. He then visited some sick and went back to Wokha. On 24 January 1963, Fr. Larrea made his second visit to Lungsa. In the chronicle of Catholic Mission Golaghat 1954-1965, Fr. Larrea (1963) commented, "People are still sympathetic. It is a pity no headway has been made so far. Precious time has been lost in this village still predominantly pagan". It was during

41 However, there is a confusion regarding the first visit of Fr. Larrea to Lungsa. In the letter written by Mothungo (Peter) Lotha from Lungsa on16 March 1969, he claimed that Fr. Larrea reached Lungsa in the year 1958. "One day in 1958 Fr. Larrea reached Lungsa. He was looking for a place to rest. I was curious to know who he was. He told me the purpose of his visit was to preach Catholic faith in the village. Upon my request he stayed with me and that very day I was converted to Catholicism. Thereafter he had no hesitation to coming to Lungsa.......let it be known to all that I am the first Catholic member who got converted in Lungsa."

this visit that he visited a sick child who was at the point of death and quietly baptised him by pronouncing the words, 'I baptise you in the name of the Father and of the Son and of the Holy Spirit' (Larrea, 1988, pg. 5) and the baby died soon after. In fact that secret baptism was the first baptism in Lungsa. It is said that night Fr. Larrea prayed to that child, already in heaven, to intercede for his family and for all the people of Lungsa. Fr. O'Hara visited Lungsa at the end of 1963 and he kept up the contact. Even though three families wanted to embrace the faith but in the end there was one Mothungo's family who were baptised on 1 January 1964 and in 1966 four more families joined.[42]

While on their way to Golaghat, the three pioneers of Lakhuti used to go through Yimbang village near Bhandari and during their stay with their relatives told them about the Catholic faith. This was the route Fr. Larrea took whenever he went to and from Lakhuti. There was one Charles Stonor (C. R. Stonor) a Catholic European, a Surveyor in the Naga Hills during the British period who had good acquaintance with Yimbang village. He and his servant one Oremo Kikon from Yimbang, used to attend Holy Mass while they were

42 Marcus Humtsoe narrates an incident in the life of Mothungo Ezung. While Fr. O'Hara was baptising Mothungo, (he said the prayer "I baptise you in the name of the Father") he ran out from the church saying to father, 'It is raining; I have put out my clothes and bedding. I will come back soon.' He came back and father continued with the baptism rites over him (personal communication, May 2, 2012.

There is a story surrounding Fr. Larrea among the people of Lungsa: One day Chumzamo Kikon poked one of the fingers of Fr. Larrea and made him sign with his blood on a paper that he won't visit Lungsa again. After sometime this man was accidently killed by his own gun (personal communication, Y. Augustine and Timothy Ezung, May 8, 2012).

in Bombay before the Second World War. We read in the chronicle of 'Catholic Mission Golaghat 1954-1965' that Stonor used to tell Oremo, "The day the Catholic priest comes to your village you must become a Catholic." Oremo narrated this story on 1 April 1954, the day he was baptised (Vincent, Personal communication, May 5, 2012).[43] Vincent also said that on 26 December 1953, Phyuchümo Peter from Lakhuti at the invitation of Mantsuo Yanthan, the church secretary of the Baptist church Yimbang, blessed the latter's house and on 31 December he was followed by three more families. Bishop Marengo and Fr. Larrea visited Yimbang on 31 March 1954 and baptised six families on 1 April 1954.

On his first visit to Pangti in 1955 Fr. Larrea was opposed by some leaders of the Baptist Church. He stayed at the house of a Gaon Bura, Nyansao Ngullie and celebrated Mass at 3 o' clock in the morning before anyone got up. On the following morning, Mensemo Kikon, an elderly man invited him to his house. He was received into the Catholic Church on 15 May 1957. A few families followed him and they formed a community assisted by the people of Lakhuti.

43 At the time of the Silver Jubilee of the Church, the Catholics of the village could not include the story of Stonor in the souvenir as it was not known to them. When they published the Golden jubilee souvenir they first wanted to include it but they decided not to do so because if published what was not in the first souvenir, they thought it might lead to some misunderstanding. Before the Independence of India Stonor came to Yimbang and stayed with Oremo's family. He left for England in early 1948. By 1950 the pioneers of Lakhuti made contact with Yimbang on their way to Golaghat. When Fr. Larrea baptised the first Catholic members on 1 April 1954, Oremo and his family too became Catholics. Later on when Oremo narrated the story of Stonor to Fr. Larrea, the latter wrote a letter to him mentioning about Oremo's baptism. In reply Stonor sent £70 to Fr. Larrea for his students. This story was told by Fr. Larrea personally to Vincent on 24 January 2000 (Y. Vincent, personal communication, May 5, 2012).

Another village under Wokha district to have received the Catholic faith was Riphyim. On 22 January 1960 Fr. Larrea went to Riphyim and preached to the people gathered but his preaching fell on deaf ears as nobody believed him as they had never before heard anything about the Catholic faith. On the evening of 24th he went down to Yikhum village and there he stopped for a while at the house of a friendly man but the Protestants sent to him a memorandum stating that there was no place for the Catholics in the village. It is mentioned in the chronicle of Catholic Mission Golaghat 1954-1965 that he then went back to Riphyim, where a non-Christian approached him and said: "There is hope for you in this village." He came back to the village once again in April 1961 to preach and to his surprise found people were more welcoming than during his previous visit. In his third visit to this village, Nanshumi, mother of Yanchamo, was baptized on request as she was sick. On 2 April 1962 four people, Yanchamo Abraham Humtsoe, Ngheo Robert Patton, Jobhao Patton and Tsatemo Peter Patton received Catholic faith (Humtsoe, 1986). As Catholics, they were denied the right to cultivate their fields.

3.1.2 Reception of Ntheo Yanthan into the Catholic Church

Ntheo Yanthan, the pastor of Lakhuti Baptist Church from 1950-51, managed to convert 27 pagan families to Christianity because of his visits and preaching. Attraction to Baptist Christianity, however, was not a welcome sign for many pagans as the former forbade the latter from drinking rice beer. In the second year of his ministry Ntheo resigned as pastor. He said, "I had no qualified degrees to be a pastor and my wish to bring more people to God could not be fulfilled as the pagans were not willing to be converted to the Baptist religion" (Ntheo, personal communication, May 3, 2012). Hence, he decided to become a Catholic as he thought more pagans would follow Christ as the Catholic Church had no aversion to rice beer. He met Bishop Marengo in 1953 and was sent to Dibrugarh for catechist training and in 1954 he was baptised and thereupon appointed catechist of Lakhuti in 1955. That was the beginning of his harassment as he was accused of being a 'deserter' by the Baptist Church.

Ntheo as the new catechist of Lakhuti encouraged the Lotha children to avail themselves of education imparted by the Catholic Church at Golaghat. He managed to convince the people that Catholic education there was equivalent to foreign education and the response was overwhelming (Ntheo, personal communication, January 10, 2007). The increasing number of people joining the Catholic Church, however, caused alarm particularly in the village Baptist Church. Henceforth, the Baptist pastor of Lakhuti wrote to the Bishop and Fr. Larrea informing them of his decision to complain to the Government against the Catholics. Consequently the Catholics responded to a series of accusations and calumnies levelled by the Baptists against them and Fr. Larrea. The chronicle of 'Catholic Mission Golaghat 1954-1965' further informs that Fr. Larrea used to prepare a series of cyclostyled notes under the title, "NTSA" (Truth) to counteract the Baptist claims. In this, he replied to the Baptist objections, explained the Catholic religion and responded to their doubts. In fact, it was a great help for the Catholics as they could use them as defence in case they were caught unawares and also to attract many Baptists in good faith.

3.1.3 Wokha

Nchemo Kinghen, the Political Assistant to the Deputy Commissioner and the authority among the Lothas was sympathetic to the Catholic cause. He insisted that the Catholic school should be shifted from Golaghat to Wokha as he saw it as the basis for future prospects of the rest of the Lotha range and the possibility of evangelisation of the Semas and the Rengmas. The chronicle of Catholic Mission, Golaghat 1954-1965 states, "Round and about Wokha there are a number of villages, non-Christian in majority, less sophisticated than those of the middle and lower ranges, and with less Protestant influence…a station in the Upper Range would open our work to the Semas and Rengmas close by."

Fr. Larrea had been insisting for years with his superiors that an Indian priest be put in charge of the mission as it was quite impossible to get a permit for the foreign priests. It did not sound well to keep a foreigner any longer and it was absolutely essential for the proper running of the mission that a priest free to visit the communities should be appointed. Since 1950 Fr. Larrea had been applying for Indian nationality but each time this was denied. When the Naga agitation began, it became all the more difficult to get a permit to visit the hills. For the whole of 1959 he could not visit the communities. In fact, some new converts had already returned to their earlier fold as there was pastoral negligence. It was also feared that more could follow suit. Finally the request was felt to be an urgent need and so in 1959 Bishop Marengo sent Fr. Roland O'Hara to join the Lotha mission at Golaghat. With his arrival frequent visits to the villages became possible. He realised that occasional visits from Golaghat would not lead to a fruitful ministry in the hills.

Though the Naga School at Golaghat catered exclusively to the Lotha boys, it was realised that no lasting work could be done without a residence in the hills. As the number of Catholics as well as the students at Golaghat increased, the urgent need to build a residence for the priests and to shift the Naga School to the hills was felt (Mattappally, 2007). After the Baptist foreign missionaries had left Wokha, the people approached Fr. Larrea with a request to open a school in Wokha in 1962 (O'Hara, 1990). In January 1963, another delegation met Fr. Larrea and they discussed the possibilities of opening a school. The conditions laid down as prerequisites were agreed upon by the people.[44] As a follow up the Bishop and Fr. Larrea had another round of meetings on 5 December 1963 in Wokha and once again the request to shift the school from Golaghat to Wokha was given serious thought.

In the meantime, many allegations had been leveled against the Catholic Church particularly on the position held on marriage and family. The Catholic Church's teaching on marriage differs with the Baptist Church particularly on indissolubility. Etssonyimo Kikon, Commissioner, Lotha Province, Federal Government of Nagaland, wrote a complaint letter addressed to Fr. Larrea on 4 January 1964 that the Roman Catholic religion was an unwelcome religion in Nagaland,

44 Some of the conditions were: land must be bought at a nominal rate, water supply should be provided, the school would start with the lower classes but would not be upgraded beyond the Middle level for the moment as it was difficult to obtain teachers unless well paid, fees must be such as to guarantee the self-sufficiency of the school, permission must be obtained for the priests to come up and stay at Wokha, grant to be obtained for the building, etc (Chronicle Catholic Mission Golaghat, 1954-1965).

because it challenges and does not respect the age old customs and traditions of the Nagas particularly of marriage (Kikon, 1964). In a written reply, Fr. Larrea clarified the position of the Church regarding marriage stating the Catholic Church had never violated any rule but only followed the Church law to keep up the sanctity of the marriage.

As the Church was reflecting on the idea of establishing a centre at Wokha and shifting the school from Golaghat, some Baptists came into the scene with strong opposition. They tried all possible means including the might of the underground to dissuade the people from selling land to the 'Romans.' Fr. O'Hara came to Wokha in 1964 to stay and he managed to get land by the end of 1964 albeit at an exorbitant rate. People were anti-Catholic and so they thought if the land price was fixed at a higher rate the Church would not buy it. O' Hara (1990) writes, "In fact, the story that spread was that, the Romans have come to disturb the peace of Wokha" (p. 17). There were no Catholics of Wokha origin then but a few of floating nature. (O'Hara, Personal communication, December 29, 2008).

3.1.4 Appointment of Bishop Hubert D' Rosaria and Shifting of the School

In the meantime there was a change of guard in the Diocese. Bishop Marengo was transferred to the new Diocese of Tezpur and in his place Bishop Hubert D'Rosario was appointed. Bishop Hubert visited Golaghat in February 1965 and decided to open a Catechist Centre in Dibrugarh and also shift the Lotha mission from Golaghat to Wokha. On 10 April the work for the school began in the midst of strong protest, both from Baptist leaders and the underground. The landowners were told to rescind the deal or else face consequences. No local support came for the construction of the school building except for a few Catholics staying at Wokha. Hence Fr. O'Hara and a few masons and labourers from the Khasi Hills did the construction. In two months' time the first building took shape which could house the primary school, Church and a hall which also served as the dormitory. On 1 September 1965, the first batch of twenty seven Lotha students arrived from Golaghat and soon started studying at the new school named as Don Bosco School in the present premise. 'Lotha' was the medium of instruction and only boys were admitted. On 8 September 1965 the parish of Wokha was officially created comprising of the districts of Wokha, Mokokchung and Tuensang and Fr. O'Hara was appointed the parish priest with Fr. T.J. Chacko, assistant (Mattappally, 2007). In 1966, the 'Lotha' medium was changed into English medium and the school began to admit girls too. Fr. O'Hara's ministry was cut short due to some serious misunderstanding he had with Fr. Larrea and Bishop Hubert.

Firstly, he favoured English as the medium of instruction in the school while Fr. Larrea preferred 'Lotha'. Secondly, Bishop Hubert strongly opposed Fr. O'Hara's healing ministry to the sick particularly women at child birth (O'Hara, personal communication, December 27, 2008). In short, Fr. O'Hara left priesthood at the end of 1968 and was replaced by Fr. Paul Bernick.

Fresh life poured in for the pastoral ministry with the coming of the Congregation of the Daughters of St. Ursula from Ranchi in January 1969. The sisters started visiting villages, giving medicines and teaching catechism ("St. Paul's Wokha",

1999). In the later years, communities were established at Bhandari Village, Bhakti, Khomchoyan, Lio-Longidang, Lio Wokha, Longayim, Merapani, Pantong, Yamhon, Yampha, Yanlum, Yimpang, Lotsu and Pynagsa villages.

3.2 Growth of the Church in Angami Areas

As several Catholic communities were founded in Lotha area, many villages in Angami area requested Fr. Marocchino to preach and teach the Catholic faith. After the Sisters' departure from the hospital, Fr. Marocchino had asked two boys to stay with him in the hospital in 1955. While Zhazolie and Zedeilie of Nerhema village stayed with him and attended the school, they also learnt about the Catholic faith. Fr. Marocchino advised them to instruct their parents and people in the village during their vacation and consequently some people showed interest. While they were catechumens, the fight between the Naga army and the Indian army started on the hills of Chiethou on 14 March 1956. This resulted in villagers finding shelter in the nearby forest. However, while they were in the forest they faced the fury of nature including starvation, disease and death and worst of all the burning down of their houses in the village by their enemies. Added to their misery was the murder of some of the Church leaders. Shockingly, Zhazolie and Zedeilie left their studies and joined the Naga army and the community was left with no visible leaders. The peoples' agony lasted for eight months and on their return they built a Church. In the meantime, Zhazolie and Zedeilie who were responsible for the advent of the Catholic Church in the village married Baptist girls and became Baptists. Even after building the Church no one had been baptised. So they selected Lhouzetuo, Suonguhie and Zavilie to lead the community. On 9 March 1959, Fr. Marocchino baptised six people. As the pagans were bitterly against the Catholic Church they did not allow the Catholics to cultivate their fields. What attracted them to the Catholic Church was spelled out by Vattoth (2010) in these words, "Among the pagans, all are not allowed to sow seeds but only an appointed person. This delays cultivation. With the Catholics, all began to sow and cultivate and thus speeded up the process. Seeing this advantage, many pagans became catechumens" (pg. 112).

Between the years 1959-1960, Kramhieo and Lhouphfelie of Zhadima Village, formerly known as Keruma Village, had the privilege of meeting Fr. Marocchino at Christ King Church Kohima and came to know of the Catholic Church. When the Baptists and pagans came to know of the plan of establishing the Catholic Church in the village they opposed it. However, Fr. Marocchino sent Vilalie Victor from Kohima village to instruct them and on 30 October 1960 Fr. Marocchino baptised seven of them who, with the exception of one, Neile-ü Nelly, left the Church after some time due to various reasons ("Catholic kehou dze", 2010). Sometime later, around thirty of them joined the Catholic Church. Since it was a strong pagan village, the Catholics had to go out of the village and start a new village and Church. The desire of Khrielhoulie Christopher to establish a Catholic school in his village Chichema led to the establishment of the Catholic Church there. Through one Thakrie, a Catholic community was formed in Merema in 1966.

Khonoma village, the first green village of Nagaland is dearly associated with late A. Z. Phizo, the Father of Naga Nationalism. Pelie Elias Chase from the village was fortunate to have had acquaintance with the first Catholic missionaries at Naga Hospital - the Spanish sisters namely Guadalupe Velasco Galos, Margerita Cifre Cerda, Pilar Gonsalez, Doleres Borga and Albino Bronte; and Mgr. Emmanuel Bars and Fr. Marocchino. Following the baptism of Pelie in January 1955, two more joined the Church. While Fr. Marocchino stayed at D' Block, Kohima, two boys from Khonoma, Niu Francis Kuotsu who later became a lecturer in Science College, Kohima and Rüüngutuo Augustine Zinyü who went on to become the Director of Medical Sciences, Government of Nagaland, came to stay with him to continue their studies in the school. The return of Theyuchie George Vakha from Kerala as a Catholic encouraged people to embrace the new faith[45] and between 1955 and 1965 many more people joined them. It was the need of the time and so in 1965 Fr. Felix started a school to impart good education to the people of the area (Alangimattathil, 1977).

With the baptism of Lhoupfelie Linus in 1965, the Catholic Church came to exist in Rukhroma. The first missionary to visit Jotsoma was Fr. Bernick along with some persons in 1967. Vitsütha and Guovi embraced the Catholic faith after instruction. However, they were disappointed when

---

45 George Vakha went to Kerala for some work and returned in the year 1954 as a Catholic. If his baptism was counted among the first Angami Catholics, he would be the second person baptised as Catholic among the Angamis, much before the first group of Angamis was baptised on 24 December 1954 at Kohima. He had received some education and so he was a translator for the priests and also served as a touring catechist. He toured villages and accompanied Fr. Marocchino to the villages showing films, translating his talks and assisting at baptism. In 1955 he stayed with Fr. Marocchino at Chotabosti. He, on his own shared his knowledge and experience of faith with the new Catholics in his village and beyond. He remained an active helper of Fr. Marocchino till his departure from Kohima (Vattoth, 2010, p. 105).

the educated people of the village who had been instigated by the Baptist Church did not permit them to open a school. Even though the efforts to open a school failed, the Church continued to grow in strength with the help of touring catechists Neichüwhelhou and Thekrunei Edward (Rino, 1992). Zubza was the next village to hear about the Catholic faith. Guovi of Jotsoma shared his faith with some of his friends and they became Catholics in 1969. Mezoma, a few kilometers away from Khonoma received the Catholic faith in 1975.

Chavi Xavier of Phesama village had got an opportunity to know the Catholic faith from Neizo Louis and Kevipralie Paulus of Kohima Village. On 24 December 1959, he and his wife were baptised by Fr. Marocchino in Christ King Church, Kohima. They were followed by a few more people in the following year. In 1961 a small Church was built and Fr. Marocchino blessed and named it as 'Sacred Heart Church.' Phesama village thus became the first village in the Southern Angami region to have received Catholic faith (Xavier, 2009).

Vicha-ü and her children from Phesama brought the Catholic faith to Viswema village when they moved in there. They were assisted by Chavi and Fr. Felix. The Catholic community of Kigwema is indebted to Kehozecha Zacharia, catechist of Jakhama village who played a key role. Visazo Paul and Thino were the first people who got baptised in Kigwema in 1965 through the instrumentality of Chavi Xavier and Kehozecha Zacharia of Jakhama.

3.3 Kohima

As the number of Catholics increased, the Catholic community of Kohima village felt the need to have a permanent site for the establishment of the mission. Fr. Marocchino paid for five acres of land at Bayavü Hill, Kohima in 1959. In order to supervise the construction work, he shifted his residence from Levi's house in D' Block to Neizo Louis' house in Pezielietsie, the present Veterinary Hospital. As the community began the work, some people raised objections against the construction saying the Catholic Church could not own land in the village. They also accused the Catholics of buying land with Roman money. Some rumors spread among the people that the land was purchased with blood money. It was decided to settle the case in the Panchayat Court and to the surprise of all, the court declared its verdict in favour of the Catholics. There was no partiality in the judgment because the case was heard by members who were mostly pagans. Their argument was that if the Baptist Church could own land the Catholics also could own it. Dominic Mezhüvilie one of the pioneer Catholics of that time has the following to recollect, "We were treated as foreigners and so were refused to own any land. This issue was taken to the Kohima village Panchayat for settlement. But God saw to it that the more it was discussed the greater was the support that it brought in our favour. Ultimately we won the case, and had the ownership of the land" (Suosahie, 1977, pg. 19). However, the Catholics could not build the Church as the said land and the surrounding area were requisitioned by the Deputy Commissioner for the Directorate of School Education. In the meantime some of the Baptist leaders sought the help of the underground army to murder Kevipralie Paulus Belho, Neizo Louis Solo and Suosahie Philip Dzuvichu who were accused of being traitors and of buying Naga land for Rome (Vattoth, 2010). Finally in their search for a new plot of land they managed to acquire it in P. Khel of Kohima village, where the present Christ King Church stands.

In 1963 Fr. Marocchino was transferred, as the Government refused to renew the permit of the foreign missionaries as a whole. At the departure of Fr. Marocchino, Fr. Paul Bernick, a Yugoslavian, working in South India, but an Indian citizen by registration was appointed as his successor and the first parish priest of Christ King on 4 January 1964. As he could not reach Christ King in time Fr. Joseph Felix was asked to look after the Kohima mission. For some time he stayed in the rented residence at Pezilietsie where Fr. Marocchino stayed. It was during Fr. Bernick's time that the Church reached out to Jotsoma, Rukhroma, Phesama, Kigwema, Zubza, Zhamai, etc. Fr. Felix was going around preaching and at the same time opening schools in many places much to the displeasure of the Church authority. The argument he gave for opening schools was that, "only through English education could the Church win over the hearts of the people and acceptance from the Baptists" (Felix, personal communication, December 28, 2008). On the occasion of Christmas he made a big star of red cloth and placed it on top of the Church for everybody to see. Red was the symbol of Marxists who were against Christians and so Fr. Bernick did not like it. In the words of Fr. Felix, "I had set up the first Magna Christmas Star over the Church in view of the town and the village. When Fr. Bernick entered Kohima on 4 January 1964, Lhisema Khel Day, with my chest out, I pointed out to the STAR from T.C.P gate. "It's a pity, it is RED", he said bitterly. His country Yugoslavia, was then under the RED communism. So, from then on I have sworn to keep my Christmas Stars BLUE!" (Cathedral Parish, Kohima, 1999, p. 41).

While Fr. Marocchino was staying at Samuel Mezhür's quarter in the War Cemetery, both together started the Kohima English School with the hope that one day the sisters would take over the school and run it. In fact when the sisters of the congregation of the Daughters of Mary Help of Christians (Salesian Sisters) came on 14 May 1964 they started teaching there, but gave up the idea of taking charge of the school as the place was not sufficient and suitable for them. So they started the Little Flower School in 1965 in the present location.

The presence of the young Catholic Church in Nagaland was felt at the International Eucharistic Congress at Bombay at the end of the year 1964 when 25 Angami delegates of Nagaland participated in the said programme. In February 1969 the Bethany Sisters took the initiative to establish the Christ King School. When Fr. Bernick was transferred to Manipur in July 1969, Fr. Ittiyachen Manjil was appointed parish priest. He started the Don Bosco School in 1971 from Class Five upwards. Students who completed Class Four at Christ King School were absorbed by Don Bosco School. Later on both became independent schools. In the year 1972, the Medial Mission Sisters opened their Medical Unit in the Child and Maternity Centre at L. Khel, Kohima Village (Suosahie, 2002).

3.4 Beginning of the Mission among the Chakhesangs

Chakhesangs are a major tribe in Nagaland and the Catholic Church's association began with them in the latter part of 1960. The first village in Phek district inhabited mainly by the Chakhesang and Pochuri tribes got contact with the Catholic Church was Zhamai village. The original name of

Zhamai is 'Zevame' meaning people of the 'enchanted lake' (Dukru, 1993, pg. 1). The preaching of the Catholic faith and the subsequent consequences faced by the Catholics of this village could be compared to that of the early Christians. The people were open to the Catholic faith because of the influence and association they had developed with the people of Mao area in Manipur, where Fr. Peter Bianchi had formed a large community (Syiemlieh, 1990). On 18 October 1964 a group of traders namely Akha, Tho-o, Theba and Thezü of Zhamai village were told about the Catholic faith by Panü of Liyai village under Mao centre on their way to Imphal. They then approached Fr. Bernick, at Christ King, Kohima, who sent a group of youngsters under the leadership of Suosahie Philip to preach the Catholic faith. Fr. Bernick baptized the first eleven members on 20 March 1966, the day the Church was blessed.

Soon after the baptism into the Catholic Church, there began an unleashing of accusations against the Catholics who were branded as 'anti Christ' The chorus of accusations was supported by the Naga army which arrested Akha, the pioneer of the Catholic faith on 16 December 1966 and took him to Khomi village, the Company Headquarter of the Naga Army, where he was placed in a dungeon. He returned on the Christmas day of 1966, giving up his faith because he was threatened that he and his family would lose their lives if they did not go back to their original faith.[46]

On 18 April 1967 K. Yevecho Nenuotso, Razou Peyu,

46 The dungeon was 8 feet in length, 6 feet in breadth and 4 feet in depth. It was covered with wood and mud and on one side a small hole functioned as a ventilator.

Phek, Federal Government of Nagaland, sent a letter to the Catholic Church at Kohima in reply to the letter sent to him in respect of Akha who was taken into custody for becoming a Catholic. Nenuotso (1967) writes, "The Federal Government of Nagaland had passed a resolution that no Catholic religion will be allowed to be practiced in our land except the Christian religion. So we, the Chakhesang people have determined to abide by the resolution of the Federal Government and no other religion will be allowed to be mixed with our religion; we ask you to keep this in mind" (pg. 1). He further said that all the land was grouped into a state and the state was divided into districts and now the Catholics, without consulting him started a new religion that would create trouble in the land.

Fr. Bernick, kept up his visits to this village despite various threats from the Baptist Church and the underground. At about the same time the Naga Baptist Church Council (NBCC) published a leaflet signed by seventeen people under the title "Citizens' Voice, The Voice of Nagaland Baptist Churches," accusing the Roman Catholic Church of "naked intrusion" into Nagaland thereby creating serious tensions. Below is an extract from the leaflet:

> The British policy towards the Nagas was designed to protect the people from outside exploiters and weld together the warring tribes into one administrative unit, where peace would prevail. To that end, the administration adhered to a policy of strictly forbidding various protestant denominations and other religious groups to enter the then Naga Hills, except one, i.e. the American Baptist Mission. Mill's statement, which clearly reflected the then official stand on the matter, says, 'an arrangement, designed to

> prevent overlapping, has long been in existience by which definitive Mission fields in Assam have been assigned to the Anglican and various Protestant Churches. The Naga Hills falls to the share of the American Baptists and they have been long at work among the Nagas.' (Mills, J. P. The Ao Nagas, pg. 411)... However, a close look at the state of affairs during the past few years show beyond any shadow of doubt that another non-protestant Body i.e. the Roman Catholic Church has intruded into Nagaland, which had long been a Baptist territory. This intrusion goes contrary to any recognised Comity arrangement (it means in an area where a church or denomination is working, no other religious body can enter the same area and start a new Mission to avoid conflict) and against the expressed desire of the Naga National Council and Yezabo, and thus, seriously jeopardising Naga unity, so essential to national existence (Ao, Longri, 5 July 1967, pg. 1).

The Catholic Church immediately responded through its reply titled, "An Echo" to "The Voice of the Naga Baptist Churches" (Sousahie, July 11, 1967). Coelho (1984) writes, "In this they refuted the allegations made against them and expressed their regret that responsible Baptist leaders should have stooped so low as to slander the Catholic Church" (pg. 38). A few words from the leaflet as reply would clarify the doubts of the seventeen signatories. "A Naga Catholic cannot quote all those documents but he simply says: I am a Catholic because I myself want it. This is divinely and humanly guaranteed right of self decision, not conditioned by human factors, this is democratic" (Sousahie, July 11, 1967). Soon after this the

NBCC brought out another leaflet entitled "Roman Pope or Christ ?" on 23 July 1967.

The underground Naga Army at this juncture joined hands with the anti-Catholics and abducted five Catholics namely Sasü Dukru, Mekho Nukhu, Nasü Dukru, Thekhru Dukru and Thoo Dome from Zhamai on 19 July 1967 and lodged them in a dungeon where they were fed with a single meal a day (Dukru, 1993).[47] About the unreasonable behaviour of the outlawed people Coelho (1984) says, "The majority of the outlawed Naga Army were Baptists and the Yehzobo (constitution) of the Naga Federal Government which proclaimed 'Nagaland for Christ' stated that in Nagaland only Baptist Christianity and the Naga religion but no other would hold a monopoly over the Naga people" (pg. 38). After 83 days of detention which consisted of two terms, they were released. While in detention they had to bear untold mental and physical torture. Bishop Hubert Rosario visited them, consoled them and as a reward for their faithfulness built a Church in 1970 in Zhamai.

When these five men were released they were told to report on 29 November 1967 but owing to the visit of the Bishop they could not report on time and got delayed. So this time together with these five people, two more men namely,

---

47 They were released after 83 days in detention which consisted of two terms: the first from 19 July to 12 September and the second from 23 September to 23 October. Then again another 40 days from 29 November to 7 January. So in total they were in the custody for 120 days. The interval had been given precisely to take rest at home as their health had failed (Deo Dukru, The coming of the Catholic Church to Phek District, A Brief History of Zhamai Village, pg. 4).

Khazi Dukru (Head Gaon Bura*)* and Limo Dukru were taken as captives to the camp. Nasü Dukru, one of the survivors of the imprisonment, said that on reaching the place they were thrown into the dungeon and as usual fed them with meagre food. They were made to carry wooden benches from Khomi to Sakraba village as a punishment (Nasü, Personal communication, June 7, 2012).[48] In the meantime the Federal Government again asked them to go back to their ancient religion. Later on Suosahie Philip along with Major Neitsülie, a Federal representative to the Peace Mission met Zasheyi, President, the Federal Government of Nagaland and apprised him of the situation of the Catholics under custody. The latter replied saying involvement in religious affairs of the people was not a matter of concern of the Federal Government. As a consequence of their meeting, the arrested Catholics were released on 7 January 1968. In all they were imprisoned for 120 days.

The Catholic community's woes did not end there but continued to haunt them. They were forbidden from harvesting

---

48 On the day the seven courageous men were released the Captain said to them, "You are really brave and strong. I appreciate your determination to put up with all hardships for the sake of the crucified Saviour and the Catholic religion." He then ordered them to be released. The underground Army General who had come to Sakraba requested them to remain as Baptists or animists for three years. He feared if they continued in their Catholic faith many would join them. Sasü at once replied, "Can you assure us that any one of us will definitely live for three more years?" Back in the village, the Circle Officer tried to prevent more people from joining the Catholic Church by spreading the rumour that they were arrested mainly because they had been stealing cows from Manipur. But truth could not be hidden. The victory had been won. They were honoured as living martyrs in their village (Personal communication,Nasü, June 7, 2012).

crops from their fields, beaten up with wooden poles, made to stand naked with hands and legs tied and exposed to inclement weather and attacks from flies etc. Once two women, Lhouzeü Lucy and Pfulhouzeü Lucy from Kohima village, came to Zhamai village to teach the Catholic faith but were forced to leave at midnight as several pleas made to let them leave next morning fell on deaf ears. All these cruel actions were carried out by Nühü and Yevecho of Khomi village, the then Captain and Razou Peyu of the Naga army respectively (Dukru, 1993). The firm faith in the Catholic Church and extraordinary courage displayed during the persecution, inspired many neighbouring villages like Zelome, Chobama, Chizami and Thenyizumi to come forward to acceptthe Catholic faith.

The next village to accept the Catholic faith was Zelome village. The name 'Zelome' originated from the word 'Ze' means 'lake', 'Lo' means 'on the side of' and 'Me' means 'the people.' Thus, 'Zelome' means 'the people who settled on the side of the lake' (Joseph, 1996). Having heard of the new faith in Zhamai, Potokho Philip and Lhinizo of Zelome met Fr. Bernick in Kohima in 1966 (Mosonyi, Personal communication, June 7, 2012). The same year Potokho and his family received baptism and that was the beginning of Catholic Church in Zelome. Soon, the first family was joined by five more families. On 29 November 1967, Fr. Bernick baptised 19 members and thus the Church was officially inaugurated. They were further strengthened in faith by the Catholics of Zhamai through their teachings, instructions and mutual support.The interference from the underground did not deter the Catholics from professing their faith. As in Zhamai, here too the underground forbade them from harvesting their crops and subjected them to various harassments. Unable to bear humiliation and harassment many returned to their earlier faith. At this crucial period in the life of the new Catholics, J. B. Jasokie, a State Minister later on a Chief Minister, made an official visit to Chizami and requested people not to discriminate against anyone on the basis of religion or tribe (Joseph, 1996). In fact his exhortation cooled down the heat of hatred towards the Catholics in Phek district.

3.5 Church in the Late 1960s

In the late 1960s the Catholic Church began its work among Chang, Rengma and Sema tribes and in Dimapur area.

3.5.1 Tuensang and Neighbouring Villages

The Catholic Church in Tuensang is the 'Mother Church' of many communities founded in places like Kiphire, Tobu, Longleng, and many villages in the region. L. J. Graves under the direction of Fr. J. Felix, founded St. John's School, the first institution in Tuensang in 1965. However, it was handed over to Bishop Hubert D' Rosario of Dibrugarh after two years. To look after the school and possible evangelisation of the people of the area the Bishop appointed Fr. Mani and sought the goodwill and service of the Adoration Sisters.

Akum Imlong, the then Tuensang Affairs Minister, took the initiative to invite priests and sisters to Tuensang, expressed his wish to Fr. Mathew Uzhunalil to get the help of sisters. Fr. Mathew informed the Bishop who sent him to Kerala to approach the Adoration congregation (Blessilia, 1992). On 28 February 1967, Fr. P. C. Mani with a group of five Adoration Sisters: Sr. Epephrasia, Sr. Rose Tresa, Sr. Blessilia, Sr. Cicily

Kattakayam and Sr. Lilly Therese, came to Tuensang and took charge of the mission and St. John's School (Blessilia, 1992). The Baptists did not favour the presence of the sisters as they did not want the establishment of a Roman Catholic institution in Tuensang and therefore, tried to destabilise it. Their firm resolution was, to let no one sell land for a permanent establishment of the Catholic Church. Fear had already gripped the minds of the people on the hearing of the arrival of the 'Romans.' Fr. Mani, however, with his gentle approach and goodwill of the civil authorities, managed to soften the hardened hearts and won them over to his side. A few bureaucrats of Tuensang district namely Aliba Imti, Lanu Toshi, N. I. Jamir IAS, and R. L. Jamir, the army, the civil officials and a host of public leaders including GBs and DBs extended all possible help to the mission. They offered the Town Club to be used as the school which started with about 130 students from Nursery to Class Five. Within a span of few months the Church's presence was made visible in Tuensang through the school as it was exceptional in all ways. Yet, some people poisoned the innocent public in the absence of Fr. Mani who was away for some official work. One day on his return from Dibrugarh, Fr. Mani noticed that no children greeted him on his return and when he called them to enquire about their indifference they all ran away from him. One boy, however, took courage and told him that many leaders from the Baptist Church had visited the houses in the locality and advised the parents not to send their children to the Catholic school. Fr. Mani was soon told by some of his friends, including Chubalan Kinghen, Circular Officer, that there were moves to send the Catholic Missionary (Fr. Mani) and 'his women' (sisters) away from Tuensang (Mani, Personal communication, November 3, 2007). By making use of this opportunity and taking it as a challenge Fr. Mani decided to collect youngsters from different tribes of Tuensang district to train them as catechists, although they were not Catholics. He managed to send twelve of them for the Catechist Training Center at Dibrugarh. However, this angered some of the officials of the civil administration and they labeled it as an act of high handedness on the part of Fr. Mani. Parenkulangara (Mani) (1999) writes,"This act of mine was pointed as 'high handednesses' by one of the officers, Lanu Toshi, in front of the Minister for Tuensang affairs. I was asked to bring the students back. However, our D. C. N. I. Jamir had the good sense to tell me that it was better that those students stay on in Dibrugarh even during holidays - of course for other reasons (pg. 37).

According to Fr. Mani, 'the lesson we should teach our students irrespective of denomination is the value of the gospel. Children are our contact persons. If children speak well of us, parents will believe what we say and do. When the goodness of God is shown, people's response will always be positive' (Personal communication, November 3, 2007). It is an undeniable fact that wherever the Catholic Church has its presence, its impact is reflected not only in the field of education but also in the spiritual, social, economic and political spheres. As the school progressed, people began to realise that the Catholic Church could also offer religion to them. On 13 April 1968 during the Easter vigil, baptism was administered to Zamila and her two sisters and two brothers who were natives of the place.

Despite all efforts by priests and religious sisters offering medical aid and educational facilities, Tuensang village, with a population of over 4000, remained indifferent if not openly hostile to the Catholic Church and its message (Mannookhuzhy, 1987). In 1972, the Society of Jesus took over the Tuensang mission from the Diocesan clergy. Even though some contacts had been lost as a result of the shift, the mission work progressed with the opening of the Loyola School at Kiphire. Meanwhile the infant Church in Tuensang suffered a heavy loss in the death of Fr. Edwin Goveas in Febraury 1973. He was a Jesuit pioneer, who died of diabetes, the first priest to die in Nagaland. The Church, however, did not discontinue her works even after his death. In mid-1974, the centre was handed back to the Diocesan clergy.

Peter Chingmak, a Baptist, in his frantic search for truth one day visited the Catholic Church in Tuensang and was attracted by the crucifix. A Lotha Catholic he met with explained to him what the Catholic Church is and the significance of the crucifix. He was satisfied with the explanation and became a Catholic in 1984. Thereafter, he was asked to return to his former church or else he would be stripped off his tribal citizenship and forfeiture of government job. He, however, stood firm with his decision. The saddest event he remembered was that when he was cursed for being a Catholic by some people, his wife left him (Chingmak, Personal communication, January 4, 2007). A somewhat similar experience happened in the life of C. Simon from Chakba under Mokokchung district. By seeing the cross and crucifix and the life of some of the Catholics who went to the Catholic Church, he felt that this is the Church he was looking for. He was received into the Church in 1981. However, he was forced to give up faith and asked to pay a heavy fine for becoming a Catholic (Simon, personal communication, January 4, 2007).[49]

In the initial stage, attempts were made to contact villages to tell them about the Catholic faith and education. Fr. Felix and Fr. Lucian Miranda (Fr. Lucian came from Bombay to assist Fr. Mathew Manianchira) undertook the first evangelisation tour of Noklak area from 2 January, 1969. A few months later, Fr. T. J. Chacko, with his indomitable spirit and missionary zeal began touring villages in Tuensang district from August 1969 to July 1971. It was Fr. T. J. Chacko who left the footprints of the mission behind for others to follow. Although he was a stranger to people, language, customs and practices yet he could meet and speak with public leaders, Gaon Buras and Dubashis, pastors and teachers about the Catholic Church and the need to send children to a good school. His traveling companions, Chollan Chang, a class X student of Chingmai village and Tsapise Sngtam, a class VII student of Phelungre village, were boarders at St. John's. On three occasions he made extensive tours of the Noklak area. In 1968 he mentioned in the chronicle of St. Thomas Church, Tuensang that from Noklak Town he moved to Noklak village where people already had

49 Simon was originally from Chakba village under Mokokchung district. Chakba Baptists invited him to a meeting and told him to give up his new faith. 'I believe in what I understood and you believe in what you understood. So please let me be free,' he said. Rev. Likok, Ao Association Executiv Secretary told him 'Catholic Church is like Hinduism, doctrine is different and it is a secular religion.' In reply he told him, 'You taught me the Bible at Impur. I believed all what you taught. I am not worthy to teach you anything. However, I hold onto what I believe.' The former secretary, Rev. Riküm asked him to pay Rs. 1500 and a cow as fine and told him to go out of the village. Later the village chairman asked from him an explanation and threatened to file a case against him. But the very following day the chairman went to the field and died so the council got frightened and thereafter didn't ask for an explanation (personal communication, C. Simon, January 4, 2007).

anti-catholic feelings. Then he toured Nongkyen, Nokhu, Khengyu, and Penso-the biggest and the mother village of all Khemungen tribe. The population was very thin in proportion to the number of houses due to large scale head-hunting practiced till 1963 and also due to high infant mortality rate. From there he went to visit Yokao, Tsawao and Lengyu villages. From all these villages the leaders agreed to send their children to the boarding-house at Tuensang. As soon as the Baptist leaders, field directors and evangelists learned about his tours, they alerted all the pastors and school masters not to accept him or cooperate with him or to be deceived by him in any way and not let him show the film. They even forbade the villagers from sending their children to the boarding-house and school. So, many among those who had agreed to come to the boarding-house backed out later.

Not discouraged by the earlier experience, Fr. Chacko began his second tour of the Noklak area from 12 to 24 February 1970 with a dual motive: to contact people, preach to them and to bring some fifteen students who had been arranged for the boarding-house. However, during his visit people boycotted his programme and those who had earlier given names for the boarding-house withdrew except at Tsawao village where three boys agreed. In all, he managed to get four Khemungen boys for the boarding-house. In spite of having arranged film shows in all the villages not a single person turned up for the event, as the pastor and other leaders had forbidden the villagers to attend the same. The people were indifferent and did not show the initial interest they had shown to him on his first visit. On 13 February the Director of Education from Kohima with his party, DIS, SIS etc. paid a visit to Noklak. Later, they went to

Nonkyan village where the Director addressed the gathering. The local RCM also asked Fr. Chacko to speak. Fr. Chacko said, "I spoke about the Catholic schools in Nagaland and the aim of the Catholic Church to give the Nagas real education and real religion" (Chacko, 2010, p. 8).

Not having the habit of giving into disappointment, Fr. Chacko undertook the third tour of the villages from 3 to 13 December 1970. This visit, however, to the villages was disheartening. The boys who agreed to tour with him in Noklak backed out. In all the villages he visited, the Baptists objected to the film show and even the non-Christians were indifferent to him. He felt that the people were untrustworthy and the Baptist leaders were very much against the Catholics. In all these tours he presented the Catholic Mission in the following words: "Progress and Development through Education and Religion." On being asked about the intention of his tour Fr. Chacko said, "My intention was to make the first contact to announce our presence at Tuensang headquarters and to get children for the boarding-house to sow the seeds of Catholic faith. In short, it is evangelisation as the vast majority of people in the villages were non-Christians" (Chacko, personal communication, November 5, 2007).

A decade later, seeing the fast progress made by the people of Tuensang owing to Catholic education, people of Noklak, inhabited by the Khiamungan tribe, asked for a school there. The work of the Catholic mission among the Khiamungans thus entered a remarkable period with the establishment of St. Paul's School on 7 March 1984 and the baptism of five families into the Catholic faith in 1997. A similar request was made from Tuensang Village where a school named St. Thomas School was dedicated on 19 March 1984. The people of Anganba, belonging to the Sangtam tribe were the next ones to ask for Catholic mission in Tuensang District. Their wish was fulfilled on 3 March 1986 when Christ King School was opened. With the baptism of 25 families a Catholic community was formed there in August 1993. The opening of St. Peter's School at Trongor on 5 March 1987 saw the long standing dreams of the people realised. Seven families accepting Catholic faith on 18 May 1993 laid the foundation of the Catholic Church in the village.

3.5.2 Among the Rengmas

From its inception in Kohima it was Pralie Paulus Angami from Kohima village, who made efforts in making the Church known to many areas of Kohima region. The Rengmas who inhabit the land between Kohima district and Wokha district heard of Catholic Church when Pralie Paulus was appointed in Tseminyu as an Agricultural Instructor in 1966. In his urge to establish a Catholic community at Tseminyu he started visiting and meeting people. When he began contacting people he faced some opposition from certain quarters and so he turned his attention towards Tesophneyu village. He won over the hearts of some of the leaders of the village like Lotsuo Dubashi, Nphuseng Dubashi, Nighewa Dubashi and Mezuchü Gaon Bura. He taught prayers in Angami dialect till Peter Tep became the touring catechist and translated prayers into Rengma dialect. After the initial instruction, Fr. Bernick from Kohima reached on 5 January 1967 and instructed them more in the faith. With the baptism of eighty three people on 19 November 1967 by Bishop Hubert D' Rosario, the

Church came to exist in Rengma area. As part of the ongoing formation and to strengthen them further in faith Fr. Bernick sent Lhosilalie Angami from Kohima who stayed in the village for two years. The Don Bosco School was started to cater to the educational needs of the children of the area. It was, however, shifted to Tseminyu in the year 1974 due to low enrolment but it was reinstated in 1986.

Many a time Pralie took a group of people from Tseminyu to Tesophenyu to instruct the newly founded community. They in turn showed keen interest and formed a group to be the future members of the Catholic Church in Tseminyu village, chief among them were Khikebu Khing, Ngabu Khing and Kejwishe Khing. A need was felt to instruct the newly formed community in their own dialect and so it was decided to send Ngabu Khing for catechist training. He resigned as a primary school teacher and received baptism from Christ King, Kohima on 31 July 1968 and took the name 'Albert.' Thus, he became the first Rengma Catholic from Tseminyu (George, 1993). After two and a half years of training in Dibrugarh, Ngabu Khing returned and was appointed the local catechist in 1971. Meanwhile instruction in Cathoic faith continued and the first batch of fifteen persons received baptism on 1 December 1968. Peter Tep after his baptism in 1970 was sent to Dibrugarh and Imphal for catechist training and on his return was made the touring catechist.

When Pralie contacted Kandinyu village, some people showed interest in embracing Catholic faith and they remained as catechumens for three years. They were baptised on 6 December 1970 by Fr. K. P. Antony from Wokha. A new Church for the community which consisted of seventeen families was blessed on 23 November 1986 by Bishop Abraham (Tep, n.d).[50] In the meantime, one Kapa from Nsunyu village learned about the Catholic faith and got baptised at Tesophenyu. He was the only Catholic in the village till his wife got baptised on 15 August 1977. On 30 May 1982, fourteen more members received baptism from Fr. Sebastain Manianchira. But today there is no Catholic community in this village. According to the writings of Bishop Abraham, Tseminyu was elevated to a parish in 1976 in thanksgiving to St. Joseph for saving Fr. P. V. Joseph, the Vicar General of the diocese of Kohima from a severe attack of peritonitis (George 1993). In the same year Missionary Sisters of Mary Help of Christians joined the parish for the mission work.

3.5.3 Semas in Lazami

Lazami is the biggest and oldest village in the Sema area. For the sake of communication the Pughoboto sub-division, which is a Sema area was placed under Kohima district by the Government. Punakha Sema, an accountant at Civil Hospital Kohima, and Vihokhu and Zekiye both primary teachers heard about the Catholic faith from Philip Suosahie and Paulus Pralie.

50 Many years ago Fr. Joseph Edakudan had written about the hidden motif of the people in becoming Catholics in Kandinyu. In the first place most people became Catholics were older people. They were pagans and their children, who were Baptists, told them to become Catholics as pagan funeral rites were costlier than rites of other religions. Secondly, there were only few Catholics and the younger generation Catholics married people of other denominations. Therefore, either the number of Catholics should increase from the existing community or new members should be brought in. If both these options were not possible, in 25 years time the community would die. In fact his prophetic words came true after 25 years.

They visited priests at Kohima and requested them to open a school in their village (Leo, 1985). When they heard that without a Catholic community the school wouldn't be opened, they began to approach people who were willing to become Catholics. Fr. Bernick, visited the village in December 1967 along with a group of people. But the underground opposed the establishment of the Catholic Church there. Ponnattil (1988) writes:

> Mr. Vihokhu, one of the would be members of the Catholic community and the leader of the group was caught by the underground and kept under their custody for three months. He was a man of strong faith and told them 'whether I live or die, it does not matter, I want to be a Catholic and I shall be one'. His friend Xekiye Swu reported the matter to the higher authorities and got him released (pg. 43).

The reasons for getting attracted to Catholicism varied from person to person in Lazami village. According to Punakha, in the beginning there was only the Baptist church in the village. Many became Baptist Christians because of social pressure and so it was a mass movement with no instruction in faith and teachings of the Church. Many people, who were expelled from the Baptist Church for their habit of drinking rice beer, wanted to become Catholics because they did not wish to go back to their earlier religion, paganism. They had also heard about the Catholic Church already founded in the Angami and Lotha areas. So, they approached some of their Angami Catholic friends and invited them to visit their village (Ponnattil, 1988). For Vihokhu, the attraction to the Catholic faith was prompted by his association with the Catholic

Church when he was a student at Sacred Heart High School Mawlai, Shillong. In the beginning, Fr. Mathew Ponnattil together with catechist Philip of Christ King Church stayed in the village for two days and instructed people. They were followed by Fr. John Med and some of the leaders of Christ King Church who regularly visited them and stayed in the village for a longer period. In 1971, Fr. Med printed a small prayer book in the Sema dialect under the title, "Short Prayers in Sema Naga" containing the morning and evening prayers and the Mass prayers (Ponnattil, 1988). After due preparation, Fr. Med baptised the first batch of seveny six catechumens on 4 April 1971 and thus the Catholic Church officially came into being in Lazami village. Among the three Khels namely: the Iyinu Khel, the Lazakito Khel, and the Izüka Khel in the village, the Iyinu Khel is commonly known as the Catholic Khel as the majority of the people are Catholics. This parish has three sub-centers namely Pughoboto, Natsumi and Ghatashi.

3.5.4 Church in Dimapur

Fr. Joseph Felix from Christ King Kohima used to visit Catholic families who had been there in places like Burma Camp, Singrijan and Samaguri, situated in and around Dimapur town, as early as 1940 ("Holy Cross Dimapur", 1999). Earlier they were attended to by the priests from the Catholic Church, Golaghat in Assam. Fr. Felix felt that for the pastoral care of these people it was essential to have a chapel built and so he built one in the compound of Thehuohie Felix Angami (near the present Christian Higher Secondary School) who was a Catholic, in 1964 (Mandal, 1993). Having perceived the urgent need for schools and good education, Fr. Felix invited his father, George Felix, who had just retired from the Tata Iron and Steel Company, Jamshedpur, to help him in his work. Accepting the request of his son, George Felix came to Nagaland and opened Holy Cross School, at Dimapur on 16 April 1966 in the premises of Felix Angami (Lucious, 1992).[51]

Meanwhile Namgangheing Zeliang, former Tribal Council President of the Zeliangrong requested Bishop Hubert D' Rosario, to establish a Catholic centre in Jalukie, but the latter told him the urgency was to establish one at Dimapur. In 1969, Fr. Mani shifted the Holy Cross School to the present site bought with the help of Namgangheing. The first group of Bethany sisters arrived in January 1969 to help in the mission. The parish took care of a community of about 1000 members, most of who were residing in the Mikir Hills (Karbi Anglong). In the subsequent years, communities were founded in places like Diphupar (Rongmei) (1970), Zeliangrong Village (1971), Diphupar (Angami) (1972), Thenyphe (1975), Razaphe (1980), Kacharigaon (1980), Chekeye village (1983), Vidima (1984) and Hakhize (1993).

3.5.5 Church in Jalukie

Initiatives taken by Namgaheing Iheilung, Chairman, Zeliangrong Tribal Council, led to the opening of the Catholic mission at Jalukie.[52] As he was convinced of the role of the

51 Fr. Felix named the school as 'Holy Cross' because he had an Anglo-Indian soldier friend in Nagaland who had studied in Holy Cross, Bangalore. So he was inspired to give the name 'Holy Cross (Felix, personal communication, April 20, 2012).

52 Namgaheing was the Chairman of the Tribal Council of Zeliang-Kuki Area. He took initiative in establishing the Catholic mission in Dimapur and Zeliangrong region in Nagaland. A few months before his death (19 October 2001), he received baptism in the Catholic Church on 29 July 2001, from Fr. Mani who was his close collaborator and friend in initiating Catholic mission in his place.

Catholic institution for the development of the area and the uplift of the people, he went to Kohima and met Fr. Felix who directed him to Bishop Hubert D' Rosario. The Bishop, however, told him that the priority of the Church was to open an institution in Dimapur and later on in other areas. So, Namgangheing took the initiative to get the present plot of land for the Holy Cross School in Dimapur. Once again, he discussed the matter with the Bishop in Dibrugarh and the latter promised that he would open a centre in Jalukie (Mao, 1994). In the words of Parenkulangara (1999), "Mr. Namgaheing was called the Bishop of Jalukie. It was this one man's persuasive skills that brought the Tribal Council members of the area together to support the opening of a Catholic school and the church in Jalukie" (pg. 37).

On 18 Octobr 1965, Namgaheing made an appeal to the Zeliangrong people living outside Nagaland to come and settle in Jalukie area. In response to this invitation some people from Longzang and Sangzee in Manipur came to settle at Samzuiram, Mhainamtsi and New Jalukie villages on 1 February 1967. Among them there were a few Catholics. The Baptists at that time passed a resolution that no Nagas of other denominations would be allowed to settle in the area in order to discourage further settlement. Conseqent upon this resolution a few Catholic families were driven out of this young community ("St. Xavier's Church Jalukie", 1999). Against this action, Mathew Chandy and Ambrose Melengmai filed a case with the Tribal Council. On 23 February 1972, Z. Sakhrie, the Sub-Division Officer of Jalukie passed an order in favour of the Catholics based on the freedom of religion guaranteed by the Indian Constitution, besides granting permission for them and others to reside at Samzuiram. Prior to this order, the Baptists had resolved to allow only three groups in the village namely, the Baptists, the Herakas and the non-Christians. After the order had been passed, the Baptist youth of Jalukie made an attempt on the life of Mathew Chandi but he managed to escape in 1973. In the same year, Anthony of Nkoreo from Manipur came to settle in New Jalukie and built a hut but it was burnt down on 24 December 1973 by unknown people. So, Namgaheing gave him a place in Nkoreo (Chandi, Personal communication, July 29, 2012). He was followed by a few more people who were also sheltered in the present Nkoreo village. Later some others came and settled in Ekiesangram, New Beijampui and Mhaikom villages (Syiemlieh, 1990).

In 1979, the Baptists of Mhainamtsi village refused to give land or accommodation to three Catholic families, who came from Charoi village in Tamenglong district of Manipur. So Bishop Abraham bought land for them in the same village for a sum of Rs. 10000 and settled them there (Chandi, Personal communication, July 29, 2012). The assistance extended by some prominent citizens such as Lungalang, the Commissioner, lIkising, Ex. Member of Legislative Assembly (MLA) and P. Nampeung, Sub Inspector in establishing the Catholic mission was praiseworthy. With the permission of the Bishop and support and wishes of late Namgaheing the mission started on 29 May 1969 with the official inauguration of the St. Xavier's School by Bishop Hubert D' Rosario on the two hundred and sixty acres of land given free of cost by Namgaheing. The Missionary Sisters of Mary Help of Christians came to assist the work in the parish. The first native Catholics were Kevipele Iheilung, Blaize and John Bosco Heikiding who received the sacrament of baptism on 15 August 1970.

3.6 The Church in the 1970s

The Church began to reach out to other parts of the state in the 1970s thanks to the efforts of the Diocesan priests, male religious congregations like the Salesians of Don Bosco, the Society of Jesus and the Missionaries of St. Francis De Sales and women religious congregations.

3.6.1 Tour of Shamator

Fr. T. J. Chacko undertook a missionary tour of the Shamator area in Tuensang district from 4 to 15 April 1970 with his touring companions, Tochi Yimchunger of Yakor village and Motrung Yimchunger of Kuthur village but was intimidated by the Baptist leaders. He was confronted at Langkhanger village and warned of dire consequences if he entered the area again. Chacko (2010) writes:

> We climbed all the way up to Shamator to go down to Langkhanger. First reached Shamator village whose authorities especially the school master had promised to keep two porters for us. So, when we reached Shamator village there was neither the master nor the porters. We tried to get someone but no hope. The girl porter wanted to go back. At last we convinced her to come with us. We were late, 3'o clock. We were just passing near just below the town, Shamator. A Baptist evangelist met me on the road and asked me to meet their missionary, that is the field director - I said, 'sorry, no time.' He said, 'please just wait and ran up.' We waited. Soon came six of them –field director Chuba Meren Ao, an evangelist, the town

pastor, the touring pastor and two local church leaders. The evangelist told me that I had broken their resolution saying that no one except Baptist pastors can go around preaching in the area which is under him. So I must not proceed but turn back – we can rest tonight and be back to Tuensang early morning. We discussed for about 45 minutes. I argued logically and calmly. "First of all, I heard of no resolution and even if there is resolution it won't affect me as I am not under the resolution makers. I have the Inner Line pass, Extra Assistant Commissioner's (EAC) permission and a recommendation letter. So from government side it is ok. Then, from the religious side I have not only permission but the orders of my Bishop who alone is my legitimate religious superior. Besides as Christians, we should help each other to preach and spread the gospel. You come and teach I will only show the pictures which you can translate." They became more and more furious sticking to their point that I had broken their resolution. They threatened the boys Tochi and Motrung with dire consequences if they dared to accompany me anymore. At last the missionary asked me to follow him to his house and took away the girl with part of my luggage to his house expecting me to follow. The town pastor took on his shoulder the rest of my luggage. To this I remarked, "This is Christian charity. You are so kind as to help us even carries our own luggage." I invited him to come with me on my next visit. This irritated them and they started shouting, "Get out you Roman…you are not Christian we are Christians we believe in Christ not in Mary only Christ saves us etc." And shook his fist within an inch or two close to my face…..Others shouted together

> "Go back...go back... Roman" My companion Motrung began to cry and Tochi pleaded with me that I should not go ahead on tour. (They told me later that they got frightened because the missionary was asking those pastors in Ao language to catch and beat me up). I turned my step towards EAC's quarters. He heard my story and told them what they did was wrong. He upheld the secular nature of the state and religious freedom. They began to blame EAC for helping and taking my side, despite he being a Baptist. Finally the EAC said, "Father, these are the type of pastors we have. I could not convince them. So, please let us, for the sake of peace, cancel the programme for this time." Father showed little reluctance and reached on a compromise: "I will go on touring but in a backward direction towards Tuensang side" (pg. 28).

Chacko further writes in the chronicle of St. Thomas Church Tuensang:

> My friend Motrung was inconsolable, sat near me and went on weeping. He dared to tell the missionary while weeping, 'This father is my teacher and is like my own father. By insulting him you insulted my father and my tribe. I was taking him around to my own tribe - you are also not my tribe (missionary is Ao). Our tribe can also chase you out.' The missionary tried to calm him explaining how the Roman will disturb peace etc. Next day morning they started on the backward path and reached the village of Sampur.

Starting a Catholic mission centre at the request of the general public was often met with objections in the form of personal confrontation and threatening letters and Shamator was not an exception. In the early part of 1980, letters had been sent by the Baptist church not to open the Catholic mission. In 1983, P. Akhum Yim, Excutive Secretary of the Yimchungru Baptist Association sent a letter to the priests at Tuensang purportedly written by him on behalf of the public of Wongphunger villages not to establish the school as it might lead to misunderstanding among the villagers and would also divide the villages on this issue. However, in the latter part of the same year, and in 1987 and the 1990s letters had been pouring in from the public of the area to start the Catholic mission with assurance of full religious freedom and protection. In February 1987, the head Gaon Bura of Shamator wrote a letter on behalf of Shamator Area public consisting of seven villages namely Shamator village, Shamator town, Myleangkur, Leangkonger, Chessor, Sangphur and Yakor villages requesting the Church to open a Catholic school in Shamator. Thus, after repeated requests and keeping it at an abeyance, the Catholic Church opened the centre in the year 2002. Today, many public leaders of the place lament that narrow-mindedness of some of their leaders had led to their area being many decades behind in education, religion and development compared to Tuensang area.

3.6.2 Jakhama and the Jesuit Mission

When many people accepted the Catholic faith in the Southern Angami region, many more villages showed interest in it, and so a need was felt to provide pastoral care for the region. In October 1965 having heard of a new religion in Kohima and Phesama, a group of people from Jakhama village invited Chavi Xavier of Phesama, to visit and to preach to them. Sensing a good opportune time Chavi approached Fr. Bernick and requested him to enlighten those who came in search of the truth. With the concerted effort of Fr. Bernick and communities of Kohima and Phesama a small community was inaugurated in Jakhama and a chapel dedicated to Mary Help of Christians was blessed on 10 April 1966.

The Jesuits are the second religious congregation after the Salesians of Don Bosco to have come to do pastoral work in the Diocese of Kohima. Bishop Hubert Rosario personally approached the Jesuit Superior General Fr. Pedro Arrupe in Rome for the service of the Jesuits.The positive signal given by the Superior General eased the burden of the Bishop. Fr. Ittyachan Manjil, parish priest of Kohima arranged meetings with prominent leaders of Kohima, including J. B. Jasokie, the Education Minister, who too had been working to secure the services of the Jesuits for educational work in Nagaland together with the Jesuit delegation which consisted of Fr. J. C. Pereira and Fr. Claude D'Souza in January 1970 (Coelho, 1984). Malcolm D' Silva, the Secretary of Education also promised all help for the educational apostolate of the Jesuits. As a follow up, Fr. J. Verstraeten was deputed to explore the possibilities of a Jesuit centre in Nagaland. An extract of his report reads, "Prospects: glorious, Peoples' needs: extreme, Educational standards: low, Co-operation: promised, Likely response: overwhelming" (Syiemlieh, 1990, p.72). Counting on the positive report and future prospects three Jesuits namely Fr. Ligouri Castelino and Brother Raymond arrived on 21 April and Fr. S. Coelho joined them on 11 May 1970 in Nagaland.

The search for a suitable location led them to Jotsoma but

having been denied entry there, they finally pitched their tent at Jakhama. The mission opened a school for the children of the area and named it as Loyola School in 1971. In the same year a small group of young men from Kidima village invited priests to instruct them in faith (Coelho, 1984). A small community was formed and St. Xavier School was founded in 1979. The community at Khuzama was formed in 1974 and Sacred Heart School was opened in 1978. Mima was the next village to invite priests to establish a Catholic Church there. A small group of people accepted the Catholic faith in 1978, amidst opposition. Selfless sacrifices of women religious congregations namely Sisters of the Apostolic Carmel (AC) in Jakhama (1971), Bethany Sisters (BS) in Viswema (1977) and the Franciscan Clarist Congregation (FCC) in Phesama (1981) who strengthened and extended pastoral work in Southern Angami area deserve commendation. St. Paul Institute of Education, a Teacher Training School was inaugurated in September 1977 by Bishop Abraham to meet the educational backwardness of the state. The Jesuits opened an Agro Industrial Training Centre, 'Eden Gardens' at Khuzama to provide non-formal and rural education to poor students.

3.6.3 Kiphire Region

The Catholic Church in Kiphire, the one that got into trouble one after another and was tossed about in accusations and threats yet always stood firm against all adversities from the beginning till today, is the mother Church for many Church communities in the Kiphire region. The Kiphire region is inhabited mostly by the Sangtam tribe followed by Yimchunger (Makory, Tikhir and Chiri) and Sema tribes. The work of evangelisation of Kiphire sub-division (now district) by the Catholic Church dates back to 1968, through priests stationed at Tuensang. The Church had its first members when Joseph Kirimog from Salumi Village and John Yesong Sangtam from Phelungre village were baptised on 9 June and 15 December respectively by Bishop Hubert Rosario at Dibrugarh in 1968. Fr. L. Miranda was the first missionary priest to tour the area and he reached Phelungre on 7 January 1969 (Mlakuzhiyil, 1997). But the priest who toured widely the Kiphire Sub-division was Fr. T. J. Chacko. In all he toured 23 villages on three occasions from1969 to 1971. His first tour of the area was from 2 to 17 December 1969 to Kiphire Town, Kiphire Village, Langkok, Singrup, Amahatore, Chanchore, Rutsütsü, Inscur, Phelungre and Anatongre with touring companion, Tsapise Sangtam. In all these places he spoke about the importance of education and religion in the lives of people. Other villages he toured include Thonoknyu, Chaliso, Tokchur, Pessu, Sanglao, Pungro village, Pungro Town, Thanamir, Penkim, Salumi, Luthor, Zanger, Chomi, and New Minic, now called Longkhimong Village. From his visits he had taken several boys to the boarding-house at Tuensang. By the end of 1971 Tuensang parish was handed over to the Jesuits and Fr. Chacko was transferred.

Fr. Castelino, who was in Tuensang, went to visit Kiphire at the pressing invitation of I. K. Chankija, the civil Sub Divisional Officer (S.D.O). In the first week of December 1971, Fr. Castelino, a frontier missionary particularly to the Pochuri and Chakhesang tribes from early 1970s through 1980s, made his maiden tour of Kiphire area from Tuensang with Fr. Edwin Govias. On his maiden visit, I. K. Changkija, the civil S.D.O. arranged a meeting with all the public leaders to discuss the prospects of opening a school at Kiphire. Castelino (1997), however, made clear the intention of the Catholic Church in the following words, "But as priests we are primarily missionaries who have come to preach the Good News of the Gospel, though we will be ready to extend our services in the field of social uplift in whatever way we can, including education" (pg. 27). During this tour he confirmed the information he had gathered from the visits of earlier priests that this area was a fertile land for missionary works.

The public as a whole promised their support and willingness to cooperate with the priests. In their eagerness to have the school they wanted it to begin from the following academic year and offered the Council Hall in Kiphire to conduct classes and to accommodate staff. The school, named as 'Loyola School' started functioning on 6 March 1972 with forty three students in the nursery.[53] Like Tuensang, the school began without a Catholic community. Sr. Blessilia and Sr. Celine Martin started serving as teachers, however, they went back to Tuensang at the end of 1972 due to lack of accommodation. Fr. Castelino

53 The Kiphire mission owes much of its success to the support and cooperation of the civil administration and the general public. Soon after opening the centre Fr. Castelino approached the SDO for help to enable him to tour other areas to conscientise people the need to send children to a good school like the Catholic School. On his request to get the help of some people for the tour, the officer informed all his subordinate officials and arranged for porters to carry the luggage and a Dubashi to guide and introduce him to the public. In the words of Fr. Castelino, 'This Dubashi leading us with a gun in his hands was like a body guard for us and wherever we went we received royal treatment with warm hospitality, which made our tour a grand success because of the good response from all the people (Chronicle, St. Peter's Parish, Kiphire).

was the first resident priest at Kiphire. With the death of Fr. Govias on 14 February 1973 in Tuensang, Fr. Castelino took his place but continued visiting the Kiphire region. When he was transferred to Chizami in July 1974 he handed over Loyola School to Fr. Mathew Keemattam. In the beginning some displeasure over the starting of the Catholic mission was expressed from certain quarters. Some people did not want the school to function as rumours spread that Catholics were not Christians. Such grudges, however, did not last when they saw the fast development of the area through the influence of the Catholic mission. Akumba, an Ex MLA admitted that the Catholic school was instrumental in changing the face of the entire Kiphire district, as it showed the door to advancement (Akumba, Personal communication, July 29, 2007).

Phelungre was the first village under Tuensang district to have a Catholic community founded. The Church's first contact with this village was on 8 January in 1969, when Fr. Miranda was allowed to preach in the Baptist church. Fr. T. J. Chacko during his two tours, from 2 to 17 December 1969 and 28 December 1970 to 13 January 1971 visited many villages including Phelungre. During the last visit he collected twelve boys from the villages for the boarding-house in Tuensang (one among them was Pewsang from Chomi village who later became instrumental in starting the Catholic Church in Chomi) and reached Phelungre on 12 January and left for Tuensang the following day (Throngsukiu, 2000). With the establishment of Loyola School at Kiphire visits to Phelungre, mostly by Fr. Castelino became frequent. Meanwhile John Yesong as the touring catechist began catechising the people who desired to embrace Catholic faith. Undoubtedly, the man responsible for the beginning of the Catholic Church there was John Yesong.[54]

Fr. Mathew Keemattam, took charge of Kiphire and visited Phelungre on 18 August 1974 and stayed there from 20 December to 25 December 1974, visiting people and giving medical aid to the sick, showing Bible films and conducting meetings with Gaon Buras and elders of the village. During this visit the first baptism in Kiphire sub-division was administered to Francis Yangtsakiu of Longthonger village during the midnight

54 John Yesong was born on 1st May 1949 at Phelungre. At a young age he and his brother became orphans due to the death of their parents. He began his schooling in the village government school and went to Tuensang and again back to Kiphire for study and completed class VI in 1966. In 1967 he went to Tuensang to stay with priests. Inspired by his religious outlook Fr. Mani sent him to Dibrugarh in 1968 for the catechist training. He was baptised at Dibrugarh by Bishop Hubert Rosario on 15 December 1968. Later he became the first trained catechist from Tuensang District. He began his work seriously struggling against enormous difficulties he had to face even from his own people. He toured many villages of the area and preached with the help of his Bible and guitar. It is said, 'he preached efficiently, instructed effectively and unequal was his ability to sing.' In the beginning he was alone, later he was joined by a group of students from Phelungre and Chomi which included S. K. James, Puesang Mathew and Rikhikiu James. He faced a huge amount of pressure to give up faith but he stood firm. He became a victim of intestinal tuberculosis and breathed his last on 23 November 1976. He was one of the first ones to have been educated in his village. It seemed that he was asked to contest the Nagaland Legislative Assembly election but rejected the offer as he wanted to devote his full time for the work of the church.

As an effort of evangelisation among his people and to establish the Catholic Church at Phelungre, John Yesong, with the help of Fr. Castelino arranged a dancing group from Phelungre village as delegates of Tuensang District on the occasion of the ordination of Bishop Abraham Alangimattathil as Bishop of Nagaland on 14 October 1973 at Kohima. In the beginning more than 20 people desired to go but only 13 of them could go willingly and attended the said function. Fr. Castelino personally took the team and a beautiful local cultural dance was performed on the day. Many among them turned out to be witnesses for the future.

mass of 24 December 1974 in the presence of a large gathering of people (Throngsukiu, 2000).[55] Driven by missionary zeal, Fr. Mathew Keemattam, John Yesong and James Kiosukiu (a student of St. John's School Tuensang), worked hard and many people expressed their desire to embrace the Catholic faith. They were taught the basis of the Catholic faith and thirty of them, including seven boys from Chomi village were baptised on 7 May 1975 by Bishop Abraham Alangimattathil. Thus the first Catholic community in Tuensang district was founded.[56]

The Catholic Church had to face many obstacles and mounting pressures at the beginning of the community at Phelungre. Gaon Buras and leaders of the Baptist church threatened Bishop Abraham and Fr. Mathew Keemattam with dire consequences if they propagated the Catholic faith in the village and so asked them to quit the village. In June 1975, the Sangtam Baptist Church Association held a meeting with the agenda, 'The birth of the Catholic Church in Phelungre village'.

---

55 Mr. Francis Yangtsakiu was a teacher at Loyola School, Kiphire. This was the first baptism in Kiphire because even though John Yesong was from Phelungre, he was already baptised in Dibrugarh (St. Thomas' Church, Phelungre, Silver Jubilee, 1975-2000, p. 25).

56 Among the seven boys, three of them namely Pewsang, Rekikiu and Shahto were students of St. John's School Tuensang. Since the school was not upgraded to a High School they went back to study at Government High School Kiphire. One day during a casual conversation with Fr. Mathew Keemattam, Pawsang said that he and few of his companions from Kiphire area were studying at St. John's. Fr. Mathew then enquired if it was possible for all of them to meet him later. In the course of their interaction and knowing each other they brought four more boys namely Michael, Peter, Emmanuel and John. Among them Michael and Peter were studying at Kiphire Govt. School and the other two in Chomi village. With the encouragement received from Fr. Mathew and John Yesong they expressed their desire to become Catholics (Keemattam, personal communication, June 15, 2012).

The Executive Committee of the United Sangtam Students' Conference (USSC) during mid 1970s complained to the Governor of Nagaland not to allow the Catholic Church and school at Phelungre village to operate. However, the governor in his wisdom said to them that the Constitution of India guaranteed freedom of religion to every citizen. S. K. Sangtam an ex-minister, president of the then USSC, cautioned the people against becoming Catholics. He exhorted to let all those who became Catholics to remain but no more new members should join and let no Catholic school be opened. If the school was opened the Catholic strength would increase and that would be a threat (Moses, Personal communication, July 22, 2007). The Catholic School in the village could not be opened until the year 2000 because of the threat by the USSC and some people of the area. At the height of this tense situation the Additional Deputy Commissioner (ADC) Kiphire wrote a letter asking people not to go against the freedom of religion guaranteed by the Constitution of India (Appendix: Document D). Here below is the letter written by the ADC, Kiphire.

The Catholic Church's first contact with Chomi village under Kiphire sub-division by Fr. T.J. Chacko was in January 1971. He was highly optimistic about the future prospects of the Church in this village as he was very much impressed by the people during his visit. He said, the people were kind, co-operative, helpful and appreciative. What amused him was that children ran to meet him out of curiosity as they had been told 'a Satan had come into the village in a white cloth'. When Pewsang joined St. John's School, Tuensang the people told him it was Satan's school (Pewsang, personal communication, July 24, 2007). Against all odds Fr. Castelino and John

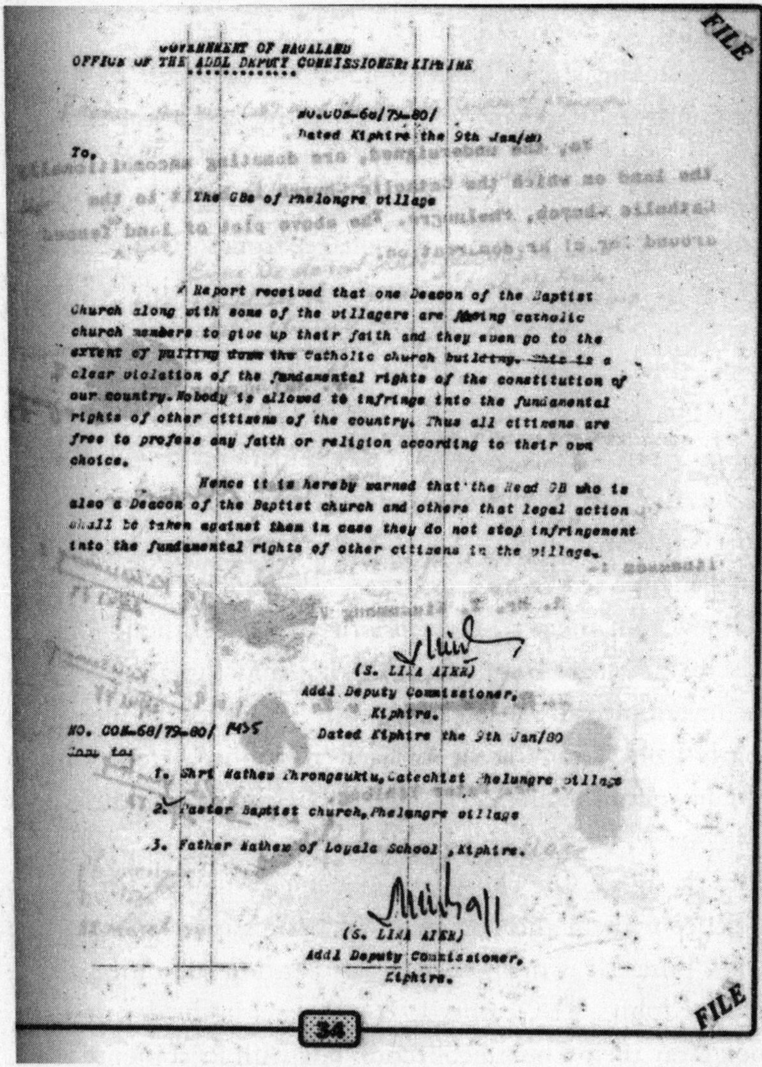

GOVERNMENT OF NAGALAND
OFFICE OF THE ADDL DEPUTY COMMISSIONER: KIPHIRE

NO.COM-60/79-80/
Dated Kiphire the 9th Jan/80

To,

The GBs of Phelongre village

Report received that one Deacon of the Baptist Church along with some of the villagers are [illegible] catholic church members to give up their faith and they even go to the extent of pulling down the Catholic church building. This is a clear violation of the fundamental rights of the constitution of our country. Nobody is allowed to infringe into the fundamental rights of other citizens of the country. Thus all citizens are free to profess any faith or religion according to their own choice.

Hence it is hereby warned that the Head GB who is also a Deacon of the Baptist church and others that legal action shall be taken against them in case they do not stop infringement into the fundamental rights of other citizens in the village.

(S. LIMA AIER)
Addl Deputy Commissioner,
Kiphire.

NO. COM-60/79-80/ 1455 Dated Kiphire the 9th Jan/80
Copy to:

1. Shri Mathew Throngsukiu, Catechist Phelungre village
2. Pastor Baptist church, Phelungre village
3. Father Mathew of Loyola School, Kiphire.

(S. LIMA AIER)
Addl Deputy Commissioner,
Kiphire.

FILE

34

Yesong instructed the people in Catholic faith in 1972. When Pewsang returned home for winter holidays in 1972 he persuaded Rukhiukiu and Y. Shahoto, his two friends to study in St. John's School Tuensang. The three youngsters learned about Catholic faith and then during their vacation back home started sharing their experience (Hosito, 2002). As a result of their faith-sharing many youth showed interest in the Catholic religion. Sensing it as a golden chance for the youth of the village who intended to become Catholics to be united, T. Korakiu, the Chairman of the village strongly supported and encouraged them to form a united youth group with P. Tsakiu, Gaon Bura as their fellowship chairman. They also selected eight youth to monitor and execute important decisions for the visible Catholic community.

In April 1975, Fr. Mathew Keemattam visited Chomi village to meet with the people at the request of Pewsang, Rukhiukiu and Shahoto. St. Peter's Church chronicle 1967-1979 mentioned that the villagers asked for a school but Fr. Mathew told them that the priority of the Catholic Church was to establish a Church in Chomi and Pungro circle. In the meantime, on 7 May 1975, thirty people including seven youth from Chomi village received baptism from Bishop Abraham at Phelungre. The youth began having their own religious service in one house but they were soon prohibited from doing so. On 11 July 1976, some of the Baptist leaders took from them the document of permission signed by the Gaon Buras. It is mentioned in the petition submitted to the ADC, Kiphire, 31 October 1976 that later in the day they also took away their Church collection box with its contents of Rs. 159.60, the Church register and several other articles. This was reported to the district administration by the end of July and on 2 August the ADC sent a message to the village to allow the Catholics to have their own worship. Again, this matter was discussed with the ADC in Kiphire in October. Finally, the items taken from the Catholics were returned at the order of Rai, Commanding Officer (CO) of Pungro. Having come back to normalcy, four boys namely James, John, Emmanuel and Andrew started a journey from Tuensang on 29 November 1976 to preach the Catholic faith in Chomi, Pungro, Vongti, Phelungre, Thonoknyu, Shamator and Leangkongre villages and their work was found to be satisfactory (Chronicle, St. Peter's Church, Kiphire).

However, several objections were raised against practice of the Catholic faith in the village. When petitioned to the administration, T. P. Imchen, the ADC issued an order on 3 December 1976 that the Catholics should be allowed to practice their faith as guaranteed by the Constitution of India. Again, when the Catholics were denied land to construct a Church in the village they filed a case in the DC court Tuensang and the latter ordered the village council through the ADC Kiphire to allot land and they managed to build a Church (Pewsang, personal communication, July 24, 2007).

By the end of 1976, forty five youth from the village decided to become Catholics. Fr. Mathew visited the village again on 23 December 1976 and celebrated Holy Mass in one of the houses that had been decorated for Christmas by the youth. On the following day, during the meeting called by the Baptists in which Fr. Mathew and Rukhiukiu were present, the former decided that the Catholics could not have the service in the village and the man who had provided the house for the service would not give his house again. Consequently on 24 December 1976 they celebrated Holy Mass on the public ground in the presence of a large gathering (Keemattam, personal communication, June 17, 2012). This further strengthened the faith of those seven young men and all those who were gathered. The Catholic youth constructed a Church on 15 February 1977 but the very next day the Baptists dismantled it. The determined Catholic youth put up another Church within a day at another place and named it as 'Christ King Church.' On the occasion of the solemn blessing of the Church thirteen families accepted the Catholic faith. A new Church was constructed and it was blessed on 8 April 1977. The spiritual guidance and missionary zeal of Fr. Mathew Keemattam and determination and faith of the seven young men were factors responsible for the establishment of the Church at Chomi.

3.6.4 Mission to the Pochuris and to the Chakhesangs

The Catholic Church's contact with the Pochuri tribe was accidental. Meluri, the headquarter of the Pochuris was only a resting place for Fr. Castelino, whenever he went to Kohima or Dimapur from Kiphire. One day in the year 1973 while on his way to Kohima he had to halt at Meluri as it was evening and came across Joseph Lushai, a Catholic Officer-in-Charge (OC) stationed at Meluri, who hailed from Manipur.[57] His frequent contact and acquaintance with the OC led Fr. Castelino to speak about the Catholic Church and finally the formation of

57 Joseph Lushai hailed from Churachandpur in Manipur. Before joining the Police Department he had been accompanying Fr. Ravalico, the veteran missionary of Manipur, as his guide and interpreter during his pioneering days. He proved to be of great help to Fr. Castelino in establishing the Catholic Church and St. Xavier School in Meluri. In fact Fr. Castelino always considered him as the founder of the mission at Meluri, since he had in some way already prepared the ground for its establishment before his arrival.

the Catholic community at Meluri despite many difficulties.

One day in December 1973 when he was in Kiphire, Fr. Castelino received a message from the EAC of Meluri to meet him the following day. On his way to Meluri, he was wondering what crime he might have committed to be summoned to the EAC's court. On reaching the spot he discovered it was a meeting arranged with the public leaders of Meluri with a request to open a Catholic school. It was in fact a blessing in disguise for him as he was requested by his superiors to begin the work among the Chakhesang tribe which included Meluri. Castelino (1999) writes, "I was too happy to oblige them, as that would provide a base from which I could operate until a more permanent location was found for the mission centre, which eventually proved to be Chizami" (pg. 22). The people insisted that he start the school at the beginning of the academic year 1974 and placed two police department buildings at his disposal for the purpose. With the permission of the Bishop and his superiors the St. Xavier School, Meluri was opened on 29 February 1974. No sooner had the school opened than a threat was issued to close down the school and mission centre immediately or else the entire complex would be burnt and destroyed. With the assurance of full cooperation of the people and involvement of the civil and local administration this threat was permanently put to rest.

Rashutho, the Ex. MLA of Meluri, confided that even though he had taken the initiative to open the centre he was later accosted by the then cabinet minister Vamuzo and an MLA of Pfutsero that the former made a mistake in inviting the Catholic Church to open a school as majority of the people in the state belonged to the Baptist religion. However, he paid no attention to them as he firmly believed in the commitment of the Catholic Church in doing a great service to the people. He told the people that only the Catholic Church could provide good education and therefore, they were right in inviting him to start the school. After the establishment of the school the pastor of the Baptist Church of Meluri came to his house and prayed and requested him to send some of his children to the Baptist school and the rest to the Catholic school. He, however, did not respond either to the threat or to the request. According to him all progress and development in Meluri region owes its credit to the Catholic Church (Rashutho, Personal communication, June 2, 2012).

Encouraged by the visit and inspired by the words of Fr. Castelino, Joseph Lushai started talking about the Catholic faith to his close friend, Khazhipa Nyusuo, a sweeper/peon at his police station.[58] Khazhipa was a worker in the Naga National Army before taking up this job. He was jailed by the Indian army and on his release requested the authorities to discharge him from duty as he was physically unfit to continue. Whenever Fr. Castelino halted for the night at Joseph Lushai's

58 Khazhipa was a worker in the Naga National Army. While on duty he was caught by the Indian Army (Maratha Regiment) along with some of his friends and taken to Kohima jail, where he was kept for two years and later on taken to a jail in Orissa where he spent three years. On his return, he requested his superiors to discharge him from service as he had no more strength to carry on with his duty as he was beaten mercileesly by the army and police while in custody to extract truth from him. At the same time he said later on many army men expressed their regret over the punishment meted out to him, as many of them were Christians. They said they had to do their duty. As per his wish he was discharged from his service. Then he took up the job of a sweeper/chowkidar at police station. While on duty at the police station he encountered the new religion.

house and celebrated Holy Mass, Khazhipa was present (Khazhipa, Personal communication, June 3, 2012). One day Fr. Castelino saw a fishing net at Khazhipa's house and asked him what he did with it. In reply he said that whenever he had no work, his only hobby was to catch fish in the Tidzu River at the foot of Meluri hill. Castelino (2000) writes, "I told him then the story of St. Peter, how Peter too was a fisherman before Jesus called him to be his disciple and how Jesus had told him that from that day he would catch not fish but man" (pg. 8). Khazhipa took these words seriously and began to work for the Church from that day.

Before he could forget the bitter experiences of the jail, Khazhipa landed in an alien religion about which he knew very little since he was illiterate. Going against the tribal resolution of the Pochuris that there should be no other religion in their land other than the Baptist religion, he decided to become a Catholic. At this crucial time, he was encouraged by the assurance of two more people, Nyiluotho, his friend and Zhulatho, his brother who also decided to embrace the new faith in 1974. Outraged by the decision of these people there came a group of leaders who asked them to promise that they would abandon their new faith. Khazhipa (2000) writes, "Having declared, some leaders one day called upon us and gave us a bullet to bite and promise, that we will not take up the Catholic faith. As our stand was firm, we replied we will not turn back whether they kill or do anything" (pg.5). Against the background of these troubles and threats eleven members were baptised in January 1975 in a small church built in Meluri village at Zheterüna within the perimeter of the non-Christians. Khazhipa took the name as Khazhipa Peter. With the appointment of Fr. Frederick Menezes in April 1975, the Church activities received a new impetus and in July 1975 the first batch of the Ursuline Franciscan Sisters arrived to work in the mission. In December 1975, the Meluri centre consisting of the whole of Pochuri region with twenty three villages was identified and placed under the heavenly patronage of St. Francis Xavier.

The new community's troubles did not end there this was just the beginning. No sooner had they received baptism than they were threatened with dire consequence that their Church would be burnt down if they did not give up their faith. Besides, the pagan king asked the Catholics either to return to their former religion or to face the following: quit the village since they became Catholics against the existing traditional law of the village, pay for if the harvest failed and be responsible for any natural calamities and epidemics that would befall the people in case their God cursed them when their rituals and worship were disturbed by the worship of the Catholics. Courageously, the neophytes shifted their dwellings from their ancestral site in the village and settled in the periphery of the village, near Meluri gate. After a few days, sensing that some more pagans were planning to join the Catholic Church (Lewis, 2000), the king called for another public meeting in 1976 and again issued an order to quit the village.

To escape from the unending troubles, Khazhipa finally decided to settle down with the new community at a new place where he had his own land and soon began the Catholic exodus from Meluri village between the years 1977-78. Thus Khumiasü, the new village, three kilometers away from Meluri, down the Kohima road was founded under Meluri sub division in July 1976. With the help of the Bishop and Catholics of Chizami the new Catholic community consisting of four families of Khazhipa, Tsivütho, Nyiluotho and Kümatho managed to settle down there (Khazhipa, Personal communication, June 3, 2012).[59] On the occasion of the Silver Jubilee celebration of the village on 20 June 2012, Yitachu, Parliamentary Secretary for Tourism, Law and Justice, the Government of Nagaland said, "It was not only celebrating the recognition of twenty five years of the village but a celebration of history as Khumiasü happened to be the first Catholic village in Pochuri tribe" ("Yitachu Graces Silver Jubilee of Khumiasü Village", 2012, June 22). After the mission centre in Meluri many sub- stations were opened in subsequent years. In May 1979, six families of Laphori embraced the Catholic faith. In the beginning of 1998, a small community was formed in Old Thewati Village with three families. Later in the year the whole village accepted the Catholic faith. Akhegwo, village with seven families came over to the Catholic Church on 29 October 2000.

While Fr. Castelino was in Meluri, he engaged himself preparing a permanent base of operations at Chizami which is 80 kilometers from Kohima. On 31 July 1974 Chizami was made the main centre/parish in Chakhesang area and Meluri was made its first sub-centre. In 1974, it had only five villages including Zhamai with a community of 300 people who were proud of having with them the first martyrs of their faith

59 At the front side of the residence of Khazhipa reads a sign board as 'Residence, First Catholic.' The first baptised Catholics, according to the order are Khazhipa, Nyiluotho, Zhulatho, Seküsü and Silatho and their families. Later, Silatho was sent for touring catechist training to Imphal (John Poji, personal communication, June 12, 2012).

(Coelho, 1984). The sparkle of faith reached Chizami through Tsilito Peter who had a friend in Zhamai who explained to him the Catholic faith. He in turn encouraged many of his friends and they accepted the Catholic faith. In the beginning, all those who joined the Catholic Church were not rich or educated (Puro, Personal communication, June 5, 2012). A few people from Mezhulomi, a village under Chizami expressed their desire to become Catholics and soon a community was formed. With the establishment of Sacred Heart School at Chizami and the arrival of the UFC Sisters helped to speed up the mission work among the Chakhesangs.

Thenyizumi is one of the villages of Chakhesang settlements in Phek district, 57 kilometers away from Kohima. The news of the persecution of seven men in Zhamai at the hands of the undergrounds for accepting the Catholic faith had its influence on Dusayi, an Agricultural Inspector from Thenyizumi who decided to become a Catholic. He and his family were baptised on 13 April 1969. In the year 1979, the Jesuit priests took over this center from the Salesian priests, and Fr. Bostu Sebastian took care of the people. With the help of the Catholic members of Thenyizumi and Zhyoti Mark, the touring catechist, communities were formed in neighbouring villages like K-Basa, Yoruba, Thevopisumi, Chozuba Town, Sakrumi and Chetaba Town. Sisters of the Holy Cross came in 1984 to work in the mission. The administration of this center was handed over to the Missionary Society of St. Francis Xavier (SFX) in October 1994. As requested by the people a school was opened at Pfutsero in 1986. The Daughters of Mary Help of Christians (FMA) arrived in August 1999, to continue the apostolic and educational works.

3.6.5 Mission among the Zeliangrongs

The parishes of Jalukie, Peren and Tenning are situated among the Zeliangrong tribes in Peren District. The name 'Zeliangrong' is a combination of three kin tribes: Zemeis, Liangmeis and Rongmeis. These three kin tribes decided to merge into one with the name 'Zeliangrong'. Leangmei means 'north', Rongmei means 'south' and Zemei means 'border.' The Zeliangrongs, particularly the Zemeis had much contact with the Kacharis who ruled from Dimapur and later from Maibong. A large number of Zemeis live scattered among the Kacharis. Thus, the Zeliangrongs have been spread over three states: Western Manipur, North Cachar in Assam and Jalukie area in Nagaland. Diphu and Lumding are supposed to be Zeliangrong names.

One Jadunang of Nungkao village in the Tamenglong area in the state of Manipur started a new faith in 1925, it came to be known as the Heraka cult. He rallied round him a big number of followers from among the Zeliangrongs ("The Empire of the Zeliangrong", 1985).[60] Jadunang declared himself as the

60 The Zeliangrong people were, perhaps, the only group of people who were opposed to any alien influences. The "Heraka Cult", a socio politico religious movement was an innovation of Jadonang to promote unity among the Zeliangrong people. This cult began as a revivalist socio-religious reform to revitalise the traditional Zeliangrong religion by abolishing irrelevant superstitions and obscure practices and thus to integrate the three tribes into one people. Haipaou Jadonang was born in a Rongmei family in 1905 at Kambiron (Puiron) village. He claimed himself as the 'Messiah' of the Zeliangrong people. As a young British soldier he was sent to Mesopotamia during First World War. British came to know of the power and influence of Jadonang's movement and so sensing a threat to their superiority he was arrested and falsely implicated in a murder case of four Manipuri traders and after a mock trial he was executed on 29 August 1931 at Imphal. The Zeliangrong movement assumed with the imprisonment of Jadonang for prophesying the end of British Raj. Today Heraka Cult is in alliance with Ramakrishna Mission (The empire of the Zeliangrong", 1985).

'messiah' of his people. The new cult had a great influence on the social, political and religious life of the people of the area. Even now there are people who practise this faith and are at times quite opposed to Christianity.

In the year 1964 Namgaheing Iheilung, invited Fr. Joseph Felix to open a Catholic school at Peren.[61] Soon after Fr. Felix's visit, Namgaheing went personally to Dibrugarh and invited Bishop Hubert to pay a visit to Peren. Complying with the request the Bishop visited Peren in January 1965 with Fr. Felix (Mao, 1970). He had a meeting with Ikising, the head Dubashi, the government officials, elders and Gaon Bura and discussed the religious, educational and cultural life of the people. The Bishop assured the gathering of his fullest cooperation in opening a school even though some present there were aggressive at his visit. When he stepped forward to shake hands with them they insulted him in public saying, "We never shake hands with a dog," reports Namganheing in his A.Z.C.C. souvenir (Parenkulangara, 1999, pg. 12). Mao

---

61 Namgaheing was a non-Christian at the time he invited Fr. Felix. It took him nearly four decades to receive baptism from Fr. Mani. He insisted that he would receive baptism from Fr. Mani if the latter was willing to come over to Jalukie from Manipur. Soon after the baptism (July 29, 2001), in the company of his children, grandchildren, Bishop Jose Mukala, and other guests he said that he was a very happy man (personal communication, Fr. Jose Edassery, parish priest, July 30, 2012).

The Council was the sole representative of the people and it not only played the role of socio-economic development but was also responsible for bringing peace among the people of the area. At that time there were two groups of insurgents commonly known as the undergrounds and the Kampai's activists. The Kampai's group was led by Rani *Gaidinliu* . These two factions, particularly in the Zeliang area, had their ideological differences resulting in much loss of precious lives. But due to active participation and cooperation given from the Council members under the leadership of Namgaheing, the state government could bring down the insurgency caused by these groups in a record time which was considered a great achievement (Asiho, 1970, p. 9).

(1970) writes, "The next morning Bishop celebrated his 'first mass' in the new soil at my residence and my two children Pauline Asosa and Anthony Kholi were given baptism" (pg. 4).

The school began with the coming of Fr. Felix's brother Bony and his wife Ivi, after having made them resign from their lucrative jobs at TELCO, Jamshedpur. So, the first Catholic School in the Zeliangrong region of Nagaland was opened in March 1965 under the name "All Saints' Home Cambridge School", in Ikising's building. It began with much hope but to the despair of many it started with barely thirty students and to counter the Catholics, the Baptists started the Baptist English School. Despite the obstacles, Bony and his wife worked hard and did their duties marvelously and people even today speak marvelously of the "Bonnie-Period" ("St. Paul's Parish Peren", 1985, pg. 2).

Though the Catholic presence had been there in Peren since 1965, it was only from 1974 that serious efforts in evangelisation began. Mathew Chandi, the touring catechist of Jalukie parish, sent by Fr. Mani Parenkulangara, the parish priest of Jalukie, initiated the mission. The first person to receive baptism from the Peren area was Peulu Franky who was baptised on 31 January 1974 at Dibrugarh ("St. Paul's Parish Peren", 2005). The spark of faith lighted by Vikietuo and his family helped the Church grow in the town. Rachi Richard and Athong Michael, two trained catechists of the parish played a significant role in establishing and strengthening the Peren mission which included six substations. On 2 March 1980, Bishop Abraham raised the Peren mission, until then a sub-station of St. Xavier's parish, Jalukie, to the status of a parish and named it St. Paul's Parish. The parish was entrusted to the care of the MSFS priests and Fr. Kurian Pattimackal was appointed the first parish priest. On 14 July 1980, the Congregation of the Mount Carmel Sisters arrived at Peren to work in the mission.

During the visit of Fr. Felix to Peren in 1964, three elders of Tenning village extended an invitation to start a mission there. All the Liangmei villages of Nagaland are situated in the southernmost part of Nagaland and there are seven villages in all. Tenning is the centre of the Liangmei tribals ("Tenning mission", 1985). Fr. Mani and Mathew Chandy evangelised this area and with the baptism of Athong Michael and Ramka Peter in 1974 the Catholic Church in Tenning took its roots. A school was opened in 1981. This mission was also entrusted to the MSFS priests. The Congregation of the Mount Carmel Sisters arrived at the centre in 1987. Due to the influence of the Heraka Cult it was not easy for Christianity to penetrate this area. Apart from the Baptists and other Christian groups, the Catholic communities of this area had to face opposition from the followers of the Heraka cult. Neverthless, the conversions were from the followers of the Heraka cult rather than from the Baptist groups ("Tenning Mission"). Of the 20 villages in this area only eight villages namely Tenning (Town and Village), Nzau, Nchangram in Liangmei area and Nsong, Njauna, Nchan and Nkialwa in Zemei area have Catholic communities.

3.6.6 Church in Medziphema

Many of the inhabitants of Medziphema, belonging to different tribes of Nagaland, are settlers including the Catholics. Medziphema town had the visible presence of a Catholic community from the early 1960s with the migration of the families of Neivonyü Savino, Chavi-u-Xavier Sanyü and Neivihu Savino from Khonoma village. The first recorded baptism at Medziphema was on 5 May 1964 when Megovotuo Petrus son of Neivihu was baptised by Fr. Joseph Felix. It was followed by a few more baptisms in the same year. However, the community didn't grow as expected. The majority of these early Catholics of Medziphema, had gone back to the Baptist church for reasons best known to them ("Catholic Mission Medziphema Parish", 2003). Perhaps it was the occasional pastoral visit of Fr. Felix and care from Kohima that helped the community which was almost a non-entity, remain afloat without much of a significant presence.

A new lease of life was given to the community at Medziphema by a group of widowed Catholic women from the place, namely Neisoü Whiso Elizabeth, Neiphenuo Rachael, Mekhrienuo, Khrieketulie-ü, Yievizo-ü, Tunuo, Vitsonuo Sara, and Khekhonuo Martha, who came together for Sunday services in some selected homes from the early part of 1970. From this time onwards priests from Dimapur parish also started caring for the community. Religious education imparted especially to children at this time by Neilhusalie Hubert of Kohima Village, who attended Co-operative training at Medziphema deserves appreciation. Significant contributions made by touring catechists Kenneth, Vikhor Francis and Keniselie Dominic helped the growth of the parish. A small Church was built and blessed on 15 December 1974 and this centre was entrusted to the MSFS priests and Providence Sisters. On 28 February 1978 a Home Science training centre for girls was opened. In February 1979, SFS School was inaugurated with the enrollment of 72 children. To foster local vocations, the SFS seminary was inaugurated on 4

November 1988. The apostolic spirit led to the establishment of communities at different places including Kukidolong, New Socünoma, Ruzaphema, Ruzaphema Block III, Punglwa, Gaili, Piphema, Pherima etc.

3.6.7 Creation of the New Diocese of Kohima-Imphal

The increase in the number of Catholic members and institutions, vast territory and the need to provide effective pastoral care prompted the decision to bifurcate the Diocese of Dibrugarh. Hence the suggestion to divide the Diocese was given approval and the new Diocese of Kohima-Imphal was created on 29 January 1973. Abraham Alangimattathil, the then Vicar General of the Diocese of Dibrugarh was appointed its first Bishop.[62]

62 Bishop Abraham was born on 11 July 1933 at Paika, Kerala, India into a traditionally Catholic family, as the youngest of seven children. After his middle schooling at home town he joined the Salesian aspirantate at Sonada, Darjeeling. He joined the novitiate at Yerccaud, Tamilnadu in 1953 after his high school studies. It was followed by his philosophical studies at sonada and did his regency in Don Bosco, Shillong. At two places, Mawlai in Meghalaya and Kotagiri in Tamilnadu he did his theological studies. After his studies he was ordained a priest on 2 December 1964, during the International Eucharistic Congress in Bombay. As a priet he worked as administrator of Don Bosco School Dibrugarh, headmaster of St. Anthony's High School, Shillong, Rector of Don Bosco Dibrugarh and Vicar General of the Diocese of Dibrugarh (1970-73).

The Diocese was given the name of the two capitals of the states as is the tradition of the Catholic Church. One of these two capitals would house the diocesan headquarters. Initially it was decided that it would be located at Kohima. Manipur Catholics objected to the idea because the number of Catholics in Manipur was far more than that of Nagaland. To have the diocesan offices at Imphal would also have created some adverse reactions from the Catholics of Nagaland. Rome was consulted. It decided temporarily to locate the Bishop's House at Dimapur, the bustling town and railhead of Nagaland plains (A Brief History of the Catholic Church in Nagaland, p. 83). It was found that Dimapur would be accepted by both the States though being in Nagaland but having its original name as 'Manipur Road.' But Rome insisted that as soon as it was convenient the headquarter should be shifted to Kohima (The Church in Kohima, by Bishop Abraham).

He was installed as Bishop on 13 October 1973 at Don Bosco School ground, Kohima village with all its tribal setting, by the Apostolic Pro-Nuncio, Most Reverend John Gordon. With the creation of the new Diocese and appointment of the new Bishop the Catholic Church in Nagaland entered into a new era of development in the pastoral, educational, medical and educational fields. Again on 29 June 1980, the Diocese was further divided into Diocese of Kohima and the Diocese of Imphal.

3.6.8 Mission among the Konyaks

Konyaks are the inhabitants of Mon District in Nagaland. They belong to two different major linguistic groups - the Upper Konyak and the Lower Konyak. Though they are the biggest tribe of Nagaland they are the most backward of the people of Nagaland. Their dialects differ from village to village. The first contact the Catholic Church had had with this tribe was at Tobu which falls under the Upper Konyak region. This region has a dialect that is almost entirely different from either of these two groups. The Church extended its service to this tribe in 1976. In the words of Puthussery (1978), the first resident priest at Tobu:

> It is to this politically hot, socio-economically under developed, culturally fertile, religiously volatile, medically helpless and educationally backward area that the Catholic Church has taken a daring leap by the opening of the upper Konyak Catholic mission with its headquarter at Tobu with one priest and five sisters engaged in religio-socio-medico, educational activities sponsored by them (pg. 2).

The first recorded entry of a Catholic missionary into the Upper Konyak region was in 1969 when Fr. Lucien Miranda stationed at Tuensang toured this area from 21 to 27 February 1969. In total he visited six villages, namely: Changlangshu, Monyakshu, Yei, Yonghong, Kenchenshu, and Chingnyu. With the exception of Changlangshu village, the people in other villages were quite indifferent and did not welcome his suggestion to take some boys to the boarding-house at Tuensang. They were as unfriendly as they had been to the first Baptist missionaries. The people of Minyakshu were quite surprisingly anti-Baptist, highly superstitious and were inclined toward black-magic. Fr. Miranda mentioned in the chronicle of St. Thomas Church Tuensang 1965-1971, that there was great scope for the Church in Changlangshu and Minyakshu.

The first acquaintance with the Konyak people was made possible through five Konyak students from Tobu studying at St. John's School Tuensang. In the chronicle of St. Teresa's convent, Tobu, we read, "The first acquaintance with Konyak people was through the students of St. John's School (Tuensang). There were five Konyak students studying in the school. They were quite smart and well behaved students. This encouraged us to get into contact with them." Consequently the invitation to open the mission centre came from the parents of those students. The Head Dubashi, Kussam Samniok, whose son Anden was a student at St. John's, one day met Bishop Abraham and expressed his displeasure over the priests' failure to visit Tobu. In his own words, "Fathers don't like us, they don't like our tribe" (Puthussery, Personal communication, April 25, 2012). Fr. Devassy asked Kussam to convene a meeting of all the leaders of the Upper Konyak region to discuss the possibilities of opening a Catholic centre. In the meeting held on 14 December 1974 in which Fr. Devassy and Sisters Rose Teresa and Blessilia were present, they said that they wanted a Catholic mission. On 14 January 1975, all the public leaders of Tobu Circle together with Anden Konyak, MLA of Moka constituency signed the resolutions for inviting the Catholic mission among the Upper Konyaks (Augustine, 2003). When Anden Konyak submitted the resolutions he wrote to Bishop Abraham, "We are eagerly awaiting your arrival here to open the eyes of this backward area people" (Cheruseril, 2001, pg. 5). Kussam, while addressing Bishop Abraham during his visit to Tobu on 4 May 1975 expressed the hope that the Catholic Church would show the people of Tobu the way to progress.

The assembly of the public leaders of the Upper Konyaks and the people of the Tobu Circle adopted another resolution on 5 May 1975 in the presence of Bishop Abraham. They resolved, "That the Catholic missionaries be given fullest freedom to preach, propagate and practice the Catholic faith in the entire area" (Cheruseril, 2001, pg. 5).[63] Accordingly on 10 February 1976, Fr. Devassy together with Sisters Mary Punnathanam, Jane Mary Kaithakary and Mercy Kottiyani

---

63 There was a set of sixteen written resolutions passed and signed by Mr. Khamba the Head G.B and Mr. Kussam the Head D.B. As the first step towards knowing the people Fr. Devassy decided to have a survey conducted in the area. He undertook the tour of the area from 6 to 17 June 1975 consisted of Dr. (Sr.) Marina MBBS, Sr. Therese MMS, catechist John Yesong, seminarian Kirimong and a person from the Gandhi Peace Centre at Tuensang. They surveyed Changlanshu, Monyakshu and Tobu. Both the MMS and SABS congregations were pleased with the place and the future prospects and so agreed to spare personnel for the mission at Tobu (Catholic Church, Tobu, Nagaland, silver Jubilee 1976-2001, p. 5).

of the Medical Mission Sisters (MMS) and Sisters Blessilia and Celine Jose of the Sisters of the Adoration of the Blessed Sacrament (SABS) arrived at Tobu to begin the mission. This centre was officially erected on 1 March 1976 and on the same day Newman School was inaugurated with 35 students in the Area Council Hall at Tobu Town. In the words of Karinthayil (2001), one of the priests who worked there:

> No mission in Nagaland has started with similar co-operation from people. The public leaders put all their resources at the disposal of the mission. The jeep of Mr. Anden MLA, the residence of Dobashi Kussam and the resources of the village of Tobu were given by Mr. Khamba, the Gaon Bura of Tobu. It is not just Tobu village but all the village leaders of Upper Konyak area came to the support of the mission (pg. 8).

The Sisters were engaged both in educational and healing ministry. The healing ministry proved to be a great blessing for the people as hundreds of them began to flock to the dispensary from far and near. There was still another invitation from the public leaders of Monyakshu village on 30 April 1976 to start the Catholic mission with an assurance of absolute freedom to propagate Catholic faith. However, there were strong objections to Catholic faith from the Konyak Union, the Konyak Students' Union and the underground. Besides, the Ao pastors who evangelised the Konyaks and many other tribes had levelled several allegations against the Catholics such as going to their school or getting treated at their dispensary were sins, the Catholics had crucified Jesus etc. Chungo Thomas Lempa, catechist of the Tobu Catholic mission said that soon after accepting Catholic faith he started receiving threats from the apex bodies of the Konyak tribe and the underground who asked him to resign from the job of a catechist of the parish and to close down the Catholic Church (Lempa, personal communication, December 30, 2006).[64] There were some leaders like Jackson, Vincent Homang and Peter Neamnei who worked hard against all sorts of threats and calumny even before they received the Catholic faith. While Vincent Homang and Francis Wanmai were doing their Teacher Training Course at Phesama, they were offered government jobs by the then minister, Yothen Konyak. This offer was made to prevent them from becoming Catholics because Yothen heard that these two were exhorting people to become Catholics. Vincent was offered an LDA post at Secretariat while Francis in the Agriculture Department in Aboi. If both were located at two different places they would be dissuaded from becoming Catholics (Homang, personal communication, December 30, 2006).

Jackson's story is different from others regarding his

---

64 Chungo Thomas is the catechist of the Catholic Church, Tobu from 1984 till date. The apex bodies of the Konyak tribe compelled the underground to close down the Catholic Church in Tobu. Consequently, Chungo received a letter from the underground to resign from the pastor's (catechist) job. But he had the support of the priests and his family who told him to stand firm and nothing to be afraid of as he was doing only God's work. Later on Fr. Peter Chinnappan, the parish priest sent a delegation to the underground leader seeking explanation for their threat to the catechist. The leader said that he did it on the pressure of the public. He assured the delegation that thereafter the Catholic Church had nothing to worry about and that the Catholics were free to visit villages, open schools and if anybody wanted to become Catholics they could do so (personal communication, Chungo Thomas, 30 December 2006).
Peter Neamnei told he too received threat from Konyak associations and so he met the underground leaders three times. He courageously told them he was ready to die for his faith (personal communication, 31 December 2006).

conversion to Catholicism. There was a serious problem between the Konyaks and the Changs of Tobu village. The Baptist Church of 'A Khel' insisted that all those who went to the Baptist Church should become Changs. At this Jackson took some twenty people from the 'A Khel' and met Fr. Chacko Karinthayil and discussed the matter of becoming Catholics as they were forced to change from one tribe to another. They started visiting the families of non-Christians and encouraged them to become Catholics (Jackson, personal communication, December 31, 2006). On 7 October 1984, the mission bore its first fruits in the Upper Konyak area at Tobu, when about a hundred and thirty five people accepted the Catholic faith. Moreover, on this day Bishop Abraham laid the foundation stone of the Holy Redeemer Church, Tobu.

On 13 May 1988, the Catholic community of Mopong came to exist with the baptism of a hundred and thirty three people and Hongkong Christ School was opened there. The Angjangyang mission was started at the initiative of three villages, Changlang, Jakphang and Angphang. In January 1993, they had collectively decided to start a new model village, a Catholic village, and requested the Catholic Church to start a school with a promise that whoever came to that village would become a Catholic. On 25 January 1994, fifty four adults from thirty families received baptism. Thus, the Catholic community was inaugurated and a primary school was opened. It is to be noted, however, that no one from Jakphang village became Catholic even though their leaders too participated in the meetings of the three villages (Augustine, 2003). Later, the Konyak Baptist Bumeinok Bangjum (KBBB), the apex body of the Konyak Baptist Churches started a Baptist Church and a Mission school in the new village with many incentives like low tuition fees, hostel facilities and admission and books on credit to the students.

Forgetting all the previous resolutions passed by the leaders of various villages that there was no objection to starting the Catholic Church in the respective villages, the Konyak Union started issuing threatening letters to the Catholic Church. The Catholic Church at Tobu received innumerable letters of such sort asking the Catholics to go back to Baptist Christianity. When the Church initiated a plan to open a mission centre at Pessao village at the request of the people in 2011, again there was a threat.

Mon town is the headquarter of the Konyak tribe. The earliest contact the Catholic Church had with the Lower Konyak area was when Fr. T. J. Chacko from Tuensang visited Mon from 5 to 7 October 1970. The ADC of Mon welcomed him but told him the following day that some local Baptist leaders had objected to his visit and therefore, he had to get permission from the field director at Wakching. Fr. Chacko told him, however, that he didn't want the permission of the Baptist leaders to tour Nagaland. The Chronicle of St. Thomas Church, Tuensang 1965-1971 mentions that his next move was to Mon village where he met with the King who had more than thirty wives and fifty children. The King was quite indifferent apparently because he wasn't presented with any gifts. So the King told him he had nothing to do with him. One consolation Fr. Chacko had from the King after meeting him was that the latter said he would send some of his children to the school at a later date. Fr. Chacko said, the King of Chui, who had thirty six wives, was, however, welcoming even though he met him on his way to the field for hunting. Then, he visited Wakching Town, Wakching Village and Thonkai. The impression he had on the visit to these villages was that the people were indifferent, unconcerned, non-cooperative and most unreliable.

There were a number of times people of Mon town requested Bishop Abraham to start a school at Mon and he thought it as an opportunity to begin evangelisation work among them. Accordingly, on 6 July 1976 along with Fr. Mathew Pulingathil, the Salesian Provincial visited Mon and met with Chingai Konyak, the leading man in Mon Town Committee, whose children had been studying at Catholic schools in Dibrugarh. He showed him two plots of land to choose from and the latter chose the one on the Mon-Tobu Road. However, the Baptist pastors compelled the Town Committee to give away the land to the Border Road Department and the other was disposed off. Later on, in 1980, another request was made to the Bishop and as such a delegation consisting of the Bishop, Fr. Mathai Kochuparambil, the Provincial of Guwahati, Fr. John the Economer, and Fr. Bianchi went to Mon to meet the mediator but were unable to meet him as he could not be traced. All, except Fr. Bianchi came away, who decided to remain until he met the person and was successful in doing so after 12 days. A meeting was arranged with the headman and the elders of Mon town and it was agreed that the mission would buy thirty acres of land on the Sonari Road (Arokiasamy, 2005). On 10 June 1980, the first group of missionaries, Fr. Peter Bianchi and Fr. Justin Lyngkhoi came to Mon to begin their work. The Church bought, 'The English Medium School' which ran up to Class VI, belonging to Chingai at a price of Rs. 20,000/ and renamed it as 'Don Bosco School, Mon.' In the year 1981 Bishop Abraham invited the Sacred Heart sisters to work in Mon. The people were, however, hostile to the Catholic mission. In the words of Fr. Bianchi, "I had some hopes when I went there, but I was very disappointed by the time I left with regard to our work there" (Bianchi, 2005, p. 8). On 2 October 1997, eleven families were received into the Church in Aboi by Fr. Abraham Kaduthodil but there is no trace of the Church today.

It is true that the Catholic Church managed to establish a school at the District Headquarters of the Konyak tribe. The Church, however, faced unfriendly approach from some Konyak associations as they wanted everyone to strictly follow their slogan 'one tribe, one religion.' The majority of the Catholic community of Mon town is originally from the Tobu area. The first Catholic families of Mon town who hailed from Tobu since 1980 had to face silent condemnation. (Liangen, personal communication, June 20, 2012.

What is more surprising is, they are not against other denominations like Revival churches or Jehovah Witnesses but only the Catholic Church. The threat against the Catholic Church is also a fundamental violation of the freedom of religion in a democratic country. The presence of different churches in a locality is a reality to be accepted.

3.6.9 To the Aos

Repeated requests from some of the Ao past pupils of St. Anthony's College, Shillong to establish a Catholic School at Tuli was given a serious thought despite opposition from the pastors of the Baptist Church. To counter their request for fear of being converted to the Catholic faith, the Baptists soon opened a school and named it 'Koinonia.' The past pupils, however, argued with the leaders of the Baptist Church, that even though they studied at a Catholic institution they did not become Catholics nor was there any pressure from any quarter to become Catholics.

When a delegation of past pupils again approached Bishop Abraham with a request, he thought it as an opportunity to reach out to the Ao tribe. As the Salesian Provincial was not interested in starting a school at Tuli when Bishop requested him, the latter approached Fr. Thomas Panakezham, the Regional of the Salesians who was on his maiden visit to the province, to let the Provincial agree to his request so that the school would remain a memorial of his visit to the province. During the visit of the Bishop to Tuli along with Fr. Mathew Pulingathil, the Provincial and Fr. Porcu Mario in September 1978, the leaders of Tuli promised freedom of evangelisation in their area and promised them that if their children expressed desire to become Catholics they could do so. However, soon after the establishment of the school the Church became aware of the hidden agenda of the people, that what they actually wanted was a Catholic school and not the Catholic Church.[65] The initial plan of the priests to stay at Jorhat and look after the school until a Catholic community was formed at Tuli was abandoned because of the insistence of the people that

65 On 30 August 1995 Mr. Paul Hongmo and family were received into the Church. He was a pastor in Mon village for ten years. He had some misunderstanding with the members of his Church; so decided to become a Catholic. But he was not a genuine person and so later went back to the Baptist Church (Mattappally, the Institutions in the Salesian province of st. Francis De Sales Dimapur, p. 244).

a priest should stay at the school premises. On 8 December 1977, Fr. Tom Karthik took charge of the centre and took his residence in the house of Mar Temjen, opposite the Paper Mill office in Tuli Town. Two rooms of the ground floor of the same building were converted and two classes were opened (Karthik, 2002) and the classes started in February 1978. From the very beginning, the Tuli mission had to face numerous troubles from the people of the area. No sooner had the priests begun the construction of the school at the new site than the problems cropped up one after another, such as demands to award contract to the land owners, exchange of a portion of campus land with land outside campus, increase in the rent, encroachment of land, cessation of work, etc. However, the priests continued to run the school with the constant interference and intimidation from the people.

Mokokchung town had the privilege of having its first Catholic School in the year 1979. The contact with the Aos dates back to October 1954, when Fr. John Larrea of Golaghat celebrated the first Mass for a small floating Catholic population of Mokokchung town. In the 1960s and 1970s, the Church had been making some contacts with the town folk through one Varkey, SDO in Public Works Department (PWD) and one Bernadette Lama, teacher at Model English School. Both of them offered their places for the missionaries passing through Mokokchung. Lama's rented house in Aongza ward served as the chapel. Sebastian (1994) writes:

> The history of the Catholic Church at Mokokchung is practically the history of the Catholic school. As early as 1965, public leaders like Mr. N. I. Jamir had requested Bishop Hubert Rosario of Dibrugarh Diocese, to open a

Catholic school at Mokokchung. In the second half of 1978, Fr. S. Coelho S. J. came to explore the possibility of opening a school there. By the beginning of 1979, the public at Mokokchung felt the urgent need to open a Catholic school and an Ad-hoc committee was formed with Mr. Kariba MLA, as chairman, Mr. M. Bendangnukshi as secretary and the following as members: Mr. A. Shanmugan, IAS, DC, Mr. Tali Longkumer, SDO, Mr. Imchalemba MLA, Mr. Takoyaba MLA, Mr. Imtimeren MLA, Mr. S. I. Sungit, Mr. Apong Pongener, Mr. Tokishe Sema, Mr. Tinuwati, Mr. L. Chuba Pongener, Mr. T. Chuba Walling, Dr. T. Walling, Mr. Tsukungpokba, Prof. Jongshi, Mr. Bendangmayang Longkhum and Mr. Temsu Kietzar. The united move by the public leaders, the government machinery and the civic bodies was perfectly matched by a positive response from the Catholic Church's side. Many rounds of meetings were held and the site finally selected was the present plot which was then occupied by the army. This land for the school was gifted by the Ao Mokokchung Village, from the Aotsuba Semchar and Achimbong Semchar families, with the helpful mediation of Mr. Maputemjen Ao as the landowner's main representative (pg. 4).

The Queen Mary School Mokokchung was thus opened on 21 May 1979 by Fr. Stanislaus Coelho on behalf of the Diocese of Kohima. As in many places, here too the people offered the Town Hall to have the classes conducted for first few months. Until Fr. Joseph Alancheril, the first resident priest took charge of the school in December 1980, Fr. Coelho supervised it from Khuzama by visiting it occasionally. The school and administration received new life with the arrival of the Ursuline Sisters on 27 January 1981.[66] Recommending the recognition of this school, A. Shanmugam IAS, the then Deputy Commissioner, wrote to the Education Department that the Queen Mary's School, "has come up due to the popular upsurge of the people and public leaders to have a Catholic School in Mokokchung town" (Abraham, 1992, pg. 2). In 1982, Fr. Joseph opened a school at Changki but due to unavoidable circumstances it was closed down.

Some of the ex-service men of Chungtia village approached the Catholic Church at Mokokchung for a school in 1981. While they were on duty at different places in the country they came to know of the Catholic faith. When they approached Bishop Abraham, he told them that without a Catholic community to support the school he would not start one. So, under the leadership of Hengen, a signature campaign was undertaken but many of the ex-service men decided not to cooperate. So, the Council Chairman Sunang Senangshiba requested that for the sake of the school a few people who were ready could become Catholics, otherwise there would be clashes between the Churches (Michael, Personal communication, January 6, 2007).

From the very beginning Hengen had expressed his desire to become a Catholic and the Village Council had no objection but forbade him to canvass more people to be converted to Catholicism. On 6 January 1983, twenty nine members came

---

66 The Ursuline Sisters under the leadership of Sr. Frieda worked tirelessly for the uplift of the school. Sr. Frieda was conferred the prestigious National Award for Teachers on 5 September 1992, by the President of India, Dr. Shankar Dayal Sharma.

forward to join the Catholic faith. On 7 August 1983, Bishop Abraham officiated at the baptism ceremony of the new converts amidst a large gathering of priests, sisters and faithful from various parishes of the Diocese. On this day, the first Ao Catholic community was born" (Sebastian, 1994, pg. 6). As per the wishes of the people, Christ King School was inaugurated on 12 February 1983.

On 29 March 1984, the Ao Baptist Arogo Mungdang (ABAM), the apex body of the Ao Baptist Church asked the Catholics to give up their faith as it did not favour the establishment of the Catholic Church. On 5 April 1984, the ABAM once again issued a threat to them to return to their fold by 31 July 1984 or else face consequences including being ostracised from the village (Ao, 2007). In reply, the Catholic Association of Nagaland (CAN) through its president R. Rocus Chasie sent a three member delegation to Chungtia (Chasie, June 8, 1984) encouraging the community to remain firm in their faith.

On 17 February 1984, Mother Teresa, accompanied by Bishop Abraham, visited Mokokchung at the invitation of the Bishop, the Rotary Club and the people of Mokokchung. Shri Mayangnokcha, the first graduate among the Aos and Mokokchung's most illustrious educationist, welcomed Mother Teresa on behalf of the public.

Later Mother inaugurated the Mother Teresa Home for the orphans and the disabled at Khensa (Sebastian, 1994). St. Joseph's School at Khensa was opened on 28 February 1987 with the Sisters of the Adoration of the Blessed Sacrament to look after the same. A small community under Queen Mary Parish, Mokokchung was formed at V.K. Town, consisting of members from the Sema tribe on 18 June 2000.

3.7 To the Semas

Coinciding with the request of the then Governor of Assam for the Sisters' help at the Naga Hospital, Kohima, in 1948, a group of past pupils of St. Edmund's College, Shillong from the Sema tribe who were already baptised as Catholics, appealed to the administration to grant permission to the Catholic priests to work in the Naga Hills. As it failed to comply with their request, they submitted a memorandum to the Secretary for Tribal Areas, the Government of Assam at Shillong with a renewed appeal. The following is the letter/memorandum submitted by them, dated 15 August 1951 (Chronicle 1951-1954, Archbishop's House, Shillong).

They had been appealing to the Church headquarters at Shillong unceasingly for the priests to be sent to instruct them in faith. The Church may have had its own constrains, for not responding positively to the repeated requests. The people of Akuluto range, however, sent another letter expressing their earnest desire to accept the Catholic faith if a priest was sent to them. How earnest they were in their quest is shown in the following letter.[67]

67 V.C. Khutovi, Head Gaonboora of Shichimi Village and Chairman of Shichimi Village Council, under Akuluto in Zunheboto District, who studied at Don Bosco School, Shillong from 1953-1957 said that the three signatories namely, K. Shikhu, H.S. Asumi and H.Khulu died long ago. K. Shikhu from Aochakilimi village became a circle Officer at Lumami and died in late 1950's. H.S. Asumi from Litami Old Village became a business man and he also died in late 1950's. H. Khulu (Heikhu Khulu) from Naghutomi Old Village became an E.A.C. at Akuluto and died somewhere between 1965 and 1970 (Personal communication, May 23, 2012).

Akuluto M.E. School
Compound
P.O. Mokokchung
Naga Hills.

Sir,

We the people of Akuluto Range beg most humbly and respectfully to state that we have been expecting and looking forward ... the best result out of everything from you. But it is our great surprised that no attention has been paid to our ... whom we have with you by our two representatives send to you from last month.

As we have been informing you that most of the people have determined to convert if you kindly allow a priest to visit our Akuluto Range and to construct us the new faith and the way of worship. We are not yet given the last decision, but have great hope that you are trying to enter in the Naga hills also.

We beg to add, that the Govt. also given us permission to accept the new faith and informed us that the Roman Catholic may enter in the Naga Hills for the religious metter. So it is your will, whether it possible to come or not. As you know well, we the Semas are the centre in the Naga Hills and we are sure, that your faith may spread to all tribe in our places, if you possible to come. We the people are ready now to accept your faith and it is our earnest hope and we trust that you will give this metter your immediate attention.

Yours faithfully,
K. Shikhu
Secretary of Akuluto
Range.

Dated
Akuluto M.E.
School Compound
10.7.37.

... Akuluto Range.

(MEMORANDUM)

Letter No. AR/PRC/51/136,
Dated Akuluto the 15th August, 1951.

To,

The Secretary,
to the Governmnt of Assam for Tribal Areas, Shillong.

Sir,

We the Baptised Roman Catholics beg to lay down the following few facts for pur kind consideration and generous order.

That Sir, neary three years have elapsed since we asked for permission to be grated to Catholic Priests to go over the Naga Hills as well, for reaching their faith. We beg to point out to your honour that it we not through the agency of R.C. Fathers but we ourselves became onverted into R.C. religion; and now we want to acquire our knowledge both spiritually and educationally.

That Sir, it is officially learnt that the Government would permit the R.C. Prests to go over to the Naga Hills after one year only: ie after eciding the political situation of Naga Hills. It is very difficut to understant why Government should intervene in religious matter. However, we assure your honour that R.C. Priests are not coming to Naga HILLS to interfere in Naga Politics, but we want them just for religious service-ministration: in accordance with the freedom of religion granted to us under the constitution of India. Consequently, we request your honour to give permission to any R.C. Father to come to Akuluto Range of Mokokchur Sub-division, Naga Hills; for our religious service-ministration.

We shall be higly obliged if you would kindly treat it as **EXTREMELY URGENT**.

Yours faithfully,

1. K Shikhu
2. H.S. asumi
3.

On behalf of whole Akuluto Range.

Letter No. AR/PRC/51/136, dated Akuluto the 15th August, 1951.

Copy forwarded to:-

1. H.E. Bishop's Secretary, Shillong for favour of H.E. Bishop's information and necessary action. He is further requested to send one Priest to Akuluto as soon as permission is g

2. H.E. the Governor of Assam, Shillong for information and necessary action: We should be most grateful for any assistance ~~given~~ that your honour could give in this connectic

3. The Deputy Commissioner, Naga Hills, Kohima for information.

4. The Sub-divisional Officer, Mokokchung for information. (Civil).

Menchangki 16-8-6

It is learnt from the first letter that as early as 1951, a small group of Sema Nagas from Akuluto Range had obtained necessary permission from the Governor of Assam for the Catholic missionaries to enter into their area and start a mission centre.

Prior to that Andersons, the Baptist missionaries built a mission school at Aizuto in 1937. It was followed by a mass conversion movement among the Semas helped and supported by the Aos, the Lothas and the Angamis. A Sema association was formed in 1946, and a Bible School started in Aizuto in 1949 (Ponnattil, 1988). In 1948 Andersons had built a mission bungalow at Aizuto which accelerated the mission work among the Semas.

It was against this background that some Sema Nagas got permission from the administration and invited the Catholic missionaries to work among them. A strained reaction was expected from the Baptist quarters at that time against the Catholic missionarics. Scnsing dangcr at thc door, De Lano, who was in charge of the Aizuto Sema mission centre wrote to the Baptist mission in America, "Uppermost in our minds is the Roman Catholic Church" (Ponnattil, 1988, p. 42). Ponnattil (1988) writes:

> Following the Governor's green signal, the Naga Hills Church Advisory Council in its meeting at Wokha took a firm stand against the entry of the Catholic missionaries into the Sema area and communicated its 'strong resolution regarding the Roman Catholic Situation' to the Sema Tribal Counicl and to the Naga National Council. As a result, in May 1950, the Deputy Commissioner at Kohima rejected the plan of the Sema group, which had favoured the entry

of the Catholic missionaries and prevented the latter from coming to the Sema area (p. 42).

Most probably due to the strong opposition, the three Catholic members who sought permission to allow the Catholic missionaries to begin work in the Sema area kept quiet because nothing is heard about them in the later days.[68] V. C. Khutovi, the present Chairman of Shichimi Village Council, who studied at Shillong, wanted to become a Catholic and favoured the establishment of the Catholic Church in his village, brought Fr. Marocchino from Kohima to Sutemi village in 1959, but the latter had to go back due to strong opposition from the people. He expressed once again his desire to Fr. Marocchino but the latter told him that it was difficult for a single Catholic to survive in a village. Besides, Khutovi's father did not want him to become Catholic. As in most cases, the parents discourage children to follow another denomination because of social status or important positions being held in their own church or the village council. Later when he became a Gaon Bura the people requested him not to become Catholic and not to take the initiative in establishing the Catholic Church in the village (Khutovi, personal communication, May 23, 2012).

---

68 V. C. Khutovi, the present Head Gaon Bura of Shichimi village and Chairman of Shichimi Village Council, under Akuluto in Zunheboto District, who studied at Don Bosco School, Shillong from 1953-1957, said that the three signatories, namely K. Shikhu, H. S. Asumi and H. Khulu are no more. K. Shikhu, from Aochakilimi village became a Circle Officer at Lumami and died in late 1950's. H.S. Asumi from Litami Old village became a business man and he also died in late 1950's. While H. Khulu (Heikhu Khulu) from Naghutomi Old village, became an E.A.C. at Akuluto and died somewhere between 1965-1970 (Personal communication, May 23, 2012).

With these turn of events, the Catholic Church's plan of entry into the Sema area was put off for a long period of time before the Church could enter it. After a wait of two decades, the people again renewed their request during the time of Hokishe Sema the then Chief Minister of Nagaland, to start a Catholic school in his home town, Akuluto. This was made possible by the constructive efforts of Viswadel from Viswema Village who was the EAC of Akuluto and was formerly a student of Don Bosco School, Shillong. As he was much interested in the development of the people, on many occasions he told them that only a good Catholic school in their area could give their children good education (Ponnattil, 1988). With the support extended by Hokishe Sema, a school was opened at Akuluto by the Church in 1972 headed by Fr. P. K. Anthony, Principal of Don Bosco School Wokha looking after from Wokha.

As the school had not acquired a permanent site, it was conducted from the government buildings at the heart of Akuluto town. During thc timc of Fr. Devassy it was shifted to its permanent site at Sutemi village, nearly two kilometers away from the town, in 1975 that drastically brought down the enrollment. The people failed to show initial enthusiasm and the mission could not rely on the support of the villagers. As a result there were suggestions to close down the school. In 1976 when Fr. Mathew Ponnattil took charge of the spiritual needs of the Catholics scattered in Zunheboto, Sataka, Aghunato and Mokokchung, he tried to revive the school from Wokha. The boarding-house at Sutemi also served children from nearby areas and many expressed their desire to become Catholics. Bokato Robert, a boarder from Akuluto was the first Sema boy to have been received into the Catholic Church in 1982 (Ponnattil, 1988).[69]

As there were several requests made from Aghunato, Zunheboto, Atoizu etc. for a priest, Fr. M. M. Michael Sdb, a veteran missionary was appointed in charge of the Sema area and started residing at Sutemi in July 1985. Upon Fr. Michael's transfer, Fr. Job Sdb assisted by Fr. C. J. Mathew began the missionary work. Fr. N. J. Francis in the place of Fr. C. J. Mathew after one year. It was in the mind of Fr. Job to shift his residence to one of the Catholic communities as there was no Catholic community in Akuluto or in Sutemi. Besides, he could not foresee any immediate possibility of evangelisation in sight. After two years of his stay, either at the end of 1990 or beginning of 1991, just before his transfer he shifted his residence to Atoizu, where there was a small Catholic community. When he was transferred, Fr. C. J. Mathew took charge of the mission assisted by Fr. N. J. Francis. However, the non-cooperation and persistent trouble and ill-treatment meted out to Fr. N. J. Francis were reasons for the decision to move from Sutemi. Finally the priests left the place, entrusting the administration of the school at Sutemi to some teachers (Job, Personal communication, October 27, 2012). With this, the first part of the Sema mission came to an end. The school ran classes till VIII (Lhovito, Personal communication, May 22, 2012).[70]

---

69 Bokato Robert was a student of Don Bosco School Sutemi. He married a Rengma woman and was staying at Tseminyu. He was not a practicing Catholic and, therefore, left the Catholic Church (Ponnattil, The Semas and Christianity, p. 43).

70 When Fr. Michael was in Sutemi there were no Catholics in the village. The land given by one Gaon Bura, *Khekishi, was for the use of school only. After the priests had left the place Hokishe's son ran the school and he bought the school land from Gaon Bura's son. After sometime the school was given to a private individual to run but finally it was closed down (Personal communication, Lhovito Mathew, May22, 2012).*

Not discouraged by the problems and difficulties faced, the Church following persistent requests from the people once again opened the centre at Akuluto (not in Sutemi) in the year 2003. Although Hokishe Sema agreed to donate land at Sutemi where the previous school stood, he withdrew his decision at a later date. It is said that he changed his mind at the insistence of the Baptists who were residents there. The present centre has been named St. Clare Church/School Akuluto. Currently there are fourteen Catholic families, including three from Sutemi village. It is now being looked after by the Capuchins (OFM).

Some of the goodwill ambassadors of the Catholic Church from its inception in Nagaland have been district administrators and past pupils of Catholic institutions, who were not Catholics. The first attempt to have the Catholic presence at Aghunato came in 1979 from Khekiye Sema the then civil SDO of Aghunato who requested Bishop Abraham to open a Catholic centre at Aghunato (Mariadoss, 2010). Fr. Mathew Ponnattil from Wokha visited Aghunato on 13 October 1981 to assess the situation. In the public meeting that followed the people expressed their eagerness to have a Catholic school. As a response to their request Fr. Mathew said that a school was possible only if there was a Catholic community.

Fr. Mathew visited Aghunato again on 20 February 1982 after the people extended a formal invitation. He spoke to people in the Baptist Church about the Catholic Church and its mission (Ponnattil, Personal communication, September 20, 2012). He also said that the priority of the Church was to establish a Catholic community and that other institutions like a school and dispensary would follow thereafter. The people argued that a school was a means to know and study the Catholic faith (Ponnattil, 1988). Fr. Mathew enjoyed the goodwill of the Pastor whom he described as a good, learned and broadminded person who allowed him to celebrate Holy Mass in his house on the following day. The contact with the priests continued and Bishop Abraham visited the place on 14 February 1984 along with Leo Kiyelho, the touring catechist. On 6 March 1985, Fr. Mathew Pulingathil the Salesian Provincial dedicated the newly constructed Catholic Church and declared that a school up to class II will be opened and Fr. Michael would soon take care of the Sema mission. The Bishop requested Leo from Lazami, Edward from Kohima and Marcus Angami Civil SDO to instruct people in the faith from 14 March. Finally in October 1985, Fr. Michael baptised four families of Hozheto - Henry, Nitovi Michael, Kikheli, and Khekiye and thus officially the Catholic Church was brought into being in Aghunato.

The school at Aghunato is one of the rarest schools in the diocese which has seen a number of openings and closures until 1998 (Sharing, 2006). The school was closed down in 1988 because of lack of cooperation from the people but in 1989 it was reopened and ran classes from LKG to class IV. In 1989, the Church was dismantled by some miscreants when none of the members of the Catholic community were present at Aghunato. Lack of cooperation and problems created one after another by the people of the area compelled the Salesian priests to withdraw from the Sema mission including Aghunato in 1993.

In 1995, the community was placed under the care of Fr. George Parakal in Mokokchung. In 1997, the school was closed again only to reopen in 1998 with LkG and UKG classes. From

1998 to 2004, the centre was looked after by the Capuchin priests from Atoizu. In the year 2005 the Diocese bifurcated Aghunato from Atoizu and elevated it as an independent centre (Sharing, July-August, Kohima, 2006). From Aghunato, the Church branched out to Zunheboto, Viyilho (Vilo), Tokiye, Sathakata and Hugher (Huker).

Atoizu is a small township between Akuluto and Zunheboto. The one who took the lead in contacting the Church in 1983 to start a school was Lhozhevi Isaac, a retired Assam police personnel, who while on duty at different places in North-East India, had been to Catholic Churches. He was overwhelmed by the discipline and behaviour of the students of Catholic schools. On his retirement, he convinced some of his friends that they should ask the priests to start a school at Atoizu. Upon their request Fr. Michael told them a community was a must to have a school.

In the meantime, the Baptists raised objections to the establishment of Catholic institutions in the place. They also instigated the people that Catholics were worshippers of Mary and there was no salvation in the Catholic Church (Lhozhevi, Personal communication, May 21, 2012). Added to that, a group of representatives was sent to the then Education Minister, K. L. Chishi, who represented the constituency to abort the plan.

As Chishi was a student of a Catholic institution, he could explain to the people the positive contributions the Catholic Church could make for the Sema area. After Fr. Michael took charge of the Sema mission he visited the village several times and instructed the people who expressed a desire to embrace the Catholic faith. When the work seriously began, the number of households reduced from seventy four to sixteen and finally at the time of baptism in 1985 it came down further to ten. Before the Salesian society left the Sema area they had shifted the centre from Akuluto to Atoizu as the majority of the Catholics lived there.

The Church took over the 'Modern English School, Atoizu' (founded in 1974 and run by some teachers up to class IV) and renamed it as 'St. Peter's School'. The centre was given to the care of the Capuchin priests in the year 1998. It is from here that Akhuhaito village was contacted.

The third centre opened by Fr. Michael was at Satakha in the year 1985. From 1998 to 2004 this community was looked after by the Capuchin priests. Touring catechists Kiyelho Leo and Hushito David served the community from 1985. The number of Catholics in the village, however, started decreasing gradually from 2000 due to various reasons especially owing to the migration of some of its members to other places like Kohima and Dimapur ("A Brief History of St. Mary's Catholic Church at Satakha", 2010).

Since 1960, the people of Zunheboto town, the headquarters of the Sema tribe, had also been asking for a Catholic school. So Fr. Felix opened St. Paul's Home Cambridge School, Zunheboto in May 1965 on his own. In September of the same year, Fr. Bernick however, entrusted the school with R. A. D'Cruze, the headmaster, as there weren't enough priests to look after it personally.

The public through their MLA expressed displeasure by writing a complaint letter to the Bishop. Yeshito (16 July 1966) writes, "This we feel is an infringement of the agreement previously done." On being asked the reason for opening schools, Fr. Felix said that only through English education, the message of the gospel could be communicated (Felix, personal communication, December 28, 2008).[71] A community was formed in 2003. In March 2010, the parish of Aghunato was bifurcated and St. Anthony's Catholic Centre Zunheboto was made as an independent centre with Satakha as its sub-centre.

3.8 Church in the 1980s and 1990s

By the end of 1970, the Catholic Church came to be known by many in most parts of the state and a good section of the people including those from the rural areas began to enjoy the fruits of its service. Braving different accusations and allegations it went on to reach out to other areas of the state.

Lozaphuhu village, situated fourteen kilometers away from Phek district headquarters came to know of Catholic faith from Vesacho Vincent Hoshi who heard about it from his relative at Lai village in Manipur. Back home, he shared his desire for the Catholic religion with Tavehu Chizo and Veniekhu Vincent Khamo. So, on one of the Sundays in August 1980, while observing Sunday service along with their respective family members they declared themselves Catholics. On 25 December 1980, they celebrated and observed their first Christmas ("A Brief History of Catholic Church Lozaphuhu village", 2007). Chiekhutso, the then MLA of Meluri, promised that if they

71 Fr. Felix, a composer and musician could play the accordion well. People flocked to hear him play on it. He could converse well in English and some of the local dialects. He said that parents were inspired to send children to our schools. He was an itinerary missionary. People used to wonder about his movements. They used to make a comment, "he is like a helicopter-today here tomorrow elsewhere (Felix, Personal communication, December 28, 2008).

formed a community he would request priests to set up a school in the village. Accordingly Fr. Castelino and Fr. Boniface visited the village and met with the people. Their proposal to establish a Catholic school first at Phek village and then at Phek Town was rejected by the leaders and landowners on the ground that people might embrace the Catholic faith and so finally it was put up at Lozaphuhu. On 7 November 1982 fifteen members received baptism in the Catholic Church ("A Brief History of Catholic Church Lozaphuhu village", 2007).

As the years went by, many Catholics from different parts of the state started settling down in Kohima town. Seeing the urgent spiritual need of this community a small chapel of Christ King Parish was built in 1975. The Mass in this chapel, located in the house of Kevipralie Paulus at D' Block was celebrated by priests from Don Bosco School. In November 1977 the laying of the foundation stone of the present Catholic Publication Centre (CPC) building, where SFS Church is located, was done by His Eminence Lawrence Cardinal Picachy, S. J. of Calcutta, when he came for the Silver Jubilee celebration of Christ King Church. Sometime in the early part of 1980, Fr. Thomas Vattoth was appointed as the first resident priest to look after the Catholic Publication Centre and the Catholic community of Kohima Town. It was on 15 August 1980 that St. Francis De Sales Parish was officially erected with the installation of Fr. Thomas as its first parish priest (Chasie, 2005). This community had people hailing from different tribes and places. In the year 1981, Savio KG School was started. The Missionary Sisters of Mary Help of Christians have been rendering services since 1982.

The Cathedral is the mother Church of a diocese. The

term 'Cathedral,' drawn from Latin, means 'chair', the 'Church where the Bishop of a diocese resides' (Parish priest, 2008). The Catholic Cathedral of Kohima Diocese is situated high on the New Minister's Hill in Kohima, which is a parish with more than 400 families belonging to different tribes and linguistic groups. This Church was inaugurated on 14 December 1989 on the occasion of the beginning of the centenary celebration of the Catholic Church coming to North East India. The aim and scope of this Church is well expressed in the words of Bishop Abraham. "My wish and prayer in building this church... it becomes a centre of prayer ...dedicated to Mary Help of Christians ... may turn out ...to be a place of pilgrimage, seeking the help of Mary Help of Christians ("Cathedral Parish, Kohima", 1999, pg. 17). The lion's share of the three crores financial expense came from the Japanese, who wished the Church to be a place of prayer especially for the Japanese War victims who laid down their lives for their nation in the Second World War battle fought in Kohima. This is affirmed in the prayer inscribed in English and Japanese scripts in the Cathedral campus, "It is with thankfulness that we heard that Catholic Cathedral was being built at Kohima, where Mass would be offered every morning in memory of the fallen..." (Parish Priest, 2008, pg. 1).

The most controversial Church of the 1980s, dragged into allegations and counter allegations and finally led to its knocking down was the Catholic Church at Penkim in the present Kiphire district. Penkim is a village situated just below Saramati, inhabited by the Yimchunger tribe. The first contact with the village was initiated by Fr. T. J. Chacko between 1969 and 1970. Fr. Kurian Mannookhuzhy was the second priest who visited this village when he stayed two days in the army camp just above the village during his visit to the Makware refugees in Fakim village, in the first week of November 1980. Between the years 1981 and 1983, five boys and one girl were brought from the village for study as requested by their parents. John Kiutsumong ACM and Yansekiu a village master visited Fr. Kurien with a request to start a community in the village. A list of 17 names of those who wanted to become Catholics was brought to him with a request to visit the village and it was arranged for 15 April, 1983.

Accompanied by students from Penkim studying at Loyola School Kiphire and Yansekiu, Fr. Kurien set out for Penkim on 15 April. However, at the residence of John Kiutsumong in Pungro, Trongwo, the Baptist pastor of Penkim intimidated Yansekiu, and as a result John Kiutsumong refused to go with Fr. Kurian for the rest of the journey (Mannookuzhy, 1983). Fr. Kurian, however, proceeded and met those who expressed their desire to become Catholics. 15 May was fixed for the next visit. During this visit, representatives of the Catholic communities of Phelungre and Chomi, a few students and Yansekiu accompanied him. On the way, there was a heated verbal exchange with the pastor and the evangelist of Pungro Town and Pungro respectively who tried to stop them. A letter from the GBS' of Penkim was also given to Fr. Kurien, though none of them had signed it. During this visit, it was decided to have a temporary Church constructed and that the Bishop would bless it on 29 June 1983.

The leaders of Penkim requested the Catholics of Phelungre and Chomi to help them in their work. In the meeting of the village elders and public on June 14, Hilumong, the Head GB was adamant in his refusal to allow the Church to be built though GB Merumong and GB Tsepanthong were in favour of allowing people to exercise their religious freedom. On 15 June, the situation was rather tense and some people including pastor Trongwo tried to manhandle the Catholics who were clearing the site for the Church that belonged to Gaon Bura Merumong who by then was a Catholic.

As suggested by others, Trongkhiba, the ex head *Dubashi* of Pungro, one of the founders of the village was brought from Kiphire to settle the issue. Before he set out for Penkim, he met with Yimkhong Temsu, the EAC of Pungro at his residence in Kiphire and told him of his plan and sought the latter's opinion. He said, "Sir, I am going to Penkim as some people in Penkim are not allowing Catholics to put up their Church. I will try my level best to settle the issue amicably but if I am not able to do so then, what shall we do"? The EAC replied, "If there are Catholics in Penkim, then they have a right to build their Church. You see that it is done and then come back" (Mannookuzhy, 1983, pg. 2). However, before starting the construction of the Church, a complaint was lodged with the Principal of Loyola School, Kiphire by someone from Penkim village stating that the public leaders and Gaon Buras had a meeting and in the said meeting most of them expressed their displeasure about opening a Catholic mission in the village. Therefore, it was desirable to wait some more time before the materials for the construction of the Church were brought (A written petition against opening of Catholic Church in Penkim, on 4 June 1983).

The Catholics from Chomi helped in building the Church in the presence of Trongkhiba and the blessing of the Church took place on 29 June, 1983 by Bishop Abraham as planned, in the presence of Catholics from other parts of Kiphire. The chronicle of St. Paul Convent, Kiphire 1973-2010, mentioned that on this day thirty three people received baptism.

Tensions continued to mount following the baptism at Penkim and on 3 September priests and sisters were blocked at Pungro village when they were on their way to Vongti village at the invitation of the people there. From the petition filed by Fr. Kurian to the ADC dated 6 December 1983, we learn that the Yimchungru Baptist Borubo Amukhongto, the Supreme Baptist organisation was unhappy about the establishment of the Catholic Church. Its main argument was that the village would be divided on religious lines. Hence, they didn't favour the presence of the Catholic Church in Yimchunger area and decided to dismantle the Church. As per their decision, the people led by Hilumong, the head Gaon Bura Pensukin and Trongwon the pastor, dismantled the Church on 8 November 1983. This incident was the most painful and unforgetable memory for those Catholics who took initiative. For example, David Yanseki and his family were expelled from the village. However, the people did not lose heart and some of them used to go to Kiphire for instruction and got baptised there in April 1984 and again a few of them were received into the Church at Penkim later. Due to continuous pressure and threat some Catholics fled the village. In 1985, the ADC of Kiphire invited the priest and the people of Penkim to settle the cases pending before his court since 1983. The ADC stood for justice and truth and finally the case was settled in favour of the Catholic Church. As such the dedication of the re-constructed Church of Penkim took place on 14 November

1985 by Bishop Abraham. On this occasion many people received baptism. In the following year, a new Church was dedicated by the Bishop and a good number of people received baptism (Thuniyampral, 2008). The community, however, became completely disintegrated as a result of internal strife among its members.

We know it was Fr. T. J. Chacko who made the first contact with Pungro region between 28 December and 13 January 1971 accompanied by his touring companion, Joseph Kirimong. This area is inhabited by the Makhori group of the Yimchumger tribe. It was in New Minic village where tension built up due to the presence of the army and underground, that Fr. Chacko baptised Joseph Kirimong's father who was a Gaon Bura of some six villages. Then he visited Thanamir, Penkim, Salumi, Luthor, Zanger and Chomi. In Chomi, he met a boy named Chiusume, studying at Impur High School in Class X, who agreed to translate his speech. Fr. Chacko in the chronicle of St. Thomas Church, Tuensang, 1965-1971 quoted the words of Chiusume, "At Impur, children taught Catholics are not Christians; they don't teach the Bible but preach about Mary and the Pope and they follow practices like drinking, worshipping statues etc." From these villages he collected twelve boys for the boarding-house. Of all the areas he visited, according to him the Pungro area was the happiest place. People were simpler, poorer, quite dignified and much more reliable. They had interest in education and they were helpful. He suggested having a centre opened at Kiphire and from there reached out to the Pungro area to recruit more boys and through them scatter the seeds of the Catholic faith. His opinion about the boys from Pungro region proved him right when he narrated an incident. Chacko (2000) writes:

> During the June 1971 summer holidays while attending the church service at Pungro Baptist Church, the boarders from St. John's heard the pastor speaking against the Catholic Church. One of them challenged the pastor saying, "Sir, what do you know about Catholic Fathers and the Catholic Church? You were never with them. We are with them and we know who they are and how they are doing. You are telling lies. The Fathers are not like you, they don't tell lies and teach like you." The pastor had to pacify them saying that if Catholics were to come they would destroy the unity and peace of the area (p. 79).

Fr. T. J. Chacko's prophecy came true when some boys who were in the boarding-house in Tuensang took the initiative to establish the Catholic Church at Chomi. Mathew Pewsang, who studied at St. John's, Tuensang, said that when Fr. Chacko visited Chomi, children ran to meet him as they were told by people that Satan came to the village in a white cloth.[72] Towards the last part of 1970, some of the early Catholics from Chomi came and settled down in Pungro town. On 28 May 1983, Bishop Abraham visited the Catholic community at Pungro town. As the number of Catholics increased the need for a new Church was felt and on 25 October 1983

72 When Pewsang went to study at St. John's, Tuensang the people in the village told him not to go there as it was a Satan's school. Whenever he came back to the village for vacation he told his friends about Catholic faith. He was one among the seven from Chomi who was baptised at Phelungre in the year 1975. He was threatened with expulsion from the village if he did not give up his new faith (Pewsang, personal communication, July 24, 2007).

Fr. Kurien blessed the newly built Church.[73] On 22 October 1983 six people from Vongti village including the head Gaon Bura received baptism.

Fr. Kurien, sisters and some Catholic leaders from Chomi and Pungro went to Vongti village for Holy Mass on 26 November 1983. Waiting at the entrance of the village were a few people from the Baptist Church who told them to go back and they had to return as their reply did not satisfy them. On the following day, accompanied by the police Fr. Kurien went to Vongti but during the service some people shouted at them and demanded a meeting there and then. After the service, the meeting was held and Fr. Kurien tried to explain the purpose and freedom of religion. The head Gaon Bura said, "I am a Catholic and I brought the Catholic religion here. By bringing this religion I have not divided the village" (Chronicle, St. Paul Convent, Kiphire). The people said that there should be only

73 When the community built a new church in the year 1989 there was a great uprising from certain quarters not to allow the community to have it blessed. Delegates came from various parishes in anticipation for the celebration. However, at this time Khekeye Sema, the ADC of Kiphire told Fr. Mathew Thuniampral to postpone or cancel the celebrations as the neighbouring villages had warned through letters that they did not want the dedication of the Catholic Church to take place in Pungro. They threatened to attack the visiting dignitaries, priests and nuns on their way to Pungro. He said that he was unable to provide security and insisted that no one should go from Kiphire to Pungro. Finally it was decided to cancel/postpone the celebration. The Catholic community understood the seriousness of the situation and remained calm, prayed and had their food. As they were having food they noticed the neighbouring Luthur village on fire. There were no men in the village as they were all waiting armed to attack the visiting dignitaries, priests and nuns along the Chomi-Pungro road, far from the village. The Catholics at Pungro rushed to the spot and helped in extinguishing the fire which engulfed about 30 houses by then. In a true Christian spirit they donated utensils, rice and some cash to the villagers which they appreciated. The church was blessed and dedicated during the next Christmas without much fanfare (St. Paul Church, Pungro, 1983-2008, pg. 17).

one religion and the Catholics, therefore, should be expelled from the village. However, on 7 April 1984 thirty eight people were baptised at Vongti again. In the meantime, Vongti village was divided and Kiutsüthong Abel, Head Dubashi and Head Gaon Bura together with some of the villagers shifted to New Vongti and thus St. John Church New Vongti came into existence in 1995. A few miles away from Pungro town, a new Church was erected at Khongjiri in 2004.

On 2 October 2002, Bishop Jose Mukala, inaugurated St. Paul Parish, Pungro and appointed Fr. Thomas Muttathil as the parish priest. Two great stalwarts of Pungro village were two brothers, Victor Ramji and his younger brother Titus Merimong. These were the first Catholics of Pungro who stood for their faith despite tremendous pressure. They were threatened with dismissal from their government jobs and expulsion from the village and even despised at, saying 'no one would be there to bury them.' By the grace of God, when they died the whole Catholic community was present in large numbers for their funerals. Both of them offered their sons to the service of God. Today Thomas Torekiu and Kurien Kokto are priests ordained for the Diocese of Kohima. Prior to the establishment of the Church at Pungro the Gaon Bura and the public leaders of the area requested the Bishop in writing for a Catholic school in 1979. However, it was only in April 1989 that Fr. Mathew Thuniampral started the Little Flower School at Vongti village but it was shifted to Pungro Town in 1990.

It was as a result of the farsightedness and missionary zeal of Fr. Mathew Thuniampral that the new community at Sitimi took its origin. In the last part of 1984, Sukuto Abraham and Shikiye Stephen from Sitimi met Fr. Mathew with a request to open a Catholic school. When he explained the need for a Catholic community to support the school, there came a spontaneous reply that they were willing to accept Catholic faith with no objection to preaching and establishing the Church in the village and that nobody would be prevented from embracing Catholicism. In the first part of January 1985, a two member delegation from the village consisting of Sukuto Abraham and Kiyehe (Head Gaon Bura, Sitimi Town) together with Fr. Mathew met with Bishop Abraham. The Bishop said, "Without a Catholic community we are not interested in opening a school as it will not grow without a community to support it" (Thuniampral, 2010, p. 12). In the presence of the Bishop Sukuto Abraham assured him that he would embrace Catholic faith.

In the aftermath of the discussion with the Bishop there was a meeting on 17 January 1985 at Sitimi Town Hall in which the assembly (council) assured that the missionaries could work fearlessly. As a result, many people expressed a desire to receive Catholic faith. On 9 March 1985, the school was inaugurated at Sitimi town. On 15 November 1985, Bishop Abraham received five families into the Catholic Church. An added advantage the Church had in Sitimi was that there were two public leaders who became Catholics, namely Shikiye Stephen, the head Dubashi, and Sukuto Abraham, the Gaon Bura. After the establishment of the community at Sitimi, communities were formed in Thonoknyu, Kiusam, and Seyochung.

The invitation to start a school at Seyochung had been expressed by the people of the area for many years. The parents of students from this area studying at Loyola School, Kiphire made contacts with the Catholic mission there. At the invitation of the students of Seyochung, Fr. Mathew Thuniyampral, Sisters Annie Paul and Sibia and Mathew accompanied by few people of Seyochung made their first visit on 20 December 1978. They visited their students' homes and met with parents and leaders of the town and village. Visits continued the following years but always at the invitation of the people. When five families expressed their desire to become Catholics, the priests, sisters and catechists started instructing them in the faith. On 30 March 1986, baptism was administered to them at Seyochung and a school was also opened. The aspirations of the peoples of Thonoknyu, Khuism and Pokfur villages were fulfilled when some of them accepted the Catholic faith in 1986 and 1987.

The Phom tribe made contact with the Catholic Church through Yingsham, an employee in the Public Health Department, Longleng, whose son Chingchei was a boarder at Tobu Catholic mission. The Dubashis and the Gaon Bura of Longleng pledged their support towards the establishment of the mission in Pongo, nine kilometers away from Longleng town. In addition, the Pongo Village Council, Hukphang Village Council and Yongphang Village Council also jointly extended their full cooperation towards this venture.

Since the Baptists would not part with land for the Catholic mission at Longleng, it was decided to establish the centre at Pongo (Chingmei, Personal communication, July 1, 2012). After the first visit on 12 November 1986, frequent visits were made for the instruction in faith. On 6 February 1987, one hundred Catholics from Tobu went to receive the new members of Phom tribe of Pongo village into Catholic faith. Concerning the establishment of the Catholic community at

Pongo village, Alencheril (1987) wrote in the chronicle of St. Thomas Church, Tuensang 1987-2012 that on 7 February 1987, Bishop Abraham inaugurated the Catholic community in Pongo Village by baptising about a hundred and fifty people and the sacrament of confirmation was administered to people twelve years of age and above. After the baptism a school was inaugurated. In the following year, another school at Longleng was started perhaps knowing fully the future possibilities of viability and management as many of the newly baptised members were permanent residents of Longleng. A convent of Missionary Sisters of Mary Help of Christians was opened on 29 January 1994 at Longleng.

On 20 February 1990, a small community of eleven families accepted the Catholic faith at Tamlu closer to Tuli. The people of Yongnyah village met with priests at Tuensang many times and requested them to open a school. According to the chronicle of St. Joseph Convent, Longleng, 1990-2010, on 17 April 1986 with sixty three students on enrollment a school was opened with the motive of future evangelisation of the area.

With repeated requests to embrace the Catholic faith some people of Yongnyah contacted priests at Longleng. During the maiden visit of Bishop Abraham on 26 October 1986 the people again renewed their demand for a Catholic Church. After due preparation and instruction, twenty seven families were baptised by Fr. James Kerketta on 4 May 1995 (Chronicle, St. Joseph's Convent, Longleng). The first visit to Sakshi village was made on 28 April 2002 and a community was soon founded.

Lotsu, a village in Wokha district under Lakhuti parish

welcomed Catholic faith in the year 1980 through the initiative of Chonrow Lapon. All those who wished to become Catholics expressed their desire to Fr. Devassy, Fr. P. K. Mathew and Sr. Pretty in Wokha. After due preparation, eight members were baptised on 17 February 1980 at Wokha by Fr. Mathew (St. Paul's Catholic Church, Silver Jubilee 1980-2005, Lotsu).

Pyangsa, adjacent to Lotsu village came to know of the Catholic faith through the visits and instructions given by Fr. Jesudhas and Daniel Yanthan from Lakhuti in 1984. Tondungo Ovung alone came forward to accept faith without support from any quarter. Fr. Jesudhas took one of Tondungo's children to Lakhuti and told him he would provide him with religion and education. Even though there was no Church or community at Pyangsa, Tondungo received baptism together with eight of his family members on 25 March 1984 (Pyangsa Catholic ekhum ko, Silver Jubilee 1984-2009). One of his sons, Mhonchumo Philip is a priest in the congregation of the MSFS.

Bhandari is the centre of Lothas of the lower range. The first Catholic community of Bhandari came into existence in 1973 with the arrival of Henry Yanthan from Yimpang village and Shanlamo Ezung from Longsa village. On Sundays, Henry used to go to Yimpang and Shanlamo to Longayim for the Church service. From the year 1979, when Nzinyimo Humtose's family was added to their fold they used to have services in each other's house. In the same year, more families joined them and they started to have services more often. With the increase of the Catholic population in 1980, they built a small chapel which was blessed by Fr. K.P. Paul on 11 January 1981. A school was opened on 18 January 1981 by the Catholics of the area and in 1983 it came under Wokha parish

(Sacred Heart Parish, Silver Jubilee 1985-2010, Bhandari). By the time many villages under Bhandari sub-division had the Catholic Church in their places, the need was felt to make Bhandari an independent centre. In the year 1984, the Bishop requested the service of the MSFS priests to care for the centre. The parish was officially inaugurated on 15 September 1985 with Fr. Davis as the first parish priest. In the following year, the Sisters of Providence came to assist the parish. The centre was handed over to the Diocese at the expiry of the contract.

It was the contact that Fr. Larrea and Fr. O'Hara had with the people of Merapani since 1961, from Golaghat on their way to and from Lakhuti and other Lotha areas that enabled some people of Merapani to embrace Catholicism. This contact continued even after the establishment of the Church in Wokha. In December 1970 Fr. Michael celebrated the Holy Mass for the first time there. From the year 1951, the people of New Lio Wokha showed a keen interest in the Catholic faith. The first priest to visit this place was Fr. John Larzar. Gradually a Church was built there and in due course, churches were also built in Bhandari Town, Bhandari Village, Khomchoyan, Lio-Longidang, Lio Wokha, Longayim, Merapani, Pantong, yamhon, Yampha andYanlum.

After making Chizami a permanent base to work among the Chakhesang tribe, some public leaders of Pfutsero approached Fr. Castelino with repeated requests to start a Catholic school. While negotiating for land for the establishment of the school and a Pastoral Centre, he received a copy of a letter addressed to the Chief Minister of Nagaland from an important dignitary of the Baptist Church Council of Phek district protesting against the opening of a centre by the Catholic Church in Pfutsero.

Because of this Fr. Castelino hesitated to open the school since it might bring misunderstanding between the Catholics and the Baptists. Moreover, the Baptists had already opened a school and they might not have been happy to see another school, fearing low enrolment. But the leaders retorted saying, "Their centre is at Bible Hill in Phek, if they object to Catholics having a school in Pfutsero, we will tell them to go back to Bible Hill" (Castelino, 1999, pg. 36). When he showed the letter from the Baptist dignitary the leaders promised that they would sort out the matter with the Chief Minister. Following this, there was no more opposition and the school was opened in 1986. St. Joseph Parish, Chumukedima was created in the year 1997 with a community drawn from different tribes like Angami, Rongmei, Lotha, Mao, Garo, and many others. A number of religious congregations like Sisters of Charity, Medical Mission Sisters, Carmelite Sisters and Sisters of the Adoration of the Blessed Sacrament now have their houses there. St. Joseph School, Chumukedima and St. Antony's School, Tenyphe are the two important institutions in this parish.

In addition to the above mentioned parishes and schools there are many more schools in the Diocese - Don Bosco Higher Secondary School Dimapur, St. Mary's Higher Secondary School Padampukhri, Carmel Higher Secondary School, 3rd Mile, St.Clare Higher Secondary School, Kacharigaon, St. Paul Higher Secondary School Dimapur, etc. In the course of time, many churches and a host of educational institutions including colleges, formation houses, convents, dispensaries, training centres etc have been established at different places in the state. In fact the most number of Churches and institutions were founded in the 1970s and 1980s.

CHAPTER FOUR

Contribution of the Catholic Church

Bishop Abraham Alangimattathil

THE BEGINNING and growth of Christianity after the arrival of Dr. Clark, the Baptist missionary in Nagaland had great significance on the erstwhile non-Christian religious traditions, beliefs, customs and practices of the people. In the course of time the vast majority of the non-Christians accepted Christianity. Conversion to the new religion was a turning point in the life of the Nagas as it took them to a new era of civilisation, progress and identity. One of the noted achievements was helping different Naga tribes of Nagaland to come together under a common identity called 'Naga' and encouraging them to give up conflicts. The contribution of Christianity towards this new era is significant. In the words of Sanyu (1996), "If one responsible dynamic factor were to be singled out for an overall change in the life of the Nagas, it would undoubtedly be the introduction of

CONTRIBUTION OF THE CATHOLIC CHURCH IN GENERAL

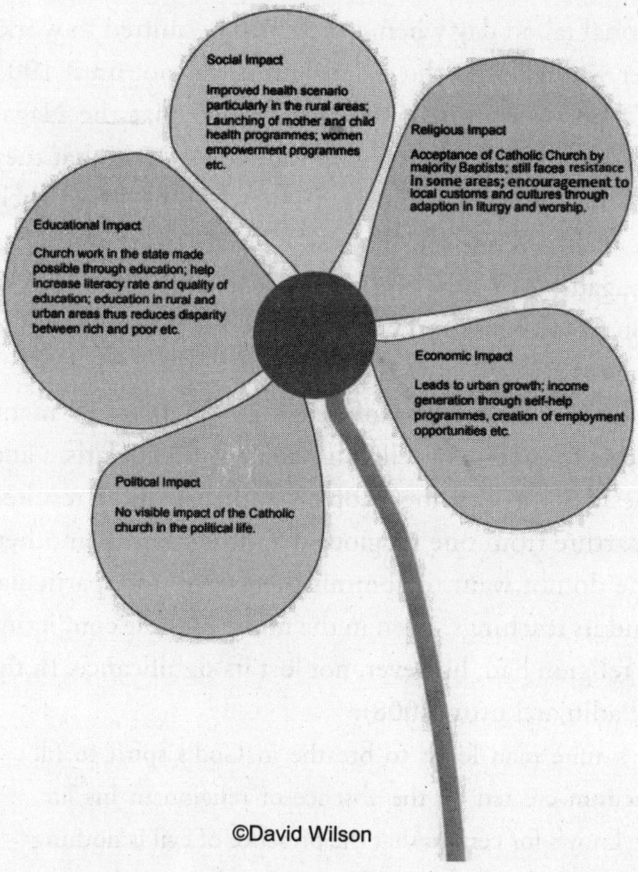

Christianity among them" (pg. 508). The new development was strengthened further with the coming of the Catholic Church as it always insists on the universal theme of 'harmony'.

Mass conversion to Baptist Christianity among the Ao and the Sema tribes in the beginning and later on among other tribes alarmed the pagans who felt it a threat and started persecutions against them. This persecution is reported by Downs (1983) in the following words, "Villages near Impur tried to force Christians to contribute to religious festivals and to observe the traditional taboo day when no one was permitted to work. The matter was taken to the courts and it was not until 1907 that the Deputy Commissioner finally ruled that the Nagas should be free to follow any religion they wished and that they should not be forced to support a religion other than their own" (pg. 128). While the Baptist Church faced resistance from the pagans, the Catholic Church faced a different form of persecution from the (other) Christians as it was not welcomed in many places at the beginning.

There is a sense of loss of religion and faith in many countries due to the rise of religious fanaticism, secularism and wealth. Besides these, some people's spiritual quest resulted in the departure from one religious denomination to another, while some do not want to commit themselves to a particular religion and its teachings. Even in the midst of these conflicting opinions, religion had, however, not lost its significance. In the words of Padinjarekuttu (2008):

> Many a time man longs to breathe in God's spirit to fill the vacuum created by the absence of religion in his life. But he knows for certain that the presence of evil is nothing compared to the presence of ever pervading goodness in the world. Humans have always been able to transcend the fragmentary experiences of life with the help of a set of moral values. This has been the primary goal of the religions of the humankind: to make meaning flow into everyday life and to provide moral norms, which impel humans to purposive and life-transforming action (pg. 18).

It was approximately after seventy five years of the presence of the Baptist Church that the Catholic Church was able to officially begin its work in the state, thanks to the invitation of Sir Akbar Hydari, Governor of Assam who requested Bishop Stephen Ferrando of Shillong to send some religious (nuns) nurses to work in the Naga Hospital.

The Catholic Church has been at the service of the people of the state for more than sixty years rendering valuable services in the religious, social, economic and educational fields and has reached out to almost all the tribes of the erstwhile undivided Diocese of Kohima-Imphal which consisted of the entire states of Nagaland and Manipur. With the formation of the Diocese of Imphal in 1980, which comprised of the entire state of Manipur, the Diocese of Kohima concentrated on its own state, Nagaland. The Catholic Church is one of the strong instruments in bringing about religious, social and economic transformation of the state.

Periodic assessment is essential for any organisation for it to be focus oriented for the future. An attempt has been made in this chapter to assess the overall functions and performances of the young Catholic Church and the contributions it has made to the state with the help of questionnaires, interviews and secondary sources.

4.1 Background to the Church Mission

Planning, discussion and deliberations precede any event before it is being actualised. All what the Catholic Church could do for the people of the state was made possible through many seen and seemingly unseen factors played at backstage.

4.1.1 Catholic Church's Entry in the State

The Catholic Church entered the state not with a spirit of competition or as a game changer. Its presence in the state can prompt one especially a non-Catholic to raise fundamental questions like what would have happened if there was no Catholic Church in the state? Or, did it bring about any substantial effect in one's life? Or, what is that outstanding quality that differentiates it from other churches so as to get converted to it? The most important reason for the entry of the Catholic Church in the state was the very inherent nature of the Church, which was explicitly found in the command of Christ, mentioned in the Gospels. The history of the origin of the Church goes back to the apostolic times. The various denominations that are found in the world today have sprung up in the course of history because of theological or doctrinal or personal reasons.

The missionary nature of the Church commands one to share one's faith and the message of the Gospel. The mind of the Gospel was reflected in the ministry of the Church to provide people with opportunities to choose one's faith which was felt to be a fundamental duty. There were a large number of people who left their religion or denomination of birth to choose another of their choice later. There weren't many who regret accepting the Catholic faith. At the same time, there are a few who have gone back to their earlier faith citing various reasons. This is evident in a few places in the state that is mentioned later in this chapter.

This phenomenon of shifting allegiance happens in all faiths. It is important to provide everyone the opportunities to know the true faith and to choose the same is one's freedom.

There is no force or incentive offered in the Catholic Church but only equal opportunities are provided. Even though Christianity is a belief in Jesus as the Saviour, worship and practice, theology and ideology differ from denomination to denomination. We all need to be open-minded to welcome people of other faiths and from other denominations to prove that it is one's absolute right to be in what one feels more comfortable with. The reality of the presence of people of other faiths is never a threat but a broader outlook for the best is yet to come. The welcome sign of unity in diversity is experienced not only in Christianity but also in other religions.

The Catholic Church, therefore, offers the people of the state with opportunities to fulfil their aspirations and spiritual quest. Getting upset with the presence of another denomination or faith is an unwanted fear. Instead one should rather consider these as occasions to see the best in others and to improve on what we believe in.

True worship of God through celebration of the Eucharist and other sacraments and sacramentals, veneration of Blessed Virgin Mary and saints, novenas, pilgrimages, traditions, hierarchical and universal nature of the Church are some of the characteristics of the Church. These are part of worship not meant to add colour to it but are intrinsic to the true worship of God and to improve the quality of Christian life. Indeed, the sacramental life has a special place for a Christian because it offers a deeper God-experience. People embraced Catholicism in the state on their own.

The presence of the Catholic Church presented the universality of the Church which was new knowledge for the people of other faiths and denominations.

4.1.2 Goal: Common Good and Welfare of All

Social activism has an important place in the Catholic Church. The Church visualises the overall development of a person through medical help, educational services and economic well-being. It is opined that although there is a concept of social activism in the Naga society it has not been fully realised yet. Hence, the Church feels it is necessary to instil it through its services for the complete wellbeing of the people (Abraham, Personal communication, September 19, 2012).

The people's indifferent attitude towards general development and amassing of wealth by a section of the people could be cited as reasons for the absence of overall development and welfare of the state. The only aim the Church has in mind while discharging its mandate is the common good and welfare of all. With this end in view, it has been involved in various humanitarian and social ministries. The Bible says in the book of James chapter 2: 14-17 "What good is it, my brothers and sisters, to profess faith without showing works? Such faith has no power to save you…so it is for faith without deeds: it is totally dead." The emphasis the Catholic Church places on different ministries has been mentioned by Puthenpurakal (1993) in the following words:

> Different aspects of the Church tells us that in contrast with the Baptist form of mission work with its emphasis mostly on the Word of God, the Catholic evangelisation, followed the traditional integral approach making use of as many opportunities as possible to be of service to the community both spiritually and materially. Hence, attention was given to the Word of God, the sacraments, inculcation of Christian virtues, emphasis on Christian

> living, education, medical care, training of lay leaders, their in-service training, promotion of local vocations, establishment of Catholic associations, celebration of feasts, efforts at inculturation, organisation of youth, teachings of saints, welfare programmes and a host of other aspects of Catholic life. As a whole, in a matter of a few years of Catholic presence in the Naga Hills where the Baptists were the vast majority, the people came to realise that the Catholic Church's approach is for the welfare of the whole man and of all men irrespective of tribal divisions. This, we believe, was a big contribution in the Baptist stronghold. It removed prejudices and opened the people's hearts to welcome the Catholic form of Christianity (pg. 228).

Hence it is to be noted that benefits the Catholic Church brought to the people of the state through its humanitarian works, were enjoyed not only by the Catholics who are hardly 4 per cent of the total population but the majority non-Catholics too.

While in the state of Meghalaya, it was from the Welsh Presbyterians that the Catholic Church faced hostility, in Nagaland it was from the American Baptists as they were the predominant denomination. The advantage the Catholic Church had in Nagaland was that in most cases the invitation to open schools came from the Baptists themselves. The Church, therefore, opened several schools and a few colleges in due course of time, besides other social service centres to cater to the needs of the people. It is absolutely true that it was through Catholic educational services that the Church could make its contacts and continue with its work.

4.1.3 Resources and Allied Services of the Catholic Mission

The traditional Naga religion is not missionary in nature while Christianity is indeed missionary. The former does not have a mandate to proclaim its teachings or message but the latter does have a special invitation to proclaim so as to be an agent of change in the world and we find references to this effect in the Bible, Mathew 28: 18-20; and Isaiah 42: 6-7. Hence the Church employs all possible means to fulfil this call. As a religious body and promoter of social welfare the Church was given an acceptance by the people of the state through open invitations. Therefore, it was essential to have sufficient manpower to realise the aspirations of the people. According to Puthenpurakal (1993), "An overall look into the evangelisation work by the Catholic Church in Nagaland shows that the principle followed has been, if we may put it, place the pastor and the sheep will follow" (p. 228). The pastor in due course of time could launch into many areas and form communities by making use of the synergy of resources at the disposal of the Church for the betterment of the people. Through various services and agencies like availability of religious personnel, personal contacts, village visits, goodwill of the general public, leadership programmes, promotion of lay leaders, training of catechists, scholarship to deserving students, lay associations, local vocations, funding agencies from abroad and within, development agency of the diocese, schools, colleges and boarding-houses, vocational training centres for men and women, teachers' training institutes, dispensaries, rehabilitation centres, orphanages, publications etc. the Church grew, created opportunities and brought development. Among these, however, the two most important factors that favoured the growth of the Church and its subsequent contribution is the Naga people's desire to have good education and the strong leadership laid by Bishop Abraham Alangimattathil (1933-1997), the first Bishop of the Diocese of Kohima for twenty three years from 1973-1997. An intelligent visionary, a pastoral and practical minded personality, a doer, a promoter of culture and a great lover of souls, he led the diocese from the front with a band of few priests, religious catechists and committed laity.

From the very beginning of the establishment of the Catholic Church all possible efforts were made for the good of the people. In all its undertakings, the hard work, diligence and commitment of a large number of religious men, women and laity particularly the catechists were seen throughout. The arrival of many religious congregations of men and women from outside to work in the diocese was one of the first signs of the growth of the Church. As diocesan priests who are the close collaborators of the Bishop were not sufficient in number, the Bishop invited a large number of religious congregations of men and women from outside the diocese to work in the mission. The Salesians of Don Bosco (SDB) - commonly known as the Don Bosco Fathers were the first to volunteer to work in the diocese, followed by the Society of Jesus (SJ) or the Jesuits, the Missionaries of St. Francis De Sales (MSFS), Order of Friars Minor Capuchin (OFM Cap), Congregation of the Mission (CM), Society of the Missionaries of St. Francis Xavier or the Society of Pilar and Montfort Brothers of St. Gabriel (SG) or The Gabriel Brothers. The first group of the Sisters of the Daughters of Mary Help of Christians (FMA) arrived in Kohima in 1964 and the Sisters of the Adoration of the Blessed Sacrament (SABS) in Tuensang in 1967 gave a new dimension to the mission. They were followed by the Carmelites of the Mother of Carmel (CMC), the Franciscan Clarist Congregation (FCC), Sisters of Bethany (BS), Medical Mission Sisters (MMS), Sisters of Charity (SCCG), Sisters of Providence (Sd.P), Missionary Sisters of Mary Help of Christians (MSMHC), Apostolic Carmel (AC), Sacred Heart Congregation (SH), Pious Disciples of Divine Master (PDDM), Missionaries of Charity (MC), Sisters of Ursuline Franciscan Congregation (UFC), Franciscan Sisters of St. Mary of the Angels (FSMA), Congregation of the Sisters of St. Joseph of Chambery (CSJ) and Sisters of Mary Immaculate (SMI). In most places, along with the Church convents, dispensaries, boarding-houses for boys and girls and in some places Home Science Centres have been built. With thirty five parishes and many centres and sub-centres, today the Church has become a symbol of unity and identity in the land of the Nagas.

In addition to these, the growth of the Church in the state owes much to the work of the committed local laity together with the catechists. Their support and cooperation proved to be a great solace and blessing during the initial stages and in times of struggles, disappointments, successes and failures. They were responsible for the establishment of communities in different villages. Furthermore, various lay associations such as Catholic Association of Nagaland (CAN), Catholic Women Association and Nagaland Catholic Youth Movement played a sacrificial role in keeping the faith alive and active. The educated laity of our Church is the main voice especially for the defenceless and downtrodden (Karotemprel, 1993).

The success of an organisation depends upon the commitment of its employees towards the responsibility they are entrusted with. The Catholic Church is distinct from other churches in terms of dedication as a result of the vow of celibacy practiced by the priests, brothers and nuns. The call to celibate life is a call to total commitment as mentioned in the Bible. Celibacy for the sake of Kingdom is a gift, a call that is not granted to all, or even most people, but is granted to some (Mathew 19: 11-12). Catholics are taught to venerate marriage as a holy institution. Astonishingly, it is precisely the holiness of marriage that makes celibacy precious, for only what is good and holy in itself can be given up for God as a sacrifice as the gift of Abel (Genesis 4: 4). Just as fasting presupposes the goodness of food, celibacy presupposes the goodness of marriage (Brom, 2004, August 10, www.catholic.com/tracts/celibacy). The dedicated celibate men and women through their life and service make a difference in the lives of people who are suspicious and hostile towards the Catholic Church. They are called to be contemplatives in active apostolate through their commitment. However, at times they may fail because of human nature. The Church makes use of every bit of opportunity at hand, puts in maximum use of available human resources and invests everything it has, to offer commendable service to humanity. Without enthusiasm, no mission will be effective and fruitful. In the words of Alengaden (2007), "In spite of a strong infrastructure and financial support many government projects and programmes fail. Schools run by the government fail to attract students, hospitals run by the government are mismanaged. On the contrary, institutions run by committed persons excel because of their passion for mission" (pg. 153). Nearly 180 priests and brothers and 260 sisters, along with many committed laity are behind the Church in Nagaland. The significant role played by the religious women in various ministries of the Church is irrefutable and has increased the people's trust in them. They tour villages and conduct catechetical programmes such as instruction in faith and morals, catechism for children, conduct of Bible camps and youth camps, training in hygiene, health and child care for women etc.

4.2 Religious and Cultural Contribution

The Catholic Church in Nagaland began its work in an organised manner with the creation of the Diocese of Kohima in 1973. A review of its overall activities helped her to move forward with renewed energy. Initially, the absence of quality education in the state was a setback for the infant Catholic Church. Many of those who opposed the Church were biased because they had been misinformed about the Catholic faith. So, when distorted information reached innocent and simple people they believed whatever they heard. Incidentally people who embraced the Catholic faith in the beginning were mostly illiterate and had neither deep faith nor good understanding of the teachings of the Church to defend themselves in the face of verbal accusations and questioning. Added to their woes, was their poor financial background which resulted in them becoming socially withdrawn and isolated. At times Catholic students were laughed at by their friends from other denominations when they couldn't satisfactorily explain certain practices of the Church. Unlike other denominations, the basis of the Catholic Church is deeper as it is centered on the Bible, sacraments, traditions and the magisterium of the Church. Notwithstanding the setback faced by the Catholics in education, particularly religious education came as a great relief to them. It enabled them to have a better understanding of the teachings of the Church and deepening of their faith. In this ministry, the most important role played by the religious sisters deserves great appreciation. They empowered and strengthened families through their visit to families, catechesis, and prayers. Regular catechism classes for Catholic children in the Church and school by sisters, catechists, and catechism teachers benefited them.

Religious harmony empowers one to appreciate one another's faith and helps draw whatever is good in other religions. Imitations of some of the practices of the Catholic Church by other denominations of late point to this reality. The importance and meaningful celebration of the Easter events, such as the observance of Palm Sunday and Good Friday enabled people to shift from a mere external celebration to a spiritual one. These days many non-Catholic churches celebrate Palm Sunday by taking out processions carrying palm leaves. Good Friday has been given its due spiritual dimension as the day is turned from a day of celebration or a picnic into a Holy Day. The Catholic Church draws inspiration from other churches about the need for lively music during liturgy. Music ministry in other churches attracts young people to the church while the Catholic Church is lagging behind in this.

4.2.1 Gradual Acceptance of the Catholic Church

Despite the fact that no force was ever used by the Catholic Church to establish mission centres in any part of the state, it has often been accused of doing so by some vested interests.

There has always been a standing invitation from every village authority which includes Gaon Buras and village council members both in word and writing to start a Catholic mission at their place. If any dispute or misunderstanding arose in the village or in the community at the news of the plan to establish a mission, the people themselves settled it and then invited the priests to start the same.

Even in recent times negative propaganda against the Catholics such as 'Catholics are like Hindus not Christians' or 'Catholics are found only in Nagaland' or 'the state's religion is Baptist Christianity,' have been given wide publicity both in rural and urban areas. From the time it came to exist as a body, the Church has been under suspicion as being foreign (Talibuddin, 1993). Majority of the peoples' opinions were formed around such verbal propaganda that was devoid of truth which further strengthened their prejudices. Yanthan (2005) opined, "Some view Catholics as outcasts, anti-Christ or a branch of Hinduism, which clearly suggests not only ignorance but also pure prejudice" (pg. 53). Catholics were considered as non-Christians in the beginning in many parts of the state because of the prejudices. Wherever people are fed with misleading information, a common doubt they often have when they come across Catholics is, 'is he a Christian or Catholic?' Or 'Are there Catholics outside Nagaland, India?'

Catholics faced ill-treatment from non-Catholics in the beginning of the establishment of the Church. Refusal to go to field together or share the field, being barred from social life, denial of opportunities in the village, unwillingness to send children to the Catholic school for fear of being converted are a few examples. This discrimination, however, lessened when the younger generation got educated and Catholics started progressing (Tsuha and Puro, Personal communication, June 6, 2012). Today, however, except in some areas of the state, fierce opposition is not witnessed. This suggests that people have been raised from the level of ignorance to understanding and from prejudice to tolerance through the educational and social services of the Church and their contacts with the Catholics. People have come to accept the reality that there exist other religions in and outside the state other than Baptist Christianity.

At times tension builds up in a village when a few members decide to follow the Catholic faith. Often the reason cited is, another faith in the same village might cause disharmony among the people, but we know that people have the fundamental right to choose and practice one's faith of choice. Here, we have an example of biased attitude towards another faith and its response. Chiten Jamir (2008) writes:

> In 1956, when a youth delegation of the Naga National Council visited Lakhuti village, a remote village in those days, we met an Italian Missionary who was a Roman Catholic, it was dismissed as a minor issue. Slowly, as the Baptist Churches were giving way to secularisation, the Roman Catholic Churches kept on growing in many parts of Nagaland. When I visited Changki in 1958, I was fortunate to meet a great man of God, Rev. Nikenmeri Ao. He said in tears that the Nagas must not allow the Roman Catholics to come to Nagaland. I told the old man that I knew of no law in India that could stop the people to become Catholics, if they choose to. Later, Rev. Longri Ao came to meet me and discussed the problems of the spread of Roman Catholicism

> in Nagaland. No law can stop the Nagas becoming Roman Catholics. Perhaps, the RCs provide the people with good education and better care for their physical needs more than what the Baptists do. Before you ask the people not to become RCs and to stop opening of good schools, the Church leaders should stop sending their children to RC schools in Shillong and other places ("The Christian state of Nagaland", February 24, pg. 4).

Pastor Joshua, educated in a Catholic school says, "If we freely mingle with all denominations, there will only be healthy relationships. One of the ways to do this is to let no church engage in politics of attack but work hard to distinguish between love and hatred" (Personal communication, July 27, 2007). The Church, for example, receives great support from many of the past pupils like bureaucrats, politicians and others. Fr. T. J. Chacko (2007) opines, "The greatest impact of the Catholic Church on Naga society is the educational efforts. Education has helped people to shed their prejudices about the Catholic Church and hence they cooperate with it for the good of all" (Personal communication, November 3).

Downs (1983) and Jala (1990) opined how Church structures have taken the tribal groups of the North East beyond the narrow confines of their villages. The very structures of the Catholic Church have narrowed down the prejudices that people have and this brought them to a realisation of the universality of mankind. The work of the foreign missionaries over the years till the middle of 1960 and the visit of Pope John Paul II in 1986 have created awareness in the minds of the people of the existence of a Church that exists beyond the borders of the North East, while being a true and fully local church. As a result the negative propaganda, suspicion and hatred towards the Catholics and Catholic missionaries have narrowed down. This has been made possible through people's contact with missionaries from India and abroad who took pains to widen people's horizon of knowledge about the Catholic religion, culture and practices. The Naga people's interaction with the foreign Catholic missionaries followed by the Indian missionaries exposed them to a different world of knowledge and truth. In addition, the active ministry of a significant number of local clergy and religious today has made people realize that the Catholic Church is not alien or foreign but universal. In the words of Lotha (2012), "The presence of the local clergy in Nagaland is the beginning of acceptance of the Catholic Church. It is a sign that the Church is rooted deeply in the land and people know, therefore, it can be Naga and it is Naga" (Personal communication, September 19, 2012).

The influence of many enlightened men and women of the state who had the privilege of studying in Catholic institutions outside the state in places like Golaghat, Shillong, Dibrugarh, Tezpur, Naharkhattia and Darjeeling, through the 1940s to 1960s, who later on became public leaders and bureaucrats helped broaden the vision of the people about the Catholic Church and narrow down prejudices. Their learning, adventure and interaction with people outside the state created feelings of interdependence and reminded everyone that it was possible to inculcate what is good in each other for one's own betterment.

The teaching staff from outside the state in the educational institutions has been a source of unity, integration and contact between the Naga tribes and mainland India. The non-availability of qualified teachers from the region in the initial stage of the opening of educational institutions compelled the missionaries to look for them outside the region (Thoppil, 2003). These teachers too were missionaries especially in the far flung areas of the state. Their great sacrifice in the absence of basic amenities like roads, running water, electricity, transport and communication and away from their family is to be recorded in the annals of the history of the Church. Often these teachers were the only non-local persons the people of the village had ever come into contact with (Thoppil, 2003). Chenjei (2012) stated, "Catholic schools have brought in teachers from all over India and they have opened the eyes of the Naga people helping them broaden their perspectives and lessened narrow-mindedness. The students' familiarity with these teachers helped them feel at home when they are outside the state for their studies" (Personal communication, June 20, 2012). The Church's overall activities enabled people to recognise the fact that its universal identity, self-sacrifice and expertise are meant for the common good and to bridge the gap between the churches and societies.

4.2.2 Church, Symbol of Unity

The Catholic Church is globally present while the Baptist Church when it began in Nagaland was primarily connected with the United States of America. The universality of the Church makes the Catholics in Nagaland feel united with all the Catholics in the world and hence it stands as a symbol of unity. "This is the sole Church of Christ, which in the Creed we profess to be one, holy, catholic and apostolic" (Theological Publications in India, 1995, pg.164), and these four characteristics are inseparably linked to each other. The visible sign of the oneness of the Church is expressed in the profession of one faith and teachings, common celebration of worship especially of the sacraments and the maintenance of fraternal concord through apostolic succession of the Holy Orders. It is holy because Christ, who is with the Father and the Spirit is holy. He loved the Church as his body and by his holiness he sanctifies it (Lumen Gentium, Vatican Council II). St. Ignatius of Antioch decreed that, 'Where there is Jesus Christ, there is the Catholic Church.' The Catholic Church receives the fullness of the means of salvation from Jesus. It is apostolic because it is founded on the apostles.

The closely linked fundamental principles which guard and rule the Church universally are the Sacred Scripture, Tradition and Magisterium or teaching authority of the Church. The Sacred scripture and tradition are interconnected and bound closely together. As a result, the Church, to which the handing on and interpretation of revelation is entrusted, does not derive all revealed truths from the holy scriptures alone. Both scripture and tradition must be accepted and honoured with equal sentiments of devotion and reverence (Catechism of the Catholic Church, No. 80, 82). Tradition refers to the whole process by which the Church 'hands on' (literal meaning of tradition) its faith to each new generation. This handing on occurs through preaching, catechesis, teaching, devotions, gestures, (for example, the sign of the Cross) doctrines, and indeed the Bible itself (Augustine, The Echo, 2009). The term 'magisterium' means 'teaching office' of the Church. It refers to the teaching role of the Pope and the bishops. As successors of the apostles, the Pope and the bishops teach authoritatively.

They teach and judge what is in accord with the gospel and what is not. Some of the important subjects covered by the magisterium are discipline, doctrine and dogma (Augustine, The Echo, 2010).

The members of this universal Church practice the same faith, follow the same tradition and learn the same teaching. Through this common bond all are united whether they are tribals or non-tribals. What makes the members feel one with everyone is the common identity known as 'Catholic.' Because of this identity, it is desired that no Church (for example in Nagaland, as elsewhere), should be labelled after the name of a tribe or community like Angami Catholic Church, or Lotha Catholic Church, or Sema Catholic Church but only 'Catholic Church.' All the Catholic Churches in different places in Nagaland come under the Diocese of Kohima.

In all Catholic Churches the same faith is practiced and the same form of worship is observed, though some rubrics may differ depending on the rites people belong to. This culture of unity has sent out a message to the people of the state who are multi lingual and multi tribal in character that it is possible to be united to live as one and achieve common goals. In the Church there is no difference between rich or poor, white or black, tribal or non-tribal. Wherever the Church may be, the members belonging to different tribes go to the same Church. This bond of unity is very significant and it can even unite people of various ethnicities. In Manipur, during the ethnic clashes in 1992, the local priests (belonging to different tribes) pledged and signed in unison for peace and this gesture had great benefits for the society and the peace process (Haokip, Personal communication, March 9, 2009). Haokip, a tribal and a professor of theology for many years opines that, "If all tribals are Catholics there are fewer chances of ethnic violence or clashes as we preach about one Church, one people, one language and no differences inside or outside the Church about any group" (Personal communication, March 9, 2009). According to Mani, the great impact the Catholic Church has had on Naga society is, "we loved all people irrespective of their faiths or denominations and they love us in turn" (Mani, Personal communication, November 3, 2007).

The adaptation to the culture is one of the achievements of the Church. The Catholic Cathedral at Kohima is a symbol of unity of all the Catholic Churches in Nagaland. It is the Mother Church which the Bishop of the Diocese of Kohima presides. It is also a parish whose members are drawn from various tribes and linguistic groups. The lion's share of the total expenses for the construction of the cathedral came from the Japanese, who wished the Church to be a place of prayer, especially for the Japanese War victims who laid down their lives for their nation in the Second World War fought in Kohima. This is affirmed in the prayer inscribed in English and Japanese scripts on the Cathedral campus, "…it is with thankfulness that we heard that a Catholic Cathedral was being built at Kohima, where Mass would be offered every morning in memory of the fallen…" (Catholic Cathedral, Kohima). Here at the Cathedral important meetings of reconciliation between the Japanese and the British war veterans took place. On the gates of the cathedral a visitor is welcomed with an inscribed prayer, "Bring before the Lord all those who gave their life and who will give their all for your safer and better Nagaland" (Catholic cathedral, Kohima). Besides this, the Blessed Sacrament is adored the whole day in this Church on behalf of all.

4.2.3 Church a Beacon of Hope

To great many people establishment of a Catholic Church in their locality was a beacon of hope as it could infuse fresh energy in their religious, educational, social and economic life. In the beginning several people objected to the establishment of the Catholic Church in their area however, they welcomed Catholic schools. This choice was deliberately notable so as to discourage another church in the village coming up that might divide the people on religious lines. At the same time, they were appreciative of the Catholic school because many of their leaders including some prominent politicians educated in the Catholic schools and colleges outside the state spoke well of Catholic education. In some places, however, the Church was first established followed by the school. Even though the Church was a new entity in the locality, many voluntarily embraced the Catholic faith. Non-interference and cooperation with people of all denominations was the characteristic feature of the Catholic Church that was very much appreciated. The establishment of income generating small scale businesses by the local people and the creation of employment opportunities improved the overall economic wellbeing. All these achievements helped people to see that the Church was here to stay and work for the welfare of all people irrespective of religious and tribal affiliations. In the given situation the overall impact felt especially on the religious, educational and economic life of the people was overwhelming.

The Church welcomes all people as it is convinced of the truth that the 'Church is for all,' and never denies entry to anyone whatsoever be the reason. It is an open truth that non-Christians who had the habit of drinking rice beer expressed their desire to become Christians had been denied entry into the Baptist church, they were, however, happily welcomed by the Catholic Church. Some might mistakenly think it was done to add numbers to the Catholic fold but it is to affirm the inclusive nature of the Church. Prior to their admittance into the Catholic Church they were branded as 'pagans' or 'heathens' the name which they didn't like to be known for when majority of the people in the village had already accepted Christianity. However, after their entry they got rid of the 'shame' and were proud of having an identity for themselves. A policy followed by the Church is to treat people as equal before God and others and it is very much reinforced through its education ministry. Division in a community occurs when everyone is not treated as equals. For example Dr. Ambedkar knew that there was no sense of equality in Hinduism and got converted to Buddhism. His words are found in The Hindu, "I was born a Hindu but will not die one" ("The Bogey of forced conversion", 2008, October 26). One notable trait of the Catholic Church is its membership which is not based on one's contribution/tithe to the Church but voluntary. The failure to pay tithe does not lead to cancellation of membership unlike it is commonly practiced by many Christian denominations.

In the past, Christians were quite indifferent to non-Christians and so tried to alienate them from social life of the village. Also a non-Christian who had enjoyed and respected his own traditions and customs became apathetic towards them after embracing Christianity. This is attributed to the failure of the earlier missionaries to understand the rich cultural heritage intrinsic to the tribals and their belief that it had nothing to do with the new faith. In the words of Haimendorf (1989, "Seeing his own customs condemned by the missionaries, he (the new convert) learnt to despise his own tribe and cultural inheritance" (pg. 52). In the beginning, when Dr. Clark founded churches, the villages were divided between the Christians and non-Christians. He even started a new village for the new converts and named it Molungyimsen. The Catholic Church, however, appreciated the rich cultural heritage of the tribals from the beginning. So, the new convert happily carried with him all that he valued in his older faith into his new faith and found himself in a caring community. Perhaps one of the positive contributions of the Church to the tribal culture is incorporation of tribal values into the life of the Church.

The Church exists for the liberation of all, liberation from diverse hurdles of life for which it tries to reach out to people in different ways. It is in the heart of the Church to uplift man and help him achieve all round wellbeing. A common word used in theology to mean liberation is evangelisation. "Evangelisation means to announce a joyful message, namely, of God and his kingdom. It is the proclamation by words, deeds and life of the Good News of salvation of men in Jesus Christ " (Vadakumpadan, 1989, pg. 52). *Evangelii Nuntiandi,* the apostolic exhortation of Pope Paul VI, which deals with the theme of evangelisation in the modern world, explains it in terms of proclamation, liberation, changing the world, reaching out to non-Christians etc. Very often people misunderstand the word evangelisation to mean 'conversion', or to convert someone from one religion to another. In fact, conversion is essentially a change of heart. Bharati (2008, October 27) confirms this view when he says, "More than a mere change of name, or place and form of worship, real 'conversion' according to true Christian faith is essentially a 'change of heart' whereby one becomes a 'new creation' (*navasrushti*) in Christ" (pg. 32), which means a true witness in word, deed and faith.

Efforts made by the Catholic Church in the state, therefore, aim at the conversion of a person in the above sense and to offer hope in concrete situations. It is to help form an identity that is worth living, an identity to be known by and an identity to hope for the best in the future, to enhance one's spiritual, social or economic life. In the course of time, however, one may express his will/desire to be a member of the Catholic Church by leaving his former religion or denomination. That should be generally taken or treated as one's freedom to practice his faith guaranteed by the Constitution of the country. Unfortunately, many people in the state get agitated when they hear about the very name, 'Catholic Church.' It is a reflection of an unseen fear and or insecurity expressed through open letters, or intimidations.

4.2.4 Enhancement of Religious Life through Local Church

The scope of the Catholic Church includes establishment of the local church through the ministry of the local clergy and religious and active collaboration of the laity. The future of the Church in Nagaland as in the rest of the North East lies in the hands of the priests, religious and dedicated laity of the state. Puthenpurakal (1979) quotes the words of Pope Leo XIII to elucidate the nature and future of the Church in

India, "Thy sons, O India, are the ministers of thy salvation" (p. 254). Puthenpurakal (1979) continues saying, despite the fact that the priests and religious personnel came from outside the state are committed, well-intentioned and successful, it would be well-nigh impossible to substitute the lack of local vocations. Bishop Abraham strongly believed that unless the Church earnestly fostered vocations to priesthood and religious life from the local Naga Catholic families, it had no future. This view was further reflected in the meeting of religious superiors of the Diocese of Kohima in 1984 in which the Bishop exhorted, "All to give great attention to the promotion of local vocations to the Diocesan clergy-to build up the local church with its own clergy" (Alangimattathil, 1984, pg. 8). It was also decided at this meeting to set up houses of formation for religious vocations.

Ferrando, (1948), in his "The mission becomes the church" says, "The missionaries come from Europe and America, but as the Church grows, the priests and nuns must be chosen from the people of the country. Unless we have an indigenous clergy, we shall have a mission, not a Church." Keeping in mind the nature of the local Church the early missionaries sowed seeds of vocation and many responded positively to this call and steadily grew in priestly and religious life. According to Moses, "If there had not been priests and nuns from outside the state working in parishes there would not have been enough local vocations" (Personal communication, July 10, 2008). One of the first steps Bishop Abraham took to build a truly local Church and enhance the Catholic faith was the founding of seminaries in the diocese. In 1978, the Good Shepherd Seminary at Dimapur was blessed and inaugurated by the then

Apostolic Pronuncio to India Rt. Rev. Mgr. Luciano Storero. Thus, the dream of a seminary for the aspirants to priesthood from the states of Nagaland and Manipur came true (Rector, 1985). From 1984, it was raised to a major seminary for philosophy and college studies. Today, this seminary forms students hailing from across the North Eastern region, besides a few from the rest of India.

The Salesian College of Higher Education, Dimapur, a seminary and a college affiliated to the Nagaland University, provides college courses in Arts with specialisation in philosophy, was founded in the year 1984 by the Salesian congregation for the same purpose. In order to nurture vocations to the priesthood at a very young age, Bishop Abraham founded the St. Xavier's Seminary at Jalukie in 1981. With the amalgamation of the Newman Bible College at Chumukedima in 2004, this seminary forms students from class eight and above. In its thirty years, more than 400 students have passed through the portals of this house. The first seminarian from this seminary was ordained a priest in 1997. Ever since, year after year, one or two past pupils are being ordained.

All those who discontinued their studies from this institute are rendering active service to the society at various capacities in different parts of the state (Rector, 2005). In the following years, many seminaries such as the SFS Seminary of MSFS (1988) at Medziphema, Jesuit Training College (pre-novitiate) (1994) at Phesama of the Jesuits, Savio Home (1995) and Emmaus Home (2003) at Zubza of the Salesian congregation and Vincentian Seminary at Dimapur of the Congregation of the Missions, have been founded to recruit young men to priesthood.

On 17 December 1989, Fr. Neisalhou Carolus and Fr. Mhonchan Abraham, the first two local priests were ordained at Cathedral Church, Kohima on the occasion of the formal inauguration of the centenary year of the Catholic Church in North East India, in the Diocese of Kohima. It was the beginning of the real presence of the local Church in Nagaland. Once ordained, a priest is set apart for all the people. He sheds his tribal identity and affinity to live for all and to be with all. On the occasion of the ordination of Shikaho Isaac Swu, Bishop Jose Mukala said, "Fr. Shikaho Isaac will no more be for Lazami or for Sumi Nagas alone but for all people in the diocese" ("First Sumi catholic priest ordained", 2008 April 28, pg. 3).

Today, the Diocese of Kohima has more than forty ordained priests from Angami, Chang, Chakhesang, Lotha, Mao, Phom, Pochuri, Rengma, Sangtam, Sema, Tikhir, Yimchunger, and Zeliangrong tribes (Kamei, 2012) and more than seventy religious nuns belonging to different tribes working in various places in the state and outside. The establishment of religious formation houses for young men and women and acceptance of religious life by them opened the minds of the people who are now convinced that, like the missionaries from outside the state, their children too could enter religious life and offer their life unconditionally to the service of God and their fellow human beings. This is, in fact, a great contribution to the state where priests and nuns from the state serve their own people for their spiritual and general wellbeing.

A trend being noticed among most people in the world is to look for comfort. A call to religious life, therefore, is no longer an attraction to a great many young minds. Furthermore, parents support their children for higher education to find a decent job that would provide a secure future. With this changing attitude, courage and dedication is required from an individual for a life of sacrifice for the Church. Yet, contrary to the expectations of the modern world there are many local men and women of the state who enter religious life in the full knowledge that life is worth living for others if lived well. They in turn have encouraged many young boys and girls to follow their example. It is indeed a great achievement and blessing for the state that has been exposed to Christianity for less than a hundred and fifty years and Catholicism for 60 years.

Apparently people don't make any distinction between native clergy and religious personnel and those from outside the state regarding commitment and preference. However, they feel more at home with the former. It is very normal for the people to feel proud of their own sons and daughters since they can understand and communicate better with them than with the missionaries from outside the state. Local priests and nuns have the great advantage of living the culture and so their approach is more homogeneous.

"They can easily understand the ethos of the people unlike priests from outside," (Roselyn, Personal communication, August 30, 2012). According to Martha, "They are more approachable and know us better" (Personal communication, August 29, 2012). Francis spoke of the advantage of being local religious people but at the same time reminded them to be cautious, "Local priests can sense areas of sensitivity. But if love of one's tribe becomes greater than the love of Christ, then the mission will suffer. One thing they should keep in mind is the disadvantages of 'tribalism.' The moment tribalism gets in justice is sacrificed. They should excel in asceticism and self-discipline, they should preach and practice what they preach" (Personal communication, August 22, 2012).

Neisalhou, a priest for twenty two years has this to say, "My decision to take the first step toward the priestly vocation and become the first Angami Naga priest was the best contribution ...my association with various churches in Nagaland and involvement with different civil organizations is appreciated by all irrespective of denomination or religion" (Personal communication, August 31, 2012). On being asked about his strength and the contribution he has made to the Church and society as priest, Keduolhou said that he is familiar with the likes and dislikes of the people and is, therefore, able to utilise this in socialisation and communication. He also stated that, "The Church and society bestow respect and honour and are happy with our involvement in various organisations in the state like the Forum for Naga Reconciliation (FNR) and the Nagaland Christian Forum (NCF) that are engaged in peace building measures, ecumenism and other humanitarian works" (Personal communication, August 22, 2012). In the words of Latsutho, "My best contribution is giving my life to the Church and making use of the opportunities I get to unfold the truths about the Church to leaders of other denominations. People feel free to approach us in matters related to our faith, the Church, the village etc" (Personal communication, September 18, 2012). Roseline says, "Being a religious sister I have helped Catholics and Baptists to clear doubts about religious life. As a single Catholic family in the village, we held on to our faith which resulted in many more joining us later" (Personal communication, October 6, 2012).

With the founding of convents and formation houses in various parts of the state by different congregations, local vocation to women religious life received considerable support and encouragement. Many of the congregations have got their major formation houses in the state where they have candidates mostly from Nagaland and North East India and a few from outside the North East. Candidates of other congregations have got their preliminary formation in the state and for higher formation they are sent to their own Province or other formation houses.

To renounce the attractions of the world, to embrace religious life that calls for poverty, obedience and chastity certainly demands in the first place a commitment and above all, a call from God. It is a challenge to attract young people to religious life through exemplary life in the modern world. Added to that, identification with the life of ordinary people in their struggles and difficulties and become one with them does entail courage, deep faith and dedication. Religious life fails when one misses the focus and falters in the earlier commitment in the face of seemingly insurmountable problems. Again, to be a witness in trying situations can be a strenuous task. And if such situations are not dealt with effectively, the end result can be counter-productive, bringing about greater harm to the community and one's life.

The religious life of the people of the state has been enhanced by the ministry of committed priests and nuns. They have challenged the young people of the state to respond to religious vocations. Thus, many local vocations have stemmed from the life of these religious people who wielded great influence in their life. Thus, a priest or a nun becomes an evangeliser and a true witness in life and in death. Mary (1991) quotes Pope Paul VI, "Modern man listens more willingly to witnesses than to teachers, and if he does listen to teachers, it is because they are witnesses" (pg. 71).

4.2.5 Encouragement of Naga Culture through Inculturation

Inculturation is a term used in Christianity, especially in the Roman Catholic Church. It is a fundamental component of the mission, which the Church has been emphasising on for years, particularly after the Second Vatican Council (1962-65). It refers to the adaptation of the way the Church's teachings are presented to non-Christian cultures and to the influence of those cultures on the evolution of these teachings ("Inculturation", 2012 December 24, www.en.wikipedia.org/wiki/inculturation). Vadakumpaden (1989) stresses the importance of inculturation when he says, "It expresses the idea that the faith, like a seed, must sprout and grow in a culture, using the resources and genius of that culture" (pg. 257), by preserving the essence of the gospel message. It is not a compromise on the uniqueness of Jesus Christ and the identity of the Church. According to Manjaly (2006), it can be pictured as, "The seed of the gospel falling into the soil of culture, which, of its own native impulse, develops expressions of Christian life and worship, in keeping with the original genius of that particular community" (pg. 72). It can be applied in worship, catechesis, theological formulation, architecture, etc. The Church needs to identify signs and symbols, stories and folklores, feasts and festivals of the people in a particular context and inculcate their values into the daily religious practices and worship.

Inculturation and culture are interdependent. The word 'culture' has been defined differently by different authors as it encompasses the entire life system of man. It revolves around belief, language, social life and attitude of man. In culture one has his identity and discovers the meaning of life. He becomes refined and capable of self-transcendence only when he fully participates in the life of the community. Culture has been defined by Luzbetak (1970) as, "Culture is a way of life, the total plan for living. It is functionally organised into a system, acquired through learning. It is the way of life of a social group not of an individual, as such" (pg. 59). "It is a sum total of ideas, images, myths, language, laws, values and institutions that express a given society's analysis of itself and of the world as it knows it" (Haokip, 2006, pg. 15). Actually, it is a way of life and is acquired through learning. By the end of the last century many thought the world was immersed in inventions and discoveries and so lost in modernisation. At the dawn of the present century, however, even the most advanced societies have clamoured to identify themselves with a history and heritage that would provide meaning to their present life and direction to their future (John, 2006).

The most important event of the 14th century was the rise of renaissance in Europe which lasted till the 17th century. The word 'renaissance' means 'to be reborn.' It was a cultural movement that began in Florence, Italy and later spread to the rest of Europe. Its influence was felt in literature, philosophy, art, music, politics, religion, science and other aspects of intellectual inquiry. So, culture influences the entire life system of human beings. Religion and culture are inter-linked. When a new religious perspective based on the cultural life is presented and subsequently accepted by a people, their socio-cultural life is bound to undergo a transformation (Rao, 1994). The greater the absorption of religion into the cultural life of the people, the greater is the God-experience of the people. The Catholic Church encouraged inculturation from the beginning while the Baptist Church did so later. Today, inculturation is also called contextual theology. A small ancient Chinese poem aptly depicts the reality of the process of the Christian faith into a local culture, "Go to the people, live among them, learn from them, love them, start with what they know, and build on what they have" (Haokip, 2004, pg. 269). Hence, one can conclude by saying that every culture exists in its own right and no culture will be justified if it dominates another. Pope John Paul II points out that the path of culture is the path of man who meets God along this path and, therefore, concludes that the Gospel of Christ, the Incarnate Word will find its home on the path of culture and from there it will continue to offer the message of salvation and eternal life. The Jewish Christian converts never seemed to have felt that by accepting Jesus they ever lost their religious, cultural, historical, national and social identity. "This is the reason why they continued to go to the Jerusalem temple, synagogue of the place and kept up the Mosaic law while they also gathered by themselves to celebrate the memory of the Jesus-event which they experienced as the turning point in their life, transforming and fulfilling every bit of it from within" (Impact of Christianity on North East India, pg. 142).

There had been allegations in the past that Christianity, the new religion in Nagaland was responsible for the destruction of the age old tribal customs and cultural values. This was primarily attributed to the ignorance of the missionaries who despised most of the older practices as 'heathen' and 'satanic', which was unacceptable to the people. The missionaries' lack of concern for the tribal culture was condemned by many anthropologists and local populace in the state through their valuable opinion. In the words of Chenjei, "The Baptist religion did not appreciate well the Naga culture. Christians were discouraged from wearing the traditional ornaments as they believed them to be a taboo. This attitude, however, today has undergone change as there is tolerance and better understanding among people" (Personal communication, June 20, 2012). Imchen (2008) shares his opinion in the following words, "The period 1947-1972 saw divisions and dissentions within the church ultimately leading to the development of indigenous churches. By this time, the cultural milieu of the Nagas had undergone such extensive changes that Christian missions were blamed for detribalising the Nagas" (pg. 161). Downs (1994) shares the views of Haimendorf on lack of appreciation of Naga culture by the missionaries in the following words:

> It is a pity the American Baptist mission has little sympathy with the aims of Government and even less appreciation for the valuable elements of Naga culture. Many of its aspects conflict in no way with the principles of Christianity and I believe that even some of the old feasts and ceremonies, certainly agricultural festivals, could have been adapted to the new faith, given a new meaning and retained by the Christian community...with a little more understanding and sympathy for Naga culture they might have brought more happiness to their flock and avoided many of the more unfortunate results of a sudden clash of cultures (pg. 219).

Christian education, in Nagaland was also criticised for being one-sided as it meant to transplant the Christian ideologies in western style. Longkumer (2003) says, "The role of Christian education was reduced to transplant the teachings of Christianity as it was developed in the west. They ignored the native context and culture" (pg. 183). It is felt that the missionaries were not sympathetic towards the tribal culture and hence they insisted that it was a prerequisite to abandon the old religion and all that was connected with it, which had shaped their life and nurtured them for years. The American Baptist missionaries were the first who forbade taking part in tribal dances, singing tribal songs and other indigenous customs (Sanyu, 1996). During the last decade of the 19th century, the Ao church decided to tighten up standard of membership based on new guidelies: "Among the Ao churches there had been frequent lapses into the prohibited practices of opium eating, rice beer drinking and participating in traditional religious rites. In 1894, it was decided to disband the Molung Church and reconstitute it on the basis of a strict covenant or agreement specifying standards of Christian conduct. When this was done only one Naga, Bendang, would accept the new covenant" (Downs, 1983, pg. 127).

Some people are of the opinion that culpability should be fixed on those who claim to be the agents of civilisation. While most people accuse the introduction of Christianity as the responsible factor for the destruction of Naga culture, some believe that British colonialism is also equally responsible. "Although envisaging a Christian identity for the Nagas, they (the Baptist missionaries) looked down on the local culture, especially the local beliefs in the same perspective as that of the

British colonials" (Iralu, 2012, July 11, pg. 7). The following view strengthens what has been said above:

> Naga cultures were being attacked from two related outside forces with conflicting views: one was the colonial administration, which took it upon itself to 'civilise' the primitive Nagas by stages, a policy that seemed in step with the contemporary currency of the process of evolution; and two, the Christian missionary project of converting the Naga heathens into children of God through the revolutionary act of baptism. The end result was the same (Pimomo, 2008, February 15, pg. 6).

It is an accepted fact that undermining people's culture means negating their civilisation that would eventually lead to discontentment and chaos. Sanyu (1996) quotes the words of M. M. Thomas, a renowned theologian and a former Governor of Nagaland, who made a valuable comment on the need for inculturation in the life and religious practices of the people saying, "The moral crises are often expressions of cultural crisis, arising from the loss of traditional, cultural roots without acquiring new roots" (pg. 510). He further said, "Naga Christianity has yet to become truly indigenous by adopting the Naga arts and festivals and cultural artefacts into its life. It has yet to know the other religion and culture in depth" (pg. 509). From his words it is understood that imposition of an alien culture would alienate the people from their roots and consequently they would lose their identity. In the words of Puthenpurackal (1993):

> The missionaries tried to put an end to what they considered something 'heathen.' Unfortunately without an in depth

> understanding of tribal customs and practices they forbade tribal songs, dances, sacrifices, celebrations connected with cultivation, construction of houses, founding new villages, feasts of merit, use of morungs, etc. Rice beer was replaced with tea, and total abstinence from the former became a 'basis of church membership'. According to the report of Mrs. Clark, even baptism was refused by Perrine and Haggard to a young man who would not put on the 'Assamese clothes. Though we have come a long way off from those early years, the uncritical attitude of the missionaries gave rise to comments in books and articles which were and are still unfavourable to Christian missionaries who are branded as 'destroyers' of Naga culture (pg. 225).

From the writings of Bishop Ferrando (1947) one could perceive the discouragement of tribal culture in the Naga Hills by the earlier missionaries:

> The American Baptists suppressed dancing and removed a very happy and healthy variant to the ordinary monotony of the village life. In fact, I hear it said by the Nagas themselves in many places: 'If only some missionaries would come who would allow us to keep our dances, our village club-houses and not break up our tribal life!' The Protestant Baptists had the absolute monopoly of spreading the Gospel amongst the Nagas. The Catholics have been entirely excluded. The Baptists made many conversions by means of their schools and hospitals. But the Baptists were not spared with bitter criticism for having destroyed the charm of a simple picturesque life. Civilisation is not in wearing trousers, abstaining from tribal dances, and not drinking rice-beer.

> Their crude dances, which are accompanied by horrifying and savage cries and the threatening brandishing of their long lances, are mostly associated with religious festivals! (pg. 94).

Bishop Ferrando, however, said that the criticism was not always fair because it is a fashion now-a-days to belittle the apostolate of the missionaries who have done pioneering and heroic work to uplift the primitive tribes. On the one hand, the missionaries came with good intentions as far as their mission was concerned. Nagas were war-like and the missionaries considered it essential to eradicate activities and practices considered to be 'heathen', in order to make them 'civilised'. The missionaries were possibly ignorant of the cultural life of the people.

On the other hand the Catholic Church being aware of the interrelationship between religion and culture, which is an essential tool for religious life, gave importance to inculturation from its very inception in the Northeast. Jala (1993) writes:

> In 1974, Pope Paul VI pleaded for efforts to bridge the gap between Gospel and culture, saying: 'the rift between the gospel and culture is undoubtedly an unhappy circumstance of our times just as it has been in other areas. Accordingly, we must devote all our resources and all our efforts to the sedulous evangelisation of human culture or rather of the various human cultures. They must be regenerated through contact with the gospel. But this contact cannot be effected unless the good news is proclaimed' (pg. 379).

Bishop Ferrando (1951, chronicle) wrote that the Church had

an incredible appreciation for Naga culture because Nagas considered it very dear and inseparable from their lives:

> The Nagas are a proud and virile race and have some of the warlike traits of the American Indian tribes. There is a strong sense of nationalism among the Nagas but let us hope that wise counsel will guide events for the mutual benefit of India and these rugged hill men. Neither a century of civilisation nor the catastrophic events of World War II followed by a new era of progressive resurgence, have taken away the glamour, picturesqueness or enthusiasm out of their ancient feasts.

He (1947) further writes:

> We had to open schools and give an education where none had ever been given, for these tribes have no literatures or alphabet of their own, but like all primitive people there have an abundance of folklore. We had to bring about a work which in the spiritual sphere may be compared to the clearing up of a thick hill-jungle and converting it into the wonderful green carpet of the Assamese tea-gardens. But, while preaching the gospel, the Catholic Church always respects the folk-lore, the simplicity of these people, because Jesus Christ belongs to all time and to every nation (pg. 11).

While the Baptist missionaries forbade much of Naga traditional and cultural life, the Catholic Church seemed to have had a much better understanding as far as the implications of culture and tradition were concerned. The Church encouraged indigenous songs, music, symbols and dialects in its worship. It incorporated them into liturgical life: vestments, altar, sanctuary, rituals, sacraments, burial services, theology, songs, music, architecture, etc. in as far as they fit well into the system. Cultural symbols like spear, mithun head, rice plate, Naga cup etc are symbolically depicted in places of worship as well as during celebrations. The Catholic missionaries have always exhorted the Catholics to hold on to their own folk lore and customs which are not against the spirit of one's faith. In the words of Bishop Ferrando (1951, chronicle):

> Pandit Nehru and other leaders are afraid that the missionaries have made Europeans out of the tribals. Now the Government of India is going to spend enormous sums for the uplift and improvement of tribals numbering 19,000,000. Let us hope that our people will be allowed to preserve in their holy faith. We Catholics have always allowed the principles so dear to Pandit Nehru to approach the tribal people with love, to preserve what is good in them, not to destroy their dances and song and joy, and at the same time to give them the advantage of civilisation.

The Catholic Church upholds its teachings on the culture and practices of the people:

> The Vatican Council II, in its Liturgical Constitutions has boldly stated the following: 'even in the liturgy the church does not wish to impose rigid uniformity in matters which do not involve the faith of the good of the whole community. Rather does she respect and foster the qualities and talents of the various races and nations. Anything in these people's way of life, which is not indissolubly bound up with superstition and error, she studies with sympathy, and, if possible, preserves intact (Jala, 1993, pg. 379).

Mawrie (2002) is of the view that, "A culture that has been evangelised becomes not merely an agent of human promotion, but it transcends its earthly potentiality and becomes an instrument of salvation itself...from being a threat to culture, the gospel should become a catalyst for the preservation, refinement and growth of a human culture" (pg. 22). In the words of Vadakumpadan (2002), "All this means that the gospel-culture encounter should not primarily result in individual conversions uprooting them from their historic-cultural life-springs. The gospel is to be addressed to the very roots of the identity of a people" (pg. 82).

The Catholic Church always attempts to encourage and maintain cultural traditions. For example, songs and dances of the land have found their way in the worship. Many of the hymns in church services are sung in tribal tunes. The altar in many churches is a symbolic expression of a Naga rice plate. The Catholic religious vestments adorned in cultural costumes are worn by priests during Church celebrations. This action symbolises the appearance of Jesus in Naga identity as every priest is another Christ. Tribal symbols are often incorporated into the structures of the Church and buildings. The Catholic Cathedral at Kohima is an example of integration of local culture and practices into Christian art and worship. Inculturation is the driving force behind the design of this Church. Its façade is shaped in line with the traditional Naga House. The roof and floor are divided into seven sections signifying the seven sacraments (Mathew, 1989). The paintings, furniture etc. are modelled after the Naga tradition and heritage. The fourteen stations, pose a real replica of Naga houses with its beautiful arrangement on the slope of the hill (particularly in earlier days the houses of the Nagas had been situated on the slopes and on top of the hill) leading to the Cathedral (parish priest, 2008). The interior design, architecture and beauty of the Cathedral church is described as follows:

> The structure centres on a unique blend of western and Naga art. From the grills on the windows to the doors are motifs of Naga art-from the hornbill to the mithun-set in unison with scenes from the bible, the Last Supper and the Baptism of Jesus Christ. The cross in the church is placed between two spears 'to signify that we all subject our weapons to the cross, the sign of our salvation.' In these mountains of the north-east where the first guns were fired in rebellion, the church is now a beacon of peace that has a large following ("Heaven, the Naga way", 2004 May, pg. 11).

The bell tower is a symbol of 'bamboo,' an inevitable thing in the life of the Nagas. Imchen (2003) observes the Naga art and culture in the Cathedral and the importance of other signs and symbols in the following words:

> One scholarly work has a photograph of an icon of Jesus and the Cross ensconced within a 'mithun' head and also a Cross hemmed in by two hornbills and 'mithun' heads in the Christian themes adapted to Naga cultural elements of the Catholic Church in Nagaland. Among the Nagas, the 'mithun', buffalo, hornbill, pig, dog, cock and lesser creatures of the earth and sky are accorded their rightful place in the social structure in descending order of significance (pg.50).

One of the features of the Catholic Church in Nagaland has been its commitment to building the local Church and at the same time remains united with the universal church. Priests directly involved in the Church and educational institutions make considerable attempts to promote local culture and evangelisation of cultures as both are dear to the community. The role of a diocesan priest is very much valued in the field of inculturation as he is one with the believing community. In the words of Manjaly (1990):

> While inserting themselves into the local church through the study of languages, culture and religious beliefs and practices of the people, they (the diocesan priests) also preserve the universal dimension of the church. Diocesan priests promote the local culture and evangelisation of cultures. Their identification with the local church as fellow believers in a community has helped very much to evangelise the local cultures. Though there is yet much to be done, a beginning has been made. With the increasing number of local priests, one can hope that much more will be done in this field and make inculturation really meaningful, not just particularisation of a universal gospel, but also universalisation cultural values (pg. 293).

Perhaps many baptised persons remain just 'Christian' in name because of the absence of cultural elements in worship. "Religious symbols from traditional religions are coolly dislodged from their cultural and recognised contexts, emptied of their religious depth and meaning, and of their relationship to religious convictions and moral principles within a believing community" (Menamparampil, 2009, pg. 14). To connect people with their roots the Church has translated many hymn books that are in use in the Church into local dialects incorporating local music to suit them. It will have to become truly a 'local church' with the involvement of more local clergy and religious persons and the active participation of the laity in the decision making process of the Church. One thing is certain that inculturation is yet to take deep roots as study of tribal philosophy, theology, legends and beliefs are still underway.

Table 1.1 in Appendix illustrates the importance the Catholic Church attaches to indigenous songs, music, symbols etc. in worship and also the encouragement given to uphold Naga culture. Accordingly many of the respondents expressed the view that the Church has very much encouraged it and felt it as important and meaningful to incorporate them into religious ceremonies as it would involve the whole person in worship. Competitions on folklore, song and dance are often conducted in churches and schools to help maintain the tradition.

A word about the modern trend toward inculturation needs to be mentioned. There is already a disregard for ancient cultures that kept societies or communities close-knit for years the world over. This change has been triggered by adaptation to modernisation, westernisation and self-sufficiency. Appreciation and encouragement of traditional cultural values, has thus been neglected as the modern generation considers them to be outdated. Nagaland is not an exception. In the urban areas of the state, people show little attention to inculturation as in any other city in the world. To maintain one's own culture in a pluralistic society is hard. So, the people tend to follow the 'modern way.' Even in the architectural designs of the buildings including churches and houses, western styles and designs are adopted. It seems the wealthy families are attracted more into western designs. The buildings in Dimapur and Kohima and the district headquarters testify to this trend in the state. Apart from the dome of a few churches and village gates the rest barely depict Naga architectural designs. The interiors of most of the churches are decorated with modern art and designs. Cultural dances and folk songs are limited to feast days and to accord welcome to the dignitaries. They have become obsolete for the modern generation and are being showcased under the pretext of preserving for the future generations. The influence of modern culture, most often without religious and cultural values has pushed the eternal meanings of Naga culture to the brink. A revival of Naga culture would demand painstaking exercises from the intellectuals of the society who could perhaps blend both modern and ancient cultures in order to make it appeal to the younger generation while preserving it for the future.

4.2.6 Personalization of God-experience and thrust to Women's Spirituality

The Church has made attempts to personalise the concept of God not through a new teaching but through reinforcement of what has already been there. For example, people generally believe in the power of the 'spirits' but the Church tries to convince them that the Holy Spirit is a personal God who is more powerful than ordinary spirits. Again it is not God who departs from His people but people who go away from Him. Some believe He visits priests and holy people who are intermediaries and bestows gifts on some people but whom and when no one knows and as such people are scared of Him. The Christian belief has personalised this God in the person of Jesus Christ who visits everyone if one lives according to His teachings. The main idea that upholds this concept is, 'love one another as I have loved you' taught by Jesus.

One of the significant contributions of the Catholic Church has been its attempts to reinforce the role of women in spirituality. The Church promotes it, especially, through its teachings on Mary, Mother of God and other holy women both married and unmarried. Devotion to Mary, Mother of God has been a new religious experience for the people. In Baptist Christianity the influence of virtuous women, particularly the declared saints by the Church is not accorded importance. There are thousands of holy women whom the Catholic Church considers as an embodiment of holiness and generosity. Some of the married women saints like St. Adelaide, St. Anne, St. Elizabeth of Portugal, St. Helena, St. Monica, St Margaret of Scotland and others are examples of courage, holiness, generosity and perseverance in prayer, some of whom were queens and mothers. St. Agatha, St. Agnes, St. Alphonsa, St. Catherine of Sienna, St. Maria Goretti, St. Mother Teresa of Kolkata, St. Teresa of Child Jesus, St. Teresa of Avila and others proved themselves loyal daughters of the Church even in the midst of wars, calamities, sufferings and illness. Their life and example enable people, especially the women folk, to lead a holy life. Life of young virgins is an attraction to embrace a life of consecrated life. The Church's teachings on them have helped people to widen their religious horizon and make their spirituality more personalised.

4.2.7 Family Life

Virtuous living is a hallmark of one's identity. Virtues are the fabric of a society, group or organisation for quality living, which are inherent in human beings also taught at home, in the school, in places of worship and work. Religion plays a significant role in acquiring virtues like honesty, truthfulness and faithfulness, humility and work culture. However, it is a difficult task to change people's mentality, if they are easily lured into procuring easy money and caught up in the web of corruption.

The effect of Catholic Church's effort in inspiring virtuous living in people through education and religious life is negligible. Positive effects, however, including quality of work culture is noticed in some individuals. An essential element that helped many people to be true to them is the sacramental life in the Church. The sacraments of Holy Eucharist and Confession (Reconciliation) draw one closer to God and help possess a clearer conscience.

Fear of God, honesty, love for one another and sense of work culture are some of the characteristics of a Christian. There are times when Government officials have appreciated Catholic employees for their honesty, hard work and commitment to duty. There are Catholics who feel proud of being members of the Catholic Church as it helps them to be good Christians. On being asked what made him different from others especially in his attitude towards his work, Thepfünilhu said, "If I were not a Catholic, I would not have been a person with a clear conscience. The sacramental life specially nurtured by the sacrament of Confession helps me to have regular examination of conscience. When one is honest with his work he becomes a good church worker (Personal communication, August 29, 2012). "I gave up my bad habits, faithful to my duty and became a regular church goer" are the words of Sepicho when he was asked what difference his Catholic faith made in him after he embraced

Catholicism (Personal communication, July 28, 2007). Pelevito has this to say, "People don't feel my presence in the office but my absence. My religion has influenced my profession, the way I think and work" (Personal communication, August 28, 2012). He also added his opinion regarding general impression formed in the minds of the people that a good number of Catholics are honest in their work and this is attributed to the Church's teachings and sacramental life. The above mentioned examples are a few among the many who made a difference in their lives because of their Catholic faith.

A few words about family cannot be ignored, as church, marriage and family are correlated. The basic unit of any society is the family. Every society or culture develops relationships, norms and codes of conduct to regulate family life within its total plan of life. In this regard, the role of Catholicism cannot be neglected. "Christianity, Catholicism in particular, brought with it some evangelical values that asked these cultural groups to review their traditional family values in the light of the gospel and the church's teachings. Some values would have to be strengthened while others would have to be purified or suppressed" (Jala, 1993, p. 389). Among other things, the insistence of Catholic teaching on the unity, indissolubility and sacredness of marriage has eventually contributed to the stability of married life among the Catholics. Jala and Shangpliang (1993) wrote on the sacredness of the marriage based on the Code of Canon Law:

> The Catholic code embodies a belief in the sacramental sacredness of the marriage bond which is one and indissoluble. Marriage and family life are expected to be stable. In the past one century particularly socio-political situations have

> led to the emergence of a world where traditional tribal organisation, for example, had to undergo a change. The church's insistence on the sacredness of marriage and the stability of family helped pave the way for a society where the family will not be easily ruptured and where people can better find means for coping with eventual crises in family life (pg. 472).

It was essential to attribute sacramental character to marriage for a stable family life. "Marriage as a sacrament was taken out of the exclusive concern of the home into the church. Thus, the family began to assume a more stable character" (Jala, 1993, p. 389). Family apostolate is an important ministry of the Church as family is referred to as the 'domestic church.' Thus, the Church gives due importance to marriage preparation courses, family counselling and family visits. The Church encourages Church weddings as fundamental for stable family life and hence live-in relationships are in no way encouraged as a way of life. Those who choose the latter are not left out but the Church encourages them to have a Church wedding and their children receive sacraments after due preparation on sacraments. The general assumption among young people is that when two people live together they are married. The Church, however, does not accept this view.

The Church's teachings on family and its sacredness within the plan of God and the duty of the parents towards children, especially in bringing them up in faith for which the unity of marriage is a prerequisite, are made known to the families. The families are thus, to a greater extent, transformed and children are better looked after. The Church's teachings especially by the Popes on various issues relating to marriage and family are guidelines for the stability of marriage especially in the context of so called broken relationships. Thus, one may notice Catholic families are quite stable and the rate of divorce among them is less. Imparting the Christian vision of life and the insistence on equal treatment of children within the family has led to the education of all children both male and female. The Catholic Church in India observes 'Girl Child Day' on September 8 realising its moral and social responsibility to educate people by dedicating a day to honour girl children. It aims at building confidence in every girl child, making her conscious of her equal rights in society so that she would feel she is cared for. It creates awareness among the people to stop crimes against her and the need to protect her. In order to make every family a home of love, sharing, mutual respect and equality, the Church organises seminars and classes on violence and atrocities perpetrated against women.

The message for the 'Girl Child Day' is that she be regarded as a sister to everyone, a compassionate and loving wife of tomorrow, a sensitive and caring mother and the one who nurtures the destiny of many, to treat her with honour, protect her with all the rights, empower her with knowledge and allow her to grow in dignity ("Catholic church observes girl child day", 2012, September 10, pg. 3).

In Nagaland, many girls give up their studies to support their siblings mostly brothers studying within the state or outside with their meagre income. There may be a few instances where brothers discontinue their studies to support sisters. The Government at the centre has initiated a program to empower girls in the country. The program is called *"Beti Bachao, Beti*

Padhao," means, 'save the girl child and educate the girl child,' to address the declining child-sex ratio and related issues of women empowerment.

The religious Sisters in the diocese engage in various apostolates like education, health, social work and family. They regularly visit families irrespective of religion or denomination and maintain contact with them. In due course, through patient listening and understanding some families strengthen their ties with them and begin to confide in them. What men find difficult to achieve women are very often able to do so because of their patience and commitment. This intimacy with the families builds up a strong relationship especially with the women folk and helps to maintain peace and harmony in the families. This approach leads to enhancement and stability of the marriage and family. In this way, the family unity is maintained and the Christian faith is transmitted to other members of the family. Through their instrumentality, many non-sacramental marriages are rectified and broken families are reunited. Instruction on the need of family prayer and praying with family helps to maintain a praying family.

To most people the essence of religion is morality. Thanks to the efforts of all the churches in the state they all speak against the practice of polygamy. It is true that in the past many people practiced polygamy even though it was not an officially accepted practice. But when conversion to Christianity took place all churches insisted on monogamy as an essential element for family stability. This is based on biblical teachings. When the Chief Minister of the state allegedly spoke in favour of polygamy by saying, "Marrying and living with more than one wife was accepted in the Naga society," the Nagaland

Baptist Church Council, Council of Naga Baptist Churches and Kohima Baptist Pastors' Fellowship vehemently criticised his statement and said: "It is obvious that government rules civil affairs. However, God is the ruler in the moral realm and wherever civil and moral affairs overlap, God's standard is to be followed" ("Church response to polygamy remark", 2009, April 14, pg. 3). The joint forum of the council said that in the present, decaying society where all kinds of evil and immorality are rampant, making such utterances by none other than the top leader of the Christian state is deplorable. It further said that God sets the rules for marriage and therefore the Church opposes polygamy. Hence, they expressed the hope that the churches in the state maintain the biblical principle of 'Holy Matrimony' and advocate the sanctity and purity of marriage as life-long commitment. The Catholic Church was compassionate towards polygamous couples and showed flexibility especially by applying the Pauline Privilege (1 Cor 7:12-15) and rectifying non-sacramental marriages.

Another area of concern was superstitious beliefs among people. The Church's efforts to do away with superstitious beliefs have met with little success. It is difficult to dismiss such deep rooted beliefs from the lives of the people. There are people who still believe that an unexpected or critical illness is caused by the devil. For example, if someone gets sick while being in the field or going through a forest then it is assumed that it is caused by an evil spirit. In order to confirm this assumption, people resort to seeking the opinion and advice of the visionaries or soothsayers. If the visionary confirms it, then the next expected step from the family would be to take the patient to a prayer centre. At times appeals made to the family to not take a patient whom they believe is possessed or under the spell of the devil to a prayer house for fasting and prayer but to a hospital for proper treatment would not satisfy them and often fell on deaf ears. There were many instances in the past where patients in critical stages were denied medication but had been taken to prayer centres to pray over. In the words of Gwasinlo, "Our priests teach us not to seek the help of visionaries or to attribute the cause of unfortunate events occur in life to the devil. We know what they say is true, however, we fall again because it is in our blood " (Personal communication, May 12, 2010). Latsutho has this to say:

> Catholics who were converted from the non-Christian belief have transmitted their beliefs and practices and concepts on life, sickness, spirits, death etc. to their children. The Church teaches, 'don't believe in the power of devil but God', however, people say, 'how can we deny the existence of devil when we have seen it for ourselves'. So, people run to visionaries and soothsayers for solution (Personal communication, September 18, 2012).

Among the respondents, many agree that the Church makes positive efforts towards the eradication of superstitious beliefs, however, the could not make much progress.

4.2.9 Ecumenism and Peace Efforts

Unity and cooperation, the two essential unifying forces enable not only different countries to promote international peace and development but also help establish good relations among the people, communities and groups. This is also a need felt for all religions as they have been divided into various sects. Christianity is not an exception as it has been divided into various denominations and sects in the course of time due to ideological and theological differences. There have been attempts made to bring together different Christian groups at least on a working relationship. The approach widely known as 'ecumenism' has been in the forefront to fight misunderstanding, jealousy, suspicion and intolerance among themselves. The word 'ecumenism' is from a Greek root –*oikoumene*, meaning "the inhabited earth," that means, people of all faiths living in harmony respecting each other's religion. Ecumenism aims at the unification of the churches of the world separated by doctrine, history, and practice ("Ecumenism", 2013, January 20, en.wikipedia.org/wiki/ecumenism). It is defined as the promotion of religious unity and cooperation among different Christian faiths. One of the ways to promote Church unity is the observance of the unity octave, a weeklong prayer observed by the churches (Augustine, 2010). Ecumenism is not interfaith pluralism. The interfaith movement strives for greater mutual respect, toleration and cooperation among the world religions. It does not lead to unity of all religions but it does promote better relations. World War II was a turning point for the churches to take initiatives towards dialogue. The vast devastation caused to humanity made all churches become more involved in social issues. Thus, the churches became a source of hope for those in need.

In 1948, the first meeting of the World Council of Churches took place in Amsterdam under the theme, "Man's Disorder and God's Design." The Council focused on the damage caused by World War II. It decided to continue the efforts of unity with the idea of helping all those in need whether it be physical, emotional, or spiritual needs. The movement led to an understanding amongst the churches that despite differences they could come together to work for hope and peace in the midst of chaos and destruction. More importantly, the council and the movement led not only to ecumenism but to the forming of councils amongst the denominations that connected churches across continental lines (http://en.wikipedia/wiki/ecumenism).

The traditional model of ecumenism limits itself to Church unity and refuses to address social divisions and mutual rivalry. In the context of multi-splinter groups in Christianity in the North East, it is imperative to have a common and practical approach towards all. So, the new concept of 'society-centred' model of ecumenism is given importance. In the North East, it is driven by the goal of social harmony and integration. Social unity is difficult in a multicultural society but social harmony is possible. This is true of what we see in Nagaland, especially in the background of the existence of different tribes. There is a very strongly felt need for the churches to come out more courageously to promote peace and harmony. "Christians have to play a more pro-active role in order to promote peace and harmony, while helping tribals by actively promoting and enabling them to achieve their aspirations for justice and development" (Jala, 2002, pg. 202).

In the past there had been rivalry and competitions among the Baptists and Catholics in the North East. Ecumenism in those days might have been a remote possibility as the rivalry was deeply rooted and with little opportunity to explore differences. In the first place the missionaries came to the Naga Hills from a situation of intense anti-Catholic propaganda in the United States; and secondly, the Baptists were the only Christian group in the Naga Hills up to about 1950 (Puthenpurakal, 1983). It was during the time of the British rule that most of the Christian missions started in the North East. "Though the situation has registered a marked change for the better in recent years, yet there exists a wall of ignorance of each other built on past prejudices making it a major obstacle to any fruitful dialogue" (Puthenpurakal, 1983, pg. 198). More the number of denominations, greater will be the differences. It was, therefore, essential to come together to fight biases. Jala (2002) opines that ecumenical dialogue is a challenge and a call to conversion for the whole church. He quotes an example in the context of a common problem faced by the churches in India when all the churches came together to oppose the so called Freedom of Religion Bill in 1978.

"There are already signs of unity in search of common solution to problems that afflict society such as violence, poverty and illness" (pg. 205). There had been a number of accusations against the Christians from Hindu organisations in the past and now. There have been organised attacks on the minorities particularly the Christians. However, when there is a common enemy working against the Christians, it is not the time to maintain each other's status quo but to wake up from our complacency and show forth our solidarity and oneness by bringing all denominations to a common platform. "The *Sangh Parivar* does not care whether we are Presbyterians, Roman Catholics, Baptists, or else, but simply targets us as Christians. So, we have to respond to it as Christians" (Tochhawng, 2004, pg. 42).

In the background of bitterness against the Christians, it is wise on the part of the churches not to work independently but seek more cooperation from each other as it is evident from the mission of the churches that their obligation is not only to spiritual well-being but also overall well-being of the people. The church should, therefore, involve in socio-political uplift of the people. For example in Mizoram, the church had been the main instrument in reconciling the insurgent group of Mizo National Front and the Central Government during the two decades of the Mizo independence movement (1966-86). According to Pachuau, "The Church was the first to condemn the violence and the first and leading instrument in bringing the peace" (Simte, 2004, p. 39). If one takes the overall efforts of the churches in achieving peace and unity, there has been some headway. Jala (2002) states, "There are already signs of unity in search of common solution to problems that afflict society such as violence, poverty and illness" (pg. 205).

The Naga reconciliation process commenced under the banner of Forum for Naga Reconciliation (FNR) consisting of the Church, Tribal Hoho (organisations), civil society activists and student bodies which played a great role in bringing different groups together. Even though the FNR is not a church organisation, the Baptist Church has made a significant contribution in the process of peace in the state.

The Nagaland Christian Forum (NCF) comprising of church leaders from all the different churches in the state is a common platform to discuss and settle common issues pertaining to all Christians. They voice their concern over attacks on Christians, discriminations, human rights violations, and social issues like corruption. Youth ministry run by brothers of Salesian College and Good Shepherd Seminary especially on Sundays is perhaps a small step towards openness to sharing and ecumenical dialogue irrespective of denominations and religions.

The Catholic world view of universality of the Church helps a great deal in instilling a spirit of unity and peace within the community and with others. The Church's emphasis on love, concern and forgiveness, helps people reflect on the need for peace. It is involved in solving inter-clan rivalries in the villages and tries to maintain a peaceful atmosphere. No lie is uttered and no mind is prejudiced against any denomination from the pulpit. The priest as the local head of the Church, local leaders and religious sisters through religious and humanitarian works try to promote unity in the village.

4.2.10 Literature

The general life of a community is largely kept alive by its oral and written literature. The people's origin, customs, practices, language and their religious, social and economic life are expressed through literature. Christian literature has a 2000 year old history and it is one of the biggest collections in the world. In order to promote Christian literature a press and a book stall, named 'Catholic Publication Centre (CPC) was opened at Kohima in 1983. The CPC and the Pastoral Centre, Dimapur promote Christian literature which includes spiritual and educational books, religious articles and audio-visual materials. The Lotha, Angami, Pochuri, etc. tribes have their own literature committees and translate and publish Church hymnals, prayer books, life of saints, etc. into their own dialects. The Bible and few literary works based on faith and teachings of the Church have been translated into some of the vernaculars using the Roman character. The Translation of the Deutro-canonical books (the seven books of the Bible not accepted by the Protestant Churches) has been translated into a few local dialects. The diocesan newsletter, 'Sharing' published bimonthly, covers the news and views of the diocese and the universal Church. The monthly circular of the Bishop gives valuable information on various activities of the Church. 'The Echo' published from the Pastoral Centre, Dimapur contains teachings of the Church on faith and morals. Books on different subjects meant to be used on various occasions and books on contributions by important lay leaders of the Church have been published. Religious cassettes, containing devotional and liturgical hymns have been released. Another major contribution in the field of music was the publication of 'All You Hills' hymn book, compiled by Fr. John Med which was used in many dioceses in the Northeast.

Many books have been published in English containing the basic teachings of the Church and answers to questions people have about the Church. Some of the books/booklets published are: 'The Bible and the Church' by T. J. Chacko, 'Christian Religion in a Biblical and Historical Nut-Shell' by Joseph Edakudan, 'The Christian Faith' by John Med, 'Searching for the Truth' by St. Thomas Church Tuensang, 'Lay Apostles and their Apostolate' by the Diocese of Kohima, 'A Brief History of the Catholic Church in Nagaland' by David Syiemlieh, 'Corruption of Christianity' by Jonas Yanthan, 'A Star Over Tenyimia' by Thomas Vattoth, 'Christianity through the Centuries' by Isaac Padinjarekuttu, 'The Original Root Church the Mother Church' by Tom Karthik, etc. An educative monthly bulletin, 'Emmanuel Dielie'in Tenyidie, aims to defend the Catholic faith and doctrines. Lotha Literature Committee, the sub-committee of the Lotha Catholic Union has published many works which include a Catechism book in Lotha dialect, My Catholic Faith, God Speaks to His Children etc. Book of Blessing, Christian Funerals, Baptism for Children, Holy Week, Catechism Books, Deutro-canonical books, Rite of Marriage, Missal and others are currently being translated. Apart from these, there has been very little progress in the Church in the field of Catholic literature. Absence of a common language could be cited as one of the reasons for lack of written literature in the Church. More needs to be done along with local dialects as the Church has its members in all the tribes in the state. The process can be accelerated if there is self-will and dedication.

By contrast, the Baptist missionaries were active from the very beginning in translating hymns and catechism books into local dialects. For example, during the short stay of Mr and Mrs W. E. Witter in Wokha they began their literary work and opened a school on 25 August 1886 with three Naga boys. Mr Witter writes, "Of course the main work of the year has been the study of the language. A considerable vocabulary has been collected and a phrase-book illustrating the syntax of the language has begun. A short catechism has been put into Naga and a beginning made on the miracles. A primer has also been written and two hymns translated" (Bendangyabang, 2002, p. 100). Before they left in 1888 they had translated the Assamese catechism into Lotha and had written the first hymn in Lotha. They had also translated several hymns and some portions of the New Testament.

4.2.11 Differences with the Church

Although the public in general have acknowledged the presence of the Catholic Church and have been visibly tolerant towards it, nevertheless it faces occasionally unfriendly reactions from some quarters. One of the reasons for this reaction is the theological and ideological differences that exist between the churches and the insistence of the village policy of 'one religion/ denomination.' Added to these there are also false propaganda spread against the Catholic Church. In the words of Chuba:

The Catholic Church faces an unfavourable situation in many areas because of the wrong seeds sowed in the minds of the ordinary people by leaders of other churches about the Catholic faith, practices and beliefs. They preach even now from the pulpit that 'the Catholics are anti-Christians, idol worshippers (like the Hindus), worshippers of Mary, no Catholics outside Nagaland,' etc. Before the arrival of the Baptist missionaries the Nagas were pagans. The missionaries provided them with basic education and a new religion. So, whatever they were taught they believed. People are generally against the Catholic Church, but not schools run by it (Personal communication, June 28, 2012).

Yabang, says, "People began to experience all round development in Kohima and Wokha after the establishment of Catholic schools. In the beginning, though the Baptist leaders opposed the Catholic mission later on they approved it. But still many are not in favour of the Catholic Church but welcome Catholic education" (Personal communication, June 29, 2012).

The religious and social contribution of the Ao pastors who were the most educated in the beginning of Christianity is praiseworthy as they evangelised and educated many of the tribes in Nagaland. The people in general heard about Jesus Christ for the first time from their lips. In their preaching and teaching, however, they wished that people follow Baptist Christianity in order to receive eternal life. Hence, it was a natural reaction to oppose and react when they heard about the Catholic religion in their village or town. Being illiterate most people could not distinguish one from the other (Angnyei, Personal communication, June 20, 2012).

Another opinion is fear among people of losing their religious and social fabric with which they have felt protected for so long, to a life of insecurity and alienation if they embraced Catholicism that has insufficient members in a given area to provide them moral and social security (Chinkai, Personal communication, June 20, 2012). A third view is that the anti-Catholic propaganda in the remote villages is caused by some church leaders (Yonwang, Personal communication, June 20, 2012). Angnyei opines that one reason for the opposition is the fear of financial insecurity of the Church. If there are more churches, the Church income will be divided and the Church would become poorer (Personal communication, June 20, 2012). It is generally believed that those who were educated in Catholic institutions or have some prior knowledge of the Catholic Church won't speak openly against it.

Even though the freedom to practice faith is one's right, various written records proved otherwise in some parts of Konyak and Phom areas. Many Catholics have gone back to Baptist Church due to verbal influence. It is quite natural for people to doubt the intention of a new Church when they hear of its entry in the locality. Beaü said, "Living together, learning together and helping each other are the best ways to acknowledge each other's contribution" (Personal communication, June 30, 2012). He told people to be open-minded when he was questioned for not sending his children to a Baptist school but to a Catholic school.

Even in recent times Catholics were threatened to return to the Baptist Church failing which they would face serious consequences. The warning letters carry the message of, 'one religion in Konyak land.' (Jackson, Personal communication, June 22, 2012). There was a strong opposition to people accepting the Catholic faith in Pesao village under Tobu division in 2011. In the meeting that followed at Pesao on 17 June 2012 they said that both Pesao Catholic Church and Tobu Catholic Church would have to be closed down. But the Pesao community said that it was their own free will that they accepted the Catholic faith and they reiterated to remain as Catholics. At this they were told to close down gradually. Wanmai said that unless the leaders changed their mind-set they would continue to say that there should be only one religion (Personal communication, June 22, 2012). According to Chenjei, "The Konyak people have benefitted much from Catholic education but from the religious point of view the Church failed to make any impression, as such people don't feel the presence of the Catholic Church in Mon town" (Personal communication, June 20, 2012). In conclusion the people in general appreciate Catholic education but don't get drawn to Catholic religious beliefs. In such a background it is not surprising when you hear about discrimination against Catholics. It is an open secret that during interviews Catholic candidates are asked to give reasons for being Catholics.

It is an undeniable fact that Catholics in some parts of the state face opposition as it is evident from the questionnaire. The 'one religion principle' of many of the villages is interpreted as an agent of unity while presence of multiple religions as a cause of disunity. One of the accusations against the Catholic Church has been that it is an intruder into the majority Baptist state. Majority of the respondents who happen to be non-Catholics, however, do not agree with this view. On the question whether the Catholic religion was an intruder and divided the Naga society, a substantial number of respondents responded in the negative (Pie Chart 1.1).

In the aftermath of the dismantling of the Catholic Church at Anatongre village under Kiphire district, on 9 July 2010 the Deputy Commissioner of Kiphire issued an order that the village council's resolution to deny the right to some of the members of the village to become Catholics and the subsequent dismantling of the Catholic Church under construction had no legal sanction because it went against the fundamental rights of the citizens.

Lotha defended the fundamental right of citizens to practise their religion and questioned the wrongful interpretation of Article 371A of the Constitution for vested interest. In 2010, he writes:

> Another argument put forward is that in Nagaland one has to keep in mind the culture of the Nagas to preserve the unity of the villages. Specifically, an argument put forth by some Nagas is that allowing a section of the people to become Catholics will destroy the unity, communal peace and harmony of the village. This kind of argument speaks of double standard practices, a misunderstanding of culture, and an abuse of culture for one's advantage. According to my observation, in many parts of Nagaland this reasoning is applied only when some people want to become Catholics.

> When in the late 1800s and the 1900s the Baptist converts in Nagaland were suffering a similar fate from the non-Christians, the Baptists didn't say they were dividing the village. The NBCC even has a target of sending 10,000 missionaries to different parts of the world. But if these Naga missionaries are destroying the cultures and unity of these mission areas, then they should be brought back immediately. Nagas should not be associated with destroying others' cultures (pp. 11-12).

It is quite unreasonable to blame the ordinary village people for prejudice against the Catholics as they act on the instigation of some leaders whom they believe.

Many people embraced the Catholic faith of their own free will but against the wishes of their parents or family and as a consequence, some of them were ostracised from the family. While some took this experience as a challenge, others gave in to the pressure of the family later on. Murilo said, "I went back to the Baptist Church because I was ostracised from the family and being cut off from the family meant great humiliation" (Personal communication, July 22, 2007). Alongkiu, a Gaon Bura and an ex-catholic, said, " I was told by the village council that I would not get a government job if I became a Catholic. Soon after leaving the Church I got a job" (Personal communication, July 22, 2007). A similar experience was shared by Thsipongkiu, a priest of the diocese. "I felt humiliated as Catholic students were ill-treated by the teachers especially during school assembly. I joined the Baptist church when I was in primary one but only to return back to the Catholic Church the very following year" (Personal communication, July 23, 2007).

Many people accepted the Catholic faith on their own free will, while some others for selfish interests like monetary advantage, free education of their children or acceptance in the community. When their expectations were not met by the Church they threatened to leave and spread lies about the Church, priests and administration. The Catholic faith and practices are different from other Christian denominations. They are based on Bible, sacraments, traditions, magisterium etc. The community, therefore, is expected to adhere to faith formation imparted by the Church from time to time.

At the same time, negligence on the part of the Church needs to be addressed. In the first place the Church's failure to understand the peoples' motive behind becoming Catholics has led to many misunderstandings and even closure of some village communities. There are instances of communities being formed without sufficient catechesis and waiting. A period of catechumenate is being practiced in the Church from the very beginning. Therefore, the hurry shown by the Church to baptise people or receive them into the Church have led to unforeseeable troubles. In many cases, delay in meeting the genuine demands of the people and negligence of the community by the Church have led to discontentment and drop in membership (Celestine, Personal communication, June 22, 2012).

The contribution of the Catholic Church in the religious and cultural field is significant. In the first place the Church is accepted by most people as an independent entity with an identity. It has shown itself to the society as a symbol of unity, universality and hope. It has its own distinct practices, worship and prayers. Catholic spirituality does not depend on external manifestations alone but inner conversion also. It has morally and spiritually affected the lives of the people. Many people bear testimony to a good and exemplary life. They have created for themselves a good impression in the society. However, the spirit of Christianity in Nagaland as a whole is shallow because of shallow ethics. It is more external than internal. It hasn't gone deep into the heart and is not fully inculturated into the local soil. Being at an infant stage it is difficult to part with the influence of the immediate past. People need God, but for many Mammon is nearer. For many people, sunday gatherings are more of a social gathering than spiritual. The time has come to introspect into the functioning of the churches at all levels. The identity of a Christian does not depend on the fact that he is a baptised person and the state need not be called a Christian state because majority of the inhabitants are Christians. Yanthan (2010, April 6) writes:

There is a dichotomy between what is being called a Christian and being called a Christian state, in actual practice. There is much puzzlement created by the notion of being citizens of a state that is numerically known to be inhabited by 90% Christian on one side while on the other hand the prevalence of 100% non-Christian ethics in every walk of Naga life, be it in the church, society or politics. The Christian life is a call to a life of constant challenges against the evil forces of personal and social or tribal selfishness, greed, jealousy, dishonesty and self-righteousness. If we have not overcome these then, there are no Christians in Nagaland, but beginners and novices (pg. 7).

4.3 EDUCATION AND ITS IMPACT

Education plays an important role in the development of a nation and its citizens. Palamattam (1993) writes, "One of the main requirements to solve the problem of national development is judicious development of resources, of physical resources and above all of human resources" (pg. 397). Etymologically, the word 'education' is derived from the Latin *'educare'* meaning 'to bring up,' which is related to *'educere,'* 'to bring out,' to bring forth what is within, to bring out one's potential (John, 2010, pg. 45). To educate means to give intellectual and moral training to someone. An ideal system of education should enable individuals to know and develop to the fullest, their physical and intellectual potentialities and promote their awareness of social and human values, so that they can develop a strong character and live better lives and function as responsible members of the society. It is by transforming the people that social transformation can be brought about (Malik, 1997). According to the National Policy on Education 1986, education is fundamental to one's all-round development, material and spiritual. "Education has an acculturating role. It refines sensitivities and perceptions that contribute to national cohesion, a scientific temper and independence of mind and spirit - thus furthering the goals of socialism, secularism and democracy enshrined in our Constitution" (National Policy on Education 1986, 1986, pg. 3). The purpose of education, therefore, is the development of the intellectual, emotional, spiritual and social spheres of person. With the Right of Children to Free and Compulsory Education Act, of April 1, 2010, India joined a select group of nations where education is a fundamental right, making elementary education an entitlement for the children in the 6-14 years age group (Competition Success Review, May 2010). If implemented correctly, the Act will ensure that no child is deprived of the right to learn in a school environment. In the all-India context, the Act could have been enacted earlier than now as India has more than nine million children who have never been to school or have dropped out. In Nagaland literacy rate today as per the 2011 census stands above the national average. The Catholic Church has played a definitive role in this great feat by providing quality education. As in most parts of country the children in the state are also deprived of modern infrastructure, committed and trained teachers and midday meals. Ingrained ignorance of people in rural areas of the need for good education is a big challenge. In addition, corruption and insufficient flow of funds from the government affect quality education. Yet, the state has progressed in education much more than many of the Indian counterparts mainly because of the great involvement of private players.

Education is by far the best agent of social transformation. It is a preparation for life and as such the child should be provided with an environment that will enable him to face life's challenges and lead a meaningful life. If connected to culture and faith one will grow up as a responsible child and citizen. One also discovers through learning that education is not a mere degree or a certificate that can be shown to others as proof. It also influences our attitude, actions, language and behaviour with others in real life.

4.3.1 Catholic Education Policy

The Christian concept of education is based on Christian

anthropology and Christian humanism. It is the integral development of the whole person (Pulimoottil, 2011, April 2). Quoting the words of Cardinal Telesphore Toppo, Mukala (2007) writes, "Catholic education is integral to the very mission of the Church. Church is both a mother and a teacher. That is why it is so involved in the education apostolate and has invested a huge amount of personnel and money in education" (pg. 3). The greatest contribution the Church of today makes to the national mainstream is efforts to build human resources by means of its educational services so that the nation will have a firm footing. "The Catholic School is a major constituent of the image of the Catholic Church in India. The longstanding commitment of so many institutions and persons down through the years has created a consistent and prominent Catholic presence in the field of education in India and has enabled the Church to make the Gospel known and to contribute to the development of persons and of the nation" (Pastoral Plan for Catholic Schools in India, 1994, pg. 11). Today, the nation is proud to have so many illustrious men and women who studied in the Church run schools and colleges and are now working in the social, political and administrative fields. Even in the North East many past pupils of the Catholic educational services are at the helm of politics and administration.

Schools are centres for building up human communities and therefore, education by its very nature is a transformative process, namely changing human persons, and through them society and its structures. "This activity of transformation is a spiritual, humanising and liberating activity and constitutes the core mission of education" (All India Catholic Education Policy 2007, pg. 11). The Second Vatican Council in its Declaration on Christian Education has spelt out in unambiguous terms the aim of education in Catholic Schools as follows, "True education aims at the formation of the human person with respect to his ultimate goal and simultaneously with respect to the good of those societies of which, as a man/woman/he/she is a member and in whose responsibilities, as an adult, he/she will share" (Anikuzhikattil, 2003, pg. 211). Pope John Paul II, makes it clear that schools are centres for building up human communities so as to form students as agents of change. A child should be given an integral formation through systematic and critical assimilation of culture in order to make him feel part of the base. "A faith that does not become culture is a faith that has not been fully accepted, not thoroughly thought and not faithfully lived" (Anikuzhikattil, 2003, pg. 211). In school, the child comes directly into contact with his culture and assimilates it to become integrated. So, the school should help in all possible ways to stimulate intelligence and provide a better understanding of the purpose of study. This will in turn enable the assimilation of learning for a meaningful and truthful life. Any school (education) that neglects this duty is a hindrance to personal development. The school should, therefore, aim at integral formation and the critical assimilation of culture. In order to realise this, a sound education must be organised around the four fundamental types or pillars of learning namely, learning to know, learning to do, learning to live with others and learning to be. The Church-run schools should try to coordinate all activities of the school around these pillars of learning to form and equip the student to live his life. "An educated person works hard to earn his living by honest means because life has taught him the values of life and that will enable him to live those values" (John, 2008, pg. 1).

In India, Catholic educational institutions are second in number behind government run schools. There are 13,004 primary and secondary Catholic schools, 243 special schools, 448 Catholic colleges, and 534 technical institutions ("Catholic school", 26 January, 2013, en.wikipedia.org/wiki/catholic school). Catholic educational institutions throughout India are known for their quality because they operate on gospel values. "Catholic schools generally enjoy a good name for the quality of education they impart, for the hard work and dedication of their educative personnel, and for the sense of discipline and good behaviour they instil in their pupils" (Pastoral Plan for Catholic Schools in India, 1994, pg. 13). In order to coordinate the activities of these educational institutions, policies, action plans and follow ups are essential. The Church, therefore, comes forward with a general policy based on the gospel values that binds all institutions under it. "Catholic education chooses to work for the total development of the young. In this process, the young are helped to discover their God-given talents and to work towards their fullest development as far as possible in order to place them at the service of the community" (Pastoral Plan for Catholic Schools in India, 1994, pg. 27). A similar view is expressed by the Catholic Bishops Conference of India (CBCI) Commission for Education and Culture, "Education by its very nature is a transformative process, namely changing human persons and through them society and its structures. This activity of transformation is a spiritual, humanising and liberating activity and constitutes the core mission of education" (All India Catholic Education Policy 2007, pg. 11). A message from the CBCI annual meeting of 2006 puts the overall purpose of the Church's educational institutions as, "Building a New India, where every child is educated, where the marginalised are empowered, where the educational system seeks to transform the society, is the Christian dream" (Thumma, 2006, December 11-17, pg. 25). The All India Catholic Education Policy of the Bishop's Conference of India insists that the Catholic schools have a special responsibility to impart religious instruction to children of its faith. The Bishops say, "We stand committed to nurture a Catholic culture of faith as a personalised way of life of Catholic students,....a complete catechetical course, a careful study of the scriptures, a profound understanding of one's eternal destiny in Christ, an enlightened fidelity to Catholic religious traditions and practices, and an introduction to an intelligent participation in the Church's liturgy and prayer-life remain key components of faith education" (All India Catholic Education Policy 2007, pg. 18). The All India Catholic Education Policy (2007) centres on the integral development of the student:

> Education, from the standpoint of Christian faith, aims at the all-round formation of the human person with a view to empowering the person to create a society inspired by the Gospel values of service in love, peace rooted in justice and fellowship based on equality. This education is meant to lead a person to an ever greater openness to the transcendent – for us Christians to God, to become one-of-us in Jesus Christ. Hence, one of the important aims of Catholic education is faith-formation, deepening the Christian commitment to Jesus in His Church (pg. 15).

Catholic education gives importance to the spiritual

formation of students of other faiths too who form the vast majority in our schools and colleges. As in conformity with the teachings of the Church, Catholic students are taught catechism in order to strengthen them in their faith, while others are given lessons in Moral Science. "The Church assists them to develop a set of personal values and principles and become persons of character and integrity, internalising the social aspects of their religious traditions and thus leading them to experience personal well-being and to make a contribution to build a better India" (All India Catholic Education Policy 2007, pg. 17). India is a multi-lingual and multi-religious country and the constitution of the country grants religious freedom to all its citizens. Therefore, all the educational institutions respect this multi-faceted character of the country.

"Plurality requires a disciplined commitment to tolerant understanding of the other. This kind of tolerance is not a matter of merely being nice to each other. It respects differences of beliefs.... and tries to understand what these beliefs mean rather than to bypass them or eliminate them" (Ryan, 2008, pp. 21-27).

Irrespective of religious practices, both Catholics and non-Catholics in Nagaland receive education based on good morals in a harmonious and respectful environment. In the words of Bishop Stephen Ferrando, "The Central Government of Delhi has a grand plan for the education, uplift of these hill tribes. The government can throw in millions and millions of money, but the moral values are on the side of the missionaries (Ferrando, 1949, July, pg. 2). At par with the intellectual and emotional growth the Church stresses character formation of students in its institutions that will help them grow in their own respective faith and promote causes of justice and equality. Our institutions should not be for a 'privileged few,' but should always have an 'option for the poor.' John (2010) quotes from the Second Vatican Council's Decree on Catholic Education (*Gravissimum Educationis, 3*), "The church as a mother is under an obligation to provide for her children education by virtue of which their whole lives may be inspired by the Spirit of Christ.

At the same time, she will offer its assistance to all people for the promotion of a well-balanced perfection of the human personality, for the good of society in this world and for the development of a world more worthy of man" (pg. 41). According to Haokip, "In our efforts, we are to project and communicate character formation and inculcation of values as qualitative signs of our schools and colleges and also by introducing positive aspects of tribal culture" (Personal communication, March 9, 2009).

There is a tendency and temptation to measure the end results of public examinations as criteria to judge the quality of the school. The validity of the Catholic school is not to be judged from immediate efficiency in discipline, results and achievements in cultural activities. Gospel values have to mark the educational atmosphere and the tone of the whole institution (Jala, 2002).

4.3.2 Catholic Education-a Gateway to North East India

The influence of the Catholic Church in North East India was mainly through its educational institutions. "Catholic schools used to be known as providers of the best education in the country and in the region carrying the brand name for quality education" (Thomas & Elizabeth, 2009, February, pg. 1). In many parts of the country including the North East, when people hear of the Catholic Church they mostly identify it with Catholic schools and colleges. "In the minds of many, especially outside the Church today, the Catholic Church seems to be synonymous with quality education" (Jala & Mukhim, 1993, pg. 338). This identification is not totally wrong as we see the monumental contribution made by the Church in the field of education.

Education is an integral part of evangelisation for the North East India in general and Nagaland in particular. According to Downs (1983), "The key to Roman Catholic success, often at the expense of established Protestant groups from which they draw some of their members was their educational policy" (pg.154). The Ministry of Education is actually an evangelisation agency that imparts the values of the Gospel and promotes the culture of love, justice and tolerance. In earlier days the only medium of contact with far-flung areas of the North East was through educational institutions. The Christian schools and colleges are the only means of contact with the non-Christian world in most places (Mary, 1991). The Catholic Church provided a platform for the people of the region to be in contact with mainland India through its education. Eventually these institutions benefited the region in many ways. Without the schools and colleges run by the Church, North East India would not have been prepared to cope with the changes following the Indian independence. "The developments in free India would have remained outside the reach of the people of the region, were it not for the education imparted to young people over the years by the Church" (Jala & Mukhim, 1990, pg. 60). Jala in his article,'Contribution of

Catholic Church to the Cultures of North East India' (Indian Missiological Review September-December 1990) mentions the educational contribution of the Catholic Church to the region primarily through primary and middle schools, in the following words:

> If the church has been able to spread and survive in Northeast India through many difficulties, credit must be given to the role played by the church-run educational institutions. One must not underscore the fact that education has best helped the various groups in Northeast India come to terms with the inevitable process of modernisation and development that is forging its way ahead especially in the present decade. Without the process of education, the various cultural groups of this region would have been behind and at the mercy of more educated groups. It is through the educational institutions that local talents were readied for taking up various posts that helped the development of economic and political autonomy in the region. The spread of literacy has helped to encourage the growth of indigenous literature. In this respect, the church has done yeoman's service through the network of primary and middle schools that are found in every region.

In the North East, the concept of 'education for all' was not opened to both the sexes by the male dominated society in the beginning, rather it was predominantly for males because female education was regarded with open contempt. A frequent reply by parents in the plains to send their girls to school was, "You will next be asking to send our cattle to school!!" The Nagas would reply, "You cannot teach our females, they are trained to bear burdens, to bring wood and water and to make the salt by which we make our sustenance" (Sangma, 1987, p. 42). This trend, however, gradually changed and equal treatment to males and females was accorded when parents were educated on the need to educate both.

4.3.3 School Education by Nagaland Government

Nagaland has made progress in the field of quality education. The State runs 1794 Primary Schools, 880 Upper Primary Schools, 547 Secondary Schools, 103 Higher Secondary Schools, 2 B.Ed/CTEs and 7 D.Ed/DIETs (Directorate of School Education, 2012). Since private schools outdo government schools in terms of performance parents prefer to send their children to them. With highly qualified teachers, the government run schools should perform better. The outcome, however, indicates a dismal performance by many of these schools, while the private schools toil hard and produce better results with little financial assistance from the government. One of the problems faced by the private schools in Nagaland is that the government absorbs all the qualified persons and appoints them to government schools which do not reflect qualitative output in comparison to the personnel, infrastructure, and finance invested. Conversely, the private schools are left with no option but to desperately search for expertise from outside the state. It has been criticised from the 1970s that the government schools lag behind private schools in the state. "Much has been said and written about the 'failing' standard of education in Nagaland in particular and in the country as a whole. A few years ago, Shürhozelie, the then Education Minister, admitted that "schools were better managed by private individuals, particularly those run by Missions" ("Lesson for the teachers", 1984, June 14, pg. 4). Discrepancies and disparities on the side of the government need to be studied and addressed and the government should also shoulder responsibility for quality education. Often with untrained teachers and insufficiency of funds, the private schools perform satisfactorily and continue to remain the chief agency for providing quality education in the state. However, there have been marked improvements recently in some government schools in Dimapur and Kohima districts. This can be seen as being the result of the positive and concrete efforts which are being made by the administration, teachers and students there.

4.3.4 Educational Initiatives of the Baptist Church till the Independence of India

Education was unheard of among the Nagas prior to their conversion to Christianity. The new religion opened the door to a world of growth, development and civilisation. The arrival of the American Baptist Missionaries marked the beginning of renaissance in Naga history. They deserve praise for opening the minds of the Nagas to learning, followed by the Catholic missionaries and others. Earlier, the only education known to youth was the teaching of their village chiefs, parents and elders about the social, religious and traditional practices in a training centre called the Morung (Ennio,2008, April 11). The people's eyes were opened when the missionaries introduced literacy among them. The educated masses were easily employed and soon they became wealthy. In the words of Thepfünilhu, "Nagas educated by the Baptist missionaries eventually became leaders of society and became wealthy too. It became fashionable to be

Christians. Children started writing their identity as Christians even though their parents were non-Christians" (Personal communication, August 29, 2012).

The British left the task of educating the tribals to the missionaries (Islam, 2003), and rendered all possible help. From the very beginning of their contact with the Nagas, the British officers perceived the need to introduce Christianity and education among the Naga tribes as the best agency for reclaiming the rugged Nagas to order and progress (Sema, 1988). In the beginning when the Nagas came into contact with the missionaries they were hostile. The non-Christians even persecuted those who had converted to Christianity for accepting the new religion and blamed them for dividing their age old religion and traditions. It was in the midst of this unwelcome approach that the missionaries began the enlightening mission of education. Interestingly, the laying of the foundation of education by the Baptist missionaries in Nagaland met with some success as many Nagas showed a keen interest in learning. This remarkable attitude encouraged both the missionaries and the government. The keen interest shown by the people was a great motivation for the missionaries to spread education to as many areas as possible. "Rev. Miles Bronson, the first American missionary to the Nagas landed at Namsang, a Naga village in 1839 is believed to have started the first school for the Nagas" (Ennio, 2008, April 11). Dr. Clark, the first missionary to the Ao Nagas, Rev. D. E. Witter, to the Lotha Nagas and Rev. C. D. King to the Angami Nagas, tirelessly worked in the midst of head-hunting to introduce education in Nagaland.

The British government introduced the western system

of education assisted by the Christian missionaries to bring the Nagas in touch with modern civilisation and to use the educated class as a link between the ruler and the ruled. The progress in education prior to 1908 was discouraging due to various factors (Uzhunnalil, 1975). It was in 1910 that Rev. Dr. S. W. Rivenburg (1886-1923) started a school in Kohima. The Angami dialect was converted to writing and some Biblical literature was translated from Greek into Angami. They jointly established as many as 161 L.P. schools, three M.E. Schools and one High School (Uzhunnalil, 1975). Barpujari (1982) wrote of the immediate need to educate the tribals in the following words, "The missionaries wanted a workable literacy among the hill men and with this end in view they opened mostly primary schools and a few training schools for teachers. Those who had received education were sent to the villages to teach as well as preach the principles of Christian religion among the Nagas" (pg. 4). Initially, however, the missionaries used the Assamese language both in teaching and preaching. The local dialects were suitably adopted afterwards converting them to the Roman (Barpujari, 1982), as the Nagas did not have a script of their own. Without much delay the teaching of the English language was undertaken in these schools.

There was a change of attitude in the educational system in the Naga Hills after the Independence of India as the government assumed the responsibility for education. Imchen (2008) mentions that, "The Baptist mission and churches gradually began to withdraw from the educational field on the ground that Christian schools were no longer necessary in the light of government's decision to take over education" (pg. 162). With this, the flow of funds for education ceased. "By

1950s, the Mission or the Association had completely ceased aiding the Ao village schools as most of their support came either from the government or the villages " (Imchen, 2008, p. 163). It was decided to discontinue the Middle English department at Impur and open a training and Bible school instead. The Vankhosung School at Wokha and Aizuto Mission School were closed down. In the years between 1950 and 1960, at the peak of Naga insurgency, the growth of education in the Naga Hills further suffered. According to Yabang, (Personal communication, June 29, 2012) it was the Baptist leaders who opened the eyes of the illiterate people in the beginning. Years later when people observed the all-round development offered by the Catholic educational institutions in Kohima and Wokha they expressed satisfaction over the quality of Catholic education. Even though many Baptist leaders opposed the entry of the Catholic mission, later on they approved of it. There are still many who are not in favour of the Catholic Church but approve of Catholic education.

4.3.5 Educational Initiatives of the Catholic Church

Nagaland has achieved an important milestone in the field of education on account of the contribution of the Catholic institutions that have been a major player since the 1960s. It is only after 1949, with the arrival of the Catholic priests and sisters that Nagaland entered into a new era of educational life. Education is an act of empowerment and liberation especially enabling the poor through formal and informal education. The monumental contribution made by the Catholic Church in the field of education in the last sixty years has surpassed all other services. As we have seen, in the beginning of Christianity among the Nagas, the Baptist Church brought the benefit of literacy to many parts of Nagaland. Even though there were already schools started by the government and the Baptist Church at different places, there was a great demand for quality education in the state. Education has always been an important part of the Catholic Church's mission (CBCI, 2006).

Christian education is meant for the overall development of the people of both urban and rural with special emphasis on the rural poor who otherwise have no ways and means to achieve it. "But in the last two decades, most of the Christian educational institutions in India were founded in the towns and urban areas. As a result, the Christian institutions in the rural areas are estimated to have got reduced from about 85% to below 55%" (Thumma, 2006, p. 25). Consequently, this drastic shift from the official stand of the Church cannot justify the claim that Christian institutions are meant to serve the marginalized in rural areas. In order not to defeat our purpose, the Church needs to concentrate on gospel values and ideals.

Nagaland being largely a rural state, the Church in the beginning itself gave equal importance to both urban and rural areas like Tuensang, Kiphire and Peren districts. The Church despite many hurdles such as transportation and communication, lack of personnel and finance invested hugely in activities that were beneficial for the people and for socio-economic development of the state. The fact of the matter is that because of this policy, the ratio of academic balance between rural and urban areas was somewhat stabilised. Thus, Catholic education has helped to achieve the socio-economic transformation of the state simultaneously both in rural and urban areas.

4.3.6 Invitation and Acceptance

Realising that education was an urgent need, the people invited the Catholic missionaries to start schools even though there were Primary and Middle Schools in most of the villages and High Schools in many towns. It was also the time the Baptist Church had withdrawn from serious educational ministry in the wake of the government's decision to take over education. The situation that favoured the Catholic Church's growth in Nagaland is the people's desire to have good and efficient Catholic educational institutions in the state. Much before Nagaland attained statehood many young people from the state, who studied in St. Anthony's College and St. Edmund's College in Shillong eventually becoming successful citizens in all walks of life as politicians, bureaucrats, social workers, educationists, academics, etc. of the state. So, there were repeated requests from the public including late J. B. Jasokie and K. L. Chishi, both ex-Chief Ministers of Nagaland who were also alumni of Catholic institutions, to start schools and colleges. In the same way, wherever the Church has the mission centre, invitations came from the public. Neiphiu Rio, the present Chief Minister and many of his cabinet colleagues and bureaucrats, police officers and administrators have had the privilege of being past pupils of Catholic institutions. The values they have inherited and the leadership qualities fostered in them by the institutions became the determining force in their lives. On the occasion of the silver jubilee of the Don Bosco School, Kohima, Jasokie (1996) writes:

> The essence and importance of education hardly needs elaboration in Nagaland, the noble task of imparting quality education to our people have fallen onto the shoulders of

> institutions like Don Bosco and other Catholic schools. Hence, the resulting responsibilities of these schools are all the heavier because it will be they and they alone who will mould the destinies of the younger and upcoming generations in Nagaland (pg. 30).

Namgaheing of Jalukie pressurised the Bishop to open Catholic missions in Jalukie and surrounding areas. When he offered one square kilometre land for the mission, Fr. Mani told him the Church may not be able to do any developmental work immediately. But he said, "Ten years or twenty years or thirty years are nothing for us. I know that the Catholic Church alone will do something good for our people when it is possible" (Parenkulangara, 1999, pg. 37). His desire to have the Catholic mission was a sign of the people's desire for knowledge and development and not, as expressed by some, a means to convert people to the Catholic faith. Tsuha has this to say, "Earlier many used to say, 'don't send your child to a catholic school, if you do so they will convert him/her.' This suspicious attitude has, however, been changed" (Personal communication, June 6, 2012).

In the words of Longkumer (1992), the Ex-chairman of the Mokokchung Town Committee, "Many of our prominent leaders had the good fortune of an early Catholic education. Even though Mokokchung already had a number of schools, people opted to invite the Catholics to impart better education to our children" (pg.13). The Church took root in the state owing to the unconditional support extended specially for establishing schools by some former bureaucrats of the state namely I. K. Changkija (Civil SDO Kiphire), Lima Aier, ADC (later, Director, Higher Education), N. I. Jamir and others. Of course, they knew well that with schools, churches will also be established. Among them the support and encouragement given by N. I. Jamir, former Deputy Commissioner, Ex-Chief Secretary and Ex-Minister, Government of Nagaland, to the Catholic mission from the beginning of the Church and stood with it in time of trouble especially in Tuensang, Kiphire, and Mokokchung were truly praiseworthy. He (1992) writes:

> The Catholic mission has opened a lot of good schools and colleges in India which has given great progresses and development in the field of education...the Catholic mission does not preach from the platforms but they help progress the people through education...in 1966 the Catholic mission came with an interest to open schools but we AOs were not so interested then. Instead the Baptist English School that we have today started to take shape. Later the Mokokchung village citizens provided a plot of land for establishing the Queen Mary's School that we have today (pg. 60).

Mayang says, "The religious contribution of the Catholic Church in the Ao area is not much as they have just one Church. But regarding the education, Queen Mary School is one of the best in the state" (Personal communication, June 29, 2012). Similar view was expressed by Leisha, "The Catholic Church's best contribution to Naga society is quality education. Today people don't make much discrimination on the ground of religion. As convener of the nomination committee for Phom People's Council, I selected a Catholic as president" (Personal communication, June 30, 2012).

4.3.6.1 School Education

The Catholic Church runs twenty eight High Schools, twenty Higher Secondary Schools, three Degree Colleges, two Teachers' Training Institutes and sixty three Primary and Middle Schools (Thuniampral, commission for catholic education, 2010), besides many Open Schools and IGNOU Study Centres. At the start of the mission schools, boarding-houses were very important as they were channels of contact in building up the Church and providing education to children from poor background (Jala & Mukhim, 1993). The first school and boarding-house was a Naga School for the Lotha children at Golaghat in Assam started in 1958. It was shifted to Wokha in 1965 and named Don Bosco School. In 1959, Fr. Marocchino started Don Bosco Elementary School at Kohima which was closed down in 1963 upon his transfer. The first school in the remote area of the state was St. John's School, at Tuensang in 1967, followed by Loyola School at Kiphire in 1971. Little Flower School at Kohima in 1965, Christ King School at Kohima in 1969 and Holy Cross School at Dimapur in 1969 were opened to impart education to the students of the urban areas. It was Fr. Felix who took initiative in founding schools in Tuensang, Peren and Dimapur with the help of some of his family members but the Church took over from him so that he could be engaged fully in pastoral works. The Church then started schools in many parts of the state and by 1985 all the district headquarters except Zunheboto and Longleng had a Catholic School each, besides a number of primary and Middle schools in many villages. From the late 1960s to 1990s Catholic schools were in the forefront in providing quality education in the state. Later on, as other private schools emerged, there began healthy competition in providing quality education and improving academic performance of the students in the state.

4.3.6.2 College Education

Besides the above mentioned schools, the Church ran three under graduate colleges in the state. All these colleges were in the forefront regarding academic performance and quality. The Salesian College of Higher Education in Dimapur was founded in May 1982 and got affiliated to Nagaland University as a full-fledged Degree College of Arts in 1995. With an emphasis on Philosophy, the college also offers honours in different Arts subjects (Principal, 2012-13, brochure). The college has an excellent library, perhaps one of the best in the state, with over 35,000 books and a host of journals, magazines, etc. With an excellent academic environment, students excel in their studies. The overall pass percentage from 1982 to 2011 is 95%.

St. Joseph's College, in Jakhama, the first under graduate college of the Catholic Church and a premier institute of higher learning in the state was founded in the year 1985. As a cradle of higher learning, it began with Plus Two courses in Arts and Commerce and in the subsequent years it was raised to a college. The mission of St. Joseph's College was to form men and women who are intellectually alert, morally upright, religiously oriented, socially conscious, culturally distinct and nationally integrated (Principal, 2009-10, brochure). From the year 2010, the college introduced science stream in Higher Secondary and in 2012 the Higher Secondary was de-linked from the College so as to make it a full-fledged under graduate college offering courses in Arts, Commerce and Science. BBA and B.Sc. were offered from the year 2009 and 2012 respectively. At present the college has nearly 3000 students hailing from all districts and belonging to all tribes of Nagaland including a few from Manipur. The overall pass percentage stands above 80%. A well-equipped library with nearly 16,000 books, over 70 national and international journals, and over 40 magazines equip the students for quality education.

St. Xavier's College, in Jalukie, affiliated to Nagaland University was founded in 2005. A co-educational institution, it admits students to Arts stream. Jalukie is a sub divisional centre under Peren district, which is home to the Zeliangrong tribe. Being a small region and economically poor, this college does not have sufficient enrolment but at the same time the Church considers it a service to the people.

4.3.6.3 Teacher Training Institutes

Teachers and educators are the beacons of light in a society as they are expected to lead others by example. Being the architects of future generations their responsibility is a dignified one. One can teach better with one's life than with lips (Principal 2010, brochure). St. Paul Institute of Education, in Phesama, is an Undergraduate Teacher Training College affiliated to the State Board of Teacher Education (SBTE). It is also recognised by the National Council for Teacher Education (NCTE), Government of India. It was founded in 1977 in order to prepare professionally qualified primary school teachers to work in North East India in general and Nagaland in particular. In the words of Coelho (1984), "This institution is meant for training local teachers for Nagaland's schools which are badly understaffed with a vast number of untrained and even unqualified teachers who, for all their goodwill and good faith, are greatly responsible for the educational bankruptcy of Nagaland" (pg. 19). The two-year residential course prepares them well to adjust to the situation in the North East and the trainees prove themselves as effective teachers. There is a centre for National Institute of Open Schooling for both Secondary and Senior Secondary located on the campus to bring the dropouts to the mainstream through distant education and Indira Gandhi National Open University (IGNOU) for degree studies. The institute also offers short term In-Service Training Programmes and refresher courses for teachers working in different schools in North East India. In the 32 years of its existence, the institute has trained more than a thousand and five hundred teachers, now working in different parts of North East India (principal, 2012, brochure).

The first B.Ed College of the Catholic Church in Nagaland, Bosco College of Teacher Education, affiliated to the Nagaland University, was founded in Dimapur in the year 2003. The college offers a wonderful opportunity for the teachers to learn and teach, keeping in mind the triple mission of a sound education: to form, inform and transform (Principal, 2010, brochure). The in-take capacity of the college is 100 and the pass percentage over the years is above 90%. So far, more than 800 teachers have been trained in this institute. The college stands as the first choice for teacher training in terms of quality and academic performance in the state.

4.3.7 Boarding-houses

Catholic boarding-houses are abodes of learning and religious formation. From the initial stage of the establishment of the Church in Nagaland they have been serving many poor and rural children who otherwise would not have gone to study. Most parishes in the diocese have two boarding-houses each – one for boys and the other for girls with approximately 50 students each. Financially well-off parents from urban and rural areas send their children to the boarding-houses in order to improve their education. Many orphans and poor children are educated free while others enjoy the benefit of concession. In the beginning of the Church's mission the boarding-houses played a key role in the evangelisation of the area as the missionaries did not know the people's language nor knew anyone personally. Through these children, villages were contacted and informed about the educational and medical facilities available on the side of the Church. Nuns during their tour to the villages used to identify poor children and encourage parents to send them to our schools and boarding-houses. Fr. T. J. Chacko speaks about the need for boarding-houses:

> It was difficult to convince parents to send children to the boarding-house as many villages were hostile to the Catholic Church. We collected boys from interior places and kept them in our boarding-house. Even though, most of them could not pay their fees, yet we looked after them. The church could reach out to non-Christians in the parish through child boarders. Boarding was a centre for direct preaching, solely with the intention of making them know of the Catholic faith so as to shred off negative thoughts they have of the Church and they in turn tell parents what the Catholic Church stands for. We have to show in all our work and contacts that we are a religious people and teaching religion is our prime duty. We need to change the perception of people who think that through our teaching

> profession we are like business and rich people enjoying a cosy and comfortable life (Personal communication, November 7, 2007).

As time went by there was a great demand for boarding-houses as parents from far flung villages requested the mission centres to accommodate their children as there weren't good schools in the villages and towns. Again in order to help the poor children with their studies, the Church opened "Self-cooking hostels" in many interior areas of the state. These are not a new phenomenon in the rural context of any state. There are hundreds of poor children especially in the remote areas of the state who are unable to go to a good school or stay in a boarding-house. Children who desire to study are admitted into the Church run school and provided with hostel facilities to stay, to cook and to study. Every weekend, parents bring food required for their children from the village. The children themselves cook before and after class and their study is monitored by the warden. They are treated like other students in the boarding-house. Don Bosco Hostel Lakhuti, St. Xavier's Hostel Meluri, St. Ignatius Hostel, Razeba, Little Flower Hostel, Pungro, Sacred Heart Hostel Chizami etc. are some examples of such hostels. Hundreds of children from these hostels have passed out in flying colours and are doing well in their higher studies and many have been employed. If the Church had not offered these facilities for those underprivileged children today many would not have come to the forefront of the society and would have remained a cause of concern for everyone. Through this noble venture, the Church has, therefore, helped out a number of poor families in the remote areas and led them from darkness to light.

During their stay with the priests and nuns many non-Christian and non-Catholic children express their desire to become Catholics, many have voluntarily received baptisms either in the boarding-house or back home during or after their studies. Some have continued their studies and formed themselves into good lay leaders even as catechists and serve dthe Church faithfully. A few committed young men among them were instrumental in establishing churches in some parts of the state, especially in Kiphire district. There were also some opportunists who received baptism in the Church with the tacit support of their parents as 'an escape route' to continue their studies in the school and stay in the boarding-house. On completion of their matriculation they left the Church. There are also boarding-houses for college going men and women at Jakhama, Jalukie and Jotsoma.

4.3.8 Scholarships

From the year 2005, the Church has founded a scholarship to aid deserving students in the state with help received from various funding agencies. It is being distributed to students of a few selected centres in Dimapur, Kohima, Peren, Phek and Kiphire districts. Each student is paid Rs. 2500 each per annum. Besides education, the programme also monitors children's health level and all round personality development (Karinthayil, 2005). 'Bishop Abraham Memorial Scholarship' for students who intend to pursue higher studies has been instituted with funds raised locally by the Church. Besides these, needy children in schools irrespective of religion and denominations are given scholarships to continue their studies.

4.3.9 Peace Education

Peace education has become a necessity in schools and colleges against the background of increasing crimes like human-trafficking, ethnic cleansing, sexual abuse and exploitation of women and children, the most vulnerable in society. Less control, substance abuse, peer group fighting, excessive individual freedom etc. found among the young are also causes of concern for teachers and parents these days.

Pope John XXIII identified the four pillars of peace namely truth, justice, love and freedom necessary to build a peaceful state. According to his view, truth will build peace for every individual who sincerely acknowledges not only his rights, but also his own duties towards others. Justice will build peace, if in practice everyone respects the rights of others and actually fulfils his duties towards them. Love will build peace, if people feel the needs of others as their own and share what they have with others, especially the values of mind and spirit, which they possess. Freedom will build peace and make it thrive if, in the choice of the means to that end, people act according to reason and assume responsibility for their own actions. Peace education will instil the pillars of peace in students to be advocates of peace. Hence, peace education has to become a part of the school curriculum, for in the absence of peace no true progress can take place and no quality education can be acquired (Jeyaseelan, 2004). In order to create awareness among children and youth of peaceful co-existence and to help them avoid the path of violence, a movement entitled 'Peace Channel' was founded. It is a movement of the youth led by the gospel values to promote peace in the troubled regions of the country (Director, 2011, brochure). It aims at transforming children, youth and individuals as peace lovers, peace makers and peace promoters. An initiative of the Diocese of Kohima, founded by Fr. C. P. Anto, on 21 September 2005, reaches out to all sections of the society. It tries to achieve its goals through formation of peace clubs in schools and colleges. The peace clubs have been formed in many schools spread across the state and also in some North Eastern states. It is gaining momentum and it has received positive response from students, teachers, parents and the public. It is trying to change the culture of violence and foster a culture of peace and reconciliation.

4.3.10 Outcome of Catholic Education

The Catholic Church through its ministry of education has undoubtedly contributed a great deal in raising the literacy and academic standard of the state.

4.3.10.1 Improvement in Literacy Rate and Academic Standard

Fifty years of service in the educational sector has brought many benefits to the people and the state. In the first place the outcome is reflected with the rise in the number of Catholic schools that are a major factor for the increased literacy rate in the state. The literacy rate in Nagaland as per 2011 Census stands at 80.11% which is higher than the National average of 70.04%. There is a marked improvement from 61.65% in 1991 to 66.59% in 2001. In 2011, the total literate population rose from 1,132,323 in 2001 to 1,357,579 in 2011, according to Census of India 2011 ("Nagaland literacy rate", 2012, July 16). This has been made possible by the contribution of the Catholic schools. By operating more than one hundred schools the Church has helped the state to be at par with many of the Indian states. The average matriculation result of the Catholic schools is 85%. This is a clear indication that the educational system in the state is moving in the right direction, helping people to shed the web of ignorance, illiteracy and superstitions. The high literacy rate in the state is helping people in taking up responsibility. There is a move among educated people especially in the urban areas, to critically evaluate the socio-economic and political activities of the government and other organizations. They begin to look at their society with a new vision, aware of the need to bring in changes towards progress. At the request of the people to provide quality education, the Church started schools, colleges, boarding-houses and self-cooking (self-catering) hostels. Education thus imparted, especially in the rural areas, balanced the gap between the haves and have-nots which in turn benefited the rural poor and helped increase the academic standard of the state.

The Pie Chart 1.2 in Appendix show the contribution of the Catholic Church in the field of educational system of the state. It is of the view that catholic education has helped to raise the academic standard and moral values and proficiency of the students.

More than 75% of personnel, time and resources are invested in the educational service. Today, more than 70,000 students are studying in these schools. Meticulous planning, saving and investment are other reasons for the success, while the state with nearly three thousand government Primary, Upper Primary, High Schools and Secondary Schools have been unable to raise the academic standard, administrative efficiency and moral standard despite employing highly qualified personnel. Catholic schools are channels for unity and strength. Many of the schools have been built in places where multilingual tribes live. The students of these schools have come to know each other and forged a sense of unity among them which in turn paves the way for tribal unity and integrity (Khiusumew, Personal communication, July 24, 2007). Interaction among students from different villages, belonging to different tribes in the same school or in the same boarding-house helps reduce tribalism and contributes positively towards unity. "The composition of the students in the school itself provided the first opportunity and ground for developing a broader outlook and national perspective. The missionaries admitted students from different villages, tribes, regions and religions in their institutions" (Thoppil, p. 279). So, education has been an important and effective means adopted by the Church for instilling unity and integration. However, there are certain divisive tendencies making national integration a great problem. To solve this problem the Secondary Education Commission suggests, "Education system must make its contribution to the development of habits, attitudes and qualities of character, which will enable its citizens to bear worthily the responsibility of democratic citizenship and to counteract all those fissiparous tendencies which hinder the emergence of a broad national and secular outlook" (Swaroop & Dargan, 2008, pg. 478). Many schools organise extracurricular activities like sports with a theme. For example, children run marathon with a theme 'Sports for Peace'. If this is done within the context of tribal conflict, it is likely to inculcate unity in young minds. Many people believe that former pupils of Catholic schools are more generous in working for the benefit of the general public when compared to others as a result of the bond they have with each other and the discipline they have acquired during schooling. In the words of Welhitso, "Students of Catholic schools have an edge over others in getting employment because of their overall performance. They have improved the living standard of the people in the towns and villages (Personal communication, June 6, 2012).

One of the objectives of Catholic education is to raise the academic standard of the state which is essentially the academic standard of the people. Education, however, is incomplete without academic relevance. The drawback of education today is it is not relevant to life situations. It is desired, therefore, that the Church impart education relevant to the people: make it directly applicable to personal aspirations, interests and profession oriented. At present even at the college level education is based on traditional courses most of which are not professional, do not equip one to find a job of his own choice but lands one at seeking government jobs.

The above table depicts the pass percentage of the Catholic Schools at the state annual matriculation which stands at 85% over the past ten years, from the year 2001 to 2010 although many schools had become full-fledged High Schools even before the year 2000.

4.3.10.2 Affordable Education and Equal Opportunities

With the aim of offering affordable education, reducing inequality and increasing literacy within the state, the Catholic Church launched its mission in both urban and remote areas. It founded many Higher Secondary, Secondary, Middle and

Table 4.1 The following table reflects the matric results of the

School	2001	2002	2003	2004	2005
SFS Medziphema	75.51	67.12	92.7	94.37	91.01
HC Dimapur	94.31	95.04	97.04	93.96	95.00
St Paul Dimapur	92.31	93.51	93.83	100.00	96.77
DBS Dimapur	92.98	84.16	80.73	98.95	94.74
Carmel Dimapur	100.00	95.59	93.98	87.67	93.33
Assisi Dimapur	95.45	86.21	93.02	75.00	88.89
St Clare Dimapur	100.00	87.50	92.59	79.31	95.00
St Mary's Dimapur			96.55	100.00	95.00
St Joseph Dimapur					
DBS Aghunato					
St Peter's Atoizu					100.00
Montfort Baghty	62.50	72.00	36.84	66.67	71.43
DBS Wokha	96.84	87.20	91.97	86.13	86.78
DBS Lakhuti	27.03	28.95	46.88	62.07	46.43
DBS Bhandari	47.30	52.00	51.16	70.00	70.45
DBS Chiephobozuo	80.00	42.86	100.00	100.00	66.67
S H Chizami	78.57	78.05	81.08	72.13	67.80
Loyola Jakhama	89.47	73.44	78.95	98.39	91.67
St. Xavier Jalukie	42.19	31.08	71.05	63.51	62.50
St. Andrew Jotsoma					
St. John Khonoma	87.50	86.67	80.00	80.00	90.91
St Xavier Kidima					
Loyola Kiphire	40.37	48.41	94.12	93.65	87.36

Catholic schools from the year 2001 to 2010

2006	2007	2008	2009	2010	Total
84.81	89.41	100.00	87.06	85.39	867.45
90.01	92.31	99.22	92.21	87.34	936.44
92.59	96.06	100.00	95.39	94.55	955.01
90.28	91.08	90.91	83.61	94.96	902.40
91.07	96.36	90.48	73.38	84.89	908.75
75.56	84.09	73.58	94.87	97.67	864.34
90.91	100.00	98.04	95.08	82.09	920.52
96.97	97.06	98.08	97.22	98.85	
			100.00	100.00	
			90.00	94.44	
100.0	100.00	63.16	74.19	91.30	
66.67	85.00	81.25	80.77	81.48	704.61
81.90	95.00	93.60	91.67	92.91	904.00
29.17	30.00	67.86	60.00	32.50	430.89
82.98	75.00	92.00	92.16	79.31	712.36
44.44	69.23	65.52	57.69	56.00	682.41
77.42	85.42	91.43	97.67	94.44	824.01
89.71	97.01	87.30	100.00	92.42	898.36
70.77	84.38	88.16	67.09	78.46	659.19
			66.6	92.86	
65.00	100.00	90.91	70.00	70.59	821.58
	60.00	88.89	50.00	55.00	
84.69	53.24	100.00	53.44	87.30	742.59

Christ King Kohima	76.79	63.1	44.79	70.37	91.36
DBS Kohima	99.00	89.01	89.09	97.87	97.94
LFS Kohima	95.76	93.62	98.55	98.39	100.00
St. Mary's, Kohima				100.00	97.22
SHS Kuzama	63.16	81.48	72.73	82.35	100.00
DBS Lazami		46.6	68.18	64.00	82.35
St. Joseph Longleng					84.62
St. Xavier Meluri	47.22	72.41	91.67	86.96	92.59
Queen MS Mokokchung	98.86	96.43	91.82	92.62	96.92
DBS Mon	83.54	78.85	78.65	96.72	94.03
St Joseph Niuland					
All Saints Peren	40.74	48.23	71.88	91.43	94.87
Nazareth Pfutsero	90.91	90.91	90.00	82.22	91.84
St Paul Phesama		100.00	80.00	100.00	96.00
LFS Pungro					
DBS Sechu	100.00	100.00	100.00	97.30	100.00
SFS Tening	26.67	58.82	80.00	72.22	
St Andrews Thenuizumi	78.57	88.89	83.33	69.23	100.00
Newman Tobu		55.56	44.44	100.00	83.33
DBS Tseminyu	90.91	90.48	100.00	100.00	97.56
St John Tuensang	95.92	85.19	78.22	96.09	95.65
DBS Tuli	84.21	75.61	64.10	85.71	89.74
St Joseph Viswema	70.27	68.29	75.61	92.31	80.43
Seyochung, St. M					

92.65	83.08	89.39	96.43	84.54	792.56
86.81	98.89	97.03	100.00	96.91	952.55
95.29	100.00	96.32	98.48	96.12	972.53
100.00	95.83	100.00	91.43	92.41	
71.88	85.71	52.94	91.89	70.59	772.73
75.00	83.33	72.00	65.63	88.00	
88.89	92.00	63.64	62.50	56.25	
91.18	89.80	98.04	97.01	92.68	859.56
92.80	95.42	97.44	82.89	78.24	923.44
87.10	96.97	91.67	94.02	98.15	899.70
				100.00	
91.98	91.11	95.83	71.43	80.00	777.50
83.33	88.89	97.73	98.21	95.74	909.78
94.12	96.15	95.65	89.74	93.94	
90.00	83.33	100.00	94.44	95.65	
100.00	100.00	97.73	93.48	89.41	976.92
62.96	73.80	76.80	57.69	31.82	
100.00	88.24	85.71	83.33	90.00	867.30
40.91	50.00	95.24	85.71	96.77	
100.00	100.00	96.23	84.78	91.30	951.26
95.59	99.12	97.28	97.50	92.86	933.42
88.37	83.67	91.84	87.76	94.74	845.75
78.95	86.27	78.00	86.05	96.67	812.85
				100.00	

Primary schools in the district headquarters and in more than one hundred villages. Thus, the greatest contribution the Church has made in the field of education is in providing education to children of both urban and rural areas at an affordable rate. This has resulted in providing equal opportunities and reducing inequality in society to a large extent. The most educated people of the state from the beginning of Christianity till the arrival of the Catholic mission were the Aos. A considerable number of bureaucrats and government employees were Aos and this was reflected in their high living standards and the education of their children in good schools and colleges. When the Catholic mission spread its wings of education, other tribes which had previously been deprived also benefitted and within three decades they achieved the same standard. This meant that others also started enjoying employment opportunities in the government and in the private sector following their education. Today, one will find bureaucrats who were past pupils of Catholic schools belonging to different tribes occupying high positions in various departments. This has created greater equity of the tribal economy and standard of living. This has raised expectations and has also empowered the less privileged to experience the greater benefits of the society. A great transformation has thus begun in the state through Catholic education. "Sans electricity, potable water, schools, hospitals and roads, the Church explored possibilities without hesitation in many interior areas to meet the spiritual, medical and educational needs of the people"(John, 2010, pg. 44). Wherever mission centres have been established, except in villages, boarding-houses were built for boys and girls. This has further reduced disparity between the rich and the poor as many poor children could avail of the facilities in the boarding-houses. Thus, the schools and boarding-houses in the remote areas have rendered a great service to reduce illiteracy and accelerate development. Added to these, thousands of children in our institutions and hundreds in our boarding-houses receive scholarships for their stay and studies. In the absence of a Catholic school in a town or village many parents try to send their children to study where there is one by letting them stay with relatives or in a hostel or in a rented house. The effect of Catholic schools is felt in some of the far flung villages where signs of economic growth and improvement in living standard are noticed.

4.3.10.3 Emerging Leadership

Of late, a threat to the educational value system has been noticed. One must remember that if our educational system diverts its attention from value based formation of students to solely academic performance it may be disastrous for the future. "Earlier value system was centred on God, cult and community. But now economy, individual, laws and rationality have become principal values of modern culture and God, cult and community are at the service of finance and economy" (Pulimoottil, 2011, April 2). Leadership is based on the value system acquired during studies. Our educational aims, therefore, should be the formation of students to be future leaders in the social, religious and political fields. To return to the original ideals, the Church has made progress by maintaining the evangelical aspect of education. One of the evangelical purposes is to educate young men and women from the community who could stand up to their expectation especially in matters of religion. With this shift many communities are taking an interest in educating young people who would be the voice for the Church tomorrow. Today, there are educated young local evangelisers/leaders capable of understanding the teachings of the Church and communicating well with the people. In many places, strong local Churches have emerged as a result of people whose education has endowed them with leadership qualities. The emerging leaders are able to help dispel 'superstitious beliefs,' especially among the rural people, by taking recourse to the Bible and other Christian literature. From the religious point we can build a strong local Church if we provide a good education with an emphasis on religious and leadership skills. In the words of Angnyei, "Catholic teachers and those with Catholic background are spiritually and morally strong to impart value based education. They have helped children become men and women of good character and God-fearing, and many have emerged as good leaders" (Personal communication, June 20, 2012). Pelaü opines that Catholic education instils in students a sense of responsibility as the legacy of the school is in them throughout. It gives a sense of purpose (Personal communication, June 20, 2012). It is felt that better behaviour, regular church attendance, work culture, respect for elders, and more sincerity are noticed among the students of Catholic institutions. It is from our institutions that local vocations to priesthood and religious life emerge. School education has influenced many people to embrace the Catholic faith. For example, in Mezoma village, under the Kohima district, some people became Catholics because of the positive changes they had noticed in their children who were studying in Catholic schools.

4.3.10.4 Recognition and Expectation

The people in the state still count on the education imparted by the Catholic institutions. In the year 2008, the local daily 'the Morung Express' under the caption 'MEx speak-out Campaign' sought the opinion of the general public about their hopes and vision for the state in order to make the government aware of the genuine needs of the people. One of the opinions mentioned is:

> Please get in touch with the Catholic schools and start some very high quality schools in the most peripheral parts of Nagaland-especially in those areas where the literacy rate is inadequate. The backward status of tribes is an insult to them. Nobody is backward-only had less opportunities. If you give excellent schools to these places-completely funded by the Government, but run independently by the Catholics, you will not have any more backward people in the next 10 years. These schools must have the state-of-the-art facilities and the teachers there should be paid twice the amount given to teachers in bigger places like Kohima, Dimapur or Mokokchung. These model projects must be completely under you (Chief Minister) and not any other minister ("Mex speak-out campaign", 2008, March 28, pg. 7).

Even though there are many government and private educational institutions in the state, still the people's desire for quality education is a felt need. Sedevi writes:

> Education in Nagaland came through the Christian missionaries-both Catholic and Protestant. The Catholics continue to give excellent service to Nagaland. They are extremely well organised and have single minded unmarried

> nuns and fathers to run their institutions and so are unbeatable...Enter into a public-private partnership with some good credible organisations in the state to run the schools. Partner with the Catholics and organisations like ECS in Tuensang. Fund them completely and scrutinise their activities aggressively so that they have to deliver the goods and maintain very high standards (2012, September 6, pg. 2).

The same opinion is shared by Pusa, while gracing the Parents' Day celebration at St. Xavier's School, Kidima in Kohima district. He said that Catholic school products have excelled in all fields and are now even contributing to the good of the state in various capacities:

> Catholic schools in Nagaland have more than proven their efficiency…one of the reasons why Catholic schools could provide quality education with special considerations for the poor and the needy were the selfless way in which the nuns and priests render their services without prejudice. This is also what makes it possible for Catholic schools to open in remote places and cater to the need of even backward areas where education is most wanting ("Catholic schools are contributory factor", 2012, November 6, pg. 3).

Neiphiu Rio, the Chief Minister of the state, appreciated the role of the Catholic Church for its contribution towards the progress of society, not only in the field of religion but also in education. Delivering his address after inaugurating the St. Paul's Catholic Church at Chiechama under Kohima district he said, "You have brought religion to save lives and the best of education" ("Rio lauds catholics", 2007, October 15, pg. 1).

The Catholic Church in the state has contributed greatly to the intellectual growth of the state especially through its schools and colleges. Thousands have gone through these power houses of learning and are serving at various capacities in the state and outside, thus contributing greatly for the socio-economic-cultural, political and religious development of the state and family. Experience and practical knowledge received from these institutions help many to be 'different' from the rest in terms of their loyalty to serving their society. One notable contribution from their side is that they send their children to these institutions and recommend many others to join them as the rich legacy and traditions of these institutions make a great impact on them. The state made tremendous progress in the field of education. The Minister for Urban Development and Higher Education Dr. Shurhozelie said that though Nagaland started late in the field of education "the progress we made within a short span is commendable" ("Progress in education commendable", 2008, December 13, pg. 2).

For a great many, 'Catholic schools and Catholic education' have been a 'brand' for quality in the state and admitting children to these schools is unquestionably prestigious. The Church was fortunate to play a qualitatively different role along with the state government from the very beginning of the state till today. Even though the government did not extend much financial assistance, it is appreciative of the work done by the Church and extends moral support. It was vital for the Church to have schools to educate Catholic children and to keep their faith intact. Education imparted by the Church is not biased towards any religion as all schools in the state follow a common syllabi. In our efforts, lasting and enduring outcome is given more importance than result oriented education. If the Church considers the schools as a source of income and prestige alone but not as a means to reach Gospel values to the people, then it would be just like anyone who runs a school making 'no difference' in the students and society. The future of the Church depends very much on how we educate and why we educate.

Puthenpurakal (1979) writes, "Let us remember that we run schools not only because we have a right to run them, but because education is dynamically linked to the mission of the church" (pg. 259). Jeyaseelan (2004) opines, "One thing they need to keep in mind is that there is neither a substitute for evangelisation nor is there another way of educating the masses than opening educational institutions" (pg. 156). The Church does not run schools solely for baptism or adding numbers to its fold. Baptism is part of evangelisation which includes education, health care, preaching, social uplift, etc (Joseph, Personal communication, March 15, 2009). It is evident from the fact that through the Church's contact with the parents and public a great deal has been achieved by getting rid of many of the prejudices people had about Catholics, especially in the initial stage of the Church. Undoubtedly Catholic schools have been a catalyst for evangelisation within the state.

4.4 SOCIAL CONTRIBUTION

Man is a social being. Education creates an awareness of the need to focus on the environment that influences his existence and growth. Farias (1999) writes, "The first dimension to education is its close association with social values, beside spiritual and moral" (pg. 120). She further writes, "Education brings about awareness, insight, a cultural transformation, offers opportunities for a better standard of life and scope for creativity " (Farias, 1999, pg. 120). The purpose of education, therefore, is to bring about an all-round development in man by infusing positive energy and eradicating negative influence. It is a powerful tool used by the Catholic Church in Nagaland to disseminate knowledge in every aspect of life, in order to attain social emancipation from various ills that has crippled society and individuals.

4.4.1 Social Teachings

Social work is not a subsidiary goal of the Church's mission but an essential vision to complement the actual mission. People frequently raise questions regarding the involvement of priests and nuns in active social ministry. Social work is an act of emancipation or liberation of human beings from various injustices. Christian social doctrines state that a Christian is called not only to denounce injustice in all forms but to actively work towards its elimination. "The church considers promotion of justice as an integral and indispensable part of its evangelising mission" (Mawrie, 2009, p. 142). Its aim is to make the local beneficiaries not mere consumers but also organisers to shoulder social leadership. For this, one needs to go to the needy, live with them, learn from them, think and plan together with them and animate them to shape a better future ("Training in project planning formulation", 1986). Social responsibility is not merely the task of the leaders of the Church alone but of the entire Christian community.

Manjaly (2010), writes, "Social responsibility is not an appendix to Christian faith...love of neighbour grounded in the love of God is a responsibility of each member and the whole ecclesiastical community" (pg. 50). This expression is evident in the Bible, "He who does not love his brother whom he has seen, cannot love God whom he has not seen" (1 John 4: 20). "Development is a continuous process of total and integrated human growth in all its social, political and spiritual dimensions. It should aim at a continuous process of change of communities with special emphasis on the deprived and the oppressed. It is an integral part of evangelisation" (Diocesan Social Service Society, 1982, 8). Manjaly (2010) quotes the words of Pope Paul VI from his encyclical '*Evangelii Nuntiandi,*' "It is impossible in evangelisation to ignore...the importance of justice, liberation, development and peace in the world" (pg. 51). "Social involvement (*diakonia*) should be an authentic witness (*martyria*) of what we proclaim (*kerygma*) and what we celebrate (*leitourgia)"* (Manjaly, 2010, p. 52).

The Church's mandate to proclaim the good news to all nations was never meant to include only the spiritual welfare of all even though it may have been understood in the past as the sole responsibility of the Church. "The Gospel transforms society and drives the missionaries to strive for reaching out to others in all spheres of life" (George, 1990, pg. 145). The Church cannot remain a mere spectator and pretend to be a liberating Church in the midst of struggles, illiteracy, poverty and unemployment. Chiten observes, "As it happened in America, in Nagaland too, the church has become complacent merely by being a Christian state and covenanting it to belong to Christ as 'Nagaland for Christ' and proclaiming it as a Missionary

Country - it has become secularised and is becoming more and more materialistic" (2008, February 24, pg. 4). Being involved in social work based on gospel values, however, does not make one materialistic but part of a liberating society.

Pope Benedict XVI opines that feeding the poor is more a moral obligation than an economic problem. Our present society has ignored the traditional concept of justice by becoming more selfish and widening the gap between the rich and the poor. The Church at times is silent about this issue and does not engage in great efforts. Haimendorf (1976) mentions the Aos' concept of justice, "For example, among the Aos a man did not gain social prestige by merely possessing wealth, but only by spending it for the benefit of the community. The aim is to outdo their neighbours in the giving of Feasts of Merit by stimulating the rich to produce rice beyond the requirements of their household and to rear mithuns, buffaloes and pigs for slaughter" (pg. 47). But today the rich become richer at the expense of the poor, all over. The church and the poor are not two separate entities when it comes to life and service. "Therefore, Solidarity with the 'poor' is the best way to exercise social responsibility and an antidote to 'insulation' and isolation. It requires identification of the weakest and the most marginalised in our society today corresponding to the 'biblical' poor" (Manjaly, 2010, pg. 54).

The Church founded by Jesus is a liberating one, by way of 'touching' the lives of the people in concrete situations. Sadly it often forgets this great responsibility. It, cannot, therefore, remain oblivious of social problems, indifferent to people's genuine needs and silent about the rampant corruption in the state. In the words of Stanislaus (2006), "Liberation theologians insist that God's concern goes far beyond compassion and charity; it involves justice. The prophets and their messages have one central theme - justice " (pg. 142). The churches in the state as a whole claim to be the voices of the people but they seem sympathetic in their actions and naïve in their decisions when they receive benefits from influential people.

The victims of injustice and oppression are always and everywhere the poor. Hence, love for the poor leads to liberation of the poor. Mere lip service and assurance of assistance are insufficient for an individual or a community who longs for a decent living and to be out of the clutches of poverty or oppression. The Church is at a disadvantaged position to involve in the complicated social, economic and political problems as they might face stiff opposition and resistance from people in authority. The responsibility of the Church is to care for the welfare of all in general and consequently it must be an activity oriented Church. It should speak on social ethos which includes common interests. "The social Gospel must stress on the public morality, problems of poverty, unemployment, low wages, disparity, secular solutions must be found for these secular problems" (Jamir, 2008, February 24). But people as a whole are mute to this reality finding no solution in sight. In the recent past ACAUT (Against Corruption and Unabated Taxation) spread awareness and spoke strongly against this menace.

The Second Vatican Council's document, *Gaudium et Spes*/Pastoral Constitution on the Church in the Modern World (GS) describes the mission of the Church as a service for human development. Building upon GS the document the Church in Asia highlights some important areas of ministry such as dignity of the human person, preferential option for the poor, peace-making, education, health care, possible dangers of globalisation, and threats to environment (Mittathany, 2000). The joys and hopes, sorrows and anxieties of the world are the concerns of a liberating Church and so it's duty is to scrutinize the "signs of the times" (Deberri, 2003, pg. 63). Church's option for the poor is explicitly mentioned in the Beatitudes of the gospel where one notices the poverty of Jesus and his concern for the poor (The Echo, 2011). So, evangelisation does not mean mere preaching. It takes concrete expression in socio-economic services which include charitable works, relief works, developmental projects, welfare programmes, and all the works the Church does for the common good. It is understood, therefore, that the advancement of individuals and society depends on peoples' concerns for the poor and needy.

4.4.2 Efforts of the Church

Any state's development can be at a slow pace due to lack of proper vision and planning, neglect of agriculture, absence of industries, longing for white-collar jobs, corruption, tribalism etc. The tag 'underdeveloped' can be removed and positive developments could take place if a common goal and interest for development are fully visualised and schemes properly implemented. Knowing that social emancipation is a prophetic mission, the Catholic Church in the state tries to empower the unemployed youth, women and poor through its educational institutions and social service agencies under its care. Even though few in numbers like yeast in the dough the Church does make positive contributions by addressing socio-economic problems.

With cooperation from social service agencies, the Church has been able to undertake many developmental projects and self-help programmes. One should not mistake the involvement of the Church in social actions with an ulterior motive to convert people to Catholicism or the Church has a hidden agenda. As previously mentioned, social emancipation liberates the poor. "On the whole, church is able to make a healthy combination of evangelisation and socio-economic developmental activities, not succumbing to the temptation to consider developmental activities as evangelisation" (George, 1990, pg. 69). Palamattam (1993) substantiates this point through the words of K. M. Panikkar:

> The work of the missionaries among the aboriginal tribes may be said to have created a tradition of social service which modern India has inherited. In the Indian Constitution included special provisions for the welfare of the tribal communities and *adivasis* and if the Centre and the states are making concerted efforts to bring them up to the general level of India, much of the credit must be given to the missionary (pg. 403).

Education is a pre-requisite to address the social issues or else the purpose would be misunderstood. Jonas (1994) asserts the importance of education in addressing the social issues when he says, "Education is the most important weapon for any social action, though, unfortunately, education today is more or less reduced to academic exercises. In its real and authentic sense it should enable us to analyse the society, interact and respond to it creatively" (pg. 13).

The Church has an immense field of action in education and health care as well as in promoting social participation. It needs to help the people to help themselves. The first effort the Church undertook towards emancipation of people in a given area was trying to educate the masses in their families and children in schools and young people in vocational training centres of the grave issues they are faced with. In the second place, the promotion of health services and health care by distributing food for women and children and establishing dispensaries primarily in rural areas like Tuensang, Mon, Tobu, Kiphire, Meluri, Chizami, Lakhuti, Thenyizumi, Wokha and Kohima, Dimapur etc. was done.

The significant contributions in the religious, social and medical services in the state would not have been possible without the role of the religious sisters. In the words of Bishop Kerketta (1998), "Religious sisters have played a very significant role in the fields of education, health care, family welfare, evangelisation, pastoral and developmental works, etc., and thus they have rendered yeoman service to the church and to the people of Northeast India" (pg. 279). With the help of social service agencies like the Development Association of Nagaland (DAN) and ANMA Integrated Development Association (AIDA), and other commissions, like the Women Commission, Health Commission, Youth Commission etc. the Church has been enabled to undertake many developmental projects and self-help programmes.

DAN is the 'development wing' of the Diocese of Kohima for planning, implementing and coordinating all activities and projects relating to social concern and development in the state, catering to all sections since its inception in 1985. It works in partnership with its thirty five parishes and twenty one health centres covering eleven districts in the state assisting them through animation, planning, implementation etc.

(Kizhakkeparampil, 2010-2011).

Partnership with Self-Help Groups (SHG) and Village Development Teams consisting of priests, sisters, lay-leaders and SHG representatives is essential in order to prioritize and execute projects satisfactorily in a given area. DAN executes its projects through the assistance received from various local, national and international funding agencies like Catholic Relief Services (CRS), *Caritas, Missio Achen, Propaganda Fidei,* Church in Need, etc.

The major thrust areas of DAN in the development sector include formation of self-help groups, animal husbandry and self-employment, microfinance and income generation; promotion of community health, safe motherhood and child survival programme, village health workers training, rural medical camps, control of communicable diseases, addiction counselling and rehabilitation services, HIV/AIDS awareness, infrastructural development, child sponsorship programmes, and peace education.

4.4.2.1 Food Programmes

Prior to the implementation of various projects in a given area the DAN conducts several animation programmes including building qualified staff to monitor the projects. This is done with a view to encourage SHG members to take up various income generating activities at the group level as well as to enlist community participation in promoting health for all.

The biggest humanitarian work in the field of socio-economic development undertaken by the DAN is the Food Programme, supported by the Catholic Relief Services (CRS) which was founded in 1943 by the Catholic Bishops of the

United States of America to assist the poor and disadvantaged outside the country. The CRS has been supporting the Church in the North East for years since the creation of the Diocese of Dibrugarh in 1951 followed by the creation of the Diocese of Kohima in 1973. Safe Motherhood and Child Survival (SMCS) or Mother and Child Health programme (MCH) aims at improving health of pregnant mothers for safe motherhood and nutritional status of children for their survival. Initially this benefit was extended to eleven centres covering thirty nine villages. As the need was felt later it was extended to twenty three centres covering nearly one hundred villages with forty nine operating partners. "The aim of this programme is health education, antenatal care, immunization, growth monitoring, supplementary food and formation of women's group and health committee. Another approach is the encouragement of self-reliance schemes like home science training for illiterate women" (Kuttiankal, 1999, pg. 48). The women are trained in basic health education, family administration and responsible parenthood. The health coordinators of the diocese in collaboration with Catholic Health Association of India, North Eastern Community Health Association and the governmental organisations, following the general principles of World Health Organisation (WHO) coordinate the activities of all the existing primary health centres in the diocese. Wheat, oil, maize, milk, biscuits etc. were sent regularly to the beneficiaries according to the need. Every year more than ten thousand people benefit from this programme. School Feeding and hostel food programme are important activities of DAN with the aim of increasing student enrolment, retention and attendance of the students.

4.4.2.2 Health Services

'Health is wealth' is the common maxim concerning health. General ethics demands that every citizen has the right and access to health. However, in India the poor are often denied this right as they have no voice and no means to fight for it. As such redemption from pitiable health conditions is a distant reality.

Prior to tribal peoples' acceptance of Christianity, their life was controlled by the animistic world view. Accordingly, most illness and sufferings were believed to be acts of spirits or gods due to the sins of the sufferer or his kin. So, cleanliness and hygiene were not a matter of serious concern. "Sickness, people think, result from offences against evil spirits and have to be propitiated. In every village, at all times, wherever the missionary goes he sees people needing medical and surgical help in great variety"(Syiemlieh, 2001, pg. 192). However, there was a paradigm shift from the earlier view to a new one when they accepted Christianity. Ghonglah (1996) wrote, "Whereas the Christian world-view brought by the first missionaries not only offers a God who suffers for our sins, but also propagates a new teaching that most illness and sufferings are due to germs, harmful water, unclean surroundings and they could be controlled or eliminated with pills, vaccinations, surgeries and at times even with prayers"(pg. 452). There is, therefore, now an awareness of the need to take precautionary measures and seek treatment to reduce suffering and death.

The role of the Church in providing primary health care is undisputable. "Health which is rightly defined in the World Health Organisation (WHO) constitution as not merely the absence of disease or infirmity, but as a state of complete physical, mental and social well-being, will be attained not by setting up high-tech hospitals but by primary health and the community's involvement in its own health" (Kuttiankal, 1999, pg. 47). In the words of Varghese (1993), "The healing ministry is not merely care of the sick in hospitals and dispensaries. Those involved in this ministry insist that preventing sickness through conscientisation of people in remote villages through health education is an equally important task that must be given top priority. Welfare programmes conducted in the villages to bring about the awareness of the need for cleanliness of the house and its surroundings, proper nutrition and care of children, etc. are part of health education" (pg. 357).

For the Catholic Church, health ministry was a means of accessibility to enter many remote villages. People's limited knowledge of health and illness necessitated the Church's intervention. The Church, therefore, despite its limitations attempted to ease the sufferings of the people by caring for the sick and trying to reach out to the remotest parts of the state. "The intimate link between healing ministry and evangelisation seems to have been an established fact, already in the New Testament. The mission of the twelve is characterised by a double command to preach and to heal" (Varghese, 1993, pg. 355). Wherever the Christian missionaries travelled or visited they used to speak about health and medicine.

The people of the state were very much in need of health services as many were superstitious about illness and death attributing the cause to the devil. This reality is confirmed in the writings of Barpujari (1982), "Another sphere of missionary's activity brought hope and new life to the Nagas hitherto steeped in superstitions and ignorance; and that was medical service" (pg. 4). In fact, in most places the missionaries were the first physicians to the tribals in the North East. For example, in Nagaland pioneer Baptist missionaries administered medicines to several patients even in the remotest villages and cured many. The Catholic Church too used this ministry effectively for the good of the people. Fr. O' Hara had a fair knowledge about traditional and modern medicines and wherever he went he treated patients. Alongwith the desire to know the new religion people flocked to him essentially for medicines. He said that the doctor at Wokha was so pleased to learn that he also had the knowledge of medicine as he could not treat the hundreds of patients spread over a number of villages. Hence, the doctor requested him to help him out by attending to the patients. The Bishop, however, banned him from practicing medicine as he was attending to many delivery cases on emergency. This led to a grave misunderstanding with the Bishop and finally coupled with many other reasons Fr. O' Hara left the priesthood (Personal communication, December 27, 2007). Even now, when Catholic missionaries visit villages to meet people or to conduct spiritual services they carry a chest of medicines. There are cases in the villages when the missionary was able to provide an intervention and prevent death.

The Catholic Church had two important objectives in mind as it started its mission in Nagaland, namely, to impart quality education and promote health care. "It is absolutely clear that when Christians learned to read and write, their health consciousness also increased. They became curious, they wore clean clothes, they took bath more often and this in turn made them desire to learn more, or to become real 'educated' persons"(Ghonglah, 1996, pg. 452).

4.4.2.3 Role of Religious Sisters

The health services of the Church in the state are rendered by a group of trained religious nuns belonging to different religious congregations. Hence, religious women occupy a unique place in the healing ministry of the state. They spread the love of God among the sick and suffering by their active service. In the initial stage, the Church took measures to create awareness of health in the villages and schools through health camps and seminars. According to a report by the Diocese of Kohima, "More than 60% of the illness that reinforces poverty in rural areas can be prevented by appropriate health education. Another 20% can be avoided by adequate health promotion programmes based on health education and social awareness" (Training in Project Planning and Formulation, 1986, pg. 4).

The Catholic Church in Nagaland began its activities with the healing ministry starting from the Naga Hospital in 1948. The arrival of the two Spanish nuns at the request of the Assam Governor in 1948 was the beginning of the Catholic Church's activities. Since then, the Church has done a commendable job in health care not through big hospitals and clinics but through dispensaries in the rural areas assisted by many religious sister nurses and health workers from the villages. As the saying goes, 'a healthy soul inside a healthy body'. Wherever the missionaries went they used to speak about health and medicine. It was a herculean task and a challenge to substitute the old world view regarding disease, health and medicine with the new one, which even now, has not been fully achieved.

Most of the time, in rural areas, the Church-run health centre was the only one which the rural poor could approach for timely and effective medical intervention. They also catered to the needs of neighbouring villages, despite a number of government run dispensaries which are not administered well and often without medicine. Every parish has a health centre with at least one trained nurse sister to render this great humanitarian service. The sick are brought to the nearest Church – run dispensary. With total dedication the sisters have reached out to the people and promoted better health care. They created awareness among the people of the need for better health, hygiene and sanitation including preventive measures and alternative system of treatment through school education and service in primary health centres. As they toured villages they exhorted the people, especially the women folk of the need to maintain personal hygiene and a clean surrounding as women spend more time at home with children and also are more prone to ill health. The women are trained in basic health education, family administration and responsible parenthood. They used to instruct people about the need for medical assistance at the time of illness instead of linking it with the power of evil or the curse of the gods. The Mother and Child Health programme initiated by DAN is also a means to educate the mothers on the need for nutritious food for both the mother and the child. A little mastery over the local dialect helped many sisters to win the confidence of the people. The health programmes of the Church concentrated on the practical aspects in order to make medical facilities affordable, accessible and acceptable to all.

By focusing on priority programmes like immunisation, control of diarrhoeal diseases, acute respiratory infections, malaria, typhoid, maternal and child health care and education about dreaded diseases, the Church aims to ensure rural people have accessibility to health services. Besides, through the school curriculum, awareness is created about the facts of growing up, first aid, hygiene, the harmful effects of tobacco, drugs and alcohol, spread of certain diseases like HIV/AIDS and other social evils (Kuttiankal, 1999). The Church has a wider plan to make health inclusive of everything which includes basic facilities like basic education, primary health care, housing, water and sanitation, adequate income, healthy food and security for all (Kuttiankal, 1999). This dream, however, requires the cooperation of all people who will set their own priorities within a given geographical area. Besides the implementation of this requires a lot of political will and support from the state since it incurs huge public expenditure which only the state can bear. The Church would of course extend whatever help is available from its side for transparent implementation.

4.4.2.4 Extension of the Healing Ministry

The first Catholic centre in Eastern Nagaland was St. John's School, Tuensang opened in 1967. While teaching children in the school, the Sisters of the Adoration of the Blessed Sacrament (SABS) also set aside a considerable amount of time for health care. Through family visits and health awareness programmes in the villages a number of communicable diseases in the area were brought under control. St. Xavier's dispensary, which they ran continues to be attended daily by a number of patients. The dispensary at Tobu inaugurated in 1976 is a source of consolation for the upper Konyak people who otherwise would have had to travel almost a day to reach Mon town for treatment. At the start of the mission centre the Medical

Mission Sisters (MMS) took up the health care, however, they soon handed over to the SABS. "Through the medical service the sisters have saved hundreds of snake-bite victims and malaria patients. Sisters visit sick people, distribute medicines and treat the patients in the dispensary" (Jessina, 2001, pg. 7). Even today this dispensary is the only reliable health centre for many villages in the region. Sisters occasionally visit villages to create awareness about health and distribute medicine to the people. Sensing an urgent need, a dispensary was opened at Kiphire in 1978. In the course of time many people from the town and villages received treatment from this dispensary.

The Bethany Sisters in Dimapur were one of the first groups of sisters to have begun the health ministry from 1969. Even though Dimapur town had already a number of small hospitals and clinics patients, especially from neighbouring villages, frequented this dispensary. By the year 2000, they extended their services to nearly 28 villages on the outskirts and surrounding areas of Dimapur with curative and preventive measures. In the southern Angami area, they started the first dispensary at Viswema in 1979. They conduct health awareness programmes, medical camps, immunisation and MCH programmes in Viswema and neighbouring villages.

With the establishment of the Church at Lakhuti and Wokha, the Bishop felt the need for dispensaries in order to control various communicable diseases and malaria in the villages. St. Angela's dispensary at Wokha, started by the Ursuline Sisters of Ranchi in 1969 was a great relief since there were no doctors and medical facilities in most villages.

The MMS have a wide-network of hospitals all over the world. Bishop Hubert Rosario, therefore, invited them to the diocese to work and to start a hospital, preferably at Kohima. In May 1970, three sisters including a sister doctor arrived at Kohima and they began their medical service in close collaboration with the Public Health Department and introduced mobile clinics to serve villages around Kohima and in the neighbouring state of Manipur. Later, they were entrusted with the administration of the Maternity and Child Welfare Centre, under the Social Welfare Department of Nagaland, at L. Khel, Kohima village, which had been somewhat non-functional since 1971. Meanwhile Sr. (Dr.) Marina Maliekal, a gynaecologist, had an opportunity to work in the Kohima Civil Hospital for a term of five years. Besides rendering her services to the patients, she provided training to local doctors. The sisters extended their services, both in the preventive and curative aspects of health care through immunisation programmes, health education and school health programmes. A notable achievement among many was that in the 1980s the sisters trained many women as health workers and community leaders who would help sisters in their respective villages and render medical service to the people in the village in their absence. In the year 1989, sisters started their own dispensary. When they began the work in Kohima Village, the pre-natal mortality was about 10/100 and infant and toddler death 10/100 (Medical Mission Sisters, Kohima 1967-1973). School feeding, regular medical examination for women, antenatal and postnatal care for women, preparing women for home deliveries etc. were some of the features of their work.

The FCC sisters took charge of the medical service in Lakhuti under Wokha district in 1985. St. Mary's Health

Centre was the only working dispensary in the area for many years. Despite bad road conditions medical assistance was extended to many inaccessible villages. Mother and child health programmes and immunization, supply of supplementary food, mobile clinic, home science training programme etc. were some of the important services rendered by the sisters at St. Mary's Health Centre, Lakhuti, 1993.

The Sisters of Charity started working in the Holy Redeemer Health Centre, Chumukedima in 1980. In the field of medicine this was the first hospital in the area. Hence people availed the facility offered here. One of the aims of this hospital was to coordinate all the dispensaries run by the Church throughout the diocese. After a survey conducted throughout the state, guidelines regarding administration of drugs, safety methods, working conditions of the sister nurses and health workers etc. were issued and all the dispensaries since then adhere to these guidelines. The sisters regularly toured the villages offering health education and medical assistance.

Most parts of Chakhesang and Pochuri areas were cared for by the Ursuline Sisters who began their work when the parish of Meluri was created in 1992. They reached out to many villages with major services like SMCS programmes, health education on hygiene, sanitation, nutritious food, immunization programmes etc. Many of the villages lie in far-flung areas consequently, the dispensaries were of great help. Later on when Thenizumi was made an independent centre, Sisters of the Cross of Chavanod opened the Holy Cross Health Centre.

Bishop Abraham invited the Sisters of Providence to work in Medziphema in 1977. Although, Medziphema lies very close to Dimapur, people found it difficult, especially those from the villages to reach Dimapur for medical help. The Congregation also extended their service to Bhandari, a malaria-prone area, under Wokha district where their service saved many lives and their work was highly appreciated.

The Congregation of Mother of Carmel (CMC) extended their health ministry to Peren in 1980 and Tening in 1987 and the adjoining villages among the Zeliangrongs; and to Razeba among the Chakhesangs. The Missionary Sisters of Mary Help of Christians (MSMHC) reached Jalukie in 1972 among the Zeliangrong people before the CMC sisters arrived at Peren. St. Xavier's dispensary served patients from different villages. The sisters extended their healing ministry in Tseminyu and Longleng when they had their convents there. The Sisters' service in Tseminyu was commendable as they covered a large area including Lazami, a Sema village and other adjacent villages. Longleng being a faraway place, the medical service was a great blessing for the people of the town and adjacent villages. The Sacred Heart Sisters started rendering valuable medical care from 1980 to the people of Mon town and adjoining villages, one of the most backward areas of the state. Later, the Congregation of the Sisters of St. Joseph of Chambery (CSJ) began their work at Bhakti under Woka district, a malaria prone area. With their work the spread of malaria and other communicable diseases has been considerably controlled.

The Indian medicine which is holistic, integrated and traditional has been neglected and thus gave way for costly allopathic medicine which the poor cannot afford with their meagre income. In an effort to provide relief to the rural poor in the state an attempt has been made in the field of herbal medicine by the Church. Global Holistic Health Centre, Jalukie, founded in the year 2000 by Vilasal Godfrey, a priest of the Diocese of Kohima, treats people with herbal medicines. The centre trains local people in the use of available herbal medicines by running seminars and classes. The trained health workers are sent to interior villages to treat patients who cannot afford costly medicine in towns and cities. This centre helps to serve the cause of socio-economic development of the people of Nagaland by fostering and promoting the health of the rural people (Treasa & Godfrey, 2010). Patients from Nagaland and parts of the North East come to this centre for treatment. Because of the centre many people have started to grow medicinal plants to sell to the centre which helps many marginal farmers to make a living.

At the request of Bishop Abraham, Missionaries of Charity, commonly known as Mother Teresa Sisters, came to Nagaland in 1988 to begin work among the poorest of the poor, the orphans, the abandoned and the sick. They focused their attention on patients suffering from incapacitating illness, the terminally ill, the disabled and the handicapped, mothers with unwanted pregnancies and the downtrodden (Kuttiankal, 1999). They have a home for the dying destitute and mobile dispensaries in Dimapur. Medicines are distributed free of cost to the needy. They visit the families of the poor as well as hospitals and bring to their centre all those who have been abandoned by the family or who have no one to care for them. This centre welcomes all without caste or religion. The humanitarian service rendered by the sisters at this centre is remarkable and greatly appreciated.

DAN has taken up projects in Community-Based

Rehabilitation for people with Disabilities under Chumukedima - Dimapur block. Its objective is to rehabilitate people with disabilities (PWDs) with support from the family and community together with financial assistance from DAN. The Socio-Economic Empowerment Programme (SEEP) initiated by DAN in 2009 aims at strengthening people's organisations and promoting good governance through active involvement of the community by accessing government facilities for education, health and livelihood by 2012. This project began to be implemented in Dimapur, Peren, Jalukie and Tening areas in 2009.

4.4.3 Detox and Rehabilitation

Shalom Rehabilitation Centre founded in 1993 at Chumukedima is an attempt by the Church to control the problem of substance abuse in Northeast India. It is managed and maintained by DAN together with the Medical Mission Sisters. This centre aims to empower dependents and their families to free themselves from their addictive behaviour and support them in their efforts to remain abstinent (Director, 2011, brochure). It offers detoxification and rehabilitation facilities and support for the family. Education and training on substance abuse prevention and HIV/AIDS is provided to the educational institutions. The inpatients of the centre hail from rural and urban background and financially sound and poor families.

Table 1.2 (Appendix), shows the services in the health field deserve high appreciation. The Church has been rendering valuable medical services to the people of the state and as a result reduced the mortality rate and improved the overall health condition of the people. Previously in villages, cattle, pigs, chicken, dogs, etc. roamed freely and polluted air and water causing diseases.

The Church has introduced the concept of health care by focusing on personal hygiene and hygienic living habits in contrast to the harmful, superstitious practices that existed previously. The role of sisters and women leaders of the parish who raise awareness through seminars, talks, training of grass-root level health workers and school health programmes is remarkable. The idiom, 'educate a mother and you educate a family' helped reduce health hazards drastically in the many villages. The prenatal and postnatal care essential for a mother made known through health education programmes has considerably reduced the rate of infant mortality. In order to increase self-reliance in the family, women were encouraged to take up income-generating activities such as kitchen gardens, plantations, saving habits, etc.

4.4.4 Skill Development Programmes

The pioneer missionaries in the Northeast were aware of the limitations of school and college education. They knew education without vocational courses would only result in an ever increasing number of educated unemployed youth. The boarding-houses in many places were intended to provide all round formation. Within this system, students, besides attending the academic classes, would also be engaged in farming, horticultural, dairy, poultry, piggery, and other useful activities (Palamattathil, 1996). For example, Eden Gardens at Khuzama was founded in order to make students self-reliant after their studies. As part of skill development programmes, the Church took initiatives to enable the underprivileged who could not pursue their studies either because of poor financial background or lack of facilities, to be self-sufficient to lead a normal life with the rest of their peer group through various skill development programmes. The ANMA Integrated Development Association (AIDA) founded in 1985 in Dimapur, the development wing of the Salesians of Don Bosco, Dimapur Province, which covers the states of Assam, Arunachal Pradesh, Manipur and Nagaland, is also involved in development activities. In order to empower the unemployed and those who failed to complete school education, various vocational training centres were opened for men and women.

Don Bosco Vocational Training Centre (DBVTC) at 3rd Mile, Dimapur, an informal vocational training centre started in 2003, offers courses in welding, carpentry, motor mechanics, driving etc. Every year a few hundred students pass out of this institute after their formal training course mainly in driving and motor mechanic. Many of the Naga youth, however, failed to show interest in lengthier courses like welding and carpentry. A few years ago, besides these long term courses, short term courses on livestock, fishery, organic farm management, vermi-composting and poultry were also offered.

Don Bosco Tech (DB Tech), recently initiated employment-linked, market-oriented vocational training of short duration to the economically and socially marginalised youth in the state supported by the Ministry of Rural Development, Government of India. DB Tech is a network of 125 Don Bosco skill training centres spread across 25 states in the country making it the largest NGO engaged in livelihood training in India. It attempts to bridge the widening divide between those who have access to opportunities and those who are increasingly being marginalized from the 'new economy' jobs (Director, 2011, brochure).

The specialised training programmes such as Hospitality-House Keeping, Hospitality-Spa and Hospitality-Food and Beverages; Office Management, Sales and Marketing, Tailoring and Nursing Assistance are conducted by different church NGOs in the state. The NGOs such as AIDA Dimapur, Peace Channel Dimapur, Women's Working Centre (WWC) Khermahal Dimapur, DBVTC 3rd Mile Dimapur, Don Bosco Youth Centre Kohima and Don Bosco Youth Centre Wokha conduct and organise some of the said programmes based on the need of the people and availability of youth. Since the launching of this programme in 2010, hundreds of youth have been trained and subsequently gained employment in different parts of the state and the country and thus helped reduce unemployment and poverty to a great extent.

Women's vocational training centres run by the sisters are designed to empower women especially the poor, illiterate and dropouts from the Northeast by providing them with training in weaving, sewing, knitting, tailoring, embroidery, handicraft, cooking, shorthand and computer education, health education, home nursing, food processing, home management, kitchen gardening, livestock management, faith formation, foundation English, open school coaching, and such like in the state. This venture has helped hundreds of women to be financially independent and self-reliant and thus reducing the burden on the family. Following training, many have started their own businesses.

Providence Vocational Training Centre (1978) at

Medziphema by the Congregation of the Sisters of Providence, Alphonsa Home Science Training Centre (1991) at Lakhuti by the Franciscan Clarist Congregation, Women's Working Centre' (WWC) (1986) at Dimapur by the Ursuline Franciscan Sisters of North-East Province, Women's Vocational Training Centre, formerly known as Nirmala Social Work Centre (2005) at Chumukedima by the Sisters of the Adoration of the Blessed Sacrament, are some of the women's vocational training centres meant for women empowerment and self-sufficiency. At the moment there has been a drastic fall in the enrolment of women candidates in the Home Science training centres and as a result many have been closed down.

4.4.5 The New Path

Over the past few years, women in the state have suffered from exploitation and discrimination. As a result of compelling circumstances many are forced into certain trades that compromise human dignity. "The New Path" is a social venture of the Ursuline Franciscan Sisters of North East Province to rehabilitate women who are forced into professions that are injurious to them and to society (Fernandes, 2002, pg. 51). In collaboration with the Church and civil authorities of Dimapur The New Path raises awareness, motivates and informs women of their rights and empowers them to act against exploitation, oppression and injustice. It also trains them in socially acceptable and gainful occupations and improves their health by preventing communicable diseases like HIV and AIDS (Fernandes, 2002). From its inception in 1999, the 'New Path' rescues women, mostly minors and teenage girls who have been forced into sex work and provides them with accommodation in the Women's Working Centre, Dimapur where they can access training in various skills.

4.4.6 Orphanages

Founded in 1979, Eden Gardens at Khuzama, is not only a home for destitute and marginalised children but an emerging agro-industrial training centre. Coelho (1983) wrote, "All we want to do at Eden Gardens is to prepare them to claim and enjoy their own rights, thereby becoming responsible, self-respecting, independent individuals in their own villages and thus save them from the ruin that awaits them" (pg. 23). In earlier days the Naga society was more accommodative and generous towards the destitute, orphans, widows and poor children who were well looked after and cared for. Also rich people would educate the children of poor relatives either by keeping with them or extending financial assistance. Nowadays, however, this trend is disappearing. Eden Gardens provides a home for the growing number of parentless, abandoned and poor village children from Nagaland and Manipur and offers them school education and vocational courses so that they would grow and develop into responsible and self-respecting individuals. They constitute half the strength of Sacred Heart School Khuzama, the Church-run school. They are given training in farming, vegetable cultivation and skill development. Some children are sent for vocational courses/training to different places, according to their preference. More than two thousand children have completed their studies from the institute. Even for the higher studies, needy children have been given financial assistance which is donated by generous benefactors. A few past pupils of this centre have found employment abroad, while a few in their own state. Most of them work in the private sector (Raymond, Personal communication, July 24, 2012).

Fr. O.C. Abraham founded St. Joseph's Children's Home in Dimapur in 2004. In order to educate all those who come into this home he started the Holy Child School. Most of the 45 children in the home are from financially poor backgrounds and the rest orphans. Children are helped to study to gain employment for themselves and then return to their family or relatives, so that they will be attached to their roots.

4.4.7 Charity Schools

There are a lot of young poor children who are exposed to risk in and around Dimapur city. In order to rescue them from all forms of abuses genuine efforts have been undertaken by the Church in recent times. In reality, they are rescue homes even though these children are not given shelter but education to make them independent and escape from abuse. We can find these street children in the slums and railway station areas. An effort by the Ursuline Sisters to educate and empower the economically backward children whose parents are either daily labourers or unemployed was realised in the establishment of the Assisi school in 1987 at Khermahal, Dimapur. "What makes it different from other competitive schools in Dimapur is the composition of its students - children of daily labourers, rickshaw pullers, scavengers, porters, tea garden employees, petty shop keepers... including child labourers of the age group 6 to 15" (History of the Assisi School-Evening Section, 2012, pg. 1). The parents of these children are immigrants who have come in search of work and are temporarily settled in colonies, bordering Nagaland and Assam. So Assisi Evening

School provides facilities for these children to be educated at low cost and at their convenience. A maximum of 80% of the students continue their studies after Class Eight to complete their matriculation while a few pursue higher education.

'Boscome' is a new venture started by Fr. T. O. Sebastian in the year 2000 to help children who could not go to a private school or a government school to study. The students here are mostly children of daily labourers who live in the slums in and around Dimapur. There are also a few Naga children who are either very poor or working as domestic helps. It is a home for the poorest children and so Fr. Sebastian calls it an 'educational shelter,' for the young. The target group is children from the age of four to fourteen irrespective of caste or religion. These children are exposed to risk. Boscome began with a small group of fifty children around the Rio colony. Today, there are eight centres actively functioning in different colonies of Dimapur. Children are taught Basic English, Mathematics, Science, Social Science, General Knowledge and Hindi besides training in various skills. All children are given free education including text books and school stationary. It is run entirely on the charity of generous benefactors. The Directorate of School education, Nagaland has given permission to run these schools and so after class four these children can be admitted to Class Five in any recognised school.

4.4.8 Youth Centres

The Church runs many youth centres mainly to support and empower youth during different stages of their life. The Diocesan Youth Centre based in Kohima mainly reaches out to the youth with an emphasis on faith formation, catechesis and family apostolate. While Don Bosco Youth Centres in Kohima, Wokha and Dimapur cater to the needs of youth as a whole. The youth centres of Kohima and Wokha offer intensive coaching for private matriculate candidates every year and the pass rate is above 80%. Many residential and non-residential vocational training programmes, especially for school and college students during summer and winter vacations are conducted. Teachers' training programmes, skill development programmes, training for various groups etc. are also carried out on request.

4.5 POLITICAL IMPACT

The Naga people had a long political history prior to the formation of statehood in 1963. The political struggle for an independent '*Nagalim*' led to armed conflict in the region and this struggle continues. After the formation of the state, Nagaland is moving towards progress. Strictly speaking, it is difficult to separate politics from religion, as religion is the watchdog of politics. Religion has to ensure that political reforms and legislations do not go against the faith and morals of the citizens of the state. According to Mahatma Gandhi, politics, divorced from religion, has absolutely no meaning (Andrews, 2007). Christianity has contributed a great deal towards political consciousness in the Northeast. Karotemprel (1996) writes:

> One important factor that contributed to the growth of political consciousness in North East India is Christianity... the process of creating political consciousness was accelerated by the considerable educational efforts of the Churches of North East India. As a result, the tribals were able to discover their tribal political identity, create political leadership,

claim their political rights and contribute towards the political and administrative re-organization of the whole of North East India (pg. 24).

4.5.1 Church Teachings on Politics

The first requirement expected from all citizens on political life is to create a political consciousness among the people for clean politics in order to allow the state to develop and make progress. Good governance can be ensured only through critical study and objective evaluation of the political parties. Although the Church cannot be involved in political issues, it has to uphold morality and the rights of all especially the marginalised. It is called to liberate people from all types of oppression. "Church and political community both serve the vocation of human. The Church has the right to pass moral judgments when human rights are at stake. Church should use the means of the Gospel to fulfil its mission" (Deberri, 2003, p. 66). The Second Vatican Council in its document *'Gaudium et spes'* (Pastoral Constitution on the Church in the Modern World) teaches that the Church has the right to enlighten the political leadership for the sake of human beings if their rights are not protected. Modern changes have increased the awareness of human dignity and the desire to establish a just political-juridical order. The political authority exists for the common good (Flannery, 1999).

4.5.2 Indifference of the Churches

The churches in the state should make their stand clear on politics. It would be appreciative if the Baptist Church, the main church body in the state could take a lead on all fronts to help frame some concrete policies since it has the advantage of having the majority of the elected legislators in successive Legislative Assemblies. A lack of political ideology among politicians and party affiliates may lead to selfishness. Politics and corruption go hand in hand and they seem inseparable. Easily acquired money coupled with a lack of public action can lead to corruption. Absence of accountability and the inability of the state government and administration in taking action against erring officials also leads to corruption. If there is corruption in the state, people should have the will to eliminate it. Many of our departments seem to be overstaffed; hence there is no need for a full time job/work commitment. An eight hour working day supposed to be put in by an employee may be shared by two or more people. Finally, a desire to be richer overnight leads to sincerity and honesty being sacrificed. According to the Supreme Court of India, corruption is human rights violation ("Corruption is human rights violation", 2012, October 21). Any election fought on money would result in the rich and powerful being elected. Everybody seems to have surrendered to the fate without a fight, saying 'there is no way.' It is a way to treat it as an acceptable reality. If the majority is silent, then the voice of the minority like the Catholic Church will not be heard. The apathy of the churches in general is mentioned by Solo: The Church in Nagaland is not effective in making any dent against corruption in Nagaland because there is counterfeit corruption in the Church itself. Unintentionally, inadvertently, unconsciously or ignorantly the Church has uncomfortably allowed a culture of formal Christianity not very different from the currents of the world in the Church. No pastor of any Church in Nagaland was heard to preach or inform the congregation to give only honestly earned donations to the Church and only unblemished tithes alone to be given to the Church and pastors would do well not to call those who do not give tithes as thieves (2012, January 13, pg. 4).

Solo further speaks about the compromising attitude of the Church. He says that the Church often gives importance to big financiers or benefactors because they are powerful people and as a result they will influence the decision making of the Church. Another drawback of the Church is that it places importance on finance, trying to be in the favour of both God and Mammon and as a result blind to one's conscience.

Education is one of the best means of conscientisation. This has been convincingly demonstrated by the well-known Brazilian educator Paulo Freire with his "conscientisation" method propounded in his famous book 'Pedagogy of the Oppressed' published in 1970. Mawrie (2009) highlights the view, "Conscientisation is the humanisation of people, transforming them from being objects to being subjects, from being dehumanised individuals trapped in the oppressive structure to being more fully human being. The effect of conscientisation is that an individual seeks to transform the system through personal and collective efforts" (pg. 133). Conscientisation through education is one of the ways chosen by the Church. However, it has not yet seen the light of day. Catholic institutions do speak and teach about work culture, honesty in dealings, being faithful to God and religion, clean politics etc. They have educated thousands of people yet corruption has not been checked. So, the reality of clean politics and administration is a distant reality.

Pie Chart 1.3 in Appendix indicates the Catholic Church's

lack of influence or no influence on the politics of the state. Perhaps the Church needs to analyse its approach towards politics and should take some positive steps towards this end. One reason is the minority status of the Church in the state and the absence of Catholic legislators to push for reforms. As a first step, the Church should inculcate good values in young minds when they are at home, in the Church and in its educational institutions. Secondly exhort and educate adults on Christian values from time to time that promote service-mindedness, equality, oneness and the good of all. In any case, it will take additional time as most educated people are of the first and second generations, and the Church is a minority.

4.6 ECONOMIC CONTRIBUTION

Economic well-being is the primary objective of a nation. Raising income, improving living standards and increasing economic activities of the people are the crucial social tasks of a nation. "Every year, aid is disbursed, investments are undertaken, policies are framed and elaborate plans are hatched so as to achieve this goal, or at least to step closer to it" (Ray, 2007, pg. 7). In this venture of securing the life of the people, no matter how small it may be, the Church has also a role to play. It is not only the religious welfare of the people that concerns the Church but also their all-round well-being. The Church has a holistic approach towards people's progress and growth. Karl Marx opined that, 'Religion is the opium of the people' because of its negative influence on the innocent and suffering people in the hands of the capitalists. Religion cannot project itself as a liberator of the hostile present-day, for something glorious to happen in the future or after death; rather it should help people to experience and enjoy the present.

Every organisation, whether social or religious is expected to work for the welfare of all, irrespective of creed or class. Mere preaching of religious scriptures without them being applied to concrete situations in life will never be a message of liberation. The message and teachings of Christianity lead to liberation from all bondage. *Gaudium et spes* (GS) teaches that all economic activity is directed towards the satisfaction of human desires. Human beings are the source, the centre and the purpose of all socio-economic life. However, the fundamental imbalance between wealth and poverty exists in today's world (GS. 63), therefore, justice necessitates a quick removal of economic inequalities (GS. 66). Unequal distribution of wealth leads to poverty, disease and illiteracy and will in turn lead to unemployment. In some states people take up arms to protect themselves from aggression, inequality and injustice. The Maoist movement mainly in Central, North and East India is a clear sign of the depression and suffering of the poor people due to the injustice they experience. At this juncture, religion should come into the lives of the people to help them earn their living and liberate them from economic bondage as material well-being is an essential component of spiritual well-being.

4.6.1 Church's Role in Development of the State

The Diocesan Social Service Society/DAN in collaboration with many governmental and non-governmental agencies has initiated many life-saving plans like Self Help Groups (SHGs) and other income generating schemes to make poor people self-reliant and improve their economic well-being. In the words of Jauhari (2002), "Development is about improving the well-being of people. Raising living standards and improving education, health and equality of opportunity are all essential components of economic development" (pg. 1). It has been proved that economically backward groups can achieve social transformation and economic independence through SHGs. They empower women and lead them to self-reliance and self-sufficiency. "Self-Help is a Trust, Belief and Conviction that the community, no matter how backward, has resources that can be mobilised for meeting an individual's local needs and that of the community, for making local improvements and bringing about social change" (Director, 2011, brochure). An SHG is a group of about 10 to 20 people, usually women, who come together to form savings and credit organisation. Economic homogeneity which means all belong to the marginalised or poorer section of the community irrespective of creed or class is essential.

The main source of income for the group is their own monthly savings that are decided by the members themselves and these savings are used to give small interest bearing loans to their members. They are also helped by the animators to seek loans and other assistance from various banks and other financial institutions. DAN used to provide some interest free loans with the help of organisations like Caritas India, CRS, NABARD etc. In 1999, the Jesuit priests at Pfutsero formed the SHGs and over a few years, twenty five of them have been formed in addition to four at Phesama. In the year 2002, DAN officially launched a programme aimed at spreading awareness, animation, and strengthening of SHGs in many places in Dimapur, Peren and Phek districts. Later SHGs were formed in Dimapur and Phek districts. Some of the activities taken up by these SHGs are saving, credit and income generation, loans, vegetable and fruit cultivation, sale of vegetables, handicrafts, detergent production, candle manufacturing, food and beverage, mushroom cultivation, piggery, fishery, poultry, honey production, weaving, vermicompost, sale of second hand clothes etc. Often raw materials for weaving are supplied at below market rate to the beneficiaries to encourage them and to make them self-sufficient. Some members take loans from DAN and invest in various businesses of their choice.

The rural economy of these places has been strengthened through the SHGs. Apart from financial gain, it helps members to gain self-confidence and improve their status in society. Self-sufficiency has enabled them to be involved in decision making at various levels, starting with their own families. It improves their bargaining power in administration at local, group and community level.

Economic self-sufficiency and urbanisation go hand in hand. The Church has played a great role in the process of urban growth despite the earlier view that involvement in economic activities was contrary to God's plan, and the establishment of God's kingdom necessitated being away from such activities. In the words of Pariyaram (1996), "In the first few centuries of its existence, the Christian Church did not give importance to institutionalised apostolic work in towns. The imposing tall buildings in cities were interpreted as a lack of faith in God's providence " (pg. 417). Later on the Church was in the forefront in urbanising an area. Pariyaram (1996) writes:

> My submission is that the Christian Church, both Catholic and Protestant, have contributed to the urban revolution in

> the North East by primarily helping the growth of a new civilisation or by helping the transformation of the tribals from a simple society to a complex one. Its contribution to a new civilisation and to urban growth mainly pertain to the following areas: the development of the art of writing and of education, the development of scientific knowledge, the beginning of new architectural designs for buildings, the growth of markets and of trading, the development of organisations based on universal criteria, development of specialisation, willing compliance to a tax system, new consciousness regarding health and hygiene, the rise of a new ethical order and the spread of new styles in music and art (pg. 418).

Many parts of Nagaland witnessed economic development owing to the presence of Catholic mission centres. Shikheho, says, "I believe the Catholic Church can bring about changes and development even to inaccessible areas in the state, much more than the Baptist Church" (Personal communication, July 27, 2007). A rural area that has a Catholic mission centre influences the economic activities and developmental plan of the area. It houses beautiful buildings like a Church, convent, school, hostels, dispensary, staff quarters, etc. and in the course of time the area gives rise to a small township and later on a big town. People from different villages around the town come down to settle there and as a result the town grows. Religious, educational, medical and marketing facilities attract people to settle near the mission centre and soon this becomes a meeting point for all economic activities in the region. To illustrate this point two examples can be cited: Tobu in Mon district was a very small place when the Church began its work in 1976. Today, it is an ADC centre and a headquarters of a number of adjacent villages. Another example is Jakhama, a rural area in Kohima district which has developed into a small township as a result of the establishment of St. Joseph's College in 1985. Today, the area has grown into a town to become an SDO centre. With an enrolment of more than 2500 students and with more than seventy teaching and non-teaching staff this college has proved to be the economic backbone of a good number of people in the village and surrounding areas. More than fifty private hostels which accommodate nearly a thousand students have provided employment and helped to improve the living standard of more than fifty families. Many other families make their livelihood on business establishments such as grocery shops, hotels and restaurants, public call offices, cyber nets, cosmetic and stationary shops etc. Villagers have little difficulty selling their products especially vegetables, as the students are the consumers. There are around fifty employees (daily wage earners) in construction and the whole area (village and its surrounding) has been urbanised/developed with the growth of this college (Singha, 2006, July 28). Many local people from the area are employed in the college and many are engaged in transport services by running taxis and buses to ferry students from different parts of Kohima and the Mao area to the college. So, the Church has provided direct and indirect employment to many people in a given area. In all likelihood people become financially sound as they have access to different business opportunities. Even poor people have better opportunities in the town compared to the village since there are more jobs available, some of them even start small businesses. This phenomenon has taken place wherever the Church has a mission centre. Thus, it has become a major player in the socio-economic development of the state and has, therefore, helped raise the living standard of the people.

Pie Chart 1.3 and Graph 1.1 in Appendix, portray the Catholic Church created direct and indirect employment opportunities for the local populace and thus helped many people to be self-sufficient and improve their living conditions. In order to make our people self-sufficient the Church has initiated rubber cultivation which brings regular income to families. Many people in Jalukie under Peren district and Lakhuti and Bhakti under Wokha district have started rubber cultivation.

4.6.2 Attraction to Urban Areas

Attraction to an urban area is a common phenomenon everywhere and Nagaland is not an exception. The state witnesses an exodus of educated people from the rural areas to the urban centres in search of work. A graduate in any discipline will only consider a government job. In fact the complaint one often hears from parents is that their child is a graduate but unable to find a government job. However, what we know from other parts of the country is that the failure to get a government job automatically pushes them to look for a job in their own place or outside the state.

One reason for the change of attitude is the absence of employment opportunities in their own village or neighbouring villages. They prefer to lead a life in the towns with meagre income from petty jobs while looking for government jobs. This has resulted in a shift from a self-sufficient village economy to a dependent economy in the urban areas because needs of modern life are taxing. Migration from the villages to the towns and the acceptance of new occupations has led to the erosion of family values. At the same time migration has enabled them to acquire new values, attitudes and way of life. A positive and notable achievement of migration is the economic growth and urbanisation which has narrowly broken down tribalism and promoted unity among the various tribes, as urban areas accommodate people from all walks of life.

The main characteristic of the state is its rural features and agriculture is the main occupation, even if the land is under-utilised.Those who are educated find it difficult to remain with their parents who are mostly agriculturists in the village. Many people do not want to work in fields using traditional methods of cultivation because they are aware that it is not going to make them self-sufficient as the state is far behind in modern agriculture, transportation and marketing facilities. The truth is that the vast majority of the people in the remote areas can hardly be called the beneficiaries of economic development as the majority of them depend on cultivation commonly known as 'jhum' or shifting cultivation, which does not yield sufficiently for most people for a whole year. People have not tried their fortune in various cash crop productions either because of their ignorance or lack of government support in terms of subsidy or impatience on their part to wait for long to have the yield. Many of the educated youth, on the other hand, in other parts of the country try their hand in agriculture particularly in cultivating cash crops and they have proved themselves fortunate and wealthy as they bring in sufficient profit. Still others become self-employed in other fields, frequently not in the field for which they are qualified.

There is a growing concern in the state that the state should enter more decisively into the mainstream for economic prosperity. Even now local and foreign help is sought by the Catholic Church to develop the mission centres. Actually the State Government owes its indebtedness and appreciation to the Catholic Church for developing the state particularly in rural areas. Employment generation, establishment of business centres, education, improved life, proximity to transportation and communication etc. are due to the service mindedness of the Church in bringing about an all-round development to the people.

CHAPTER FIVE

The Catholic Church and Nagaland Today

COLONIALISM, INDIAN independence, and the Christian mission have exercised great influence on the people of North East India in general and the tribal people in particular. Of these, the key factor that paved the way for the transformation of the tribal society was undoubtedly the Christian mission. The introduction of Christianity helped in the development of a common identity for the people and thus brought qualitative changes to their lives. In the words of Pugh (1992), "Christianity spread rapidly in the region particularly among the hill tribes as educational, social and economic advancement came to the adherents of this new religion" (pg. 51). The social, political, cultural, economic and educational revolution of the region began with the establishment of churches, schools, colleges, technical schools and charitable institutions run by the Christian mission. Among these, quality education imparted by the mission was an instrument of enlightenment for the people. Today, North East India continues to progress as a result of the invaluable contributions of the Catholic Church and other denominations and it is now moving forward along with other Indian states in terms of development, facilities, and opportunities. The contribution of the Christian mission as a whole in making a new India in this region cannot be ignored. In the words of Bishop Kerketta, "Recognition must be given to the missionaries of yesterday for the work they have done notwithstanding their human failures and mistakes. Recognition must be given to them both in so far as they belonged to a particular group of people or to a particular nation. Recognition implies respect" (Kerketta, 1998, p. 281).

5.1 Identity of the Catholic Church

Both numerically and demographically the Catholic Church is a significant entity in North East India. The areas of the Church activities include health care, higher education, economy and livelihood, preservation and promotion of languages, translation into the vernaculars, inculturation, research on indigenous cultures, promotion of gender equality, care for the environment, development work, social justice, creation of socio-political consciousness etc. Kottupallil (1993) cited the words of F. S. Downs, an eminent historian on Christianity in North East India, on the Catholic Church, "Without question, the most important post-war development has been the rapid expansion of the Roman Catholic Church" (pg. 53).

The God of Christianity easily got rooted into the belief system of the Nagas as He was presented with qualitative attributes such as love, mercy, forgiveness, acceptance, and mutual service. In the words of Barpujari (1982), "Christianity has struck its roots deep in the Naga soil...prior to their conversion they were 'lost souls'; they have now learnt the value of peace, toleration and co-existence with their own men and neighbours in the plains" (pg. 3). The Christian influence was a major force in effecting fundamental changes in the Naga way of life. It led the Nagas from a traditional and animistic way of life to a new religious and modern life by the missionary work of E. W. Clark, Mary Mead and Godhula Brown and they were followed by C. D. King, W. E. Witter, and Dickson.

The great work of these missionaries was followed by the Catholic Church, definitely not as an intruder but as an invited Church to work for the people of the state. Yes, at times defenseless and humiliated, it journeyed forward with its goal in mind. In the words of Fr. T. J. Chacko, "Catholics are the latecomers in many areas and often looked down upon as inferior. The Church should, therefore, improve the quality of life of those Catholics" (Personal communication, 3 November 2007).The Church attempts to educate every Catholic child. The end result is satisfactory as the majority of those who have been educated are successful in life.

5.2 Slow and Steady Growth through overall Development

In spite of several mission centers and investment of vast human resources at the service of the people, the growth of the Church in the state compared to other areas in the North East has not been exceptional. There are about fifty five thousand Catholics spread approximately over two hundred villages out of a total population of nearly two million. One of the significant contributions of the Catholic Church has been the care for its members. The words of Jala (1993) is a reminder of this great truth, "If Christian faith demanded the abandonment of many traditional religious rituals, Catholicism did not leave the people in the lurch and empty handed. It accompanied them from birth to death with rituals that breathed hope and confidence" (pg. 385).

Among various ministries of the Church, the notable benefit the people received is from educational service started from the 1960s and college education from the 1980s, followed by health services. Through a wide network of primary, middle, secondary and higher secondary education, Catholic schools have raised the academic standard of the state and helped increase the literacy rate above national average. And so, evaluation of the role of the Church on development of Nagaland is essentially an evaluation of the kind of education, the Church imparts. One question the Church needs to ask itself is, 'Is our education relevant to the present situation?' According to the National Policy on Education, there should be systematic programme of non-formal education for school drop-outs, for children from habitations without schools, working children and girls who cannot attend whole-day schools.

Ecumenical dialogue promotes healthier coordination between different denominations. The relationship between the non-Catholic denominations and the Catholic Church in Nagaland has formerly been tense. Both were suspicious of each other and the work of evangelisation was carried out on a competitive basis (Puthenpurakal, 1983). Today a small beginning has been made as both come together for discussion and planning for the common good although doctrinal differences exist between the two. Some of the alumni of Catholic educational institutions in Nagaland declare they are not 'anti-Catholic' nor are they against the existence of the Catholic Church in their region. They recall memories of their school and college days and report that while they were studying or staying in the boarding-houses, nobody ever asked them to get converted to Catholicism.

The greatest contribution that religious women have made in North East India is the great enhancement it has given to the dignity and role of women (Kottuppallil, 1991). Children are better cared for where schools are being run by the Church. The Church works hard to maintain stability and indissolubility of marriage among Christians to uphold the dignity of family life. The dispensaries or health centres in each parish looked after by a trained nurse sister, who is often the sole hope of an entire area in times of emergency, have not only saved lives, but also have contributed much to building up a healthy society. Conscientising the villagers about health, hygiene, good diet etc. could not have been improved by anyone else, especially in the early stage of the mission. As a major contributor in the health sector all over the world, the Church collaborates closely with the government and the public. In order to empower women in general the Church follows the principle, 'Educate a woman, save a family.' The empowerment of women through SHGs has raised the living standard of the people particularly women and led to the transformation of many families.

Frequently while noticing the fast development of a Catholic centre some tend to interpret the activities of the Catholic Church parallel to the 'state government.' Schools, colleges, dispensaries and other social projects of the Church have been graded above many government and private institutions and organizations. Some think of 'unknown source of money' available to the Catholic Church. The truth of the matter is that it is not the availability of an abundance of money, but the 'responsible management' of the limited available resources that is the key to the success of the Catholic Church (Yimso, 2012, July, 8).

5.3 Suggestions

Listed below are a few points that would perhaps help the Church to concentrate on specific areas in order to bring about great good for the people in general. In the first place the Naga people as a whole are proud to profess themselves as Christians irrespective of denominations. There is, however, more to be done in improving Christian life. In the words of Jamir, "Nagas consider themselves as a Christian state, covenanted Nagaland for Christ…we have miserably and shamefully failed to uphold the principles of Christian way of life ("The Christian state of Nagaland: Is it theocratic or secular?" 2008, February 24). A religion is not simply to be observed but to be lived. The spirit of Christianity should be in the hearts and minds of the people. Most probably churches had been busy in the past getting members to their fold and failed to convince them of the importance of ethics in public life and consequently failed to make them real 'Christians.' Padinjarekuttu (2006) writes, "The crisis of credibility touches the whole evangelisation enterprise: words do not match action, the received teachings do not change the life of the believers, rituals do not energise life and Christian values do not seem to transform. There is no honesty, fidelity, justice and compassion" (pg. 171). It is time to evaluate the role of the Church in real life situations of the people whom it serves.

Does the Church come closer to the people or away from them? In many situations the Church is far from the people and, therefore, needs to change its approach if there is to be a meeting between the two. A beginning has to be made. Even though the Catholic Church has only a minority status, like the yeast in the dough, it must promote values of justice and honesty for the total transformation of society. Otherwise, Mahatma Gandhi's caution to a Christian missionary will continue to haunt us, "I love Christ. It's just that so many of you Christians are so unlike Christ. If Christians would really live according to the teachings of Christ, as found in the Gospels, all of India would be Christian today" (Raj, 2012).

Raising the standard of education to the national and international level is an area that is to be given importance. We do produce good academic results. It has been felt that the Church ought to venture into imparting quality education that can compete both at the national and international levels so that the illiterate will follow the literate and the uneducated will follow the educated. One of the serious problems faced by the schools is overcrowding. The ratio between the teacher and the students needs to be balanced as an urgent step.

Secondly, it is possible to build links with schools in and outside the state and country. Many schools in India have built up partnership with other schools and thus learning from each other. Of course, this is possible mainly between town or city schools. While in rural areas make funding schools a priority because in order to provide quality education the school needs to appoint qualified teachers, build sufficient classrooms and other facilities, and involve community in the decision making process and funding.

Inclusion of vocational courses in our education system can improve the quality of education. The absence of vocational education in the state is a major setback for those students who are suited to a more practical based skill training. Omission of vocational education in the schools and colleges would only contribute to the already existing educated unemployed in the state. This negligence would increase the burden not only on the government but also on the village or town they reside in. The present form of education is just insufficient to meet modern needs. In the words of Rume (2012), "Skill-based job-oriented vocational training facilities should be made available to the youth so that they are given enough options and opportunities to either opt for higher studies or vocational training for self-employment and their livelihood" (November 6, pg. 7). Vocational educational programmes are crucial in preparing students for identified occupations. They are designed to enhance individual employability and provide an alternative for those pursuing higher education without particular interest or purpose. Until the government initiates or gives priority to this it will not be feasible for private educational institutions to take up the responsibility. In the absence of a prescribed norm in the curriculum, the Catholic Church cannot introduce vocational courses in schools (and colleges). Implementation of this programme would bring benefits to our students, improve our economy and reduce the unemployment rate in the state. "No country can improve its quality of life and standards of living, unless its human resources are wedded to its natural resources ("A seminar on development through social justice", 1982, pg. 5).

The state lags behind other states in technical education. With the increasing number of educated youth in Nagaland failing to find employment, Chief Minister Neiphiu Rio said that the "critical gaps" in the state's education system was largely responsible for educated Naga youth being unable to find gainful employment or suitable placement in the job market. "Although, Nagaland has already achieved a reasonably high rate of literacy, much above the national level, there are still critical gaps in our education system, mostly due to the syllabus not being adequately updated to suit the ever changing job requirements," ("Critical gaps in state's education system: Rio", 2008, October 15, pg. 1). In this context the Church is called upon to rise up to the occasion to meet the needs of the time.

Another area to be looked into is development of agriculture. One of the ways to bring an agricultural revolution in the state is to go beyond institutions and motivate farmers and students on advantages of modern agriculture. As many farmers are still ignorant of the use of high yielding varieties of seeds and cash crop cultivation, motivation and implementation of the same would lead to rural development and decrease in unemployment. Self-sufficiency through empowerment of women is possible through SHGs especially in the rural areas of the state including the backward districts. That does not mean the urban poor should be neglected, rather the focus here should be on gainful employment.

Today, the Catholic Church invests more than 75% of its religious personnel in the educational sector. Over seventy thousand students studying in our institutions carry the message of the Church to at least twenty five thousand families. It may be possible to improve the living standard of these families and others through formation of SHGs.

On the whole the Catholic Church has been successful in bridging evangelisation and socio-economic development from its inception and thus making positive change in the state and contributing much to the welfare of its people. Within a relatively short time span the Church has reached out to all tribes of the state albeit not expansively and has been a beacon of hope.

REFERENCES

Alemchiba, M. (1970). *A Brief Historical Account of Nagaland.* Kohima: Naga Institute of Culture.

Alengaden, V. (2007). *God in Flesh and Blood, Vol. 4.* Indore: Universal Solidarity Movement.

All India Catholic Education Policy. (2007). New Delhi: CBCI Centre.

Aluckal, J. (1982). *Announcing the Good News in the Context of North East India.* Shillong: Oriens Theological College.

Aluckal, J. (2006). *The Catholic Church in North East India.* Shillong: ArchBishop's House.

Anand, V. K. (1980). *Conflict in Nagaland a Study of Insurgency and Counter-insurgency.* Delhi: Chanakya Publications.

Andrews, C. F. (2007). *Mahatma Gandhi his Life and Ideas.* Mumbai: Jaico Publishing House.

Anikuzhikattil, J. (2003). *Understanding Tribal Cultures for Effective Education.* Shillong: DBCIC Publications.

Ao, A. B. (2002). *History of Christianity in Nagaland*. Mokokchung: Shalom Ministry Publication.

Barpujari, S. K. (2003). *The Nagas.The Evolution of their History and Administration (1832-1939).*Delhi: Spectrum Publications.

Becker, C. (1980). *History of the Catholic Missions in North East India.* Shilling: Vendrame Institute.

Becker, C. (1989). *Early History of the Catholic Missions in North East India.* Shilling: Vendrame Institute.

Chacko, T. J. (1990). *The Bible and the Church*. Pallel: St. Paul's Church.

Chakho, T. J. (2000). *My Vocation my Mission*. Imphal: Archdiocese of Imphal.

Chaudhuri, K. C. (1993). *History of Ancient India*. Calcutta: Central Educational Enterprises.

Coelho, S. (1984). *Even to the North East,the Story of the Jesuits in Nagaland.* Kohima: 1984.

D'Souza, A. (2001). *Traditional Systems of Forest Conservation in North East India: the Angami Tribe of Nagaland*. Guwahati: North-Eastern Social Research Centre.

Daili-Mao, A. (1992). *Nagas Problems and Politics.* New Delhi: Ashish Publishing House.

Deberri, E. P.(2003). *Catholic Social Teaching*. New York: Orbis Books.

Desrochers, J. (1982). *The Social Teachings of the Church.* Bangalore: C.S.C. Publications.

Downs, F. S. (1983). *Christianity in North East India*. Delhi: ISPCK.

Elwin, V. (1997). *Nagaland.* Delhi: Spectrum Publications.

Farias, K. (1999). *The Christian Impact in South Canara.* Mumbai: Church History Association of India.

Flannery, A. (Ed.). (1999). *Vatican Council II: The Conciliar and Post Conciliar documents.*Mumbai: St. Pauls.

George, M. C. (Ed.). (2007). *Golden Memoirs 1957-2007.* Imphal: DonBoscoChingmeirong.

George, M. C. (Ed.). (1990).*Centenary of the Catholic Church in North East 1890-1990.* Shillong: ArchBishop's House.

Ghosh, B. B. (1982). *History of Nagaland.* New Delhi: S. Chand and Company.

Haimendorf, C. F. (1976). Return to the Naked Nagas. New Delhi: Vikas Publishing House.

Horam, M. (1977). *Social and Cultural Life of the Nagas: the Tangkhul Nagas.* Delhi: B.R. Publishing Corporation.

Hussain, M. (1988). *Nagaland, Habitat, Society and Shifting Cultivation.* New Delhi: Rima Publishing House.

Hutton, J. H. (1969). *The Angami Nagas.* Bombay: Oxford University Press.

Imchen, P. (1993). *Ancient Ao Naga Religion and Culture.* New Delhi: Har-Anand Publications.

Imnayongdang. (1990). *Levels of Rural Development in Nagaland:A spatial analysis.* Meerut: A. S. Prakashan.

Jauhari, V. P. (2002). *Sustainable Development of Water Resources.* New Delhi: Mittal Publications.

Jha, D. N. (1977). *Ancient India: An Introductory Outline.* New Delhi: People's Publishing House.

Joshi, H. (2001). *Nagaland Past and Present.* New Delhi: Akansha Publishing House.

Kottuppallil, G. (1988). *History of the Catholic Missions in Central Bengal 1855-1886.* Shillong: Vendrame Institute.

Kuriakose, M. K. (2003). *History of Christianity in India: Source materials.* Delhi: ISPCK.

Lotha, A. (2007). *History of Naga Anthropology [1832-1947].* Dimapur: Chumpo Museum.

Luzbetak, L. J. (1970). *The Church and Cultures.* South Pasadena: William Carey Library.

Lotsüro, A. (2000). *The Nagas: a Missionary Challenge.* Shillong: Vendrame Institute Publications.

Mahajan, V. D. (1993). *Ancient India.* New Delhi: S. Chand & Company.

Maitra, K. (1991). *Nagaland Darling of the North East.* New Delhi: Mittal Publications.

Maliekal, G. (2005). *History of the Catholic Church among the Khasis.* Shillong: Don Bosco Centre for Indigenous Cultures Publications.

Malik, J. P. (1997). *The Education Commission and After.* New Delhi: A.P.H. Publishing Corporation.

Mattappally, J. (Ed.). (2007). *The Institutions in the Salesian Province of St. Francis De Sales Dimapur.* Dimapur: Salesians of Don Bosco.

Mawrie, B. L. (2002). *A Pastor Rooted in Culture*, Shillong: Vandrame.

McBrien, R. P. (1994). *Catholicism.* London: Geoffrey Chapman.

Muttumana, M. (1984). *Christianity in Assam and Inter-faith Dialogue*. Indore: Satprakashan Sanchar Kendra.

Nagaland. (2001). Kohima: NagalandBoard of School Education. New Delhi:

Namo, D. (1987). *The Prisoner from Nagaland.* Tuli: Namo Dalle.

National Policy on education - 1986. (1986). Ministry of Human Resource Development Government of India, Department of Education.

Nuh, V. K. (2002). *Origin of the Nagas.* Kohima: Vision Press.

Nuh, V. K. (2003). *The Naga Chronicle.* New Delhi: Regency Publications.

Padinjarekuttu, I. (2008). *Challenges to Religion Church and Theology.* Mumbai: St. Paul Publications.

Pastoral Plan for Catholic Schools in India. (1994). New Delhi: CBCI Centre.

Paviotti, O. (1987). *The Work of his Hands.* Shillong: ArchBishop's House.

Philip, P. T. (1983). *The Growth of Baptist Churches in Nagaland.* Guwahati: Christian Literature Centre.

Plathottam, G. (2001). *You are Peter.* Guwahati: Don Bosco Publications.

Puthenpurakal, J. (1984). *Baptist Missions in Nagaland.* Shillong: Vendrame Missiological Institute.

Puthenpurakal, J. (2000). *Bishop Orestes Marengo North East India's Unparalleled Missionary.* Shillong: Vendrame Institute Publications.

Puthenpurakal, J., & Mampra, A. (Eds.). (2006). *Sanctity in India.* Yercaud: The Retreat.

Raatan, T. (2006). *History, Religion and Culture of North East India.* Delhi: Isha Books.

Ramunny, M. (1988). *The world of Nagas.* New Delhi: Northern Book Centre.

Rao, O. M. (1994). *Fofcus on North East Indian Christianity.* Delhi: ISPCK

Ray, D. (2007). *Development Economics.* New Delhi: Oxford University Press.

Saleh, S. I. (1989). *Nagaland's Economy in Transition since 1964.* Delhi: Omsons Publications.

Sangma, M.S. (1987). *History of American Baptist Mission in North-east India* (Vol. 1). Delhi: Mittal Publications.

Sangma, M.S. (1992). *History of American Baptist Mission in North East India* (Vol. II). New Delhi: Mittal Publications.

Sanyu, V. (1996). *A History of Nagas and Nagaland.* New Delhi: Commonwealth Publishers.

Sebastian, A. J. (Ed.). (1999). *In his Name.* Dimapur: Don Bosco Publications.

Sema, H. (1986). *Emergence of Nagaland.* New Delhi: Vikas Publishing House.

Sen, S. (1987). *Tribes of Nagaland.* Delhi: Mittal Publications.

Sheedy, F. (1978). *Questions Catholics Ask.* Indiana: Our Sunday Visitor.

Shimmi, R. (1988). *Comparative History of the Nagas from Ancient Period till 1826.* New Delhi: Inter-India Publications.

Singh, C. (1981). *Political Evolution of Nagaland.* New Delhi: Lancers Publishers.

Singh, K. R. (1987). *The Nagas of Nagaland.* New Delhi: Deep and Deep Publications.

Smith, V. A. (1990). *The Oxford History of India, Fourth Edition.* Delhi: Oxford University Press.

Sunguist, S. W. (Ed.). (2001). *A Dictionary of Asian Christianity.* Michigan: William B. Berdmans Publishing Company.

Swaroop, N. R. & Dargan, A. S. (2008). *Education in Emerging Indian society.* Meerut: Vinay Rakheja.

Syiemlieh, D. (1990). *A Brief History of the Catholic Church in Nagaland.* Shillong: Vendrame Institute Publications.

Theological Publications in India. (1995). *Catechism of the Catholic Church.* Bangalore: Theological Publications in India.

Thong, J. S. (1997). *Head Hunters' Culture.* Kohima: Khinyi Woch.

Vadakumpadan, P. (1989). *Evangelization Today.* Shillong: Vendrame Institute.

Vattoth, T. (2010). *A Star over Tenyimia.* Shillong: DBCIC Publications.

Venuh, N. (2005). *British Colonization and Restructuring of Naga Polity.* New Delhi: Mittal Publications.

Wolpert, S. (1989). *A New History of India.* New York: Oxford University Press.

Yanthan, J. (2005). *Corruption of Christianity.* Kohima: Catholic Publication Centre.

Yonuo, A. (1984). *The Rising Nagas.* Delhi: Manas Publications.

EDITED BOOKS

Bednarz, J. (1993). Salvatorians and North East India. In S. Karotemprel (Ed.), *Catholic Church in North East India 1890-1990* (pp. 76-83). Shillong: Vendrame Institute.

Bhattacharjee, J. B. (1993). Predicaments of the Catholic Missions in Colonial India. In S. Karotemprel (Ed.), *Catholic Church in North East India from 1890-1990* (pp. 96-101). Shillong: Vendrame Institute.

Castelino, L. (1999). In J. Poonthuruthil, N. K. George, N. K. Abraham, & S. Vizo (Eds.), *In memory: A Loving Tribute to Bishop Abraham Alangimattathil.* (p. 36). Guwahati: Don Bosco Publications.

Cathedral parish, Kohima. (1999). In J. Poonthuruthil, N. K. George, N. K. Abraham, & S. Vizo (Eds.), *In Memory: A Loving Tribute to Bishop Abraham Alangimattathil* (p. 17). Guwahati: Don Bosco Publications.

Changkija, S. (2006). Environmental Conservation and its Impact: Environmental Friendly Indigenous Sustainable Mountain Farming System Practices in Nagaland. In E*conomic Development in Nagaland Prospects and Constraints* (pp. 89-96). Kohima: Nagaland University Teachers' Association.

Christ king parish, Kohima. (1999). In J. Poonthuruthil, N. K. George, N. K. Abraham, &S. Vizo (Eds.), *In Memory: A Loving Tribute to Bishop Abraham Alangimattathil* (p. 15-17). Guwahati: Don Bosco Publications.

Curran, C. (1993). A Century of Catholic Educational Endeavour in North East India. In S. Karotemprel (Ed.), *Catholic Church in North East India from 1890-1990* (pp. 344-354). Shillong:

Vendrame Institute.

Ghonglah, H. (1996). The Church and Health Care in North East India. In J. Puthenpurakal (Ed.), *Impact of Christianity on North East India* (pp. 450-459). Shillong: Vendrame Institute Publications.

Haokip, P. (2004). Building up the Local Church. In T. Manjaly, P. Haokip, & J. Thoppil (Eds.), *Towards Building up the Local Church* (pp. 262-283). Shillong: Oriens Publications.

Haokip, P. (2006). Formation in Tune with Culture. In T. Manjaly, K. Poovathumkudy, & P. Haokip (Eds.), *In the Service of the Mission* (pp. 12-27). Shillong: Oriens Publications.

Holy cross, Dimapur. (1999). In J. Poonthuruthil, N. K. George, N. K., Abraham, & S. Vizo (Eds.), *In Memory: A Loving Tribute to Bishop Abraham Alangimattathil.* (pp. 10-11). Guwahati: Don Bosco Publications.

Imchen, C.L. (2003). The Nagas and the Legacy of Civilizing Mission of the Western World. In J. Anikuzhikattil, G. Palackapillil & J. Puthenpurakal (Eds.), *Understanding Tribal Cultures for Effective Education* (pp. 48-69). Shillong: DBCIC Publication.

Jala, D., & Mukhim, P. (1990). Contribution of Catholic Church towards Education in North East India. In M. C. George (Ed.), *Centenary of the Catholic Church in North East India 1890-1990* (pp. 56-61). Shillong: ArchBishop's House.

Jala, D. (1993). Contribution of the Catholic Church to the Cultures of North East India. In S. Karotemprel (Ed.), *Catholic Church in North East India from 1890-1990* (pp. 378-391). Shillong: Vendrame Institute.

Jala, D. (2002). Mission among the Tribals an Assessment. In P. Vadakumpadan, K. Mathew, & P. Joseph (Eds.), *Breaking New Ground in Mission* (pp. 189-210). Shillong: Vendrame Institute.

Jala, D., &Mukhim, P. (1993). Contribution of the Catholic Church towards Education in North East India. In S. Karotemprel (Ed.), *Catholic Church in North East India from 1890-1990* (pp. 338-343). Shillong: Vendrame Institute.

Jala, D., &Shangpliang, J. S. (1993). The Contribution of the Catholic Church towards Socio-cultural Development in North East India. In S. Karotemprel (Ed.), *Catholic Churchin North East India from 1890-1990* (pp. 469-480). Shillong: Vendrame Institute.

Jeyaseelan, L. (2004). Education for Transformation a Pastoral Priority. In T. Manjaly, P. Haokip, & J. Thoppil (Eds.), *Towards Building up the Local Church* (pp. 155-169). Shillong: Oriens Publications.

Karokaran, A. Inculturation, Implications for Mission and Community Building. In P. Vadakumpadan, K. Mathew, & P. Joseph (Eds.), *Breaking New Ground in Mission* (pp. 75-90). Shillong: Vendrame Institute.

Karotemprel, S. (1996). Impact of Christianity on the Tribes of North East India. In J. Puthenpurakal (Ed.), *Impact of Christianity on North East India* (pp. 16-48). Shillong: Vendrame Institute Publications.

Kerketta, R. (1998). The Assam Mission: Contributing Factors. In F. Fernandez, & J. Varickasseril (Eds.), *Mission a Service of Love* (pp. 268-281). Shillong: Vendrame Institute.

Kottupallil, G. (1990). A Historical Survey of the Catholic Church in North East India from 1627-1983. In M.C. George (Ed.), *Centenary of the Catholic ChurchNorth East India 1890-1990* (pp. 7-53). Shillong: ArchBishop's House.

Kottupallil, G. (1993). A Historical Survey of the Catholic Church in North East India from 1627-1969. In S. Karotemprel (Ed.), *Catholic Church in North East India 1890-1990* (pp. 31-75). Shillong: Vendrame Institute.

Kuttiankal, F. (1999). Toward Health for all: Twenty-five Silver Years in Retrospect. In J. Poonthuruthil, N. K. George, N. K. Abraham, & S. Vizo (Eds.), *In Memory: A Loving Tribute to Bishop Abraham Alangimattathil* (pp. 47-53). Guwahati: Don Bosco Publications.

Manjaly, T. (1990). Diocesan Priests in North East India. In S. Karotemprel (Ed.), *CatholicChurch in North East India from 1890-1990* (pp. 282-295). Shillong: Vendrame Institute.

Manjaly, T. (1990).Diocesan Priests in North East India. In M. C George (Ed.),*Centenary of the Catholic Church in North-East India 1890-1990*(pp. 64-72). Shillong: ArchBishop's House.

Mawrie, B. (2009). Christianity and Socio-political Consciousness in North East India. In T. B. Subha, J. Puthenpurakal, & S. J. Puykunnel (Eds.), *Christianity and Change in North East India* (pp. 132-145). New Delhi: Concept Publishing Company.

Menamparampil, T. (2009). Challenges of Catechesis in North East India. In T. Manjaly, G. Augustine, & T. Palely (Eds.), *Challenges to Faith Formation in North East India* (pp. 11-39). Shillong: Oriens Publications.

Padinjarekuttu, I. (2006). Christianization or Northeasternization? A Challenge for the Church. In T. Manjaly, K. Poovathumkudy,

& P. Haokip (Eds.), *In the Service of the Mission* (pp. 162-172). Shillong: Oriens Publications.

Pal, J. (2005). The Idea of the Culture of Unity in Diversity. In Vanlalnghak,& George S. K. (Eds.), *Tribe, Culture, Art* (pp. 236-243). Guwahati: DVS Publishers.

Palamattam, G. (1993). Church and Development. In S. Karotemprel (Ed.), *Catholic Church in North East India from 1890-1990* (pp. 394-409). Shillong: Vendrame Institute.

Palamattathil, G. (1996). Christian Contribution to the Development of Technical and Vocational Education in North East India. In J. Puthenpurakal (Ed.), *Impact of Christianity on north east India* (pp. 400-413). Shillong: Vendrame Institute Publications.

Parenkulangara, M. (1999). Heart Full of Tuensang & Jalukie. In J. Poonthuruthil, N. K. George, N. K. Abraham, & S. Vizo (Eds.), *In Memory: A Loving Tribute to Bishop Abraham Alangimattathil.* (p. 37). Guwahati: Don Bosco Publications.

Pariyaram, C. (1996). Christianity and Urbanization in North East India. In J. Puthenpurakal (Ed.), *Impact of Christianity on North East India* (pp. 414-426). Shillong: Vendrame Institute Publications.

Passah, P. (1996). The Contribution of Christianity to Socio-economic Development of North East India. In J. Puthenpurakal (Ed.), *Impact of Christianity on North East India* (pp. 427-449). Shillong: Vendrame Institute Publications.

Puthenpurackal, J. (1993). Evangelization among the Nagaland Tribes. In S. Karotemprel (Ed.), *Catholic Church in North East India from 1890-1990* (pp. 216-238). Shillong: Vendrame Institute.

Sanyu, V. (1996). Christian Impact and Conflict Resolution in Nagaland. In J. Puthenpurakal (Ed.), *Impact of Christianity on North East India* (pp. 508-515). Shillong: Vendrame Institute Publications.

Stanislaus, L. (2006). Mission of the Church: Pointers from Liberation Theology. In T. Manjaly, K. Poovathumkudy, & P. Haokip (Eds.), *In the Service of the Mission* (pp. 136-161). Shillong: Oriens Publications.

St. Paul's Wokha. (1999). In J. Poonthuruthil, N. K. George, N. K, Abraham, & S. Vizo (Eds.), *In Memory: A Loving Tribute to Bishop Abraham Alangimattathil.* (p. 30). Guwahati: Don Bosco Publications.

St. Xavier's Church, Jalukie. (1999). In J. Poonthuruthil, N. K. George, N. K, Abraham, &S. Vizo (Eds.), *In Memory: A Loving Tribute to Bishop Abraham Alangimattathil.* (p. 12). Guwahati: Don Bosco Publications.

Syiemlieh, D. (2004). Education and Tribal Societies in North East. In L. Stanislaus (Ed.), *Education as Mission* (pp. 112-133). Delhi: Ishvani Kendra/ISPCK.

Thoppil, J. (2003). The Church in North East India and National Integration. In P. Vadakumpadan, & J. Varickaseril (Eds.), *Apostle of Christ* (pp.264-286). Shillong: Vendrame Institute.

Varghese, P. D. (1993). The Church's Involvement in the Healing Ministry in North East India. In S. Karotemprel (Ed.), *Catholic Church in North East India from 1890-1990* (pp. 355-362). Shillong: Vendrame Institute.

JOURNALS

Horam, M. (1974). The Nagas and their Origin, *The Thinker, Journal of Thinkers Forum, 2* (3), 13-26.

Jala, D. (1990). Contribution of the Catholic Church to the Cultures of North East India. *Indian Missiological Review,12* (3&4), 173-185.

Kottuppallil, G. (1990). A Historical Survey of the Catholic Church in North East India from 1627 to 1969. *Indian Missiological Review,12* (3&4), 25-56.

Kottuppallil, G. (1991). The Church in North East India: A Historical Perspective. *Indian Missiological Review,13* (1), 4-14.

Longkumer, L. (2003). In Search of a Holistic Educational Ministry in the Churches of Nagaland. *Journal of Tribal Studies,7*(1), 177-191.

Manjaly, T. (2010). Social Responsibility: Jesus' Jubilee Message: Biblical Orientations and Pastoral Implications. *Diocesan Priest, 24*, 31-60.

Mary, J. (1991). Contribution of Religious Women to the Growth of the Church in North East India. *Indian Missiological Review, 13* (1), 62-77.

Puthenpurakal, J. (1979). Evangelization in Nagaland and Manipur. *Indian Missiological Review, 1* (3), 247-266.

Puthenpurakal, J. (1983). Evangelization Work in Nagaland.*Indian Missiological Review,5* (3), 195-203.

Ryan, M. (2008). Future Catholic Schools: Exclusive, Inclusive and Plural Options. *Journal of Religious Education,56* (4), 21-27.

Simte, L. L. (2004). Christianity and National Integration in

North East India. *Mizoram Theological Journal, 7*(7), 32-41.

Tochhawng, R. (2004). Religious Fundamentalism and Ethnic Communalism in North East India: A Challenge for Christian Solidarity. *Mizoram TheologicalJournal, 8,* 37-47

UNPUBLISHED DOCTORAL DISSERTATION

Imchen, I. W. (2008). *Christian Missions and Social Change in Nagaland.* Unpublished Doctoral Dissertation, North Eastern Hill University, Shillong, Meghalaya.

PROCEEDINGS PUBLISHED REGULARLY

Earnest, W.T. (1993). The Sons of the Soil and Salt of the Earth: A Reflection on the Life and Mission of the Church with Special Reference to North East India. *Proceedings of NEIHA,* 13, 309-307.

Syiemlieh, D. (2001). The American Baptist Medical Mission in the North East India. *Proceedings of NEIHA,* 21, 190-197.

UNPUBLISHED MANUSCRIPTS NOT SUBMITTED FOR PUBLICATION

Ao, S. (2006). *Catholic Church, Chungtia:Early History of the Catholic Church in Chungtia, Mokokchung.*Unpublished Manuscript.

Mao, S. (1970). *How Catholic Mission Started in the Zeliang Soil?* Unpublished Manuscript.

Assisi, School. (2012). *History of the Assisi School-evening Section.* Unpublished Manuscript.

Augustine, R. R. (2003). *The Angjangyang Catholic Mission: To whom it may Concern.* Unpublished Manuscript.

Augustine, R. R. (2003). *Tobu Catholic Mission.* Unpublished Manuscript.

Barpujari, S. K. (1982). *Christianity and its Impact on the Nagas.* Unpublished Manuscript.

Chacko, T. J. (2010). A Short Report of Fr. T. J. Chacko's Tours in Tuensang District, Nagaland, August 1969 to 1971 November. Unpublished Manuscript.

Civil Hospital Kohima, II. (1949-50). *Don Bosco-Mandaluyong.* Unpublished Manuscript.

Deo D. D. (1993). The Coming of the Catholic Church to Phek District: A Brief History of Zhamai . Unpublished Manuscript.

Diocese of Kohima-Imphal: A Glance into the History of the Missions of North East India.(1973).Unpublished Manuscript.

Directorate of School Education. (2012). *Status of Schools in the state.* Unpublished Manuscript.

Edward, N., Philip, K., Francis, R., & Cheruseril, S. (2007). *A Tribute: A Brief History of Catholic Church, Lozaphuhu* . Unpublished Manuscript.

Ferrando, S. (1947). *The Silver Jubilee of the Salesian Mission of Assam.* Unpublished Manuscript.

Ferrando, S. (1948). *The Mission Becomes the Church.* Unpublished Manuscript.

Ferrando, S. (1951). *Bishop Ferrando Writes from Assam.* Unpublished Manuscript.

Islam, S. (2003). *Yearning for a New Dawn.* Unpublished Manuscript.

John, T. (2008). *Education and Character Formation.* Unpublished Manuscript

Joseph, T. (1996). *A Brief History of the Catholic Church in Zelome* .

Unpublished Manuscript.

Kikon, E. (1964). *Complaint Letter Addressed to Fr. Larrrea on 4th January 1964.* Unpublished Manuscript.

Kohima-Nagaland. (1984). *Missionaires of Christ Jesus.* Unpublished Manuscript.

Larrea, J. (1960). *A Brief History of Lungsa Catholic Church.* Unpublished Manuscript.

Larrea, J. (1988). *Lungsa yano Katholik Ekhumko chi Motsü chi.* Unpublished Manuscript.

Leo, K. (1985). *A Short Church History of Holy Redeemer Church Lazami from 1967- 1985: The Formation of Catholic Religion in Lazami and Neighbouring Areas.* Unpublished Manuscript.

Mannookuzhy, K. (1983). *St. Paul's Church, Penkim.* Unpublished Manuscript.

Marengo, O. (1955). *Assam Church History,* Unpublished Manuscript.

Memoirs from Sisters of Christ Jesus, Shilling. (n.d). Unpublished Manuscript.

Menamparampil, T. (2006). *An Introduction to North East India, Culture & History.* Unpublished Manuscript.

Missionaires of Christ Jesus. (1984). *Entry of Catholic Church and Pioneer Missionaries of Christ Jesus: Extract from the History of the Institute of Missionaries of Christ Jesus.* Unpublished Manuscript.

Nkomo, H. (1949). *Establishment of Catholic Church in Nagaland.* Unpublished Manuscript.

Pallikunnel, L. (n.d). *A Brief History of the Lotha Mission.* Unpublished Manuscript.

Ponnattil, M. (1988). *The Semas and Christianity*. Unpublished Manuscript.

Puthussery, D. (1978). *Konyak Catholic Mission: A Glimpse.* Unpublished Manuscript.

Rector. (1985). *A Short History of the Good Shepherd Seminary-Dimapur, Nagaland.*Unpublished Manuscript.

Sacred, Heart College. (1984). *Fr. Marocchino Visits Kohima again.* Unpublished Manuscript.

Sebastian. (1994). *Brief History of the Catholic Church at Mokokchung, Nagaland.*Unpublished Manuscript.

St. Mary's Church. (2010). *A Brief History of St. Mary's Catholic Church at Satakha and Catholic Mission in the Sumi Region,* 1985-2010. Unpublished Manuscript.

St. Paul Parish. (1985). *The Empire of the Zeliangrongs.* Unpublished Manuscript.

St. Paul Parish. (1985). *Peren.* Unpublished Manuscript.

St. Thomas Chronicle, Tuensang. (1971). *Fr. T.J. Chacko's Tours in Tuensang District, Nagaland from August 1969 to November 1971.* Unpublished Manuscript.

St. Thomas Church, Tuensang. (1985). *Searching for the Truth.* Unpublished Manuscript.

Tenning Mission. (1985). *Tenning.* Unpublished Manuscript

Tep, P. (n.d). *History of the Catholic Church in Rengma Area.* Unpublished Manuscript.

Thomas, V. M., & Gorge, E. (2009). *North Eastern Education Commission: North East Catholic Bishops' Conference*. Unpublished Manuscript.

Treasa, J., & Vilasal, G. (2010). *A Glimpse at the Global Holistic Health Centre, Jalukie*, Unpublished Manuscript.

Visitors' Book of the Dibrugarh State Hospital. (1932). *Extract from the Inspection Remarks made by the Inspector General of Civil Hospitals Assam*. Unpublished Manuscript.

PAPERS PRESENTED AT MEETING

Alangimattathil, A. (1984, March). *Evangelization for the Coming Ten Years.* Paper Presented at the Meeting of Religious Superiors in the Diocese of Kohima, Dimapur, Nagaland.

Mathew, P. K. (1989, August). *The Catholic Centenary Celebrations and the Cathedral Church, a Report.* Paper Presented at the Parish Council Meeting, Kohima, Nagaland.

Coelho, S. (1982, June). *Evaluation of the Role of the Church in Development in Nagalad.* Paper Presented at the Seminar on Development through Social Justice, Dimapur, Nagaland.

Diocese of Kohima. (1986, July). *Training in Project Planning and Formulation a Report.* Kohima, Nagaland.

Karinthayil, C. (2005, December). *Report of the Development Association of Nagaland.*Report Presented at the General Body Meeting of DAN, Dimapur, Nagaland.

Kizhakkeparampil, S. (2010-2011). *Annual Report of the Development Association of Nagaland.* Annual Report Presented during the Priest Meeting, Dimapur, Nagaland.

Lotha Baptist Church Council. (1951). *Minutes of the General Meeting of the Lotha baptist Church Council.* Wokha, Nagaland.

Mannookuzhy, K. (1987, July). *Evangelization in Tuensang District by st. Peter's Church, Kiphire*, Paper Presented on the Occasion of a

Seminar on Evangelization, Dimapur, Nagaland.

Medical Mission Sisters, Kohima. (1967-1973). *Annual Report of the Medial Mission Sisters*. Report Presented at the Superiors' Meeting, Kohima, Nagaland.

Mittathany, J. (2000, August). *The Mission of the Church in the Third Millennium.* Paper Presented at the Meeting of the Regional Assembly of the Catholic Church in North East India, Shillong, Meghalaya.

St. Mary's Health Centre, Lakhuti. (1993). Annual Report for the Year 1993. Report Presented at the Meetig of Health Workers, Wokha, Nagaland.

Uzhunnalil, M. (1975, March). *Christianity and Education in North East India.*Paper Presented during Second Annual Conference of the North East India Sociological Association, Dibrugarh, Assam.

MAGAZINES

Bharati, S. S. (2008, October 27). A Hindu-Christian Joint Mission. *Indian Currents, 20*(44), 32.

Bora, P. (2004, May). Heaven, the Naga Way. *India Today Travel Plus, Nagaland,* 11-13.

Competition Success Review. (2010, May). New Delhi.

John, T. (2006). *Cultural Identity and Glorious Past.* Department of History, St. Joseph's College, 8.

Lesson for the Teachers. (1984, June 14). *Kohima Weekly,* 7 (25), 4.

Pugh, B. M. (1992, December). Christianity and the Tribes of North East India. *Eastern Panorama,* 51-52.

Raj, J. F. (2012, January 23). Key Role of Catholics in India. *Indian Currents, 24* (5), 21-25.

Thumma, A. (2006, December, 11-17). Christian Education a New Perspective. *Indian Currents, 18*(51), 24-29.

NEWLETTER ARTICLES

Ao, L. (1967, July 5). Citizens' Voice: The voice of Nagaland Baptist Churches.

Augustine, R. R. (2009, November-December). *The Echo,* 3.

Augustine, R. R. (2010, July-August). *The Echo, 4* (4), 1.

Augustine, R. R. (2011), November-December). *The Echo,* 5.

Chasie, R.R. (1984, June 8). CAN Report.

Diocese of Kohima. (2006, July-August). *Sharing,*

Ferrando, S. (1942). Christian Facts and Figures from Assam. *Don Bosco in India,12* (1), 12.

Ferrando, S. (1947). The Naked Nagas: The Hill Tribes of Assam. *Salesian Bulletin,* 94.

Ferrando, S. (1949). The Naked Nagas: The Hill Tribes of Assam. *Don Bosco in India, 19* (7), 2.

Ferrando, S. (1951). Bishop Ferrando Writes from Assam: Among the Angami Nagas. *Don Bosco in India,* 5, 6-10.

Ferrando, S. (1953, April). Diocese of Dibruharh. *Family News,* 2.

Ferrando, S. (1955, February). Naga Christmas. *Family News,* 5.

Keemattam, M. (1976, October). Petition Submitted to the ADC, Kiphire. *An Earnest Request to Guarantee Freedom of Worship.*

Kithan, N. (1950, October) "Nstitav yi". *Lotha Khristian Yithen,*1.

Kohima: A Naga Christmas. (1954, February). *Family News,* 3.

Kohima. (1954, March). *Family News,* 6.

Kohima. (1956, October). *Family News,* 5.

Kohima. (1957, November). *Family News,* 7.

Lotha, A. (2010, July-August). Religion and its Abuse of Naga Culture. *Sharing,* 11-12.

Mannookhuzhy, K. (1983, June 4). Petition to ADC, Kiphire.

Mannookhuzhy, K. (1983, December 6). Petition to ADC, Kiphire, 1-4.

Mukala, J. (2007, June). All India Catholic Education Policy. *Diocese of Kohima: BPKOH/Circular, 4* (7), 3.

Naga Christmas. (1955, February). *Family News,* 5.

Nenuotso, K. (1967, April). Letter Addressed to the Catholic Church Leaders, Kohima.

Rosario, H. D. (1965, February). Minutes of the Meetings of the Heads of the Hill Districts of Manipur and Nagaland of the Diocese of Dibrugarh Convened by Bishop. *Important Circulars/ Letters from 1965-1976.*

Sousahie, P. (1967, July 11). An Echo to the Voice of the Naga Baptist Churches.

Yeshito, S. (1966, July). *To the Rt. Rev. Hubert D' Rosario, Bishop's House, Dibrugarh, Assam.* St. Paul Home Cambridge School, Zunheboto. (pp. 1-2).

NEWSPAPERS

Catholic Church Observes 'Girl Child Day'. (2012, September 10). *Eastern Mirror*, p. 3.

Catholic Schools are Contributory Factor for Nagaland's High Literacy Rate. (2012, November 6). *Morung Express, p. 3.*

Church Response to 'Polygamy' Remark. (2009, April 14). *Nagaland Post,* p. 3.

Chutia, R. (2002, May 9). Rich Culture and Heritage of Naga. *The Meghalaya Guardian,* p. 4.

Corruption is Human Rights Violation: Sc. (2012, October 21). *Morung Express,* p. 1.

Critical Gaps in State's Education System: Rio. (2008, October 15). *Nagaland Post,* p. 1.

Ennio, Y. (2008, April 11). Progress of Education in Nagaland-Past and Present Context. *Nagaland Post,* p. 6.

First Sumi Catholic Priest Ordained, (2008, April 28). *Morung Express,* p. 3.

Iralu, A. (2012, July 11). Culture and Religion. *Morung Express,* p. 7.

Iralu, K. (2010, June 2). A Short Treatise on Naga and Manipur Histories. *Morung Express,* p. 6.

Jamir, R. C. (2008, February 24). The Christian State of Nagaland: Is it Theocratic or Secular? *Nagaland Post,* p. 4.

MEx Speak- out Campaign, Write to the Chief Minister Share your Hopes and Vision Make your Voice Heard. (2008, March 28). *Morung Express,* p. 7.

Molungyimsen-'Bethlehem of Nagaland': Neiphiu Rio. (2011, March 20). *Nagaland Post,* p. 1.

Nagaland Literacy Rate at 80.11% Higher than National Average. (2012, July 16). *Morung Express,* p. 1.

Pimomo, P. (2008, February 15). History of Naga Anthropology. *Morung Express,*p. 6

Progress in Education Commendable. (2008, December 13). *Nagaland Post,* p. 2.

Pulimoottil, A. (2011, April 2). Education for Social Transformation. *Nagaland Post,* p. 4.

Rio lauds Catholics. (2007, October 15). *Nagaland Post,* p. 1.

Rume, Z. (2012, November 6). Pace and Development in North East with Special Reference to Nagaland. *Morung Express,* p. 7

Sedevi, A. (2012, September 6). Education in Nagaland. *Nagaland Post,* p. 2.

Singha, K. (2006, July 28). Missionary Institutions and Economic Development in Nagaland. *Nagaland Post,* p. 6.

Solo, T. (2012, January 13). Defects of Church in Nagaland. *Nagaland Post,* p. 4.

The Baptists of Nagaland: Life in Nagaland Before Baptists Arrived. (2008, August 24). *Morung Express,* p. 8.

Yanthan, J. (2010, April 6). No Christians in Nagaland Except novices. *Eastern Mirror,* p. 7.

Yimso, F. (2012, July 8). The Bulb of Faith at Shamator. *Nagaland Sunday Post,* p. 1.

Yitachu Graces Silver Jubilee of Khumiasü . (2012, June 22). *Nagaland Post,* p. 2.

CHRONICLES

Alencheril, J. (1987). *St. Thomas Church Tuensang 1987-2010.* (Chronicle).

Bollini, F. (1954). *Catholic Mission Golaghat1954-1965.* (Chronicle).

Castelino, L. (1972). *St. Peter's Parish Kiphire 1967-1979.* (Chronicle).

Chacko, T. J. (1968). *St. Thomas Church Tuensang 1965-1971.* (Chronicle).

Ferrando, S. (1935). *Diocese of Shillong 1934-1937.* (Chronicle).

Ferrando, S. (1951). *Diocese of Shillong 1951-1954.* (Chronicle).

Ferrando, S. (1951). From the Mission of Assam, our Christian Farmers. *History of the Diocese of Shillong, 1951-1953.* (Chronicle).

Ferrando, S. (1951). Missionaries among the Hill Tribes. *History of the Diocese of Shillong 1951-1953.* (Chronicle).

Ferrando, S. (1951). Will the Once Head Hunters of Assam Become Catholics? *History of the Diocese of Shilling 1951-1953.* (Chronicle).

Neyens, P. (1949). *Catholic Mission Golaghat 1941-1958.* (Chronicle).

Pianazzi, A. (1948). Nagas of Assam. *History of the Diocese of Shillong 1951-1953.* (Chronicle).

St. Peter's Church. (1967). *St. Peter's Parish 1967-1979.* (Chronicle).

St. Thomas Church. (1987). *St. Thomas Church, Tuensang 1987-2012.* (Chronicle).

Superior. (1973). *St. Paul Convent, Kiphire 1973- 2010.* (Chronicle).

Superior. (1976). *St. Teresa's Convent, Tobu 1976-1985.* (Chronicle).

Superior. (1990). *St. Joseph's Convent, Longleng 1990-2010.* (Chronicle).

BROCHURE

Anma Integrated Development Association. (2011). *SkillTtraining Centres in the salesian Province of Dimapur, Arunachal Pradesh, Assam (Upper), Manipur, Nagaland* (Brochure). Dimapur: Salesian Province of Dimapur.

Director. (2011). *Peace Channel* (Brochure). Dimapur: Bishop's House.

Director. (2011). *Self-help Group* (Brochure). Phesama: St. Pauls.

Director. (2011). *Shalom Rehabilitation Centre* (Brochure). Dimapur: Shalom.

Parish Priest. (2008). *Catholic Cathedral, Kohima*, Nagaland (Brochure). Kohima: St. Mary's Cathedral Church.

Principal. (2009). *St. Joseph's College, Jakhama, Calender 2009-2010* (Brochure). Jakhama: St. Joseph's College.

Principal. (2010), *Bosco College of Teacher Education, Prospectus and Syllabus.* (Brochure). Dimapur: Bosco College of Teacher Education.

Principal. (2012). *Salesian College of Higher Education, Handbook &Calendar, 2012-2013* (Brochure). Dimapur: Salesian College Publications.

Principal. (2012). *St. Paul Institute of Education, Prospectus* (Brochure). Phesama: Nagaland Jesuit Educational and Charitable Society.

Rector. (2005). St. Xavier Seminary (Brochure). Jalukie: St. Xavier's.

SOUVENIR

Abraham, O. M. (1992). Message from the Principal. In S. Joseph (Ed.), *Queen Mary's School Mokokchung 1992 Annual Magazine* (pp. 2-3). Mokokchung: Queen Mary's School.

Alangimattathil, A. (1977). Khonoma. In A. Abraham, (Ed.), *Catholic Church Kohima, 1952-1977* (p. 24). Kohima: Diocese of Kohima.

Arokiasamy, S. (2005). Don Bosco Centre Mon. In S. Arokiasamy (Ed.), *Don Bosco School Mon 1980-2005* (pp. 4-10). Mon: Don Bosco School.

Bianchi, P. (2005). In *Silver Jubilee Celebrations 1980-2005, Catholic Church, Salesian Presence & Sacred Heart Convent Mon*, Nagaland. Mon: Don Bosco School.

Blessilia. (1992). Beginning of St. John's-a Short History. In Blessilia (Ed.), *Catholic Mission Tuensang 1967-1992* (pp. 24-25). Tuensang: St. John's School.

Bollini, F. (1991) Lanes… In T. Ganlari (Ed.), *Golden Jubilee 1941-1991: Catholic Church Golaghat* (p. 10). Golaghat: Catholic Church.

Castelino, L. (1997). From the Chronicle of St. Peter's Church. In S. K. James (Ed.), *St. Peter'sPparish, Loyola School, Kiphire 1972-1997* (pp. 26-27). Kiphire: St. Peter's Church.

Castelino, L. (1999). Beginning of the Catholic Mission and St. Xavier School at Meluri. In J. Charalel (Ed.), *St. Xavier School Meluri Silver Jubilee 1974-1999* (pp. 21-23). Meluri: St. Xavier School.

Castelino, L. (2000). The Pastor and Catholic Community Khumiasü . In K. Peter (Ed.), *St. Michael's Church Khumiasü Silver*

Jubilee 1975-2000 (pp. 7-8). Meluri: St. Xavier's Parish.

Catholic Kehou Dze. (2010). (History of Catholic Church) Zhadima (Keruma) . In Souvenir Committee (Ed.), *Sts. Peter & Paul Church Zhadima Golden Jubilee 1960-2010* (pp. 18-20). Chiephobozou: St. Dominic Church.

Catholic Mission, Medziphema Parish. (2003). In *Catholic mission, Medziphema Parish 1978-2003* (pp. 7-10). Medziphema: SFS School.

Chasie, R. (2005). A Brief History of st. Francis De Sales Parish, Kohima town. In J. Vadakumpadan (Ed.), *St. Francis De Sales Church, Kohima Silver Jubilee 1980-2005* (pp. 19-29). Kohima: Catholic Publication Centre.

Cheruseril, S. (2001). A Brief History of Catholic Church, Tobu. In R. R. Augustine (Ed.), *Catholic Church Tobu* (pp. 4-7). Tobu: Catholic Church, Tobu.

Fernandes, M. (2002). The Unique Activities of the Ursuline Franciscan Sisters of North East Province. In Z. John (Ed.), *Christ King Church, Kohima: Golden Jubilee Magazine 1952-2002* (p. 51). Kohima: Golden Jubilee Literature Committee.

George, K. (1993). A Brief History of the Catholic Church at Tseminyu. In K. George (Ed.), *Catholic Church Tseminyu Silver Jubilee 1968-1993* (pp. 10-13). Tseminyu: St. Joseph's Church.

Hosito, E. (2002). Catholic Faith at Chomi. In N. John (Ed.), *Christ King Church-Chomi 1977-2002* (pp. 17-20). Kiphire: St. Peter's Parish.

Humtsoe, J. (1976). Lotha Catholic Ekhumkho Motsu etso yi. In J. Humtsoe (Ed.), *Catholic Church, Lakhuti, Silver Jubilee 1951-1976* (pp. 10-27). Wokha: St. Mary's Church.

Humtsoe, Y. (1986). Riphyim Yimtong Catholic Dhoromo Soyingten Motsu. In N. Urbanus (Ed.), *Riphyim Catholic Church Silver Jubilee 1962-1986* (pp. 4-7). Wokha: St. Paul's Church.

Jamir, N. I. (1992). Catholic Mission. In S. Joseph (Ed.), *Queen Mary's School Mokokchung 1992 Annual Magazine* (p. 60). Mokokchung: Queen Mary's School.

Jasokie, J. (1996). Don Bosco School, Kohima. In B. Lakra (Ed.), *On a Trail of Excellence, Don Bosco Kohma 1971-1996* (p. 30). Don Bosco School.

Jessina. (2001). SABS and the Tobu Mission. In R. R. Augustine (Ed.), *Catholic Church Tobu* (p. 7). Tobu: Catholic Church, Tobu.

John, T. (2010). Catholic Education and its Contribution to Nagaland. In A. Dukru (Ed.), *25 Years at the Service of Higher Education: A Flash Back* (pp. 41-45). Jakhama: St. Joseph's College.

Karinthayil, C. (2001). My Memories of Tobu. In R. R. Augustine (Ed.), *Catholic Church Tobu* (p. 8). Tobu: Catholic Church, Tobu.

Karthik, T. (2002). Don Bosco Tuli. In N. J. Cyriac (Ed.), *Don Bosco School Tuli 1977- 2002* (pp. 15-16). Tuli: Don Bosco School.

Khazhipa. (2000). 25 Years of Catholic Community at Khumiasü and in Pochuri. In K. Peter (Ed.), *St. Michael's Church Khumiasü silver Jubilee 1975-2000* (pp. 5-6). Meluri: St. Xavier's Parish.

Larrea, J. (2003). Sunglup Jubilee chi. In J. Yanthan (Ed.), *St. John Catholic Ekhumkho- Sunglup Golden Jubilee 1953-2003* (p. 4). Lakhuti: St. Mary's Church.

Lewis, B. (2000). The Cost of Discipleship. In K. Peter (Ed.), *St. Michael's Church Khumiasü Silver Jubilee 1975-2000* (pp. 9-11). Meluri: St. Xavier's Parish.

Longkumer, M. (1992). Origin of Queen Mary's School. In S. Joseph (Ed.), *Queen Mary's School Mokokchung 1992 Annual Magazine* (p. 13). Mokokchung: Queen Mary's School.

Lucious. (1992). A Historical Flash Back. In P. C. Jose (Ed.), *Holy Cross School Dimapur, Silver Jubilee 1966-1991* (pp. 27-29). Dimapur: Holy Cross School.

Mandal, P. (1993). Holy Cross Parish. In P. Mandal (Ed.), *Holy Cross Church Silver Jubilee 1968-1993* (pp. 30-38). Dimapur: Holy Cross Church.

Mao, L. (1994). A Brief History. In A. Iheilung (Ed.), *St. Xavier's High School Jalukie 1969-1994 (pp. 26-28).* Jalukie: St. Xavier's School.

Marengo, O. (1976). Memories of an Old Tramp at Large in the Brahmaputra Valley. In R. Kerketta (Ed.), *Diocese of Dibrugarh Silver Jubilee 1951-1976* (pp. 33-38). Dibrugarh: Diocese of Dibrugarh.

Marengo, O. (1989). Few Fond Reminiscences. In J. Thoppil (Ed.), *25 Years of Loving Service to God and Man, Sacerdotal Silver Jubilee Abraham Alangimattathil* (pp. 34-37). Dimapur: Diocese of Kohima.

Mariadoss, P. (2010). A Brief History of the Catholic Church, Aghunato. In N. Augustine (Ed.), *St. Joseph Church Aghunato, Silver Jubilee 1985-2010* (pp. 22-25). Aghunato: St. Joseph's Church.

Menamparampil, T. (1981). Father Krick, the First Catholic Missionary in Dibrugarh. In Editorial Board (Ed.), *Dibrugarh Parish 50 years: 1931-1981* (pp. 26-28). Dibrugarh: Diocese of Dibrugarh.

Mlakuzhiyil, J. (1997). From the Chronicle of St. Peter's Church. In S. K. James (Ed.), *St.Peter's Parish, Loyola School, Kiphire 1972-*

1997 (pp. 23-25). Kiphire: St. Peter's Church.

O'Hara. (1990). The Early Days of Don Bosco Wokha. In J. Thettayil (Ed.), *Don Bosco School Wokha, Silver Jubilee 1965-1990* (pp. 17-20). Wokha: Don Bosco School.

Pyangsa Catholic Ekhum ko. (2009). *Pyangsa Catholic Ekhum ko, Silver Jubilee 1984-2009*. Pyangsa: Catholic Church.

Rino, L. (1992). Khrista thuo Pesiekeshü Kehou-u Jotsoma rüna nu Vorkelie. In M. Rino (Ed.), *Jotsoma Catholic Church, Silver Jubilee 1967-1992* (pp. 25-27). Kohima: Catholic Church Jotsoma.

St. Paul's Catholic Church. (2005). In *St Paul Catholic Church Golden Jubilee 1955-2005* (pp. 25-28). Mekokla: St. Paul's Church.

St. Paul's Parish Peren. (2005). In *St. Paul's Parish Peren Silver Jubilee 1980-2005* (pp. 1-4). Peren: All Saints' School.

St. Paul's Catholic Church Lotsu. (2005). In *St. Paul's Catholic Church Silver Jubilee 1980-2005*. Lotsu: Catholic Church.

Suosahie, P. (1994). The Beginning of Catholic Church at Kohima. In A. Xavier (Ed.), *Christ King school Kohima: Silver Jubilee 1969-1994* (pp. 28-30). Kohima: Christ King School.

Suosahie, P. (2002). History of the Catholic Church in Kohima. In Z. John (Ed.), *Christ king Church, Kohima: Golden Jubilee Magazine 1952-2002* (pp. 1-6). Kohima: Golden Jubilee Literature Committee.

Suosahie, P., Visielie, V., & Neinguzolie N. (1994). God's Guiding Ways. In A. Xavier (Ed.), *Christ King School Kohima: Silver Jubilee 1969-1994* (pp. 44-48). Kohima: Christ King School.

Throngsukiu, M. (2000). Faith of Catholic Church at Phelungre. In J. Kyosukiu (Ed.), *St. Thomas' Church Phelungre 1975-2000* (pp. 23-33). Kiphire: St. Peter's Church.

Thuniampral, M. (2008). We Remember We Celebrate We Believe. In J. Lotha (Ed.), *St. Paul Church-Pungro 1983-2008* (pp. 14-17). Pungro: St. Paul Parish.

Thuniampral, M. (2010). Commission for Education Diocese of Kohima, Nagaland. In A. Kakuho (Ed.), *San Jose Church, Sitimi Town, Silver Jubilee, 1985-2010 (pp.2-14).* Kiphire: St. Peter's Church.

Xavier, C. (2009). Catechist Chavi Xavier and the Spread of Catholics in Southern Angami Region. In C. Xavier, (Ed.), Golden Jubilee of Chavi Xavier (pp. 2-5). Phesama: St. Pauls' Church.

Yanthan, J. (1994). Youth for a Just Society. In H. Ashuli (Ed.), *Nagaland Catholic Youth Convention* (pp. 13-14). Kohima: Catholic Youth Association.

Yanthan, J. (2003). Sunglup Yimtongo Catholic Dhorum Soying motsu. In J. Yanthan (Ed.), *St. John Catholic Ekhumkho-Sunglup Golden Jubilee 1953-2003* (pp.10-11. Lakhuti: St. Mary's Church.

ELECTRONIC SOURCE

Brom, R.H. (2004, August 10). Clibacy and the Priesthood. Retrieved January 26, 2013, from http://en.wikipedia.org.

Inculturation. (2012, December 24). Retrieved November 26, 2012, from en. Wikipedia.org.

Ecumenism. (2011, January 20). Retrieved December 2, 2012, from http: en.wikipedia.org

Catholic School. (2012, August 10). Retrieved September 11, 2012, from http: en.wikipedia.org.

APPENDIX

Appendix: Document A

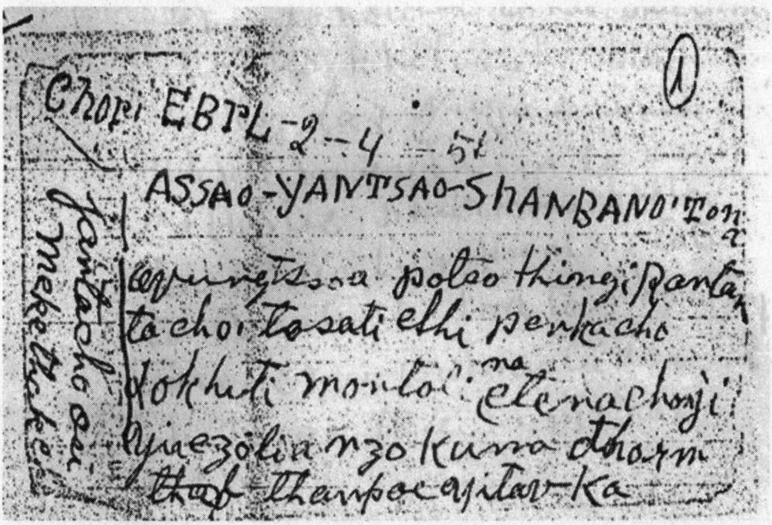

Chori EBPL 2-4-51

ASSAO-YANTSAO-SHANBANO'Tona

A resolution stating that Yantsao, Shanpano and Chenisao had repeatedly requested their church to take them back but to no avail. The resolution claimed that they would join a new denomination.

Appendix: Document B

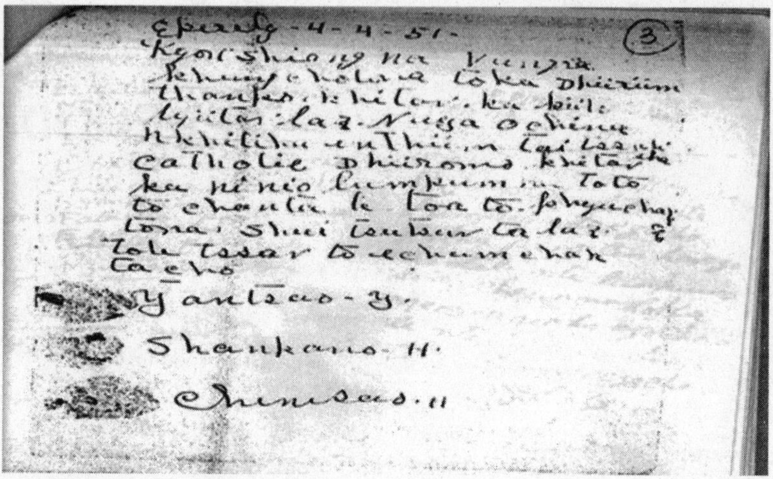

Yantsao, Shanpano and Chenisao's thumb impression while joining the Catholic Church.

Appendix: Document C

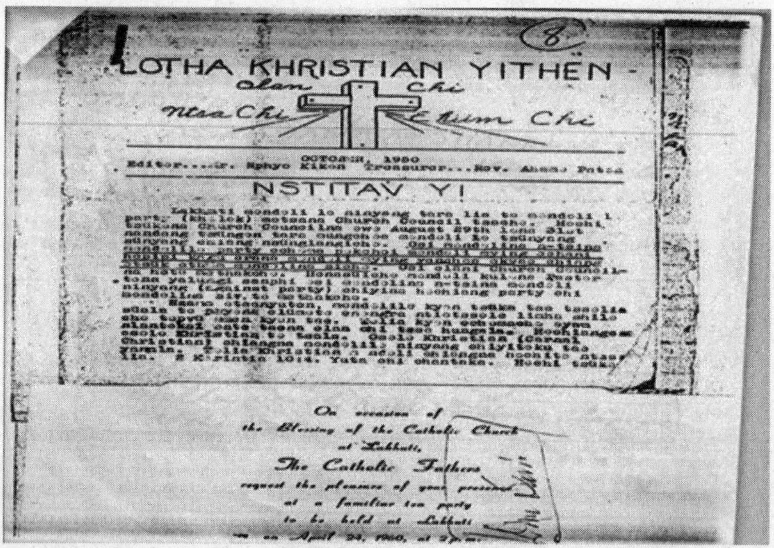

October 1950 edition of the notification from Vankosung, the Lotha Baptist headquarters.

Appendix: Table 1.1

Encourages indigenous songs and music	Encourages cultural elements like symbols, myths, folklore, dialects etc. in worship/religious life					Total
	No response	Nil	Little	Much	Great	
Very much	2(2.0)	2(2.0)	31(29.0)	47(44.0)	24(23.0)	106(100.0)
Not much	2(2.0)	0(.0)	45(48.0)	36(38.0)	11(12.0)	94(100.0)
Never	2(10.0)	7(35.0)	7(35.0)	1(5.0)	3(15.0)	20(100.0)
Rarely	0(.0)	2(4.0)	34(69.0)	10(21.0)	3(6.0)	49(100.0)
No response	8(73.0)	0(.0)	3(27.0)	0(.0)	0(.0)	11(100.0)
Total	14	11	120	94	41	280
X2= 201.065a	df= 16		p= .000		C=.646	

Catholic Church's encouragement of indigenous culture and its practices

Appendix: Pie Chart 1.1

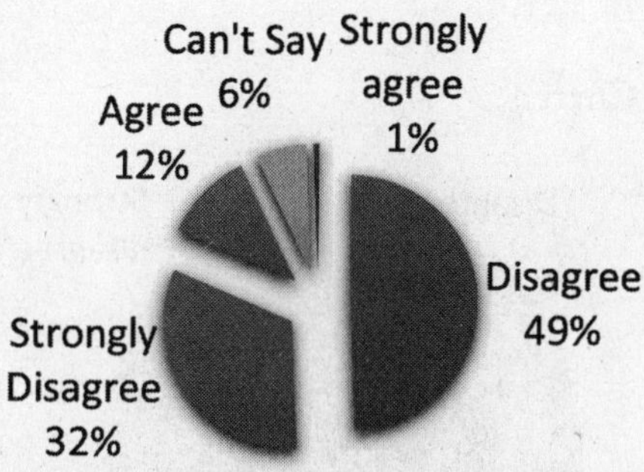

Whether the Catholic religion was an intruder and divided the Naga society?

Appendix: Pie Chart 1.2

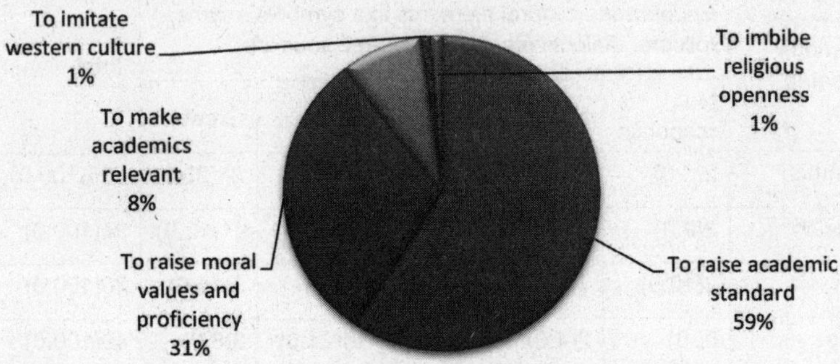

Contribution of the Catholic Church in the field of educational system of the state

Appendix: Table 1.2

Response	Distribution of Respondents	
	Frequency	Percentage
Very good	222	79.3
Good	44	15.7
Satisfactory	14	5.0
Total	280	100.0

Catholic church services in the health field.

Appendix: Pie Chart 1.3

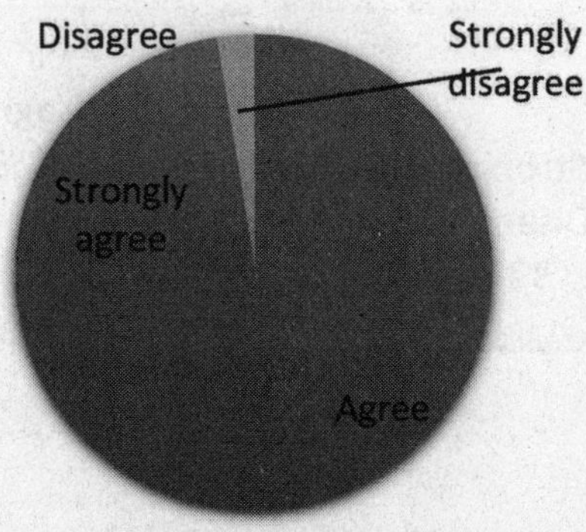

Catholic Church's influence on the politics of the state.

Appendix: Graph 1.1

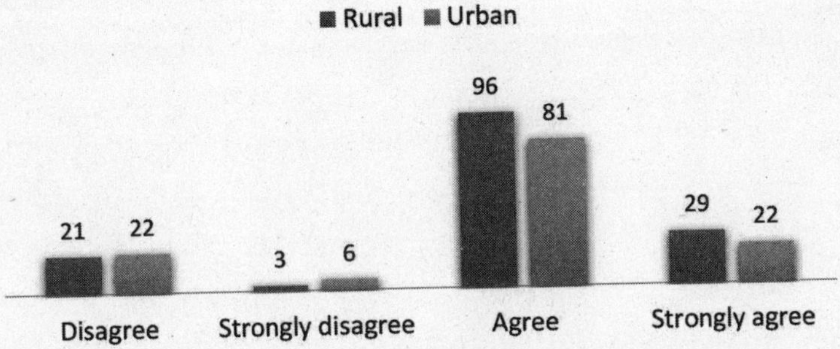

Catholic Church's direct and indirect employment opportunities for local populace.

Appendix: Document D

Letter Written by the ADC

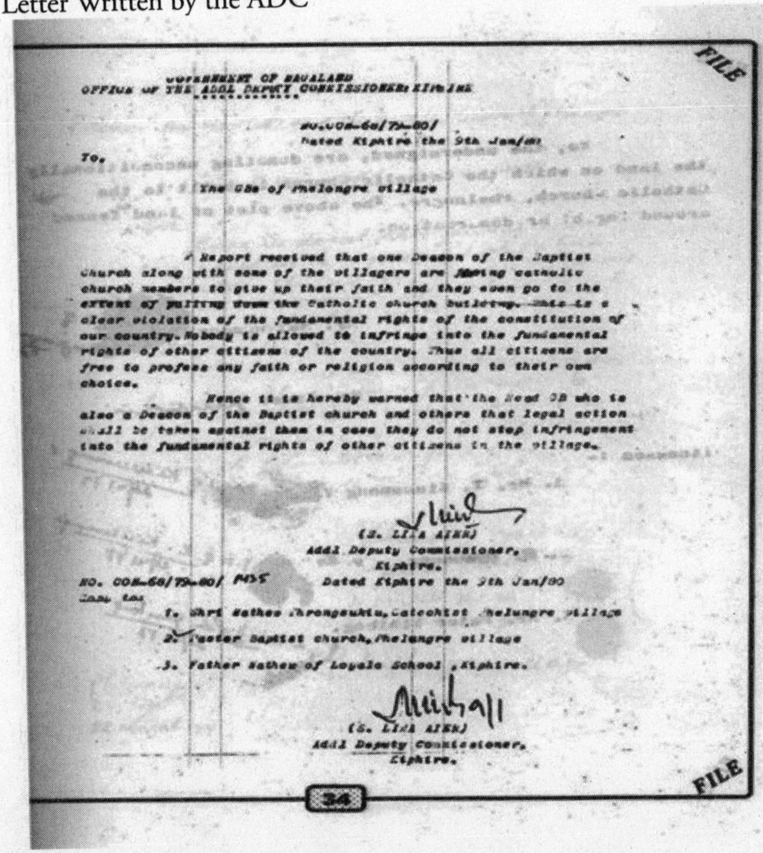

GOVERNMENT OF NAGALAND
OFFICE OF THE ADDL DEPUTY COMMISSIONER: KIPHIRE
****

NO.COM-68/79-80/
Dated Kiphire the 9th Jan/80

To,

The GBs of Phelungre village

A Report received that one Deacon of the Baptist Church along with some of the villagers are [illegible] catholic church members to give up their faith and they even go to the extent of pulling down the Catholic church building. This is a clear violation of the fundamental rights of the constitution of our country. Nobody is allowed to infringe into the fundamental rights of other citizens of the country. Thus all citizens are free to profess any faith or religion according to their own choice.

Hence it is hereby warned that the Head GB who is also a Deacon of the Baptist church and others that legal action shall be taken against them in case they do not stop infringement into the fundamental rights of other citizens in the village.

(S. LIRA AIER)
Addl Deputy Commissioner,
Kiphire.

NO. COM-68/79-80/ 8435 Dated Kiphire the 9th Jan/80
Copy to:

1. Shri Mathew Throngsuklu, Catechist Phelungre village
2. Pastor Baptist church, Phelungre village
3. Father Mathew of Loyala School, Kiphire.

(S. LIRA AIER)
Addl Deputy Commissioner,
Kiphire.

FILE

34

GLOSSARY

Dobashi: A judicial personnel to adjudicate cases relating to customary laws at the area, or circle, or district level, holding his appointment from the government. They are dressed in red coats.

Gaon Bura: A elder or of the or of a 'khel' holding his appointment from the government. They are draped in red shawls as a symbol of their office.

Genna: A non-working day observed by the community. It is an Assamese word for *Kenna* meaning forbidden. It is for the propitiation of the spirits.It is one of the functions of priest to announce the *genna.* They are also observed for the benefit of everybody

Jhuming: It is also known sometimes as 'slash-and-burn' or 'shifting' cultivation. Jhum cultivation is a method in which a piece of land is cleared of all trees and grasses; burnt and then a variety crops are planted.

Khel: An Assamese word for exogamous group among the Naga tribes. People belonging to khel live separately in a fixed territory in the . It is almost a quarter in a.

Mithun: The scientific name is Bos Frontalis, a semi-domesticated animal found in the North Eastern states.

Morung: Bachelor's dormitory is where young men, in some tribes women, stayed during young adulthood, and learned knowledge on customary laws and were trained in arts, war and wrestling.

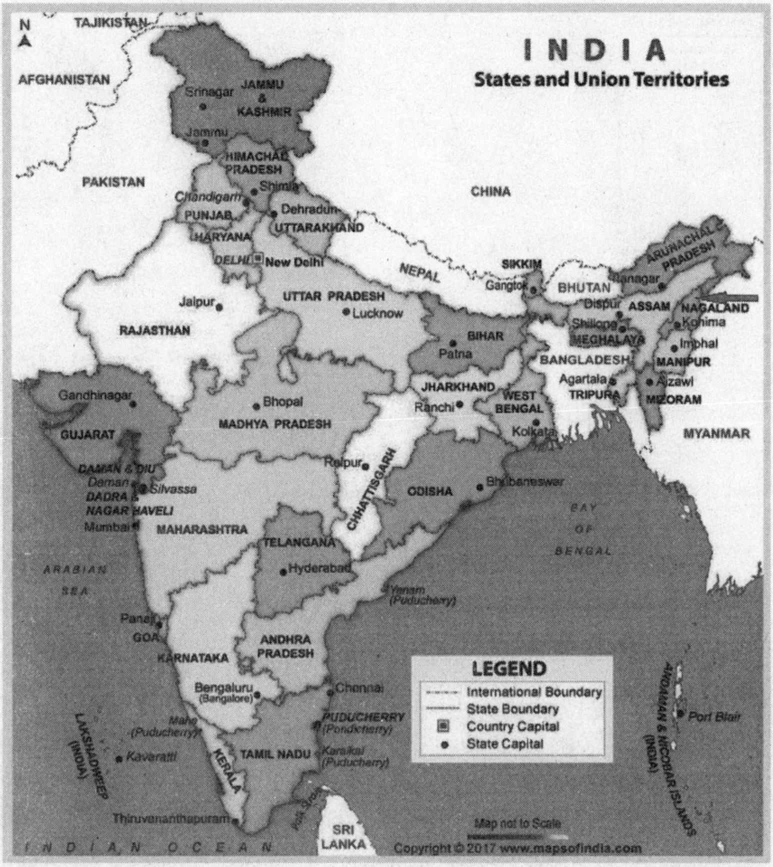
INDIA
States and Union Territories
N
TAJIKISTAN
AFGHANISTAN
PAKISTAN
CHINA
NEPAL
BHUTAN
BANGLADESH
MYANMAR
SRI LANKA
JAMMU & KASHMIR
Srinagar
Jammu
HIMACHAL PRADESH
Shimla
Chandigarh
PUNJAB
HARYANA
DELHI
New Delhi
Dehradun
UTTARAKHAND
UTTAR PRADESH
Lucknow
RAJASTHAN
Jaipur
SIKKIM
Gangtok
ARUNACHAL PRADESH
Itanagar
ASSAM
Dispur
NAGALAND
Kohima
Shillong
MEGHALAYA
Imphal
MANIPUR
BIHAR
Patna
Aizawl
MIZORAM
Agartala
TRIPURA
JHARKHAND
Ranchi
WEST BENGAL
Kolkata
Gandhinagar
GUJARAT
Bhopal
MADHYA PRADESH
Raipur
CHHATTISGARH
DAMAN & DIU
Daman
Silvassa
DADRA & NAGAR HAVELI
Mumbai
MAHARASHTRA
ODISHA
Bhubaneswar
BAY OF BENGAL
TELANGANA
Hyderabad
Yanam (Puducherry)
ARABIAN SEA
Panaji
GOA
KARNATAKA
ANDHRA PRADESH
Bengaluru (Bangalore)
Chennai
PUDUCHERRY (Pondicherry)
Mahe (Puducherry)
LAKSHADWEEP (INDIA)
Kavaratti
KERALA
TAMIL NADU
Karaikal (Puducherry)
Thiruvananthapuram
ANDAMAN & NICOBAR ISLANDS (INDIA)
Port Blair
LEGEND
International Boundary
State Boundary
Country Capital
State Capital
Map not to Scale
INDIAN OCEAN
Copyright © 2017 www.mapsofindia.com

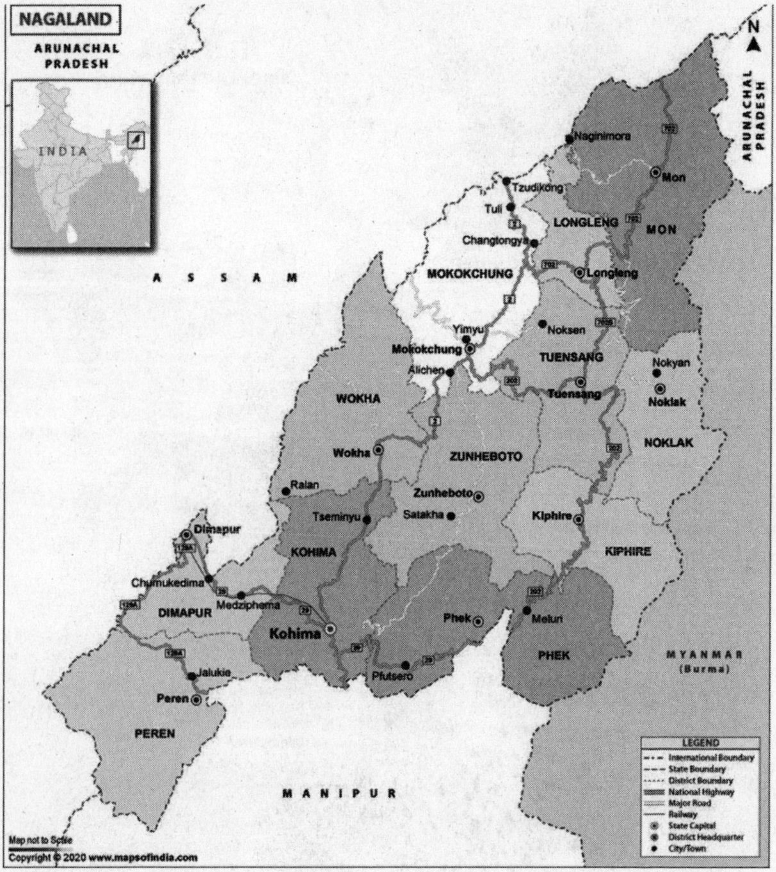
NAGALAND
ARUNACHAL PRADESH
INDIA
ASSAM
ARUNACHAL PRADESH
N
Naginimora
Mon
Tzudikong
Tuli
LONGLENG
MON
Changtongya
MOKOKCHUNG
Longleng
Noksen
Yimyu
Mokokchung
TUENSANG
Alichen
Nokyan
Tuensang
Noklak
WOKHA
NOKLAK
Wokha
ZUNHEBOTO
Ralan
Zunheboto
Tseminyu
Satakha
Kiphire
Dimapur
KOHIMA
KIPHIRE
Chumukedima
Medziphema
DIMAPUR
Kohima
Phek
Meluri
PHEK
MYANMAR (Burma)
Pfutsero
Jalukie
Peren
PEREN
MANIPUR
LEGEND
International Boundary
State Boundary
District Boundary
National Highway
Major Road
Railway
State Capital
District Headquarter
City/Town
Map not to Scale
Copyright © 2020 www.mapsofindia.com